COUNTRY BEFORE PARTY

STUDIES IN MODERN HISTORY

General editors: John Morrill and David Cannadine

This series, intended primarily for students, will tackle significant historical issues in concise volumes which are both stimulating and scholarly. The authors combine a broad approach, explaining the current state of our knowledge in the area, with their own research and judgements: and the topics chosen range widely in subject, period and place.

Titles already published

FRANCE IN THE AGE OF HENRY IV (2nd Edn) *Mark Greengrass*

VICTORIAN RADICALISM *Paul Adelman*

WHITE SOCIETY IN THE ANTEBELLUM SOUTH *Bruce Collins*

BLACK LEADERSHIP IN AMERICA: FROM BOOKER T. WASHINGTON TO JESSE JACKSON (2nd Edn) John White

THE TUDOR PARLIAMENTS *Michael A.R. Graves*

LIBERTY AND ORDER IN EARLY MODERN EUROPE *J.H. Shennan*

POPULAR RADICALISM *D.G. Wright*

'PAX BRITANNICA'? BRITISH FOREIGN POLICY 1789–1914 *Muriel E. Chamberlain*

IRELAND SINCE 1800 *K. Theodore Hoppen*

IMPERIAL MERIDIAN: THE BRITISH EMPIRE AND THE WORLD 1780–1830 *C.A. Bayly*

A SYSTEM OF AMBITION? BRITISH FOREIGN POLICY 1660–1793 *Jeremy Black*

BRITANNIA OVERRULED: BRITISH POLICY AND WORLD POWER IN THE 20TH CENTURY *David Reynolds*

POOR CITIZENS: THE STATE AND THE POOR IN TWENTIETH-CENTURY BRITAIN *David Vincent*

THE HOUSE OF LORDS IN BRITISH POLITICS AND SOCIETY 1815–1911 *E.A. Smith*

POLITICS UNDER THE LATER STUARTS: PARTY CONFLICT IN A DIVIDED SOCIETY 1660–1715 *Tim Harris*

BRITAIN AND LATIN AMERICA IN THE NINETEENTH AND TWENTIETH CENTURIES *Rory Miller*

THE BRITISH IN THE AMERICAS 1480–1815 *Anthony McFarlane*

COUNTRY BEFORE PARTY: COALITION AND THE IDEA OF 'NATIONAL GOVERNMENT' IN MODERN BRITAIN, 1885–1987 *G.R. Searle*

COUNTRY BEFORE PARTY:
Coalition and the idea of 'National Government' in Modern Britain, 1885–1987

G.R. Searle

Longman
London and New York

Longman Group Limited,
Longman House, Burnt Mill,
Harlow, Essex CM20 2JE, England
and Associated Companies throughout the world.

Published in the United States of America
by Longman Publishing, New York

© Longman Group Limited 1995

First published 1995

ISBN 0 582 209528 CSD
ISBN 0 582 20951X PPR

British Library Cataloguing-in-Publication Data

A catalogue record for this book is
available from the British Library

Library of Congress Cataloging-in-Publication Data

Searle, G. R. (Geoffrey Russell)
    Country before party : coalition and the idea of 'national
government' in modern Britain, 1885–1987 / G. R. Searle.
        p.   cm. — (Studies in modern history)
    Includes bibliographical references (p.) and index.
    ISBN 0–582–20952–8 (CSD): £38.00. — ISBN 0–582–20951–X (PPR) :
£14.99
        1. Great Britain—Politics and government—20th century.
    2. Coalition governments—Great Britain—History—20th century.
    3. Political parties—Great Britain—History—20th century.
    4. Nationalism—Great Britain—History—20th century.   5. Great
Britain—Politics and government—1837–1901.   I. Title.
    II. Series: Studies in modern history (Longman (Firm))
DA566.7.S37   1995
320.941'09'04—dc20   94–22618
                                                                CIP   AC

Set by 5B in 10/12 Bembo
Produced by Longman Singapore Publications (Pte) Ltd.
Printed in Singapore

Contents

Acknowledgements

The theme of this book is one that has fascinated me ever since I began my doctoral dissertation on "National Efficiency" over thirty years ago. Some of the chapters draw upon my own earlier publications and on my more recent research; the framework of interpretation is also my own. But, of course, in a work of this scope I have obviously incurred debts to the many other historians who have been working in the field of modern British political history over the last few decades. I acknowledge the most important of these debts in my brief Bibliography. But I would particularly like to mention Philip Williamson's outstanding book, *National Crisis and National Government: British Politics, the Economy and Empire, 1926–1932* (Cambridge, 1992), which figures significantly in Chapters 7 and 8.

I must also thank most warmly the friends and colleagues who read early drafts of the book and gave me the advantage of their criticisms and advice – in particular, Mr Matthew Carter, Dr John Charmley and Dr Terry Jenkins. Papers delivered to the University of Warwick History Society and to the Cambridge University Modern British History Seminar group also elicited useful ideas and suggestions. I have received much encouragement and support from Professor David Cannadine and staff at Longman. Finally I am grateful to my own university, the University of East Anglia, for giving me the study leave during which I was able to complete this book.

Records for the Lloyd George papers are in the custody of the House of Lords Record Office. Extracts written **by** Lloyd George are reproduced by permission of the Clerk of the Records, acting on behalf of the Beaverbrook Foundation Trustees.

G. R. Searle   University of East Anglia, Norwich
April 1994

Reader should note that where references are given in the footnotes, the place of publication is London unless otherwise stated.

CHAPTER ONE
Introduction

THE CULT OF TWO-PARTY POLITICS

'The party tie is the strongest sentiment in this country – stronger than patriotism or even self-interest', Joseph Chamberlain told Lord Randolph Churchill on 26 December 1886.[1] Few politicians in modern times have needed reminding of this truth.

No modern democratic state has found a way of dispensing altogether with party. But in Britain, aided by the existence of the first-past-the-post (or 'plurality') electoral system, political life has normally centred around a competitive struggle between just *two* dominant parties, one forming the Government, the other the Opposition. And, to quote the words of the Edwardian political commentator, Sidney Low, this presupposes the existence of 'two great well-balanced forces, always mobilised and on the war footing', each ready and able to take power at any moment.[2] Such arrangements have set Britain apart from many other democratic states – for example, the Third Republic in France, with its proliferation of parliamentary groupings, some so small that they had more words in their title than deputies in the Chamber.

Moreover, as Low also noted, in British parliamentary politics the principles of party government are carried to their logical extreme, in the sense that there is 'no attempt to concede to the defeated combatant in the electoral struggle any shred of political power'.[3] In local politics all parties are represented on the key committees roughly in proportion to their total strength and so share in the

1 Winston Spencer Churchill, *Lord Randolph Churchill* (1906), II, pp. 252–3.
2 Sidney Low, *The Governance of England* (1904), p. 123.
3 *Ibid.*, pp. 114-15.

running of the council's business, a system which some reformers (like the pioneer socialist, Fred Jowett of Bradford) would have liked to see extended to Westminster and Whitehall. But the principle of 'winner takes all' continues to regulate the distribution of *ministerial* office.

Admittedly, the maintenance of a clear distinction between the political head of a department and the 'permanent' civil service has prevented the development of a 'spoils system' in Britain like the one which operates in the United States. On the other hand, whereas an American President can appoint *anyone he chooses* to even the highest political office, British convention stipulates that in normal circumstances the Cabinet should be chosen from members of the same party[4] – yet another manifestation of the centrality of party in British national life. Indeed, so accustomed are British politicians to treating single-party government as the norm that, even when a general election leads to a 'hung parliament', the largest single party, rather than participate in a coalition government proper, invariably forms its own Ministry, supported openly or tacitly by one of the smaller parliamentary groups.[5] This convention, too, makes Britain different from most other democratic states.

During the last century and a half numerous attempts have been made to explain and justify Britain's distinctive two-party system. At the practical level, the most convincing and most frequently used defence has been that it at least produces clear-cut electoral verdicts. Indeed, one might argue that the stability of British public life owes much to a system which removes the need for the protracted wheeler-dealing characterising countries which operate a multi-party system. For, once it has won a general election, the government has behind it a body of parliamentary followers who can generally be relied upon to sustain its majority in the legislature – aided, of course, by the exertions of the party whips. The great historian G.M. Trevelyan boasted that, through the development of party, England had thus shown the world how 'efficiency could be combined with freedom'.[6]

In addition, if its advocates are to be believed, two-party rivalries have served to protect the country from falling into the hands of

---

4 John Morley, *Walpole* (1889), p. 156.

5 This happened after the General Elections of 1885, 1886, 1892, the two elections of 1910, 1929 and February 1974. The 1923 General Election led to the second largest party (Labour) being helped into office by the third largest party (the Liberals).

6 G.M. Trevelyan, 'The Two-Party System in English Political History' (1926), in *An Autobiography & Other Essays* (1949), pp. 186–7.

opportunistic office-seekers. In a famous formulation, Edmund Burke defined party as 'a body of men united, for promoting by their joint endeavours the national interest, upon some particular principle in which they are all agreed'.[7] To those who share this view of politics, the suspension of the normal healthy clash of great parties, each united around a coherent set of policies and principles, risks exposing the country to the dangers of factionalism and corruption. 'Maintain the line of demarcation between parties', Disraeli urged the Commons in one of his great philippics against Peel, 'for it is only by maintaining the independence of party that you can maintain the integrity of public men, and the power and influence of Parliament itself.'[8]

Yet why should such a conception of politics mean the dominance of only *two* parties? Obviously the issues that have marked the line of cleavage between parties have changed very considerably over the last couple of centuries. Nevertheless, one could perhaps demonstrate that there has always been, broadly speaking, a party of tradition, a confederation of those who are fearful of change or who would stand to lose from it, locked in conflict with a party composed of people with a psychological or material interest in reform. When the party of 'novelty' has been too long in office, there is a desire for tranquillity, and this brings the party of 'habit' back to power until such time as the need or the desire for change makes itself felt once more,[9] so allowing for a healthy alternation of periods of innovation and periods of consolidation. Other political commentators have even argued that the two-party system reflects the duality of the human mind.

But, more often than not, British political arrangements have simply been *taken for granted*. If challenged, defenders of the status quo are prone to talk about the venerable antiquity of the two-party system, treating it almost as though it were on a par with the Crown, Parliament, the jury system and other elements of the country's unwritten constitution. We can find Gladstone, for example, arguing

7 Edmund Burke, *Thoughts on the Cause of the Present Discontents* (1770: ed. F.G. Selby, 1951), p. 81.

8 22 Jan. 1846, cited in William Flavelle Monypenny, *The Life of Benjamin Disraeli Earl of Beaconsfield. Vol. II, 1837–1846* (1912), pp. 356–7. Similar arguments were later used, unsuccessfully, against Disraeli over his 'betrayal' of the Conservative Party during the Reform Crisis of 1866–67. See 'The Conservative Surrender', *Quarterly Review*, Oct. 1867, in Paul Smith (ed.), *Lord Salisbury on Politics: A selection from his articles in the Quarterly Review 1860–1883* (Cambridge, 1972), pp. 269–76.

9 Ivor Jennings, *Party Politics: III, The Stuff of Politics* (Cambridge, 1962), p. 15.

in 1856 that party was 'dignified by traditional recollections';[10] and writing a half century later, Lord Rosebery declared that Britain's party system was one 'of immemorial tradition'.[11] Such an interpretation has been underwritten by many professional historians. Trevelyan claimed in 1926 that the two main parties, despite all their changes of creed and programme, had 'continued as the strongest and most lasting element in our public life from the days of Danby and Shaftesbury to the days of Salisbury and Gladstone'.[12]

Similarly, the British conception of party is often portrayed as an expression of the *national character*, something rooted in a distinctive British way of life. Trevelyan believed that our two main parties historically reflected 'the dualism in the religious life of the nation', resting on the Church-Chapel division.[13] Others have drawn parallels between the party rituals of Westminster and Britain's idiosyncratic *legal* system. 'Justice, pure justice, is the result of the contest between two sets of advocates on two different sides', wrote Lord Rosebery in 1906: 'the only difference is that the politicians professedly speak from conviction, while the lawyers professedly speak from their briefs.'[14] The physical shape of the House of Commons, so different from the circular legislative chambers of the United States and Continental Europe, is also thought by many to have encouraged an adversarial political approach.

Yet another common defence of party involves the claim that the average Briton, before anything else, is a *sportsman* who loves the drama of a head-to-head *contest*. As Lloyd George once observed: 'The Briton is a fighting man. He likes a fighting speech. Politics is his football match.'[15] This is an interesting observation because it neatly draws together the two areas of activity which have always supplied politicians and political commentators with most of their metaphors and analogies: sport and warfare. In a war, of course, there

---

10 William Gladstone, 'The Declining Efficiency of Parliament', *Quarterly Review*, XCIX (Sept. 1856), 560.

11 Lord Rosebery, *Lord Randolph Churchill* (1906), p. 165.

12 Trevelyan, *Autobiography*, p. 184.

13 Ibid., pp. 198–9.

14 Rosebery, *Randolph Churchill*, p. 165. The political scientist, A.L. Lowell agreed, adding that in both cases the opposing advocates often enjoyed a friendly personal relationship (A. Lawrence Lowell, *Government of England* (New York, 1908), II, pp. 96–7).

15 10 April 1920, Lord Riddell, *Intimate Diary of the Peace Conference and After 1918–1923* (1933), p. 181.

are normally two quite easily distinguishable sets of contestants, and that is true of many games.[16] In both cases, participation is highly valued: similarly with politics, where refusal to take sides in the party contest may lay a person open to the imputation of being un-English and unmanly – even cowardly. Such was the theory of government entertained by Trollope's party manager, Barrington Erle, who thought that 'the House of Commons should be divided by a marked line, and every member should be required to stand on one side of it or on the other. "If not with me, at any rate be against me," he would have said to every representative of the people in the name of the great leader whom he followed.'[17]

Thus party, or rather a confrontational conception of party as involving a clash between two rival teams, armies, sects or sets of advocates, has put down profound roots into British life. By the late Victorian period, it had already lodged itself in the national folk-memory in the form of oft-cited (though usually misunderstood) adages like Disraeli's observation that 'England does not love Coalitions'[18] and W.S. Gilbert's jingle about the propensity of boys and gals to be born as 'either little Liberals, or else as little Conservatives'.

This is a view of politics which has also coloured historical writing. When we think about the country's political past, we tend to assume the alternation in power of two major parties of government, brought about by the 'swing of the pendulum'[19] – originally a contest between Whigs and Tories, followed, after a confused period of transition, by a renewed two-party system based on the rivalry between Conservatives and Labour. No wonder that most works of political history which are not concerned with a specific area of policy (Ireland, industrial relations, and so on) are primarily concerned with party loyalty and party conflict.[20]

16 For an analogy between politics and a boxing contest, see George Wyndham to father, 15 Oct. 1903, in J.W. Mackail and Guy Wyndham, *Life and Letters of George Wyndham* (n.d.), II, pp. 469–70.

17 Anthony Trollope, *Phineas Finn* (1869: World's Classics edn), p. 15.

18 See Robert Blake, '1783–1902', in David Butler (ed.), *Coalitions in British Politics* (1978), p. 1.

19 The latter was a concept invented by Lord Salisbury (Low, *Governance of England*, pp. 129–30).

20 For an intelligent discussion of the distorting effect of this approach on historical understanding, see Brian Harrison, 'The Centrist Theme in Modern British Politics', in *Peaceable Kingdom: Stability and Change in Modern Britain* (Oxford, 1982), pp. 353–5.

THE INADEQUACIES OF THE PARTY INTERPRETATION

But in some respects this preoccupation with party gives a distorted view of modern British political life, especially of the period principally covered in this book. So much is immediately apparent if one lists the ministries holding office in the years separating the 1885 General Election (the first to be held on a semi-democratic franchise) and the end of the Second World War.

Salisbury's Caretaker Ministry (December 1885–February 1886): minority Conservative, with Irish Nationalists holding the balance of seats.

Gladstone's Third Ministry (February-July 1886): minority Liberal, sustained by the Irish Nationalist Party.

Salisbury's Second Ministry (July 1886–August 1892): minority Conservative, sustained by the Liberal Unionist Party.

Gladstone and Rosebery's Liberal Ministries (August 1892–July 1895): minority Liberal, sustained by Irish Nationalists.

Salisbury's Third and Balfour's Ministry (July 1895–December 1905): coalition of Conservatives and Liberal Unionists.

Campbell-Bannerman's and Asquith's Ministries (December 1905–January 1910): Liberal.

Asquith's Ministry (January 1910–May 1915): minority Liberal, sustained by Irish Nationalist and Labour.

Asquith's and Lloyd George's Ministries (May 1915–October. 1922): coalition of Liberal, Conservative and Labour – Labour withdrawing in late 1918.

Bonar Law's and Baldwin's First Ministry (October 1922–January 1924): Conservative.

MacDonald's First Ministry (January-November 1924): minority Labour, sustained by Liberals, with Conservatives the largest party in Commons.

Baldwin's Second Ministry (November 1924–June 1929): Conservative.

MacDonald's Second Ministry (June 1929–August 1931): minority Labour, sustained by Liberals.

'National Ministries' of MacDonald, Baldwin and Neville Chamberlain (August 1931–May 1940): coalition, though increasingly Conservative-dominated.

Churchill's Ministry (May 1940–May 1945): coalition.

Churchill's Caretaker 'National' Ministry (May–July 1945): coalition of Conservatives, Liberal Nationals and non-party.

Clearly between 1885 and 1945 party ministries did *not* alternate at more or less regular intervals as a result of the swing of the pendulum. The period begins with the Home Rule schism, which ushered in twenty years of Unionist domination; there followed ten years of Liberal rule; then, from May 1915 to July 1945 the Conservatives, with an intermission of only three-and-a-half years, were continually in office, either by themselves or as partners, usually the dominant partners, in a coalition ministry.

Nor are we here talking simply about a party *imbalance*. For during the sixty years between 1885 and 1945, *only ten* were occupied by party administrations commanding a Commons majority; for the rest of the time, the country was ruled either by coalitions or by minority governments.[21] So startlingly at variance are such statistics with the conventional view of British political life that academic commentators have been tempted to explain them away.[22]

It is true that no modern coalition ministry has ever come into existence as the result of an indecisive general election – though general elections have sometimes ratified coalitions already in existence. Non-party administrations (most obviously the two wartime coalitions) have usually arisen, not from parliamentary deadlock, but out of a sense of national crisis so acute that the normal play of party rivalries has seemed dangerous or inappropriate.

From this some historians have deducted that coalition governments have been set up in modern Britain *solely to deal with temporary emergencies*: even their creators, it is said, have seen them as an

---

21 David Butler reaches similar conclusions, in Butler (ed.), *Coalitions*, pp. 112–13. See also David Marquand, *The Case for Coalition* (1981), p. 2; Vernon Bogdanor (ed.), *Coalition Government in Western Europe* (1983), pp. 10–12.

22 See Chapter 12.

interruption of normal business.[23] According to David Butler, the most important question to be asked about a coalition is when and how it breaks up: 'the shadow of the next election must hang, in greater or less degree, over all coalitions'.[24]

But this judgement hardly applies to peacetime 'national' administrations, some of which looked like becoming semi-permanencies: for example, the Lloyd George Coalition which carried on after the signing of the Armistice in 1918, and the 'National Government' established in the middle of the 1931 financial crisis which survived until Churchill came to power in May 1940. Clearly, something is lacking in an approach which treats the phenomenon of coalition *merely* as a short-term response to a transient emergency.

And so this is a book which does not confine itself to an analysis of the options available to politicians when confronting a deadlocked Commons. Still less is it a chronicle of the rise and fall of particular coalition ministries, treated as isolated episodes. Instead, coalition governments are seen as a manifestation of a persistent quest to break free from the 'sterility' of party strife – a quest long predating the formation of the SDP and the emergence of the 'Alliance' in the 1980s. For, as we shall see, almost as strong as party feeling (and at times much stronger) has been the antipathy which party has aroused.

THE CRITIQUE OF PARTY

Sidney Low may have believed that party had traditionally been central to British political life. But he was also impressed by how *unpopular* party had always been. From the time of the Duke of Marlborough onwards, he observed, there had 'been an unbroken stream of theoretical condemnation. No sentiment is likely to elicit more applause at a public meeting, than the statement that "this, Mr Chairman, is not a party question, and I do not propose to treat it from a party standpoint".'[25] Even Disraeli, in general a staunch apologist of party, also contributed to its discrediting by his invention

23 See A.J. Beattie, 'The Two-Party System: Room for Scepticism?', in S.E. Finer (ed.), *Adversary Politics and Electoral Reform* (1975), p. 300.

24 Butler (ed.), *Coalitions*, pp. 116–17.

25 Low, *Governance of England*, p. 117.

of Tadpole and Taper.[26] Recent Alliance attacks on 'yah-boo' politics clearly go back a very long way.

In fact, throughout the nineteenth and twentieth Centuries nearly all the standard arguments in support of two-party politics have come under challenge. For example, analogies between the law courts and the House of Commons have hardly endeared party to those countless people who hate lawyers and equate legal advocacy with insincerity and mercenariness. Moreover, it is possible to argue, as F.S.Oliver once did, that the British are a business people, who instinctively prefer the method of discussion and negotiation employed in resolving business disputes to legalistic processes which invariably widen the differences between the contending parties.[27]

Moreover, the element of sporting rivalry and ritualised combat which to some has been one of the attractions of the party system has also deterred others. To treat politics as though it were some kind of sporting contest can be seen as a trivialisation of serious issues. Nor does everyone revel vicariously in the heroism and excitement of battle. Henry Maine once cast the eye of a professional anthropologist over party and came to the judgement that it was an 'atavism': 'party feeling', he suspected, was 'probably far more a survival of the primitive combativeness of mankind than a consequence of conscious intellectual differences between man and man'.[28] Many women, it seems, are particularly exasperated by the ritualised aggression fomented by party strife, which they find childish.

Even the argument that party discipline and loyalty serve as a barrier against corruption has often been queried. Why, for example, should electors be forced to choose between two party programmes, with many items of which they are bound to disagree? Ostrogorski went further, questioning 'the theory of the natural dualism of the human mind' which the champions of party were fond of advancing and wondering whether it was 'natural that the same persons should always, in all things, take, the one set the negative, the other the affirmative side'.[29] It was this consideration which persuaded

---

26 In *Coningsby* (1844).

27 Frederick S. Oliver, *What Federalism Is* Not (1914), pp. 25–6. For the belief of many mid-Victorian businessmen that it was better to settle commercial disputes, informally, by resort to arbitration, so avoiding the expense and delay inherent in judicial processes, see G.R. Searle, *Entrepreneurial Politics in Mid-Victorian Britain* (Oxford, 1993), pp. 176–81.

28 Henry Sumner Maine, *Popular Government* (1885), p. 31.

29 M. Ostrogorski, *Democracy and the Organization of Political Parties* (1902), II, p. 617.

A.V. Dicey of the desirability of tempering party politics with the Referendum.

Moreover, what could be more dishonest than an MP having to subordinate his judgement and conscience to the demands of the party whips? In fact, ever since the tightening of party discipline in the last third of the nineteenth century, there have been individualistic MPs, members of the 'Awkward Squad', like Captain 'Tommy' Bowles, Hilaire Belloc, Josiah Wedgwood and W.J. Brown, who have loudly objected to the restraints which party officials seek to impose. Brown spoke for them all when he asked why anyone went to the bother of electing MPs in the first place when it would have been more convenient to install 615 gramophones.[30]

However, politicians who express a distaste for party are not necessarily motivated by the same hopes and aversions. Broadly speaking they fall into one of three separate groups. First, we have the 'grumblers', those who chafe at the restrictions imposed upon them by the need to toe the party line. For the last century or more, a surprisingly large number of senior politicians (as well as independent-minded backbenchers) have affected to despise their own party, just as many politicians have expressed horror at having to contest general elections. But in the absence of any alternative, these 'grumblers' invariably stick by their chosen party when the chips are down.

The second group of party critics may be called the 'rhetoricians'. There is a discourse about 'the national interest' which many politicians employ when they think it will bring them rewards. The aim is to distance oneself from a *narrow* conception of party, knowing that the wider electorate tends to find partisanship distasteful and divisive. This, in part, was what Disraeli was doing when he claimed that the Tory Party was the 'national party' because it supported the institutions of the country which guaranteed the people's freedom.[31] Indeed, almost every Conservative Leader from Disraeli onwards has

---

30 W.J. Brown, *So Far* . . . (1943), p. 253.

31 The young Disraeli had drawn a stark contrast between his own party and the Whigs, the 'Venetian Oligarchy', with their 'Dutch Finance' and their cosmopolitan, 'anti-national' outlook (Benjamin Disraeli, *Vindication of the English Constitution* . . . (1835), cited in part in William Flavelle Monypenny, *The Life of Benjamin Disraeli Earl of Beaconsfield. Vol. 1, 1804–37* (1910), pp. 311–17). Disraeli later repeated these fanciful claims in his famous speech at the Crystal Palace of 24 June 1872 which included the ringing phrase: 'The Tory Party, unless it is a National Party, is nothing.'

occasionally attached the label 'national' to his party – much to the exasperation of the Conservatives' opponents.

Nor is the Conservative claim that their party represents 'the nation', whereas Labour merely embodies a sectional interest, entirely fanciful. For Conservatives have always been very much more successful in attracting working-class votes than Labour has been in attracting middle-class votes. (Though in recent times the Liberals, and later the 'Alliance', have far excelled both major parties in the 'evenness' of their electoral support.) Moreover, psephological surveys suggest that during the 1960s Conservative voters, as well as the leadership, really did believe that their party was a 'national' party above politics because it functioned as 'the governing agent of an integrated if stratified social order', unlike Labour which operated far more with a 'them and us', class-conflict model of society.[32]

But the rhetorical invocation of 'the national interest' has not been confined to Conservatives. As we shall see, some Liberals have also employed this strategy. So, on behalf of the Labour Party, did Stafford Cripps in 1947–49 and Harold Wilson in the mid-1970s.[33] Nevertheless its most consistent practitioners have been pragmatic, middle-of-the-road, consensual Conservatives like Baldwin, Eden, Macmillan and, more recently, the 'Tory Wets'.

Now, this is the point at which some observers of British politics might be tempted to argue that playing the 'national card' amounts to little more than a ploy in the party game: it does not involve a radical rejection of party itself. Of course, even if this be true, the rhetorical invocation of the 'national interest' is still significant inasmuch as it assumes that large swathes of the electorate are 'switched off' by partisan politics.

However, a third group can be identified among the critics of party which must be differentiated from both the 'grumblers' and the 'rhetoricians'. These are the politicians who have a sincere and considered aversion to two-party politics and have invested time and energy in trying to devise an alternative, commonly designated by such phrases as a 'national party' and a 'national government'. Interestingly enough, included in their ranks have been some of the most powerful politicians of their day: for example, Joseph

32 David Butler and Donald Stokes, *Political Change in Britain: Forces Shaping Electoral Choice* (1969; 1971 edn), pp. 122–4.

33 See Chapter 11. When Heath tried to float his 'Government of National Unity' in 1974, Wilson replied that *he* was already running a 'national government'! (John Campbell, *Edward Heath: A Biography* (1993), pp. 636–7).

Chamberlain, Lloyd George and Winston Churchill, all of whom (in their different ways) favoured the establishment of a new kind of 'national' grouping.

One cannot explain the convictions of *these* critics of party by imagining a sharp disjunction between rhetoric and ideas, since they took the same line in private that they were adopting in public – indeed, if anything they have tended to be *more* critical of party in their private utterances (diaries, confidential letters, informal conversation) than in their public speeches, where prudence has often required them to uphold the orthodox party line.

This book deals only intermittently with the 'grumblers' and 'rhetoricians'. Its main purpose is to explore the minds and to chronicle the activities of those who view the two-party system with deep antipathy. Some chapters (for example, 5, 6, 8 and 9) are about the operation of actual coalitions or quasi-coalitions: others deal with what, in retrospect, have the appearance of abortive schemes (3, 4 and 11). But both accounts are necessary. For even the failed initiatives often had important though unintended consequences. For example, the tariff crusade, analysed in Chapter 3, fractured the Conservative and Unionist Party for an entire generation, and the emergence of the SDP and the 'Alliance' (Chapter 11) laid the foundations for the Conservative hegemony of the 1980s.

Moreover, during some of these periods of apparent 'failure', ideas incubated which burst out of their shells *at a later date*. Political life during the Great War and the early 1920s, for example, makes little sense if one ignores the new reform agenda which had taken shape in the Edwardian years; that is why this latter period is treated at considerable length in Chapter 4.

But, more important still, it is essential to realise that the quest for a 'national government' (whether successful or not) has been a continuous feature of modern British politics. We do not just write about the victories achieved by Liberals, Conservatives and Socialists. Dislike of party deserves to be treated in a similar way by being given its own history – a history which encompasses many disappointments and partial achievements but which has also had its moments of triumphant vindication.

CHAPTER TWO
The Mid-Victorian Prelude

MID-VICTORIAN CRITIQUES OF PARTY

Given the fact of Britain's supposedly strong attachment to the two-party system, how does one explain the widespread feeling that a 'National Government' should be formed? And why did it manifest itself so powerfully in the late nineteenth and twentieth centuries? It is sometimes assumed that these 'anti-party' ideas came like a bolt from the blue, partly in response to changing international realities. But, in fact, like the cult of party, antipathy to party also had deep *historical* roots, going back at least until the middle of the nineteenth century. One can trace the origins of these feelings to four separate sources.

First, in the mid-Victorian years there still existed an older 'Hanoverian' Tory tradition, which assigned priority to the task of establishing an effective executive *independent of party*. The Leader of the Conservative Party, Sir Robert Peel, brought just such a 'ministerial ethic' to the running of his premiership between 1841 and 1846. The principal duty of 'ministers of the Crown', Peel believed, was that of carrying on the 'Queen's Government', which meant that the national interest should always take precedence over mere party considerations.[1] As one historian has put it, Peel's was 'an authoritarian view of party'.[2]

---

1 See Angus Hawkins, '"Parliamentary Government" and Victorian Political Parties, c. 1830–c. 1880', *English Historical Review*, 104 (1989), 652–6.

2 Jonathan Parry, *The Rise and Fall of Liberal Government in Victorian Britain* (New Haven and London, 1993), p. 157.

Such a political approach may already have begun to look a little old-fashioned even in the 1840s, and in pursuing it Peel strained the loyalty of his followers to breaking point in 1846. But it also won him numerous admirers. Thomas Carlyle, himself a stringent critic of the idiocies of party, saluted Peel (on his premature death in 1850) as the nearest that contemporary Britain had got to producing a 'heroic' statesman.[3] Moreover, the Peelite conception of government was faithfully maintained by his followers, in particular by Lord Aberdeen, who formed a coalition ministry in December 1852 that many contemporaries hoped would permanently obliterate traditional party rivalries. The Prince Consort, who did not die until 1861, also stayed loyal to Peel's memory. Indeed, well into the twentieth century Peel was still being fondly remembered as the courageous statesman who had sacrificed his career by putting country before party; as such he has a privileged place in the ideology of 'national government'.[4]

The second reservoir of anti-party sentiment in mid-Victorian Britain was 'entrepreneurial Radicalism'. Significantly, many prominent Radical businessmen held Peel in great admiration. Following the Repeal of the Corn Laws in 1846, Richard Cobden urged Peel to put himself at the head of the 'middle class' in recognition of the fact that he, more than any of his contemporaries, represented 'the Idea of the age'.[5] Nor was this an idiosyncratic gesture, since a similar stance was taken by several Radical journals, including the *Westminster Review*.[6]

For in such circles the prejudice died hard that parties were aristocratic factions inspired by nothing but desire for office and official salaries – supposedly the besetting sin of the Whig 'cousin-hood'.[7] This conviction was shared by Charles Dickens, who also came under the influence of Carlyle. Party conflict at Westminster, Dickens believed, was a ritualised game played out within the landed elite, an assumption which underlay his mockery of the Coodles and

---

3 Jules Seigel, 'Carlyle and Peel: The Prophet's Search for a Heroic Politician and an Unpublished Fragment', *Victorian Studies*, 26 (1982–3), 181–95.

4 See Chapter 12.

5 Cobden to Peel, 23 June 1846, cited in John Morley, *The Life of Richard Cobden* (1896 edn), I, pp. 390–7.

6 Randall E. McGowen and Walter L. Arnstein, 'The Mid-Victorians and the Two-Party System', *Albion*, 11 (1979), 242–58.

7 This view of politics can be traced back to the Philosophical Radicals of the 1830s, if not earlier. See William Thomas's essay in Patricia Hollis (ed.), *Pressure From Without in Early Victorian England* (1974), pp. 52–79.

the Doodles in *Bleak House* (1853).[8] What Radicals valued was the 'honesty' and moral courage which enabled an MP to resist the temptations of office: 'independence', not party loyalty, was the virtue they most admired.[9] Indeed, as Brian Harrison notes, the successful campaigns against slavery and the corn laws owed little or nothing to party – which may explain why 'contempt for party was widespread among late Victorian reforming movements'.[10]

In time the Radicals' distaste for party was to fade away, as the composition of the parliamentary elite slowly changed. However, this distaste did leave behind it two important residues. First, it encouraged the belief that political life was lagging behind the commercial progress of the day and needed *modernising*: the country could only be saved if government was established on 'sound business lines', alleged these Radical critics. Such views were particularly prevalent during the Crimean War fiascos when there was a public outcry against aristocratic incompetence. To channel this discontent, a body called the Administrative Reform Association (ARA) was set up in the summer of 1855. Cobden and Bright, who disapproved in principle of the Crimean War, held aloof, but many other middle-class Radicals (Dickens included) rallied to its standards. The ARA claimed that 'merit and efficiency' were 'being sacrificed, in public appointments, to party and family influences', whereas what was needed was the introduction into government of business experience and expertise. This line of argument was to enjoy a very long life.

But such a political approach merges with a third source of hostility to party during the mid-Victorian years, one which can best be examined through the pages of *The Economist*, a moderate paper widely read by the business community for its commercial intelligence. During the course of the 1850s *The Economist* came

8 Shaw, in his 1912 Preface to *Hard Times*, declared that Dickens's 'description of our party system, with its Coodle, Doodle, Foodle, etc., has never been surpassed for accuracy and for penetration of superficial pretence'.

9 On the continuing popular mistrust of party and the survival of the rhetoric of 'Independency', see James Vernon, *Politics and the People: A study in English political culture, c. 1815–1867* (Cambridge, 1993), especially Chapter 4.

10 Brian Harrison, 'Women's Suffrage at Westminster, 1866–1928', in Michael Bentley and John Stevenson (eds), *High and Low Politics in Modern Britain* (Oxford, 1983), p. 92. But Harrison goes on to argue that the suffragettes were mistaken to follow these precedents, since 'after the 1860s the political parties had themselves become the vehicles of popular participation, the instruments of an aroused public opinion; their democratized structure henceforward relegated the non-party pressure group to a subordinate role . . .' (ibid., p. 93).

to believe that party government was dying for want of any great differences of principle to sustain it. 'The strife of parties', it wrote in 1856, 'belongs to a particular and inevitable phase in the life and progress of all free countries – but a phase which essentially belongs to a transitory and imperfect condition of the body politic – a phase which, if permanent, would be indicative of failure and ominous of ruin.' All the electorate could now do was to choose between competent and incompetent candidates, since party, and even perhaps politics themselves, had become meaningless: 'where all think so much alike, it matters much less what a man *thinks* than what he *can do*'.[11]

Here is an early staking-out of the claim (of which much more was to be heard in the future) that the developing national consensus was undermining the rationale for party and that, in consequence, some more intelligent way needed to be found of handling the country's affairs – a more managerial way, perhaps. Thus, *The Economist* clearly had in mind the *idea* of a 'National Government', though it seems not to have used these exact *words*.

Fourthly, there was an influential group of 'University Liberals' and progressive intellectuals, who, alerted to what was happening in the United States of America by De Toqueville's famous study of *Democracy*, worried over what they called 'the tyranny of the majority'. How, they wondered, could the man of distinction who went into public life avoid being driven into conformity with the dull platitudes of the day by the pressure of party organisation? More generally still, how, in a democratic age, could 'individuality' be fostered and 'collective mediocrity' checked?

An early response to this dilemma was the book by the barrister Thomas Hare, *A Treatise on the Election of Representatives, Parliamentary and Municipal*, published in 1859. This was an eloquent protest against the British electoral system which, Hare claimed, subordinated the opinions of MPs to the needs of party, here dismissively referred to as a mere 'contrivance'. To counter this menace, Hare recommended a form of Proportional Representation (what later became known as the Single Transferable Vote, or STV) to enhance the role of the individual Member. His elaborate scheme was taken up with

11 *The Economist*, 1 Nov. 1856, 1201–2. This was written in response to Gladstone's *Quarterly Review* article earlier in the year, bemoaning the decline of party. On 13 June 1857, *The Economist* warned of 'the invention of spurious party-bonds' (643).

enthusiasm by John Stuart Mill,[12] who shared Hare's belief that PR would improve the quality of candidates and MPs by curtailing the activities and influence of political parties; in *Representative Government* he argued that electoral reform would ensure the representation not of 'two great parties alone . . . but of every minority in the whole nation', thereby enabling 'able men of independent thought' who had 'sworn allegiance to no political party' to get into Parliament.[13]

Moreover, although Mill and most of the University Liberals advocated franchise extension during the Reform Crisis of the mid-1860s (though not on the scale of Disraeli's Reform Act of 1867), it is surely significant that their famous compilation, *Essays on Reform*, contains no reference whatever to party. Of course, these men of letters were still proud to call themselves Liberals, but it would seem as if party affiliations and party interests were not realities with which they found it easy to come to terms. Mill (not, in fact a contributor to the volume himself) supposed that political differences were gradually disappearing and wanted to revive healthy debate – but not through the adversarial clash of party. In short, Mill believed in liberalism as an intellectual ideal that could reshape the world, but he had less interest in the Liberal Party.[14] Trollope's fictional character, Phineas Finn, took the same line: 'If I go into Parliament, I shall go there as a sound Liberal, – not to support a party, but to do the best I can for the country.'[15]

PARTY GOVERNMENT OR PARLIAMENTARY GOVERNMENT?

So much for the main repositories of anti-party feeling. Of course, all this notwithstanding, party loyalties *did* continue to flourish even in the mid-Victorian years. Indeed, in an important article in the *English Historical Review*, Angus Hawkins has argued that the unexpected death of Peel in 1850 'made possible the near-unanimous acceptance within Westminster of parliamentary parties as the necessary and

12 Jenifer Hart, *Proportional Representation: Critics of the British Electoral System 1820–1945* (Oxford, 1992), Chapter 2.

13 J.S. Mill, *Representative Government* (1861: Everyman edn), pp. 263–5.

14 A slightly different view of Mill is given in Bruce L. Kinzer, 'J.S. Mill and the Problem of Party', *Journal of British Studies*, 21 (1981), 106–22.

15 Anthony Trollope, *Phineas Finn* (1869: World's Classics edn), p. 14.

desirable source of executive authority'. Such a doctrine, traditionally associated with the Whigs, now enjoyed the support of *both* Front Benches.[16]

But, as Hawkins goes on to show, here was a conception of party which emphasised the sovereignty of *Parliament*, not the wishes of the electorate. This emphasis on 'parliamentary government' made good sense at the time, for though in the mid–Victorian period party manoeuvres often destroyed ministries, these activities took place on the floor of the House of Commons and were not the consequence of direct popular or electoral pressure. Governments were rarely driven from office simply by being defeated in a general election. (Nor, in fact, was there any regular alternation of party ministries, the Whig–Liberal combination being almost continuously in government between 1846 and 1866.)[17] And within Parliament itself Ministers sought to guide the House by example, advocacy and personal reputation, not to curtail free debate through a strict system of 'whipping', even though they knew that this might involve them in the 'superficial indignity of occasional defeat'.[18]

It was precisely such a system of politics which Walter Bagehot celebrated in the mid-1860s in the essays which eventually appeared in book form under the title of *The English Constitution*. Abandoning the earlier editorial line of *The Economist*, which he now edited, Bagehot portrayed party as the 'essence' of the House of Commons. On the other hand, he insisted that Britain's party system only functioned efficiently because the party leaders were, 'for the most part', essentially 'mild' men, not 'eager to carry party conclusions too far': 'they are in contact with reality', he explained.[19]

This seems a reasonably accurate characterisation of political life during the years of Palmerston's ascendancy. Palmerston himself was in many ways not a party man at all.[20] Partly for that reason, there was a good deal of cross-party collaboration during his Second Ministry, especially in 1860–61. Indeed, there is something to be said for A.V. Dicey's later view: namely, that Palmerston had been maintained

16 Hawkins, 'Parliamentary Government', pp. 638–69, especially p. 656.

17 The Conservatives did not win a single general election between 1841 and 1874.

18 The quotation comes from Parry, describing the approach of Lord Althorp as Leader of the Commons in the 1830s: *Liberal Government*, p. 105: see also ibid., pp. 10–11, 232.

19 Walter Bagehot, *The English Constitution* (1867; 1963 edn), pp. 158, 160–1.

20 Parry, *Liberal Government*, p. 178.

in power by Liberals who dreaded the prospect of being led by Gladstone or Bright and by Conservatives who mistrusted Disraeli, a situation which had allowed the views of the people to prevail over party factions.[21] Such 'collusion' was a frequent occurrence in early and mid-Victorian politics.[22]

Out of this style of parliamentary politics there arose a a phenomenon which the historian Brian Harrison has labelled 'centrism'. It depended upon a self-conscious awareness of the consensual elements underlying party rivalry. Its practitioners (of whom a good representative would be the Whig, Lord Hartington) knew that no one party enjoyed a monopoly of wisdom. They accordingly treated their opponents with respect and courtesy – as befitted relations between politicians coming from very similar social backgrounds. Many 'centrist' politicians had anyhow learned from their long experience of office how difficult it often was to implement party pledges. Good government, they came to accept, involved a certain amount of pragmatic caution, and so they shrank from doctrinaire extremism, realising that even in strict party terms it might be unwise to use a transient parliamentary majority to force through policies which were blankly rejected by all the other parties – since changes, if they were to endure, had to command a modicum of national acquiescence, if not actual approval. Finally, the 'centrists' of whom Harrison writes also believed that there were certain areas of public life, like foreign affairs, which ideally ought not to be *politicised* at all.[23]

Now, it is Harrison's contention that this style of political activity long outlasted the Victorian years when it had flourished in all its splendour. There may be some truth in this claim – one thinks of, say, Stanley Baldwin in the 1920s, or Herbert Morrison in the 1940s, both conciliatory politicians quite popular with many of their opponents. But it was also a style of politics which was, in some respects, period-bound. And in the latter half of the 1860s and the 1870s developments took place which put an end to Bagehot's world of 'parliamentary government' and to the 'centrism' which throve in that particular environment.

---

21 A.V. Dicey, *Letters on Unionist Delusions* (1887), pp. 79–80. But compare with the rather different treatment of this theme in P.M. Gurowich, 'The Continuation of War by other means: Party and Politics, 1855–1865', *Historical Journal*, 27 (1984), 603–31.

22 Hugh Berrington, 'Partnership and Dissidence in the Nineteenth-Century House of Commons', *Parliamentary Affairs*, 21 (1967–68), 338–73.

23 Brian Harrison, 'The Centrist Theme in Modern British Politics', in *Peaceable Kingdom: Stability and Change in Modern Britain* (Oxford, 1982), pp. 309–77.

THE SHARPENING OF PARTY ANTAGONISMS AFTER 1870

The first of these developments was the accession to the premiership of Gladstone, who at once set about the deliberate polarisation of the two parties, initially over the Irish Church question. As political commentators of the time immediately saw, this meant the restoration, with a vengeance, of sharp ideological distinctions between the two parties. Add to this the intense personal dislike that had grown up between Gladstone and Disraeli, and it can readily be seen how the more 'consensual' political culture of the Palmerstonian era came to be weakened. Even more important were the policy clashes between the two parties over foreign affairs following Gladstone's Midlothian campaign of 1879–80. By the 1880s it was possible to interpret party strife as a struggle between a Radical Party keen on domestic reform but hostile to overseas entanglements and high defence expenditure, and a Conservative Party mainly concerned to identify itself with a strong Empire and a 'robust' foreign policy.

Lord Salisbury was hardly a disinterested spectator, but he had a valid point to make when he spoke in 1882 of 'a new policy, an entire departure from old principles, whether Liberal or Tory', which Gladstone had initiated.[24] There was also some substance in the contrast which he later drew between the Gladstonian claptrap which had brought the Liberals their recent electoral victory and 'the traditions of Lord Palmerston and Lord Clarendon', who had adhered to 'the well-established methods and traditional principles which ha[d] guided English policy on both sides for many generations'.[25]

But even these developments by themselves might not have destroyed the older type of 'parliamentary government', had they not been accompanied by a number of other changes. One was franchise reform, which saw the proportion of the adult male population eligible to vote rise from 20 per cent in the 1860s to 36 per cent after the Second Reform Act and to 60 per cent after 1884. Some commentators feared that this process of democratisation would inexorably lead to a coarsening of politics. Democracies, argued the political scientist A.L. Lowell, lacked the time, knowledge or

---

24 *The Times*, 8 Aug. 1882. I am grateful to Dr E.D. Steele for drawing my attention to this speech and the one cited in note 21.

25 Ibid., 31 Jan. 1884.

intelligence to examine complex issues on their merits, preferring instead 'broad contrasts, sharply defined alternatives, clearly marked issues and the frank opposition of party leaders'.[26] Conservative commentators feared the consequential emergence of a new kind of narrow and unscrupulous partisanship. 'Up till about the close of Lord Palmerston's career each of the two political parties had definiteness and cohesion', argued one such person in 1887. 'Knowledge and opinion on affairs of State were practically in the hands of the leisured classes'; but despite being divided into two competing groups 'by certain simple principles that seemed then to be immutable', the aristocrats who governed Britain in Palmerston's time shared a commitment to upholding the interests of the state – a happy situation which had since passed away.[27]

This leads on naturally to a discussion of another development which was changing the face of British politics in the closing decades of the nineteenth century: the emergence of strong *extra-parliamentary* organisations seeking to tie MPs to the party programme. Most notable of these was the Birmingham 'caucus', the nucleus of what later became the National Liberal Federation. As a result of its machinations, writes one academic commentator, the House of Commons ceased to be 'an assembly where gentlemen gathered to exercise their independent prerogative and reason upon each other', becoming instead 'an arena where members displayed their loyalty and obedience to their respective parties'.[28] This may exaggerate the ability of the NLF to 'coerce' MPs or to influence the world of 'high politics', where the impact of the 'caucus', initially at least, was perhaps mainly psychological.[29] All the same, the Conservatives were genuinely horrified by the emergence of the caucus, while some Liberals were no less worried by a political invention which they saw as being essentially *illiberal*. For example, James Bryce, in a preface to Ostrogorski's classic (and highly critical) study of modern parties, can be found complaining that 'organisation and discipline' entailed increased 'subordination' and 'obedience', along with the growth of an 'irrational' party spirit which compelled men 'to vote from

---

26 A. Lawrence Lowell, *The Government of England* (New York, 1908), II, p. 84. This was also the view of other contemporary intellectuals, such as Henry Maine.

27 W. Earl Hodgson, 'Party Politics and National Life', *National Review*, 9 (April 1887), 243–4.

28 John D. Fair, *British Interparty Conferences* (Oxford, 1980), p. 263.

29 Parry, *Liberal Government*, pp. 223, 275.

considerations which ha[d] little to do with the love of truth or a sense of justice'.[30]

It was in an attempt to shield minority groups from domination by the majority that Parliament had adopted the 'minority vote' in 1867 and 'cumulative voting' for School Board elections in 1870.[31] Yet, ironically, these constitutional innovations simply had the effect of encouraging the Birmingham Liberals, Joseph Chamberlain included, to 'organise' party more tightly still with the aim of frustrating what they saw as a contemptible dodge for 'cheating the People' of their rightful prizes. For Chamberlain and his friends believed that *collective* action was needed to secure significant reforms, a conviction which set them apart from the older 'University Liberals', with their essentially 'individualist' perspective on public life, who were further confirmed in their antipathy to 'raw democracy'.

In fact, an interesting volte-face was taking place in the 1870s and 1880s. Once they saw that they had a realistic chance of using party machinery to capture control of the state, a younger generation of militant Radicals became enthusiastic *advocates* of party.[32] Meanwhile the defence of parliamentary 'independence' was passing to the Liberal intelligentsia – from whose ranks there emerged the leadership of the Proportional Representation Society, founded in 1884.

A.V. Dicey, a prominent University Liberal, would have no truck with PR[33] but, instead, became a strong advocate of the Referendum – another device that seemed to offer an escape from the tyranny of machine politics and a return to the sort of 'parliamentary government' characteristic of the mid-Victorian years. 'Personally I think that I should have preferred real Parliamentary government as it existed up to 1868', wrote Dicey revealingly in 1894:

---

30 Christopher Harvie, *The Lights of Liberalism: University Liberals and the Challenge of Democracy 1860–86* (1976), p. 186.

31 The 'minority vote' system obliged electors to cast one fewer vote than there were seats to be filled in multi-member constituencies:i.e. a voter had only two votes in a three-member borough. The 'cumulative vote' gave electors in multi-member constituencies as many votes as there were seats, and allowed them, if they wished, to allot all these votes to a single candidate.

32 On earlier Radical indifference towards party organisation, see John Vincent, *The Formation of the British Liberal Party 1857–68* (1966; 1972 edn), p. 119.

33 Hart, *Proportional Representation*, p. 143. Of course, *some* forms of electoral reform cannot but *increase* the power of party wirepullers: for example, any kind of national list system. For this reason alone many Liberal MPs in the late Victorian period preferred to trust to the 'independence' and 'character' of individual MPs (Parry, *Liberal Government*, p. 284).

But I have not the remotest doubt that under the present condition
of things sham Parliamentary government means a very vicious form
of government by party, and from this I believe the referendum
may partly save us. It has the great merit of being the only check
on party management which is in perfect harmony with democratic
sentiment . . .[34]

But these were vain attempts to stem the tide. For the final two
decades of the century saw a rapid growth of party conformity
in Parliament. The Conservatives and Irish had always been more
cohesive in their voting behaviour than the Liberals: the Radical gadfly
Labouchere ventured the opinion in 1886 that while the Conservatives
were 'an army', the Liberals and Radicals were little better than 'a
mob'.[35] But by the mid 1890s 'partisan dissidence' was becoming
unusual on *both* sides of the House. The chronology of the change
is not entirely clear, but one student of the subject thinks that the
session of 1890 marks the watershed.[36] What is indisputable is that
by 1903 both Conservatives and Liberals were obeying their Whips
in as many as 90 per cent of all divisions.[37]

These developments were accelerated by the reform of the House's
procedures in the 1880s and by the adoption of Balfour's 'Parliamentary Railway Timetable' in 1902, two changes which strengthened the executive's control of the House of Commons and thus
reduced the scope for backbencher initiatives. 'The parliamentary
system in its present form', observed Lowell in 1908, 'require[d]
a party discipline far more strict than it did fifty years ago, and
perhaps more strict than will always be possible.'[38] Low went further,
arguing that the current Commons was scarcely a legislative chamber
at all, but rather 'a machine for discussing the legislative projects of
ministers'.[39]

From the late nineteenth century onwards there has been a stream
of individualistic backbenchers objecting to the way in which party
has fettered their independence. But some Front Bench leaders viewed

34 Dicey to Strachey, 29 Jan. 1894, in Richard A. Cosgrove, *The Rule of Law:
Albert Venn Dicey, Victorian Jurist* (1980), p. 107. Also, see Dicey's article, 'English
Party Government', *Quarterly Review* (April 1910), 210, 604–27.

35 W.C. Lubenow, *Parliamentary Politics and the Home Rule Crisis: The British
House of Commons in 1886* (Oxford, 1988), p. 151: see also pp. 128–30.

36 Berrington, 'Partisanship and Dissidence', 353.

37 Ibid., 342. Strictly speaking, these statistics cover the Unionist Party as a
whole, not just the Conservative MPs.

38 Lowell, *Government*, II, p. 86.

39 Sidney Low, *The Governance of England* (1904), p. 75.

the 'caucus' with an equally jaundiced eye. They had good reason to do so since, as one political scientist has observed, the decline of 'dissidence' in the late nineteenth century came about less through the 'regimentation of the backbencher in support of Front Bench measures' than through 'the transformation of the party leaders into the collaborators of their backbench followers'.[40] Some prominent statesmen, whether in office or occupying the Opposition Front Bench, thus came to feel that they were being hamstrung by party commitments which were pointless, impractical or even mischievous. It was frustrations of this kind which lay behind Lord Randolph Churchill's cynical observation to Henry James in November 1885 that he 'must clear [his] mind of the ordinary polemics which are good enough for elections, but do not form part of statesmanship'.[41]

Only in the Lords did a fairly strict party system coexist with an older consensual style of political rivalry. This was particularly marked in foreign policy debates in the Upper Chamber, where the usually genuine bipartisan agreement was reinforced by the reluctance of the two Front Benches to embarrass one another if this risked damaging national interests.[42] Significantly many of the fiercest critics of the abuses of party in the late 1890s turn out to be peers – most notably, Lord Rosebery, himself a former Foreign Secretary who strove desperately to preserve 'continuity of policy' in all matters affecting the country's external interests.

It was in response to this new situation that attempts were made to limit party differences by the conference method. In 1869 private consultations had taken place between the two Front Benches to settle the question of the Irish Church. More formal meetings were later employed to secure a cross-party agreement over the terms of Redistribution in 1884, and during the next few decades conferences became accepted as a useful way of securing a national consensus in support of important constitutional changes.[43]

But conferences, almost by definition, could only be held at times of emergency to resolve specific conflicts – for example, conflicts between the two Houses of Parliament. And as the nation entered the choppy seas whipped up by the acrimonious Irish dispute of 1885–86 there were politicians on both sides of the party divide who

40 Berrington, 'Partisanship and Dissidence', 373.

41 Cited in Lubenow, *Parliamentary Politics*, p. 127.

42 Andrew Adonis, *Making Aristocracy Work: The Peerage and the Political System in Britain 1884–1914* (Oxford, 1993), pp. 18–19, 72–4.

43 Fair, *British Interparty Conferences*, pp. 6–7.

began to look for more radical ways of bypassing, or at the very least mitigating, the damaging impact of adversarial strife.

This forms the background to the new interest in coalition government. Not that the word 'coalition' itself was often used. This is because earlier in the century coalition had been widely viewed as one of the more sinister *manifestations* of party: an attempt by confederacies or 'juntos' to deprive the honest freeborn Englishman of his Liberties and 'Independence'.[44] And though by the 1890s this rhetoric of 'Independency' had lost much of its former potency, so closely had 'coalition' become identified in the popular mind with trickery and 'unfair play' that critics of two-party politics usually preferred to talk about 'national government'. How, though, did they think that such a fundamental restructuring of the political system might be achieved?

44 Vernon, *Politics and the People*, pp. 176–7.

CHAPTER THREE

Chamberlain and the Legacy of the Home Rule Crisis, 1885–1906

HOME RULE AND THE PARTY REALIGNMENT OF 1885–86

Although most political history is written as a history of two-party competition, such an approach does not commit one to the position that party allegiances and boundaries are fixed and immutable. Individuals finding themselves in a party with which they no longer sympathise will detach themselves and start looking for a more congenial home; in fact, crossing the floor of the House was very common in the nineteenth century, though it has become rarer since 1918. In addition, there will be occasional party breakdowns producing 'secessions', when disaffected politicians abandon their original party and spend a number of years in some new political grouping before crossing over to the other side. It could be argued that if a two-party system is to survive at all, there will almost inevitably be secessions like these from time to time – otherwise the 'system' itself would atrophy and die.

Now, it is commonly argued that the party realignment of 1885–86 (like the Conservative schism in 1846 and the Liberal split of 1931–32) was just such an event. When Gladstone declared his conversion to Irish Home Rule, he threw his Liberal followers into disarray. Almost one-third of Liberal MPs, including Joseph Chamberlain, broke away to form the Liberal Unionist Party, under the leadership of Lord Hartington (in December 1891 he became the 8th Duke of Devonshire). The Liberal Unionists then sustained Salisbury's Conservative Administration in office between 1886 and 1892, and co-operated with it in a 'Unionist Coalition' between 1895 and 1905. From the very start there had been an electoral pact between

Conservatives and Liberal Unionists, and, although each retained its separate organisations both inside and outside Parliament, the two parties worked together in reasonable harmony until in 1912 they finally merged – to form the Conservative and Unionist Party. At the same time a rival 'alliance' came into existence, one composed of Gladstonian Liberals, Irish Nationalists and, after 1900, Labour.

From one point of view, then, the 'realignment' of 1885–86 can be treated as though it were a confused and messy episode out of which a new two-party system quite quickly emerged.[1] Some historians go further and contend that this new system was actually more rational or logical than the one it replaced, in the sense that 'moderate' Liberals who had for some years felt uneasy over Radical aggression and Gladstone's unpredictable behaviour now had the chance of aligning themselves with the Conservatives, with whom they had rather more in common.

It is true that earlier in the decade some of the great Whig aristocrats, unhappy with the performance of Gladstone's Ministry, had already crossed the floor of the House,[2] and it seemed likely that others would follow suit. True, 'the Tories needed the Whigs more urgently than the Whigs needed to escape the Liberal Party'.[3] All the same, senior Conservatives – Sir Stafford Northcote as much as Salisbury – had solid grounds for hoping that Radical 'extremism' might shortly goad many of the Whigs into leaving the Liberal Party *en bloc* and joining forces with the Conservative Party to form a new defensive alliance, though quite when and how this would happen remained unclear.[4] To some extent, the exodus from the official Liberal Party of many wealthy Whig landowners, including Hartington in 1886, can plausibly be seen as the moment when these hopes became realised.

Nor is it surprising that one of the most energetic architects of Liberal Unionism should have been the merchant banker, George

---

1 See Vernon Bogdanor, *Multi-party politics and the Constitution* (Cambridge, 1983), p. 10.

2 Donald Southgate, *The Passing of the Whigs 1832–1886* (1962), pp. 374–6. For a different view of Whig–Liberal relations, see T.A. Jenkins, *Gladstone, Whiggery and the Liberal Party 1874–1886* (Oxford, 1988), Chapter 5, and Jonathan Parry, *The Rise and Fall of Liberal Government in Victorian Britain* (New Haven and London, 1993), Chapter 12.

3 John France, 'Salisbury and the Unionist Alliance', in Robert Blake and Hugh Cecil (eds), *Salisbury* (1987), p. 223.

4 Ibid., pp. 222–4. Salisbury had held these views ever since the 1860s. See Robert Stewart, '"The Conservative Reaction": Lord Robert Cecil and Party Politics', ibid., p. 112.

Joachim Goschen, who had refused to serve in Gladstone's Government in 1880 – evidence of the mounting disquiet felt by some traditional middle-class Liberals with the leadership of their own party. When Salisbury shortly afterwards appointed Goschen Chancellor of the Exchequer, following Lord Randolph Churchill's resignation, he became the first Liberal Unionist to serve in a Conservative Administration.

Many members of the Liberal intelligentsia also 'changed sides' over Home Rule. These were men who, as we have seen, had earlier reacted with great distaste to Chamberlain's caucus-style politics. They also tended to distrust Gladstonian 'sentimentality', which they thought was endangering Britain's position as an imperial power. Among such malcontents was the pioneering proponent of the referendum, A.V. Dicey, who quickly established himself as a formidable spokesman for the Unionist cause, and George Brodrick – of whom more later.

Moreover, the realignment of 1885–86 was not confined to the world of Westminster politics, for the electoral evidence shows that, particularly in the London suburbs, thousands of middle-class Liberals took advantage of the Irish issue to abandon their traditional party allegiance.

But the politics of the next quarter of a century cannot properly be understood if this interpretation is taken to represent the whole truth. For a start, it reduces Liberal Unionism to the role of a 'transit camp' through which disgruntled right-wing Liberals found it convenient to pass before taking the plunge and joining the Conservative Party. In fact, however, Liberal Unionism retained a quite strong identity of its own, particularly during the first decade of its existence; this was especially the case in Scotland, where disagreements over disestablishment, temperance and land reform created considerable conflict between the two Unionist Parties.[5] Moreover, at national level, even a 'moderate' Liberal Unionist like Hartington cannot be treated as a 'closet Conservative' who simply lacked the courage to 'come out'.

Secondly, it is important to realise that, though contemporaries had been expecting some kind of party realignment, the one that occurred in 1885–86 took most politicians and observers by surprise. The point was well made by Brodrick in his Memoirs, published in 1900: 'Had

---

5 I.G.C. Hutchison, *A Political History of Scotland 1832–1924* (Edinburgh, 1986), pp. 207–12.

I been challenged beforehand to name those of my Liberal friends who would suddenly "find salvation" in Home Rule, and those who would remain faithful to Unionist principles as professed up to 1886 by the whole Liberal Party', he wrote, 'I should assuredly have made numerous and egregious mistakes. Even now, I find it impossible to discern the lines along which the cleavage took place.'[6]

The most glaring of these many 'anomalies' concerned the position of Joseph Chamberlain and his fellow 'Radical Unionists'. Along with the activists of their local associations, these men still *felt* themselves to be 'advanced Liberals' even after the great party schism, as presumably did thousands of the electors who voted for them. Co-operation with a Whig patrician like Hartington was an unappealing prospect to many of these Radical defectors, and propping up a Tory Ministry could only fill them with dismay. Little wonder that Chamberlain and another Radical Unionist, G.O. Trevelyan, should have joined the Gladstonians at the Round Table Conference of early 1887 in search of a formula around which the Liberal Party could reunite. Little wonder, either, that the failure of these talks should have driven several Radical Unionists, Trevelyan included, back to Gladstone; by 1892 as many as ten of the Liberal MPs who had voted against the First Home Rule Bill were actually standing as Gladstonian candidates.[7]

Chamberlain, who found it impossible to rejoin the official Liberals, was left in an unenviable position. While serving as President of the Board of Trade in Gladstone's Second Administration in early 1885, he had been hoping to use the 'caucus' to impose his own advanced reform proposals on Gladstone and on a Liberal leadership with whom his policies and methods met with little favour and also to spearhead an assault on 'feudalism'. Indeed, many of the items in Chamberlain's 'Radical Programme' – the disestablishment and disendowment of the Anglican Church (Chamberlain was a Dissenter), rating reform, land reform and the modernisation of local government – seemed particularly designed to weaken the aristocracy and the landed interest to which the great Whig magnates belonged. And although Chamberlain may have been reconciled to serving in an administration headed by Hartington[8] when Gladstone eventually

6 George C. Brodrick, *Memories and Impressions, 1831–1900* (1900), p. 335.

7 W.C. Lubenow, *Parliamentary Politics and the Home Rule Crisis: The British House of Commons in 1886* (Oxford, 1988), p. 287.

8 Chamberlain had always enjoyed a satisfactory relationship with Hartington, a point emphasised by Roland Quinault in his iconoclastic essay, 'Joseph Chamberlain: A Reassessment', in T.R. Gourvish and Alan O'Day (eds), *Later Victorian Britain, 1867–1900* (1988), p. 81.

retired, he clearly hoped that a situation would be created in which his own brand of Radicalism would prevail. Even if Hartington had been prepared to do a deal with Chamberlain, how many of the Whigs would he have carried with him? Yet Gladstone's dramatic Irish *démarche*, plus a tissue of personal miscalculations, had brought about an extraordinary situation in which Chamberlain, the former Radical Mayor of Birmingham, found himself by the end of 1886 sharing the leadership of the new Liberal Unionist Party with Hartington.[9]

The failure of the Round Table Conference meant that Chamberlain had no alternative but to work with the 'Whiggish' Unionists, while at the same time ingratiating himself with his new Conservative allies. But that did not make him a Conservative; still less did it dampen his ardour as a domestic reformer. Instead, Chamberlain declared himself to be, first and foremost, a Unionist, the guardian of a new 'national' creed which transcended the traditional party faiths. And so, out of a personal embarrassment, Chamberlain created, or at least developed, a new political idiom which captured the sympathy of a large number of his fellow countrymen.

To understand how this happened, we must first consider more closely the wider political impact of the Home Rule Crisis. On the one hand, Gladstone's initiative generated great bitterness in the political world, the like of which had not been seen for generations. Many Unionists believed that they were facing 'the assaults of revolutionists whose efforts menace[d] the integrity and the power of the United Kingdom'. To maintain the Union, they said, the claims of party needed to be completely overridden.[10] When Gladstone later came out in support of the 'Plan of Campaign', Unionist fury became even more intense: some opponents convinced themselves that they were at war in defence of the Ten Commandments. Moreover, in the view of *The Times*, Gladstone's assault on the Union had 'encouraged every political quack with an axe to grind in the belief that the whole machinery of national life exists only to turn his grindstone', thereby forcing Unionists 'to meet the steady sap of anarchical folly as well as the direct assault of treasonable schemers'.[11]

9 However, by December 1891, when Chamberlain became Leader of the Party in the Commons following Hartington's elevation to the Lords as the 8th Duke of Devonshire, he was spending much of the year in London, where he had been born and brought up (Quinault, 'Joseph Chamberlain', pp. 71–4).

10 A.V. Dicey, *Letters on Unionist Delusions* (1887), p. vi.

11 *The Times*, 19 Sept. 1889.

In this feverish political atmosphere bipartisanship all but vanished, and the exchanges between the two Front Benches grew unprecedentedly acrimonious. As one historian puts it, Gladstone's espousal of Home Rule 'broke the ruling class consensus' at Westminster.[12] In the country, too, opinion was sharply polarised, with families split asunder and lifelong friendships destroyed. Many Liberal Unionists subjected the Gladstonians to a 'social boycott'. In short, so strongly did Unionists feel about the wickedness and folly of Home Rule that they virtually denied their opponents the 'right' to form a Government at all.

Yet the very violence of these passions eventually produced its own reaction, with many of the combatants on both sides taking fright at the probable consequences of their own behaviour. Even a Unionist journal like *The Economist*, for example, thought that the absence of a viable alternative government carried dangers, since 'in England up till now, . . . no one party has had a monopoly of ability and patriotism'. Who would there be to form an alternative ministry, it asked, should the existing one falter?[13] Each major party also felt some distaste at the prospect of being dragged into extreme actions at the behest of its respective Irish allies. So though Ireland bitterly divided the parties, in time it would be the issue upon which the two Front Benches, alarmed by the virulence of party strife, would seek a 'national settlement'.

Ireland had a paradoxical impact on British party politics in other ways. For, however intense the emotions which it aroused, the Irish quarrel did not initially look as though it would be more than a transient incident. Chamberlain himself certainly seems to have felt that in breaking with Gladstone and official Liberalism in 1886 he was only taking temporary leave of the Liberal Party: either Gladstone would carry his measure, which would remove Ireland from the political agenda, or he would fail and be replaced. 'I think I shall win this fight', he told his friend Dilke in May 1886, 'and shall in the long run have an increase of public influence.'[14] In any case, since

12 Hugh Berrington, 'Partisanship and Dissidence in the Nineteenth-Century House of Commons', *Parliamentary Affairs*, 21 (1967–68), 371. Lubenow agrees that Home Rule 'galvanized partisan action', *Parliamentary Politics*, p. 144. See also John D. Fair, 'Party Voting Behaviour in the British House of Commons, 1886–1918', *Parliamentary History*, 5 (1986), 67.

13 *The Economist*, 18 June 1887, 775.

14 Richard Jay, *Joseph Chamberlain: A Political Study* (Oxford, 1981), p. 136.

Gladstone was then seventy-six, he was not expected to remain as Leader for much longer, whatever happened.[15]

Moreover, the divisions over Ireland among the senior politicians were not quite as clear-cut as they superficially appeared. This was especially true of the Liberal Front Bench, where figures like Lord Rosebery entertained doubts about the wisdom of Gladstonian Home Rule which closely resembled those of some of the Liberal seceders.[16] As for the Liberal Unionists, they were, as Hartington well knew, an incoherent party, disunited even over Ireland, the only issue which even vaguely held them together. Significantly, Chamberlain himself had briefly served in Gladstone's Third Administration, from which he had only resigned in March 1886 when he saw the *details* of the Home Rule Bill, while he continued to express support for some sort of federal arrangement on the Canadian model – a stance which put him at odds with the likes of Hartington who were prepared to fight in defence of the status quo.

More fundamentally, questions were bound to be asked as to whether Ireland should be allowed to overshadow all other issues, many of which seemed to be far more pressing. For the Agricultural Depression which hit Britain in the late 1870s had not only helped spark off the Land War in Ireland: it had also led to a rebellion against landlord power in the crofter counties in Scotland and to a tenants' rights movement among many of the farmers of England and Wales.

In addition, as the industrial depression deepened, with unemployment even among skilled workers rising above 10 per cent, social unrest spread to the major cities and industrial centres, finding outlet in such disparate activities as a revived protectionist movement and trade union agitation. In 1883 Britain's first Marxist Party, the Social Democratic Federation, had been founded; the Fabian Society emerged a year later. Thus by the time of the 1885 General Election, the first to be held on the basis of the extended franchise, politicians were aware that the country faced acute social and economic difficulties, as well as an uncertain political future.

15 Similarly, Haldane (who stayed loyal to Gladstone) initially thought the Home Rule division a temporary difficulty, which is why he did not want the official Liberals to widen the gulf with Chamberlain unnecessarily (R.B. Haldane, 'Is a National Party Possible?', *Fortnightly Review*, 42 (1 Sept. 1887), 317–28.

16 Jay, *Chamberlain*, p. 126. Initially Chamberlain's main reason for breaking with Gladstone may have been his sense that Home Rule would be electorally damaging, not strong feelings about Ireland itself.

In fact, prior to the eruption of the Irish Crisis, a vigorous debate had been in progress about how best to cope with what was sometimes called the 'challenge of democracy'. Broadly speaking, two competing strategies had emerged. On the one hand, some politicians believed in 'incorporating' the newly enfranchised masses by attempting to mobilise them behind a 'democratic programme' which offered them some chance of a change in their lives. On the other hand, there were those of more cautious temperament who favoured a strategy of 'resistance': of defending both Constitution and property rights against the forces of subversion. To add to the complexity, this split between a 'strategy of incorporation' and a 'strategy of containment' divided each of the parties internally as well as setting them in opposition to one another.

However, as we have seen, Gladstone's raising of the banner of Home Rule cut across this particular debate – as he had perhaps intended. In consequence, there were many, on both sides of the 'Unionist'/'Home Ruler' divide, who continued to feel, right up to 1914 and beyond, that the line of demarcation had been drawn in the wrong place and that party animosities were therefore, in some sense, 'artificial' and 'unreal'.

CHAMBERLAIN AND THE QUEST FOR A 'NATIONAL' PARTY

No one felt this more strongly than Chamberlain who tried, in a series of major speeches in the summer of 1887, to define the parameters of a new kind of politics. The old party names had 'lost their force and meaning', he declared. 'The Old Toryism' was 'a dead creed', while the 'new Radicalism' had degenerated into 'an opposition to all government and authority'. But, said Chamberlain, 'the wreck of the Liberal Party' had created an opportunity to form some new combination 'no less anxious for progressive reforms on all social and political subjects than the great Liberals of the past; and no less determined that they were to resist anarchy in every form, to maintain the integrity of the kingdom and the supremacy of Parliament'. Fortunately, in Chamberlain's view, there was a party 'greater, more numerous and more influential than Tory or Liberal', a party to which 'national interests' could safely be entrusted, and that was 'the party of the Union'. This, he believed, formed the nucleus of a new 'national party' which would embrace all sensible citizens, excluding 'only the extreme sections of the party of reaction on the one hand, and the party of anarchy on the other'.[17]

Now, as historians have noted, Chamberlain's speeches and activities in the summer of 1887 can be interpreted at one level as a skilful device for rationalising his own precarious position by integrating his Birmingham followers into a new kind of Unionist alliance.[18] But they had a far wider significance than that, as the *Fortnightly Review* recognised in an article which it published in July 1887. 'The idea of "a national party" ha[d] been "in the air" for many years', noted the *Fortnightly*, and it had 'taken root in many minds throughout the country'. Quoting the late Prince Consort and Carlyle in his support, the editor contended that 'the system of party government', which had been on its 'trial', had 'stood the trial very badly'. And why had the party system failed? Because, he concluded, there was an artificial division between Conservatives who 'represented exclusively the prudence and patriotism of the English people', and Liberals who wanted moderate reforms to raise the lot of the poor and miserable: 'from the sharply-marked opposition of the two parties has come a perpetual and dangerous oscillation'.[19] These were precisely the anxieties upon which Chamberlain was trying to capitalise.

LORD RANDOLPH CHURCHILL AND THE 'CENTRE PARTY' NEGOTIATIONS

But Chamberlain was not alone. For at the end of 1886 Lord Randolph Churchill resigned from Salisbury's Government and also put himself forward as the proponent of a new kind of 'national politics'.

In fact, well before the party realignment, Churchill had been trying to carve out a distinctive role for himself by propagating the creed of 'Tory Democracy'.[20] By this he meant that the Conservative Party would have to modernise its practices and institutions. Churchill also

17 Speech in Birmingham, cited in *Fortnightly Review*, 42 (1 July 1887), 146. Speech at Willis's Rooms, cited in *The Economist*, 18 June 1887, 774.

18 Jay, *Chamberlain*, p. 343.

19 Frank Harris, 'Home Affairs: A National Party', *Fortnightly Review* (42), 148–9.

20 Though Foster argues that it was in his 1887 speeches that Churchill elaborated his doctrines of 'Tory Democracy' in their most uncompromisingly Radical form (R.F. Foster, *Lord Randolph Churchill: A Political Life*, Oxford, 1981, p. 339).

urged it to imitate the alleged example of Disraeli by combining a robust prosecution of Britain's global interests with a policy of wooing the working classes with a concessionary policy of social reform; for a purely defensive approach, rooted in fear of the new electorate, would, he feared, spell disaster. If the Conservatives were to 'keep the boroughs as well as to win the counties', Churchill privately remarked to Salisbury following the 1885 Election, this could 'only be done by an active progressive – I risk the word, a democratic – policy, a casting-off and burning of those old, worn-out, aristocratic and class garments from which the Derby-Dizzy lot, with their following of county families, could never, or never cared to extricate themselves'.[21]

With good reason, historians have questioned the sincerity of this enterprise. Yet there is a sense in which Tory Democracy quickly acquired a life of its own, quite distinct from the personality and career ambitions of any single politician.[22] At a time when the franchise was about to be extended, Churchill's message held a particular attraction to many young Conservative politicians, notably those from the big cities, who wondered how the party was going to survive, given the contraction of its old county base.[23]

Now, it is surely significant that, long before 1886, Chamberlain and Churchill had formed a deep regard for one another, despite coming from very different social backgrounds. As Richard Jay argues, this was because 'both were intent on driving the "old guard" from their respective parties, and were prepared not only to exploit the others' existence as an argument in their own party for more radical methods, but even, at least in appearance, to work out tactics to their mutual advantage'.[24]

Such habits of informal co-operation, well-established before the Home Rule split, were continued thereafter. Thus, Chamberlain wrote to Churchill immediately after the latter's resignation, declaring that the government was 'doomed' and suggesting that 'we may have to re-form parties on a new basis.' 'You and I are equally adrift from the old organisations', he observed.[25] To another correspondent,

21 Churchill to Salisbury, 9 Dec. 1885, Lubenow, *Parliamentary Politics*, p. 130.

22 See Bruce Coleman, *Conservatism and the Conservative Party in Nineteenth-Century Britain* (1988), p. 168.

23 E.H.H. Green, 'Radical Conservatism: The Electoral Genesis of Tariff Reform', *Historical Journal*, 28 (1985), 667–92.

24 Jay, *Chamberlain*, p. 121.

25 Winston Spencer Churchill, *Lord Randolph Churchill* (1906), II, p. 252.

Chamberlain wrote: 'The old combination is irretrievably smashed. I hardly know what new ones may be possible in the future.'[26]

Yet Churchill believed that *he* could discern the outlines of a more modern system. In a letter to the Conservative Whip Akers-Douglas on 1 January 1887 (a letter subsequently published in the *Pall Mall Gazette*), he announced that he had left himself free to join any 'coalition, fusion or reconstruction . . . which by its composition and its policy will be an earnest and a guarantee to the country that a period of peaceful, progressive administration has in reality set in'. Impatient of 'the "principles" of stupid Toryism' (the ostensible ground for his resignation), Churchill now espoused 'a policy of rational Liberalism in Home and Foreign affairs'.[27]

Chamberlain did not come to Churchill's assistance in the opening weeks of 1887 when this might have made a material difference. But, following the breakdown of the Round Table Conference and Churchill's return from a holiday in North Africa in the spring of that year, the two men began a semi-public courtship. Privately Churchill was talking in April about 'a Chamberlain–Hartington–Randolph league against both parties', an idea which he later aired at Nottingham. Soon afterwards, in a speech at Trowbridge, he took the idea further, advocating a closer union with the Liberal Unionists, as a prelude to the creation of 'a great National Party' that could implement popular reforms at home.[28] Chamberlain meanwhile was ruminating about the possibility of 'the formation of a Central Party, with Conservative foreign & Liberal Home policy . . .'[29]

This tortuous manoeuvring led to nothing. The venture was probably doomed by Churchill's volatility, on the one hand, and, on the other, by Chamberlain's realisation that in the long run he had more to gain from working with Salisbury than with the wayward ex-Chancellor.[30] A combination between the two men would anyhow have required the support of Hartington, who periodically gave the idea of a 'National Party' a guarded public welcome but was

26 Chamberlain to Brett, 23 Dec. 1886, in Maurice V. Brett (ed.), *Journals and Letters of Reginald Viscount Esher* (1934), I, p. 129.

27 Foster, *Churchill*, pp. 321–2.

28 Ibid., p. 339.

29 Lord Ebrington's diary, 24 May 1887, cited in T.A. Jenkins, 'Hartington, Chamberlain and the Unionist Alliance, 1886–1895', *Parliamentary History*, 11 (1992), 116. On 11 June Chamberlain told his son that he was looking 'to the possibility of a strong Central Party which may be master of the situation after Mr Gladstone goes' (Jay, *Chamberlain*, p. 153).

30 Jay, *Chamberlain*, p. 162.

unprepared to take the matter further.[31] Since his prime objective was the preservation of the Union, Hartington saw no purpose in joining an embittered Churchill apparently hell-bent on undermining Salisbury's authority. 'Surely it is better, if it is at all possible', wrote Hartington to Chamberlain on 13 July, 'to keep the present Government in this session, and let a reconstruction come, if it is to come, with more deliberation and time to construct a definite and popular policy'.[32] Disheartened perhaps by these difficulties, Chamberlain by the end of August 1887 had 'lost all desire for coalition',[33] and before long he and Churchill were violently quarrelling. Churchill's career then rapidly went into tragic decline. By January 1895 he was dead.

The 'Centre Party' talks of 1887 perhaps acquired more significance retrospectively than they possessed at the time.[34] But the episode illustrates the extreme fluidity of political life in 1886–87 before politics settled down into a new kind of 'two-party' competition, structured around the 'Unionist' and 'Home Rule' alliances.

Now, Chamberlain realistically adapted himself to the changed situation. True, he continued to talk about the need to create a 'National Party'. But by this he now meant *transforming the Unionist alliance*, not bringing about a new political grouping that would embrace large numbers of former Gladstonian Liberals. Yet this, too, was a strategy which was to prove very destabilising for two-party politics.

CHAMBERLAIN AND 'SOCIAL IMPERIALISM'

We can trace back the new phase in Chamberlain's career to his speaking tour of Yorkshire of September 1888, when he expressed the hope that 'out of the clash of parties which has been brought about by the unfortunate action of Mr Gladstone' there would arise 'a party which is greater than all other parties – a party of the nation, a party which shall have national interests, national security and national faith

31 For example, in his speech at Blackburn on 25 June 1887.

32 J.L. Garvin, *The Life of Joseph Chamberlain* (1933), II, p. 434.

33 Foster, *Churchill*, p. 341.

34 See Chapter 6 for Churchill's invocation of this episode during the attempt at 'fusion' in 1920.

as the only watchwords to which it owes its existence'.[35] (He did, however, concede that 'a new party' could not be 'manufactured' but would have to 'come, if it comes at all, by a process of natural evolution, and with the good-will and assent of all concerned'.)[36]

In the course of elaborating this new strategy, Chamberlain picked up bits and pieces from the rhetoric of 'Tory Democracy'. As an ally of the Conservative Party, he was anyhow obliged to stop attacking the aristocracy, and Churchill's reformulation of the romantic Disraelian conception of a 'Union of Classes' now suited his current political circumstances much better.

On the other hand, there were other aspects of the Disraeli-Churchill ideological heritage from which Chamberlain wisely diverged – in particular, the claim that some mystical affinity existed between the interests of the 'masses' and the aristocracy, grounded in a common antipathy to the materialistic middle classes. Instead Chamberlain unfolded a pan-class philosophy in which a central place was allocated to progressive capitalists (like himself!). For, unlike Churchill, Chamberlain idolised 'the manager and owner of commercial wealth as the mainspring of the national life and the true embodiment of its long-term interests', to quote Jay, and so helped propagate the 'ideology of a reformist capitalism'.[37] In short, Chamberlain's creed was a managerial creed which extolled modernisation and efficiency and sought to create an 'interventionist state'. Much more was to be heard of this objective in the future.

Chamberlain was also more 'modern' than Churchill (though not perhaps Disraeli) in another sense. He realised that a pacific foreign policy, low defence spending and 'retrenchment', the issues on which Churchill had based his ill-judged resignation, held little popular appeal to the new electorate, stemming as they did from an older 'Manchester School' vein of Radicalism. For although in 1887 Chamberlain still believed that war would be unpopular, he quickly saw the expediency of identifying himself with a sturdy defence of British interests in the world – following the example of Palmerston rather than that of his fellow Birmingham MP, John Bright.[38] There had, arguably, been 'a strand of patriotic nationalism inherent in Chamberlain's Radicalism' from a very early stage in his

35 Peter Fraser, *Joseph Chamberlain* (1966), p. 130.

36 Cited in Montague Crackanthorpe, 'The New National Party', *Fortnightly Review*, 26 (1889), 751.

37 Jay, *Chamberlain*, pp. 343–4.

38 Foster, *Churchill*, p. 319.

career.[39] To this Chamberlain now added a fervent identification with Empire, which he presented as a quintessentially 'national' cause.[40]

Circumstances obliged Chamberlain to make yet one more prudent adjustment. In 1887 the case for a 'Centre' or 'National' Party had rested on the belief that, while the Gladstonians were too irresponsible, Salisbury's Conservatives were too 'reactionary' and 'stupid' to govern the country. However, as Churchill himself publicly admitted shortly afterwards,[41] the Salisbury Ministry had turned out to be far less negative and destructive than the Prime Minister's speeches in Opposition had led people to expect – even if Churchill felt that this was mainly because the Ministry, lacking a parliamentary majority, knew that it must earn Liberal support.

In practice, the Conservative Leader had often used Chamberlain's presence to cajole his followers into accepting certain moderate reforms (the Local Government Act of 1888, free education, and Irish Land Purchase, and so on), reforms which he anyhow thought to be desirable or expedient in the new democratic age. For Salisbury took the despairing view that it would be suicidal to row against the democratic tide: 'against a fashion it is almost impossible to argue', as he once wrote.[42] In that sense, some of the social legislation passed by Salisbury can be described as mildly 'Liberal', owing nothing to any authentically Conservative strategy of 'resistance'.[43] *The Times* certainly took this view of the matter: 'The truth is that the old high-and-dry Conservatism has disappeared', it declared in April 1888, and the 'prevailing doctrines' of the contemporary Conservative Party were almost identical to the sort of 'moderate Liberalism' recently subscribed to by most Liberals and currently underwritten by Liberal Unionists such as Hartington.[44]

But if, as Dicey argued, democracy had 'effaced old lines of demarcation' between the two historic parties,[45] then why not throw

---

39 Jay, *Chamberlain*, p. 37.

40 See Chamberlain's famous speech on Empire at the Devonshire Club, 9 April 1888, in Charles W. Boyd (ed.), *Mr Chamberlain's Speeches* (1914), I, pp. 318–24.

41 See Churchill's speech to the Conservative Edgbaston Club in April 1888, where he admitted that Salisbury's Government was now 'on the high road' to realising 'the dream of Tory Democracy' (*The Times*, 9 April 1888).

42 France, 'Salisbury and the Unionist Alliance', pp. 230–40, especially pp. 231, 236.

43 One historian goes so far as to claim that this represented '"Tory Democracy" with Lord Randolph Churchill left out of it': Jenkins, 'Hartington', 127.

44 *The Times*, 9 April 1888.

45 Dicey, *Unionist Delusions*, p. 70.

away party labels altogether? Salisbury was actually invited by some of his admirers to preside over an entire recasting of the party system which would 'fuse' the two Unionist parties in such a way as to retain the services of the ablest and most vigorous men in both. Since the terms 'Conservatism', 'Liberalism' and 'Radicalism' currently meant very little and only confused the public, there was a case for creating a new 'National' Party, whose members would simply be called 'Nationals'. Such a reconstituted party, it was claimed, would ensure that the interests of the country were placed for the foreseeable future 'above party interests and personal ambitions'. Ending the 'abnormal and unnatural' division between the two Unionist parties would also bring with it many practical advantages. 'To keep double machinery going in the constituencies is but waste of power', one writer argued: 'joint Unionist committees should at once be formed throughout the country.'[46]

Dicey and Brodrick, two of the contributors to *Essays on Reform*, also came out in 1888 in support of an alliance between Liberal Unionists and Conservatives; 'the birth of a great national party', they said, was absolutely essential now that the 'old lines of demarcation' had been obliterated.[47] Dicey, advocating union in the face of a common danger, claimed that 'an alliance based on concern for national interest' would break down the lines of party connection and so revive 'a sense of allegiance to the nation'.[48] And at Oxford University Brodrick turned words into deeds when he created a 'Unionist League', in the hope that this might be the basis of 'a National Party' which would shortly be operating country-wide.[49]

Without being so naive as to formulate his case in this way, Chamberlain, too, continued to hint at the desirability of some such development. The most important statement of his views came a few years later, after the Liberals had returned to office once more. Speaking to the Conservative Club of Edgbaston in January 1894, Chamberlain presented 'the Unionist cause' as 'the most remarkable fact of contemporary politics'. After lambasting

46 'Home Affairs', *Fortnightly Review*, 149–50; Crackanthorpe, 'The New National Party', 746–53. See also *National Review*, 9 (Aug. 1887), 734.

47 Christopher Harvie, *The Lights of Liberalism: University Liberals and the Challenge of Democracy 1860–86* (1976), p. 232.

48 Dicey, *Unionist Delusions*, especially p. 87.

49 George C. Brodrick, *Unionism: The Basis of a National Party: An Address Delivered at the First Meeting of the Oxford University Unionist League on December 1, 1888* (Oxford, 1888), pp. 6, 12–13.

the Liberals for advocating 'a policy of disintegration at home and disruption abroad', he continued:

> I am, and shall be in the future, proud to call myself a Unionist, and be satisfied with that title alone, believing that it is a wider and nobler title than that either of Conservative or Liberal, since it includes them both, and since it includes all men who are determined to maintain an undivided Empire, and who are ready to promote the welfare and the union, not of one class, but of all classes in the community.

Encouraged by the cheers of his predominantly Conservative audience, Chamberlain ventured the hope that there might arise 'a great national and patriotic party, a party that will put country before the interests of any faction, before any personal consideration; a party that will not barter its conscience for votes'. Such an innovation would be a step towards the establishment of a 'strong Government, not partisan in the old sense of the word, but a Government which really represents the strength and the best intelligence of the British people', and which could therefore deal in an 'impartial' way not only with the major questions of foreign policy but also with social problems like 'the conditions of the poor, the distribution of wealth, [and] the relations between Capital and Labour'. Chamberlain urged his audience to do all that was possible to support this 'ideal party'.[50]

Such an attempt to redefine the meaning of Unionism was timely. For it can be argued that all the political leaders had made too much depend on the Irish issue. After all, Unionism was a fine rallying cry when Home Rule seemed on the point of attainment, but it meant very little once the issue began to recede into the background, as it was shortly to do. By the late 1890s Salisbury and his colleagues were in danger of having worked themselves out of a job since, once the Union was (temporarily) safe, what point was there in having a Unionist Alliance and what did Unionism *signify*? It had no coherent political programme and no firm basis of class allegiance to hold together the disparate elements from which it had been formed. It was this vacuum which Chamberlain set out to fill with his programme of imperial unity abroad and a 'union of classes' at home – a programme which a later generation would call 'social imperialism'.

What were its chances of success? Bearing in mind the nature of the Conservative Party, it is obvious that Chamberlain stood no chance of persuading his new allies to go in for disestablishment or secular education: the sectarian items from the Radical Programme would have to be jettisoned without ceremony. But it was not beyond the

50 *The Times*, 30 Jan. 1894.

realms of possibility that the Conservatives might be won over to the idea of taking a more positive interest in social reform.

It was therefore significant that as early as 1891 Chamberlain should have made a number of speeches highlighting the 'social question', with specific reference to workmen's compensation, a statutory restriction of the working hours of certain occupational groups, and old age pensions. Some of these proposals (compensation for accidents, for example) he had acquired from Disraeli's old comrade-in-arms, John Gorst, who in turn had borrowed them from Bismarck's legislation.[51] The following year Chamberlain elaborated on these ideas in a much-publicised article in the *Nineteenth Century*, which argued that the Conservatives had always been more progressive in social reform matters than the Liberals and that 'the Conservative leaders in their latest legislation have only gone back to the old Tory traditions' – a line of argument which recalled Churchill's earlier speeches.[52]

Chamberlain, it would seem, still set little store by Hartington. But in the early 1890s, privately as well as publicly, he was beginning to woo sympathetic spirits in the Conservative Party, offering them whole-hearted co-operation, if only they would join him in pushing for a progressive social policy. Chamberlain particularly beamed his propaganda at Salisbury's nephew Arthur Balfour, telling him that the working classes could be persuaded to vote for Conservatism or Unionism – provided that the Unionists took up 'the question of Social Reform in a Conservative spirit, and [met] the unreasonable and dangerous proposals of the extremists with practical proposals of their own'.[53]

Many young Unionists, Conservatives as well as Liberal Unionists, found this message attractive. Whereas the older men still remembered with horror and disgust Chamberlain's 'ransom' speeches from the 1880s when he was still the terrible Radical Jacobin, the younger generation tended not to bear such resentments, and in any case *their* gaze was fixed, not on the past, but on the future. As E.H.H.

51 See his speech at Portsmouth emphasising the 'Labour Question', in which he mentioned Old Age Pensions and industrial accident insurance as items for inclusion in an election programme (Jay, *Chamberlain*, pp. 174, 176). Randolph Churchill, too, may have been influenced by the Bismarckian example.

52 Chamberlain, 'The Labour Question', *Nineteenth Century*, 32 (Nov. 1892), 709. By late 1894 Chamberlain's programme had come to embrace the control of alien immigration, employers' liability and compensation for accidents.

53 Chamberlain to Balfour, 8 Dec. 1894, in Alan Sykes, *Tariff Reform in British Politics, 1903–1913* (Oxford, 1979), p. 12.

Green argues, they needed a 'constructive' programme on which to campaign since they feared that the challenge of socialism and 'disruption' had been postponed but not averted by the party realignment of 1885–86, and Chamberlain's combination of social reform and imperialism seemed to offer a solution of this difficulty. 'To accept a purely negative attitude – to meet with destructive criticism every well-meant suggestion without proposing any alternative – is neither statesmanlike nor just, and will deservedly involve the defeat and the discredit of any party which adopts it', Chamberlain argued.[54] Many younger Conservatives agreed.

Yet there were two reasons why the dissolution of the old parties with a view to creating a new synthesis of Liberalism and Conservatism was unlikely to take place in the mid-1890s. First, the very suggestion of such a thing caused apoplexy in the higher reaches of the Conservative Party, where Chamberlain's past Radical demagoguery had been neither forgotten or forgiven. Even Hartington was viewed by many Conservatives with some unease, since he struck them as a dangerous 'liberal' rival; and so whereas most Conservative MPs accepted the case for some kind of Unionist alliance, they still felt strongly that such a combination should be led by Salisbury, not Hartington.[55]

Chamberlain was still more of a threat. In fact, according to Peter Marsh, 'Chamberlain's talk of a National Party, whose domestic policy would bear his imprint', coupled with his recent support for the Welsh Disestablishment Bill, caused a considerable upset in Conservative ranks in the spring of 1895, coinciding as it did with a quarrel between Liberal Unionists and Conservatives over which party had the right to nominate to the vacant seat at Warwick and Leamington. This led to personal attacks on Chamberlain's character in the Conservative *Standard*, attacks which privately amused Balfour and Salisbury but which the highly sensitive Chamberlain much resented.[56]

54 Chamberlain, 'Labour Question', 710.

55 See, for example, Akers-Douglas's warning letter to Salisbury of 30 Dec. 1886, in 3rd Viscount Chilston, *Chief Whip* (1961), pp. 102–3. It must also be remembered that, even as late as 1895, Devonshire had designs on the premiership which might have succeeded, had Salisbury not acted quickly to forestall him (Jenkins, 'Hartington', 137).

56 See Peter Marsh, *The Discipline of Popular Government: Lord Salisbury's Domestic Statecraft 1881–1902* (Hassocks, 1978), pp. 237–8, for the hostile treatment Chamberlain received from many Conservative sections of the press in the spring of 1895. Balfour, in a speech to the Primrose League in April, was more conciliatory: see *National Review*, 24 (June 1895), 440.

Against the backcloth of this political jealousy and tension, little chance existed of persuading Conservatives of the need to collapse their organisation into some new National Party. In any case, Salisbury and most Conservatives, though no 'reactionaries', shied away from the kind of Radical programme which Chamberlain was trying to foist upon them. In the event, it was Devonshire, not Salisbury, who allowed himself to be 'bounced' into espousing an advanced social programme in late 1894:[57] the Conservative Leader prudently reserved his position.

From the point of view of the Conservative leadership, Chamberlain was in many ways an invaluable ally. He had ousted the Liberal Party from its dominant position in Birmingham and was securing for the Unionist Alliance electoral support which the Conservatives could not themselves have tapped. Yet Chamberlain was a Radical Unionist, not a Conservative, and, as Sykes argues, 'implicit in Chamberlain's approach, was a distinction between "Unionism" and "Conservatism" that gave scant recognition to the traditional role of the Conservative Party as the party of resistance to change'.[58] Traditional Conservatives, like the more Whiggish members of the Liberal Unionist Party, were particularly disconcerted by Chamberlain's occasional habit of blurting out his enthusiasm for Disestablishment.[59]

Hence, the primary division within Unionism increasingly became one separating moderate from radical Unionists, not the organisational division between the Conservative and Liberal Unionist parties. But in the mid-1890s the 'moderates' were still in the ascendant.

Chamberlain was a realist. He knew that his hour had not yet come and that Salisbury was unlikely to give him the chance to carry through Old Age Pensions or other items from his advanced social programme. And so, offered a Cabinet post in 1895, he surprised Salisbury by asking, not for a domestic department like the Home Office or the Board of Trade, but for the Colonial Office.[60]

This was an important decision because it marked, temporarily at least, Chamberlain's abandonment of the role of social reformer for that of arch-exponent of the 'New Imperialism'. For the immediate future Chamberlain largely abandoned the field of domestic politics to his more numerous Conservative rivals and concentrated on his

---

57 Jay, *Chamberlain*, pp. 182–3.

58 Sykes, *Tariff Reform*, p. 5.

59 See Jenkins, 'Hartington', 129. Chamberlain voted for the Welsh Disestablishment Bill in 1895 (Jay, *Chamberlain*, p. 168).

60 Maxse, too, was surprised: *National Review*, 24 (Aug. 1895), 740.

work as Colonial Secretary. The only significant piece of legislation passed in these years was the 1897 Workman's Compensation Act, for which (significantly) Chamberlain assumed responsibility.

Yet Chamberlain's immersion in the work of the Colonial Office should not be seen exactly as a *renunciation* of his Radical convictions. It was more a question of redirecting his radical energies into new fields. There is thus a case for saying that Chamberlain's imperialism grew organically out of the enthusiasms which had shaped his earlier career. As A.P. Thornton has noted, Chamberlain apparently 'saw in Empire another great slum-ridden Birmingham', ripe for modernisation and improvement.[61] It can even be argued that what he was doing after 1895 was coming forward with a new 'Unauthorised Programme' for the Empire. This drew Chamberlain into intermittent conflict with Salisbury, whose imperialism was of a quite different stamp.[62]

The climacteric came with the Second Boer War – a conflict which, significantly, was more Chamberlain's handiwork than Salisbury's, but which destroyed the political world over which Salisbury had for so long presided. It also encouraged Chamberlain to drop his preoccupation with colonial possessions overseas and to turn back once more to domestic politics, or rather to relate his imperial obsessions more closely to Britain's internal affairs.

The fact is that problems were mounting for the British Empire in the 1890s as other powers emerged to challenge her commercial and strategic supremacy. In particular, the Admiralty was struggling to maintain the Two-Power Standard, upon which, in the last analysis, the whole majestic, but precarious, edifice of Empire rested. But the setbacks of the Boer War (described in the next chapter) exposed the vulnerability of Britain's position in the world in ways which startled even the clear-sighted Salisbury. With renewed anxieties about trade unionism at home and declining commercial competitiveness abroad, it seemed as though the moment for a new political initiative had arrived.

TARIFF REFORM

In fact, it was the Boer War which, by creating an acute budgetary crisis, indirectly gave Chamberlain the chance for which he had long

61 A.P. Thornton, *The Imperial Idea and its Enemies* (1959), p. 100.
62 Jay, *Chamberlain*, pp. 222–3.

been looking. Responsibility for this problem rested with Sir Michael Hicks Beach, the Chancellor of the Exchequer, a one-time friend and ally of Lord Randolph Churchill, but a statesman who, in the twilight of a long and distinguished career, now stood for Conservatism of a traditional kind. Believing his main task to be the offering of resistance to reckless adventures which might jeopardise the stability of the social order, Beach tried to ensure that the nation's finances were managed in a prudent and thrifty way.

In September 1901 the Chancellor sat down and composed a trenchant Memorandum on this theme, which was circulated among the Cabinet. The Memorandum revealed that since 1895 even *ordinary* expenditure had risen by 40 per cent (ironically, this was partly because of the Conservative policy of rate-aid to education and agriculture); in addition there was the heavy cost of the war (which eventually came to about £220 million). Hicks Beach warned that unless the constant demands for expansion and expenditure were sternly opposed, the Government would soon be obliged to undertake a complete overhaul of its fiscal policies. He even hinted at the possibility that there might have to be revenue tariffs – perhaps small duties on corn, or meat or petroleum. 'On the political objections' to this 'I need not dwell', was his laconic conclusion.[63] In fact, during the following year the Government did indeed impose a Corn Duty as a temporary revenue-raising expedient.

When Hicks Beach issued these admonitions, his angry and re-proachful gaze must have settled particularly on the Colonial Secretary. For it was Chamberlain's South African policies which had led to the war and many of the current fiscal difficulties, just as it was his truculent tone which was doing much to increase international tension, which in turn gave urgency to the Service Departments' requests for additional funds. Young imperialists might applaud Chamberlain's visionary enthusiasms and welcome his attempts to develop Britain's tropical estates; but, again, all this cost more money. Finally, there was the renewed call for a state-funded old age pension scheme, which Chamberlain himself still favoured. The matter had not yet progressed any further if only because, as Balfour neatly put it, 'Joe's War had killed Joe's pensions.' But in 1902 the Colonial Secretary again committed himself publicly to this piece of social legislation, making it clear that some method of funding it would have to be devised.

63 Sykes, *Tariff Reform*, pp. 24–7.

In fact, Chamberlain was one of the few Ministers to challenge Hicks Beach's famous Memorandum. He disputed, in particular, the Chancellor's prediction that once the war was over the electorate would insist upon a lowering of the current levels of taxation. Popular and parliamentary opinion, Chamberlain shrewdly remarked, would more likely side with the experts 'in any serious conflict between the Government and its naval and military advisers on the subject of efficient preparation'.[64] Though he did not say this explicitly, Chamberlain also sensed that old age pensions might be a vote-winner. Granted that imperialism abroad and social reform at home cost money: new sources of revenue would have to be found. Chamberlain, for one, was prepared to act on the logic of his political beliefs.

Here, perhaps, in the long run, was the most important political legacy of the Boer War: that it obliged all the leading politicians to re-examine their basic assumptions and, as a result, sharpened the conflict between the 'moderates' and 'Radicals' in the Unionist Party. For under the pressure of war, traditionalists like Salisbury and Beach became more prudent, cautious and defensive. At the same time 'Radical Joe' became more radical. Yet now, in contrast to 1892 or 1895, Chamberlain had a strong hand to play. For by 1902 he knew that he could count upon the support of a substantial section of the Unionist Party – not just his own Radical Unionists from Birmingham, but many younger Conservatives as well. The 'Radicals' sensed with good reason that time was on their side. Even their opponents within the party tacitly conceded that this was so. There was a strain of defeatism in the Hicks Beach Memorandum. The Chancellor was warning Cabinet Ministers of the financial consequences of their own profligacy, but he seems to have sensed that his warnings would probably be disregarded. Salisbury was equally pessimistic. 'Beach's tale is very alarming', he ruminated in a letter to a colleague: 'I think we shall have a Parliamentary explosion before long.'[65]

The explosion duly occurred. In May 1903, in a big speech at Birmingham, Chamberlain presented to the public his new 'Unauthorised Programme'. All the problems which were wracking the brains of the intelligent patriot were surmountable, he announced. The answer was Tariff Reform. This would strengthen the empire

---

64 Marsh, *Discipline of Popular Government*, p. 309.
65 Ibid., p. 310.

(through a system of imperial preferences), so reviving British power in the world. British businessmen would be protected against 'unfair' competition (an idea, incidentally, which Randolph Churchill had tentatively broached nearly twenty years earlier). And the revenue generated by a tariff would broaden the basis of taxation in such a way that money could be found for expensive social reforms without the risk of capital being frightened out of the country. Chamberlain clearly assumed that all this would guarantee that the Unionists became a popular party, with an overwhelming electoral appeal – not immediately perhaps, but as soon as the party had been thoroughly converted to the new radical policies.

In fact, Tariff Reform played straight into the Liberals' hands by giving a further boost to their electoral fortunes, which had already started to revive as a result of the controversies surrounding the 1902 Education Act. By contrast, both the Conservatives and the Liberal Unionists were at sixes and sevens following the Birmingham speech. Some Unionists reacted with wild enthusiasm. Others, including Devonshire, resolutely stood by the Free Trade cause. (There was shortly to be some desultory discussion about the possibility of a reunion between the Liberal Unionist 'Free Fooders' and the official Liberal Party.) Meanwhile Balfour desperately searched for common ground, with a view to maintaining the integrity of the Unionist Alliance.

In causing this turmoil, what did Chamberlain hope to achieve? True to his Radical past, he wanted to capture the working-class vote, or a large part of it, by revitalising Unionism and giving it a progressive social programme. Tariff Reform, he told trade union audiences, naturally complemented protection of Labour: 'You cannot have free trade in goods, and at the same time have protection of labour'.[66] Chamberlain reminded working men of how the Chartists had stood out against the Repeal of the Corn Laws in the 1840s. Early on in his campaign he also recklessly declared his willingness to leave the verdict in working-class hands: 'You are the judges, you are the Caesar to which I appeal.'

But, of course, Chamberlain was not appealing to trade unionists *alone*. The whole point of the Tariff Reform campaign was to persuade capitalists and working men alike that they had a common enemy, the foreigner, who supposedly robbed British workers of wages and employment but who also robbed employers of their

66 Sykes, *Tariff Reform*, p. 56.

48

profits and capital. What Chamberlain was therefore doing was urging the different social classes to subordinate their immediate interests to the good of the nation as a whole, secure in the knowledge that patriotism would pay in the end. His, then, was an appeal that combined Radicalism and imperialism; indeed, Chamberlain now claimed that there was not a shadow of an antagonism between social reform, on the one hand, and imperialism, on the other.

CHAMBERLAIN AND 'NATIONAL POLITICS'

Chamberlain sometimes found himself denounced as an ambitious careerist. This was in some respects unfair, in that, more than many successful politicians, he was genuinely interested in *policy*. The problem, at least after 1886, was that Chamberlain was trying to combine policies drawn from different points of the political compass, with the result that he fitted into *neither* of the two main party blocs.[67] But this owed less to Chamberlain's own eccentricities or inconsistencies than to the confused state of the party system following the Home Rule schism.

It was this situation which forced Chamberlain to come out as an advocate of 'national' politics, of which the supreme expression was Tariff Reform. In what way was Tariff Reform 'national'? First, because it supplied an economic programme which, with its 'Britain First' emphasis, supposedly elevated national over sectional or 'cosmopolitan' interests; a disciple later spoke of the need to 'look at industry in a national spirit which aims at the *maximum* of production and employment, not in the purely commercial spirit which thinks of nothing but cheapness'.[68] Like the Mercantilists before them, the Tariff Reformers thus aimed to make wealth subserve national power, rather than seeking the maximisation of wealth as an end in itself.

Secondly, Tariff Reform *transcended* the ideologies of Conservatism and Radicalism, as Chamberlain had long wanted 'Unionism' to do. So, too, did Chamberlain's own political personality. Indeed, it was his aloofness from the old party creeds which made 'Radical Joe' a hero to the many thousands of political enthusiasts who felt 'disenfranchised' by the party system because they could not

67 Jay, *Chamberlain*, p. 351.

68 Milner's speech at Wolverhampton, 17 Dec. 1906, Lord Milner, *The Nation and the Empire* (1913), p. 162.

understand why patriotism and zeal for empire could not be fused with a sustained attack on social injustice and inequality. Among the more remarkable and influential of these enthusiasts was J.L. Garvin, one of the outstanding journalists of the century and later Chamberlain's official biographer.

Finally, as we shall see in the following chapter, the conviction grew that the twin challenges of democracy at home and foreign dangers abroad required a different kind of leadership from the one that had recently been provided by parliamentarians like Gladstone. 'Democracy is a woman which is always wanting a man!', declared Garvin.[69] Chamberlain seemed to be just such a figure, a Carlylean hero for the modern age, strong-willed, virile, resolute; in 1904 Kipling sang the praises of the 'Man', who 'broke the Oracles in two, And bared the paltry wires and strings'.[70] Chamberlain, it seemed, somehow stood apart from the mediocrity of the world of party politics, embodying as he did a new kind of imperial statesmanship.

CHAMBERLAIN'S LEGACY

Yet Tariff Reform was to fail. Chamberlain's original goal, remember, had been to draw the different classes together in a 'productive' alliance. This proved to be an impossibility. For Tariff Reform never secured working-class support on the scale that Chamberlain required, and it was rejected with contempt by the world of Organised Labour.

The outcome was a tragedy to Chamberlain and all who shared his aspirations. With some justification Chamberlain believed that traditional Conservatism had lost its relevance once the Boer War had broken out; so in 1903 he made his own bid to bind the future. But Radical Unionism, in the form of Tariff Reform, proved to be an even *greater* failure. And this failure enabled the Liberal Party to appropriate (or recapture) the mantle of the People's Party: the party dedicated to improving living conditions at home. Thus, imperialism and social reform, far from coming closer together after 1903, actually

69 Garvin to Northcliffe, 1 Dec. 1906, in Robert J. Scally, *The Origins of the Lloyd George Coalition: The Politics of Social-Imperialism, 1900–1918* (Princeton, 1975), p. 133.

70 Rudyard Kipling, 'Things and the Man' (1904), in *The Years Between* (1919), pp. 93–5.

drifted further apart. The Unionists were now definitely perceived by the public as the party of empire, while the Liberals were increasingly to monopolise the issue of social reform – particularly after they had won their stunning electoral victory in 1906. This was the very polarisation of opinion which Chamberlain's 'national politics' had been designed to prevent.

In July 1906 Chamberlain's active career was ended by a stroke. Many of his loyal followers bravely tried to carry forward the 'great idea', but without much success. For, as Garvin acknowledged, 'by absorbing the middle classes' during the preceding twenty years, the Unionist Party had become 'much less vital and daring in the sphere of social reform than it was when it passed the Factory Acts, when Randolph Churchill's Tory Democratic campaign was at its height and when Mr. Chamberlain's Unionist radicalism was fresh'.[71] A modified version of Tariff Reform (as reformulated by Balfour) could make an appeal to frightened property-owners and middle-class taxpayers determined to defend the status quo. But that was emphatically not what Chamberlain had originally envisaged, and his more dedicated followers knew as much.

Embittered by electoral failure and by what they saw as the cowardice of a Unionist Front Bench unwilling to fight for the big ideals which Tariff Reform enshrined, many of the 'whole hoggers' began to turn radically against the party system itself. The temptation to do this was particularly strong in the case of those who, for one reason or another, stood at some distance from the main centres of political power.

What did the stricken Chamberlain make of this 'new departure'? It is unlikely that he wholly approved. True, throughout his career Chamberlain had been the target of many venomous attacks because of the disruptive role he seemed to be playing in the world of Westminster politics. Twice he had made a significant contribution to the undermining of his party. Chamberlain's behaviour in 1903 particularly infuriated many orthodox Conservatives, who believed that the Tariff Reformers were trying to hijack their party over the fiscal question: 'I am not going to sacrifice Toryism to an unknown Liberalism temporarily in alliance with my party', fumed one of them.[72]

71 Sykes, *Tariff Reform*, pp. 117–18.

72 Ibid., pp. 108–9. On the anger of a Conservative politician who blamed Chamberlain for the severity of the 1906 defeat, see J.A. Bridges, *Reminiscences of a Country Politician* (1906).

At the same time, Chamberlain continued to view party with great respect, as befitted the man who had once played so important a role in the development of the 'caucus'. Even after 1903 he remained far too confident of his ability to achieve his ends by working *through* the party organisation even to contemplate 'going it alone'. Indeed, Chamberlain's last significant action, his involvement in the exchange of the 'Valentine Letters' with Balfour in February 1906, testifies to his 'insider's' instinct for working within the 'system'. For although in the aftermath of the 1906 Election Chamberlain issued frequent public denials that he intended to supplant Balfour as Leader, speaking instead of his anxiety 'to restore the Party to its old efficiency and predominance',[73] his real aim was probably to take control of the Unionist organisation – an aim which he might have realised, but for the illness which crippled him five months later.[74]

In other words, what Chamberlain meant by 'national politics' was the construction of a programme which, by transcending traditional Liberalism and Conservatism, would enable him to appeal to voters across the entire political spectrum, including many who identified with neither of the major parties. But he hoped to implement his programme by *capturing* one of the major parties (after 1895 this could only mean capturing the Conservative and Unionist Parties) and using it as an instrument for the fulfilment of his plans. It is significant that, with the possible exception of the 'Centre Party' episode of 1887, Chamberlain never showed much interest in a party realignment, still less in a formal 'fusion' of Liberalism and Unionism. In that sense he remained something of a traditionalist.

And so although, as his Conservative critics complained, Chamberlain, with his 'catastrophical theory of politics', undoubtedly contributed to the mood of national crisis upon which critics of party thrived,[75] he would probably, had his health not given way, have discouraged his admirers from mounting a vigorous assault on the entire party system, as many of them were shortly to do. Nor did Chamberlain even have much sympathy with contemporaries who reacted to the Boer War setbacks by trying to establish a 'National Government', the enterprise which featured so largely in Edwardian political life.

73 Jay, *Chamberlain*, p. 306.
74 David Dutton, 'Unionist Politics and the Aftermath of the General Election of 1906: A Reassessment', *Historical Journal*, 22 (1979), 861–76.
75 Salisbury to Selborne, 10 Aug. 1904, cited in Sykes, *Tariff Reform*, p. 106.

CHAPTER FOUR

National Efficiency, 1899–1914

THE BOER WAR CULT OF EFFICIENCY

In October 1899 the British Empire went to war with the two Boer Republics, the Transvaal and the Orange Free State. By the summer of 1902 both had been successfully annexed, though at a very high cost in lives and treasure. The nadir came in 'Black Week', December 1899, when the British Army sustained no fewer than three significant military defeats. But these seemed to be not simply military failures, but also indications of organisational weaknesses which ran right through the British machinery of government. 'England herself is on trial', warned Garvin. 'The war has destroyed much in the national repute.'[1]

In fact, events in South Africa brought to a head a range of anxieties which, for at least a decade, had been giving rise to fears of 'decadence' and 'national decline' – fears articulated by Chamberlain himself. The growth of socialism, the narrowing of Britain's margin of naval supremacy, the dangers of 'isolation', all contributed to the mood of 'crisis'.[2] So did Britain's deteriorating trading position as other more recently industrialised countries, notably Germany, started to challenge her in her traditional markets. 'Will England Last the Century?', the *Fortnightly Review* asked its readers in January 1901.[3] The omens did not seem particularly propitious.

1 'Calchas', 'The Test of Efficiency', *Fortnightly Review*, 72 (Sept. 1902), 412. 'Calchas' was one of Garvin's pen-names.

2 Aaron L. Friedberg, *The Weary Titan: Britain and the experience of relative decline, 1895–1905* (Princeton, 1988).

3 Ibid., 69 (Jan. 1901), 20–34.

Contemporary Jeremiahs claimed to discern evidence that something more fundamental still was amiss with the national character. They complained of a fatal spirit of complacency, insularity and anti-intellectualism, a belief in 'rule-of-thumb' methods and 'muddling through' as the response to all problems. The elderly George Brodrick struck a responsive chord when he claimed in a much-quoted article of October 1900 that England was 'a nation of amateurs'.[4] Sidney Low agreed: 'In nearly every department of public life, and in others as well, we are suffering from the lack of that quality of effectiveness, which is based upon scientific method', he wrote. 'It has become a commonplace to say that Britain must "wake up" if she is to hold her own.'[5] The need, in short, was for much greater 'National Efficiency'.

The 'efficiency movement' drew from a variety of different concerns, which is why historians have had some difficulty in classifying it. In part it rested upon a celebration of 'expertise' and 'science', the principles of which, some claimed, should be applied to the task of modernising the British state. 'How few candidates for a seat in the House of Commons have the smallest notion of qualifying themselves for it by professional training, or of treating politics as a serious and lifelong career!', lamented Brodrick.[6] The deficiencies of Ministers and their permanent advisers seemed even more glaring.

Some historians think that such a managerial or technocratic view of political life reflected the aspirations of the expanding class of white-collar workers, managers and technocrats – of men whose occupational status made them feel neutral in the struggle between Capital and Organised Labour yet at the same time contemptuous of the old elites which had traditionally dominated the British state. Prominent Fabians like the Webbs and H.G. Wells have been discussed in just such a context; these writers latched on to the cry for 'Efficiency', it has been claimed, because, like the new *salariat* which they represented, they wanted a new elite of merit and scientific training to replace the old elite of status and birth.[7]

4 George C. Brodrick, 'A Nation of Amateurs', *Nineteenth Century*, 48 (Oct. 1900), 521–35.

5 Sidney Low, 'A Conservative Reform Programme', ibid., 52 (Oct. 1902), 684.

6 Brodrick, 'Nation of Amateurs', 532.

7 Jonathan Rose, *The Edwardian Temperament: 1895–1919*. (Athens, Ohio, 1986), Chapter 4, especially pp. 118–22. As Frank Turner shows, an influential lobby of scientists had started attacking the amateurishness and ignorance of party politicians
continued

But if 'science' supplied one model for the proponents of 'National Efficiency', the cult of 'business methods' provided another. 'Wanted – A Business Government', proclaimed one journalist: 'We want the introduction of new men who can approach the solution of these great difficulties with an open mind and a free hand.' This, he continued, could best be effected by 'a non-party Government formed to meet the unexampled difficulties of the situation – in other words, a business Government or Ministry of Affairs'.[8] Disappointed by Salisbury's reshuffled Government (no fewer than four of its ministers were close relatives of the Prime Minister![9]), Garvin, too, denounced the Unionist Ministry: 'This is not the sort of new Board of Directors called for to "put the Empire upon a business footing"', he complained.[10]

In fact, a new Administrative Reform Association came into existence in 1900 under Lord Rosebery's presidency, in self-conscious imitation of the identically named organisation created during the Crimean War. By the end of the following year it had enrolled one thousand members, many of them distinguished figures from public life.[11] And although Rosebery's refusal to address a public meeting on the subject led to the Association's being disbanded before it could accomplish anything significant,[12] the idea underlying it proved more tenacious. Thus, Rosebery himself speculated in a speech at Edinburgh on 14 November 1901 about the possibility of recruiting prominent businessmen such as Andrew Carnegie and Thomas Lipton to government posts. Similar proposals were later put forward by

continued

from the 1880s onwards, in an attempt to raise their own professional status. The periodical, *Nature*, was the principal literary organ of this group; the 'British Science Guild', founded in 1905, with Haldane as President, later emerged as its most effective pressure-group. See 'Public science in Britain: 1880–1919', in Frank M. Turner, *Contesting Cultural Authority* (Cambridge, 1993), Chapter 8.

8 Edmund Robertson, 'Wanted – A Business Government', *Nineteenth Century*, 50 (Nov. 1901), 714.

9 His nephews, Arthur and Gerald Balfour, his son, Viscount Cranborne, and his son-in-law, Lord Selborne.

10 'Calchas', 'A Cabinet of Commonplace', *Fortnightly Review*, 68 (Dec. 1900), 902.

11 G.R. Searle, *The Quest for National Efficiency: A Study in British Politics and British Political Thought, 1899–1914* (Oxford,1971: new edn, London and Atlantic Highlands, NJ, 1990), pp. 88–9.

12 H.C.G. Matthew, *The Liberal Imperialists: The ideas and politics of a post-Gladstonian elite* (Oxford, 1973), p. 257.

the Midlands industrialist, Dudley Docker,[13] and the concept of a 'business government' was exploited even more crudely by the demagogue, Horatio Bottomley, whose magazine *John Bull* combined it with non-stop attacks on the party system ('Oh, what a game it is!').

Yet not all advocates of 'National Efficiency' were angry outsiders (whether scientists, technicians, or businessmen) seeking entry into the exclusive social world inhabited by legislators and ministers. On the contrary, many members of the governing elites, Rosebery included, probably took up the 'Efficiency' cry in the belief that *they* were naturally the most 'efficient' members of society, or at least would become so once they had 'buckled down' and begun shouldering their responsibilities with greater earnestness. Moreover, the slogan of 'efficiency' had important *military* connotations since it conjured up qualities such as discipline, hierarchy and leadership, which had traditionally been valued in landed society.

There was also a coarsely anti-democratic strand in the cult of 'National Efficiency', encouraged by Rosebery himself, with his call for 'a dictator, a tyrant . . . a man of large mind or iron will who would see what had to be done and do it'.[14] Significantly, this remark was made at the Cromwell Tercentary celebration in November 1899. In fact, Rosebery had earlier stirred up considerable controversy by putting himself at the head of the campaign to erect a statue in Cromwell's memory. 'We could find employment for a few Cromwells now', men 'strenuous' and 'sincere', he publicly observed when this statue eventually came to be unveiled.[15] A few years later Rosebery again revealed a mildly authoritarian streak by coming forward as an extravagant admirer of the autocratic Japanese state.

Rosebery also echoed what many of his contemporaries were saying when he suggested that the great military hero, Kitchener, his recent triumph at Omdurman still fresh in the mind, should be asked to

13 R.P.T. Davenport-Hines, *Dudley Docker: The Life and Times of A Trade Warrior* (Cambridge, 1984), pp. 67–74.

14 Matthew, *Liberal Imperialists*, p. 146.

15 *The Times*, 14 Nov. 1899; Lord Rosebery, *Miscellanies Literary & Historical* (1921), I, pp. 98–9. To Rosebery, Cromwell was one of his 'historical demigods' and also a pioneering imperialist. In January 1900 a naive admirer of Rosebery's called on him to emulate Cromwell by becoming 'the People's Protector': see Roger Howell, Jr, '"Who needs another Cromwell?" The nineteenth-century image of Oliver Cromwell', in R.C. Richardson (ed.), *Images of Oliver Cromwell* (Manchester, 1993), p. 96.

clean out the 'Augean stables' of the War Office.[16] Typical of the new enthusiasm for giving power to 'experts' was an article in the *Fortnightly Review*, 'A Plea for a National Party', which argued that Kitchener and Cromer (Britain's 'Consul-General' in Egypt since 1883) should be included in a Centre National Cabinet: 'What a following awaits a leader who shows his determination to lead by stating boldly his disinterested convictions on important questions of policy', it remarked.[17] The *National Review*, too, urged the promotion to ministerial office of famous Imperial Proconsuls, men who were 'free from party ties' but who had 'vindicated their title to be considered real rulers and governors of men', something which made them vastly superior to 'wordy country squires and sedulous political wire-pullers'.[18]

So many meanings did 'National Efficiency' possess that there were those like the *Spectator* who were tempted to dismiss it as 'gossip', 'babble' and a 'fashionable fad'.[19] But the very breadth of these meanings also proved a strength, since 'Efficiency' constituted a 'cohering ideology' into which different social groups could read their own aspirations.

In fact, the movement for greater 'National Efficiency', far from being hot air, can be shown to have led to many significant *institutional* changes in the spheres of education, social policy, military organisa-tion and imperial defence.[20] There were also two ways in which the cult of 'National Efficiency' was important at the *political* level. First, it helped discredit Gladstonian 'shibboleths' and old-fashioned individualism, encouraging instead a new kind of 'collectivist' outlook in which an enhanced role was allotted to the *state*. Secondly, as will already be apparent, it stimulated bitter attacks on the party system, which many contemporaries blamed for the poor condition in which Britain had entered the South African War.

The anonymous author of the pamphlet, *Drifting*, voiced the standard complaint: 'We have made party citizens, not empire citizens' of the British people, and encouraged them to cast their votes for

16 Though there was little contact between the two men. Matthew, *Liberal Imperialists*, p. 220 and note 5.

17 *Fortnightly Review*, 75 (June 1904), 1036.

18 'Carltonensis', 'Ought We To Have A Coalition?', *National Review*, 34 (Jan. 1900), 669. But the author seems to have wanted a strengthening of the Government, not a Coalition.

19 'After the Coronation', *Spectator*, 16 Aug. 1902.

20 See Searle, *National Efficiency*, pp. 216–35.

one of the two parties and then keep 'quiet', while 'amateurs' were given a free hand to mismanage affairs of state. The only remedy for this scandalous situation, he contended, was the formation of a 'Patriotic Party' which 'the best of us, irrespective of our previous party creed', could join.[21] A hackneyed rhetoric of abuse of the party system came into circulation: 'Mandarins' and 'the Old Gang', for example, were terms freely applied to people over-influenced by narrow party considerations. 'Indifference to party has for the time come into fashion', noted the *Spectator*, 'and it is no uncommon thing to hear men declare that they do not care a fig for the old names, and only want to see the best men in power.'[22]

ROSEBERY AND 'NATIONAL POLITICS', 1899–1903

Given the contemporary political situation, the prevalence of these views need occasion no surprise. For as the new century dawned, Irish Home Rule (the issue around which the two-party system had been structured since 1886) had all but fallen off the agenda. What, then, did the two main political parties now stand for? Their differences seemed trivial by comparison with the crisis into which the nation had been plunged. 'The war has checked party habit and sapped party attachments', wrote Garvin. 'The party system may not be extinct, but it is in abeyance, and will remain so for the reason that politics are not now a question of abstract principles. They are a matter of management, and the real choice is between competence and folly'.[23]

There was also the oddity that although the Unionists had won a renewed term of office in the autumn of 1900, mainly because their opponents were so weak and divided, the Government failed to command much popular enthusiasm. In fact, a steady stream of revelations of military and administrative bungling seriously damaged the reputations of nearly all the Unionist Ministers, Salisbury and Balfour included. Only the Colonial Secretary was widely (if mistakenly) exonerated: 'Mr Chamberlain is the one statesman in a

---

21 *Drifting*, pp. 32, 34.

22 'Lord Rosebery's position', *Spectator*, 28 April 1900.

23 Anon (probably Garvin), 'Lord Rosebery and a National Cabinet', *Fortnightly Review*, 67 (June 1900), 1070, 1082. More abusive still, W.S. Lilly, 'The Price of Party Government', ibid., 922–32.

crowd of chattering politicians.'[24] Indeed, there were grounds for doubting whether such an accident-prone Administration would be able to take the country successfully through the war. What would happen then?

Many journalistic commentators thought that salvation lay through the return to office of the ex-Premier, Lord Rosebery. If Lord Salisbury's successor could be appointed by plebiscite or referendum, wrote the *Fortnightly Review*, there could be no doubt that he would emerge the winner.[25] This view was echoed by the *National Review*, which argued that Rosebery 'would be welcomed by the nation', not least by Unionists, once he had convinced them 'that he [was] ready to become an active leader of a great National Party'.[26]

Was there any chance of this happening? To answer that question we must analyse the position occupied in the late 1890s by the Liberal Imperialist group, to which Rosebery was loosely attached. The starting point for most Liberal Imperialists was a deep regret that, to quote Rosebery's own words, the Liberal Party had ceased to be 'what . . . it has always been and must really be . . . the national party'.[27] Accordingly, the group sought to win back alienated middle-class voters put off by the Liberals' image as 'a party of protest'.[28] In other words, as far as most Liberal Imperialists were concerned, the main priority was the revival of the Liberal Party under their own direction. In May 1899 even Rosebery was still hoping 'to modify his party's policy, and to widen the basis of its electoral support by a return to the situation before 1886'.[29]

But, once the Boer War had broken out, the possibility arose of a major party *realignment* triggered off by the formation of an emergency coalition government. It was a possibility which left the Liberal Imperialist group seriously divided. Asquith, always a party loyalist at heart, probably never seriously intended to break away

24 *Drifting*, p. 207.
25 'Rosebery and National Cabinet', 1079–80.
26 'An Old Parliamentary Hand', 'Lord Rosebery's Opportunity', *National Review*, 37 (Aug. 1901), 844. See also Robertson, 'Wanted – A Business Government', 721.
27 *The Times*, 19 Oct. 1895, cited in Matthew, *Liberal Imperialists*, p. 127. In Asquith's words, this meant looking at 'the interests of the community from the point of view of the community as a whole' (Asquith at Hull, *The Times*, 23 Jan. 1895, ibid., p. 128).
28 19 Oct. 1901, Matthew, *Liberal Imperialists*, pp. 130–3.
29 Ibid., p. 38. Matthew is paraphrasing Rosebery's speech to the City Liberal Club, which, interestingly enough, still had many Liberal Unionist members.

from official Liberalism. Like Robert Perks and Sir Henry Fowler, he valued the Liberal League because he saw it as a device for saving pro-war Liberals from expulsion.[30]

But another Liberal Imperialist, Haldane, viewed things differently; in January 1900 his mind was running over the possibility of a non-party ministry which might include Milner and have Rosebery as its Chief.[31] And two years later Edward Grey, responding to Rosebery's 'definite separation' letter of 21 February 1902, felt that a Liberal break-up was imminent: 'perhaps', he told Milner, 'a corresponding split may come amongst the Conservatives and a large middle party come into being for a while'.[32] Meanwhile other Liberal Imperialists were simply confused, unsure of whether organisations like the Liberal League were 'trying to permeate or proscribe'.[33]

The position of Rosebery himself was obviously crucial. As a former Prime Minister and Foreign Secretary, he enjoyed considerable prestige. His melodramatic resignation as Liberal Leader in 1896 had also propelled him into a cross-bench position. He had then carefully protected this position of 'neutrality' by refusing the Liberal leadership of the Lords when Lord Kimberley tried to retire. Later, during the Boer War, partly under the influence of Haldane, Rosebery delivered a series of very well-publicised speeches which established him as the very embodiment of 'National Efficiency'. As such, he was an attractive figure not only to moderate Liberals but also to many Conservatives and to those without fixed party affiliations.

Rosebery's own long-term ambitions (if he had any) remain shrouded in mystery. But in March 1901 his friend, Edward Hamilton, noted in his diary that Rosebery was contemplating the prospect of 'a sort of coalition government formed of the best men of both parties, who might perhaps unite under him, because he had taken no side decidedly'.[34] Rosebery's otherwise rather strange behaviour in the course of that year only makes sense if one assumes that he was preparing himself for some such eventuality.[35]

What is not in doubt is that Rosebery believed party itself to be disappearing, a process which he traced back to Disraeli and 1867.[36]

---

30 Ibid., pp. 49–55.

31 Ibid., p. 47. For his later views, see ibid., pp. 144–55.

32 Grey to Milner, 16 March 1902, Grey to Rosebery, cited in ibid., p. 144.

33 Ibid., p. 289.

34 Ibid., p. 62, note 3, and Searle, *National Efficiency*, p. 114.

35 See the discussion in Matthew, *Liberal Imperialists*, pp. 70–1, Searle, *National Efficiency*, pp. 111–12.

36 Matthew, *Liberal Imperialists*, p. 147.

It was a theme on which he elaborated in his 1905 introduction to Alfred Stead's *Great Japan: A Study in National Efficiency* (admittedly when his effective political career had already ended). 'Party is an evil', Rosebery raged, 'perhaps, even probably, a necessary evil, but still an evil. It is the curse of our country that so many, especially in high places, should worship it as a god.' The party system, Rosebery continued, 'blights efficiency. It keeps out of employment a great mass of precious ability. It puts into place not the fittest but the most eligible, from the party point of view – that is, very often, the worst.' As a solution to the 'evil', he drew attention to Chatham's Ministry in the mid-eighteenth century when the Duke of Newcastle handled party business, leaving the elder Pitt 'free to do the country's work'.[37]

Unfortunately from the viewpoint of those who passionately wanted a major party realignment, Rosebery attracted to his banner many Liberals whose prime concern was the continuation of the vendetta against the official Leader Campbell-Bannerman and even a few 'Little Englanders'. Some 'Roseberyites' also had allegiances to Non-conformity which got in the way of the sincere attempts being made by Haldane and others to reshape the nation's educational system in the interests of 'efficiency'. As for Rosebery himself, cynics might well doubt whether he ever intended 'efficiency' to be 'much more than rhetorical'.[38]

Those who hoped for national salvation through the overthrow of the two-party system often spoke of engineering some sort of coalition which would include both Rosebery and Chamberlain. During the Boer War period the press was full of speculation along these lines. Such a prospect particularly interested Garvin, who constantly wrote about it, sometimes with optimism, sometimes despondently. 'The combination of the Colonial Secretary and the ex-Premier would create, as nothing else really could create, a National Cabinet, a National Party, a National policy', was the burden of his song.[39] After all, Rosebery had identified his name with the idea of 'a business Cabinet', while Chamberlain was 'the most complete example of the business man in politics that has yet

37 Alfred Stead, *Great Japan: A Study in National Efficiency* (1905), pp. ix–xi. Rosebery later wrote a study of Chatham, published in 1910.
38 Matthew, *Liberal Imperialists*, p. 11.
39 'Rosebery and National Cabinet', 1082.

been seen in the public life of this or perhaps of any country'.[40] Logic suggested that the two men should be able to pull along together.

But political reality knew nothing of this kind of logic. In fact, most of the Liberal Imperialists mistrusted Chamberlain, blaming the outbreak of war on his bungling diplomacy. They also deeply resented his demagogic behaviour at the time of the 1900 ('Khaki') Election.[41] For his part, the Colonial Secretary furiously resented the fact that a man like Haldane should have impugned his family honour over the Kynochs Contracts affair;[42] nor did he have a high opinion of Rosebery. But in any case, as should by now be clear, Chamberlain's conception of 'national politics' was rather different from the Roseberyite yearning for 'fusion' and 'consensus'.

In the event, most of the Liberal Imperialists (with the notable exception of Rosebery) opted for a strategy of backing the High Commissioner in South Africa, Lord Milner, with whom they enjoyed close personal and social ties, perhaps in the hope that this would create the impression that they were taking a 'national' line on the war.[43] It was a mistaken strategy, since the Liberal Imperialists nearly found themselves driven out of their party through support of a man whose views on South African policy and on politics generally they did not really share – though it took the Chinese Labour Affair a few years later to make this clear.[44]

The main weakness of the movement to achieve greater 'National Efficiency' was its lack of a secure political base. Early in 1902, it is true, Sidney Webb had created the Co-Efficient Club, a dining circle whose members periodically met to discuss, on a non-party basis, ways in which various aspects of public life could be overhauled and modernised. Originally, there were twelve members, some of them Fabians, some Liberal Imperialists, some acolytes of Milner, but each supposedly an 'expert' in his particular field. According to Milner's friend, L.S. Amery (the military correspondent of *The Times*), they aimed to function as a kind of 'General Staff' in preparation for the

---

· 40 'Calchas', 'Lord Rosebery and Political Reconstruction', *Fortnightly Review*, 71 (Jan. 1902), 3. In more pessimistic vein was his 'An Open Letter to Lord Rosebery', ibid., 70 (Sept. 1901), 375–86. See also Henry Birchenough, 'Mr Chamberlain as an Empire Builder', *Nineteenth Century*, 51 (March 1902), 366.

41 Matthew, *Liberal Imperialists*, p. 129.

42 Searle, *National Efficiency*, p. 122. G.R. Searle, *Corruption in British Politics, 1895–1930*, (Oxford, 1987), pp. 52–64.

43 Matthew, *Liberal Imperialists*, p. 173.

44 Ibid., pp. 187, 194, 291.

Government of 'National Efficiency' which they hoped would later materialise.

But although the 'Co-Efficients' lingered on for many years as a dining club, they obviously had no such portentous role to perform. The 'benevolent conspiracy' of like-minded people continued to ensure some co-operation across the party divide throughout the Edwardian period. But the prospect of a Rosebery-led National Coalition faded with the ending of the Boer War in June 1902[45] and with the eruption of the controversies surrounding Balfour's Education Act; it completely disappeared when Chamberlain launched his Tariff Reform crusade in May 1903.

There is some evidence that on the fiscal issue Rosebery, and perhaps even Grey, initially wavered.[46] But all the leading Liberal Imperialists ultimately rallied behind Free Trade, Haldane almost as enthusiastically as Asquith. For the next six years or so party opinion was to be sharply polarised. Symbolically, the Co-Efficients split right down the middle. In so far as 'fusion' remained on the agenda, it now meant creating some kind of 'Centre' alliance between the Unionist Free Fooders and the Liberal Imperialists, under the leadership of Rosebery or Devonshire – a hopeless project, as soon became apparent.[47]

Rosebery's willingness even to contemplate linking up with Devonshire perhaps shows how superficial his commitment to the ideals of 'National Efficiency' had always been. At any rate, figures like Garvin soon gave him up in disgust. The real political struggle henceforward took place between the Free Trade Liberal Party and a Unionist Party inside which Chamberlain's Tariff Reform friends steadily increased their influence. Chamberlain's 'national crusade' had thus put paid to the prospects of a 'National Government' – at least for the foreseeable future.

MILNER AND NATIONAL RECONSTRUCTION, 1903–10

Between 1903 and 1909, then, the 'efficiency advocates' tended to go their separate ways. Chamberlain embarked on his heroic attempts to

---

45 This was the occasion of Salisbury's retirement and his smooth replacement by Balfour.

46 The *Spectator* commented caustically on the ambivalence of Rosebery's Burnley speech (23 May 1903).

47 Matthew, *Liberal Imperialists*, pp. 103–8.

win the Unionist Party over to Tariff Reform; Rosebery drifted off into ineffectual isolation; and the other Liberal Imperialists became absorbed in the official work of the Liberal Party, as a reward for which most of the leading figures received ministerial posts when Campbell-Bannerman formed his Administration in December 1905. Meanwhile the Fabian intelligentsia concentrated on the task of 'permeating' the two main parties with a 'constructive' social policy, with the Webbs preocuppied from 1905 onwards with reforming the Poor Law.

It was Lord Milner, who returned from South Africa in April 1905, who now emerged as the most articulate critic of the party system. Milner had started life as a Liberal until he followed Goschen (for whom he acted as Private Secretary) into Liberal Unionism over the Home Rule issue. But subsequent work as an imperial administrator, first in Egypt, later in South Africa, soon removed most elements of traditional liberalism from his thinking.

The gravamen of Milner's charge was that the '*Rotten Assembly at Westminster*', with its silly party rivalries and animosities, was jeopardising 'the whole future of the Empire' by allowing MPs to meddle in imperial affairs which they did not understand simply because they had 'been elected for their competence in dealing with Metropolitan Tramways or country pubs'.[48] Grim, humourless, dedicated and honest, Milner became obsessed 'with a vision of non-party government without having invented any device for securing it', as Beatrice Webb noted.[49]

The worship of all things German had been a feature of much turn-of-the-century 'efficiency' rhetoric: Germany's was 'the most efficient and exacting administration in the world', Garvin misleadingly claimed in 1900.[50] But Milner, himself German-born, carried this commitment very much further, and with some justification his Liberal opponents could categorise the former Proconsul as a 'pure bureaucrat and a pure idealogue' possessing an 'essentially un-English character'.[51]

All of this would have been of no more than biographical interest

---

48 Milner to Parkins, 24 July 1905, cited in Robert J. Scally, *The Origins of the Lloyd George Coalition: The Politics of Social-Imperialism, 1900–1918* (Princeton, 1975), p. 107.

49 Diary, 4 Oct. 1905, cited ibid., 107.

50 'Calchas', 'Cabinet of Commonplace', 905.

51 *Speaker*, 3 March 1906, cited in A.M. Gollin, *Proconsul in Politics: A Study of Lord Milner in Opposition and in Power* (1964), pp. 80–1.

but for the fact that Milner, whose dourness on the platform belied the considerable charm which he could exert in the company of intimates, came to establish a remarkable ascendancy over a band of young, mainly Oxford-educated young men, many of whom had met him or worked for him in South Africa. Several members of the 'Milner Kindergarten' eventually reached positions of importance in public life: L.S. Amery as a Conservative Cabinet Minister, Philip Kerr (Lord Lothian) as British Ambassador in Washington, Geoffrey Dawson as editor of *The Times*. To these disciples Milner communicated something of his own deeply-felt convictions: for example, his sense of the centrality of 'national service', his belief in 'constructive' social reform, his dedication to the goal of imperial unity, and, of course, his contempt for party.

After 1906 Milner was not a truly cross-bench figure since he was on such very bad terms with Liberal Ministers (including his one-time Liberal Imperialist backers). On the other hand, after Joseph Chamberlain had been removed from active politics by a stroke in July 1906 he did not have that much in common with the official Unionist leadership either. Balfour learned in January 1907 that although Milner would 'lead no movements that [would] cut across the programme of a united Unionist party', the latter saw himself as 'a Free Lance, anxious to impress upon public opinion (which in Imperial matters is quite rotten) certain strong views he has'.[52] In a letter to Lord Lansdowne, Unionist Leader in the Lords, Milner gave this account of his political position: 'The very fact that I am so little of a party man brings me into touch with a great many of the neutral unpartizan [*sic*] people, whose wobbling to and fro turns elections.'[53] Meanwhile, in speeches to the wider public Milner presented himself as a 'political Ishmaelite, who [had] found hospitality in the Unionist camp' but knew that he was 'a hopeless detrimental [*sic*] from the party point of view'.[54]

In exchanges with his friends Milner could afford to be more frank. In October 1909 he told Dawson: 'My own interest in what I call *Local* British politics is rather faint. It is only in their bearing on the bigger issues that they seem much to matter. Of course *good social legislation* in the U.K. is essential, but as regards that it is rather a case of Tweedle

52 Sandars to Balfour (summarising Iwan-Muller), 13 Jan. 1907, cited in Gollin, *Milner*, p. 113.
53 Milner to Lansdowne, 22 Nov. 1908, ibid., p. 155.
54 Speech at Wolverhampton, 17 Dec. 1906, Lord Milner, *The Nation and the Empire* (1913), pp. 153–4.

& Tweedle & both pretty bad.'[55] Indeed, despite his commitment to an austere conception of Tariff Reform, Milner was actually prepared to go 'into the wilderness' rather than follow the Unionist Party in a sterile 'anti-socialist' crusade. Believing that 'Unionism on its present lines' was 'hopeless', he therefore wanted to reform the party, give it a new programme, and reconstitute it 'with perhaps a strong contingent of the saner workmen, on a broader basis than that of Conservative Mandarinism and middle-class timidity, lethargy & narrow mindedness'.[56] Garvin broadly agreed on the necessity for this Chamberlainite strategy.

WINSTON CHURCHILL AND LLOYD GEORGE

Meanwhile during the 1906–10 years the idea of creating a new 'Centre Party' never entirely died. It resurfaced in 1908–09 when, ironically enough, desultory negotiations took place between the *old-fashioned individualists* on both sides of the party fence – that is, between Unionist Free Fooders, alarmed at Tariff Reform encroachments, and Liberal Cobdenites, repelled by the social legislation emanating from Lloyd George and Churchill. Had such a 'Centre Party' materialised, it would have been a kind of 'Government of National *Inefficiency*'.[57]

However, in 1910 the situation dramatically changed once more. The Lords' rejection of Lloyd George's People's Budget and the indecisive General Election of January 1910 created a party and constitutional deadlock, while also fostering a mood of deep 'national crisis'. The political forces working for 'Reconstruction' reassembled; 'national politics' was about to enter an entirely new phase.

In fact, even before the onset of the Constitutional Crisis, there were two politicians who, partly unbeknown to the wider public, had developed an interest in the idea of 'National Government' (an interest which they were to retain for many years to come): Winston Churchill and Lloyd George.

Churchill's involvement dates back to the opening years of the century when he was gathering material for his father's (Lord

---

55 Milner to Dawson, 30 October 1909, Gollin, *Milner*, p. 160.

56 Milner to Amery, 25 Sept.1907, ibid., p. 153.

57 On this episode, see Alan Sykes, *Tariff Reform in British Politics 1903–1913* (Oxford, 1979), pp. 170–4.

Randolph's) biography. This work had brought him into contact with Rosebery, one of his father's close personal friends. Like so many young men of his generation, Churchill soon fell under the spell of the older man. In any case, Churchill's ambition to achieve political greatness had never been matched by any deep enthusiasm for the Conservative Party under whose banner he had been elected to Parliament in the 1900 General Election, and his views (then as later) were a strange mishmash of Conservatism and Radicalism.[58] Moreover, and in this he was not alone, Churchill quickly became disillusioned with the performance of the accident-prone Salisbury and Balfour Ministries and frustrated at his own lack of opportunity for office.

Perhaps as a result of that frustration, when Rosebery delivered his Chesterfield Speech in December, Churchill gave it an effusive welcome, both publicly and in private. 'I wish most sincerely I could review the political situation without having to consider the claims and influences of party and party machinery', he confessed.[59] A week later he was writing to a friend about his personal belief in 'a well balanced policy . . . something that will coordinate development and expansion with the progress of social comfort and health',[60] vague words which echoed those used earlier by his father.

Long after many of his contemporaries had become disillusioned with Rosebery, Churchill kept in touch. In October 1902 he was dangling before the ex-Premier the possibility of a 'central coalition' emerging from the existing confusion, a 'coalition' in which he had clearly allotted *himself* a historic role! 'Only the conviction that you are upholding the flag for which my father fought so long and disastrously would nerve me to the plunge', wrote Churchill to Rosebery: 'The Government of the Middle – the party wh[ich] shall be free at once from the sordid selfishness and callousness of Toryism on the one hand, and the blind appetites of the Radical masses on the other' might be an 'ideal' which was not, in the short run, attainable, but it was an ideal 'which [was] nevertheless worth working for'.[61] However, the two men agreed that the 'psychological moment' for such a venture had not yet arrived.

---

58 See John Charmley, *Churchill: The End of Glory* (1993), Chapter 3.

59 Churchill to Rosebery, 17 Dec. 1901, cited in Paul Addison, *Churchill on the Home Front 1900–1955* (1992), p. 21.

60 Churchill to J. Moore Bayley, 23 Dec. 1901, Randolph Churchill, *Winston S. Churchill: Young Statesman, 1901–1914* (1967), p. 32.

61 Churchill to Rosebery, 10 Oct. 1902, ibid., p. 47.

Country before Party

The Birmingham Speech five months later initially seemed to offer the requisite opening. Churchill, as a Free Trader, found himself increasingly at odds with his own party, and for a while hoped for the creation of a 'Central Government' dedicated to Free Trade, to be headed by Rosebery and Devonshire.[62] When this failed to materialise, Churchill crossed the floor of the House, reconciling himself to a career in the Liberal Party, in whose interests he now spoke with an almost exaggerated eloquence and zeal.

In the spring of 1908, after serving as Under-Secretary at the Colonial Office, Churchill was appointed President of the Board of Trade in succession to Lloyd George, with whom he had recently struck up a close friendship. This was also the moment when Churchill first began to wander away from the path of orthodox Liberalism. For example, he encouraged Sidney Webb to give him advice, and was soon invoking the Webbian concept of a 'National Minimum'. Churchill also developed a deep interest (as, momentarily, had his father) in Bismarckian social policy. 'Constructive' social reform on the German model, he believed, would strengthen the social organisation of the country and boost 'National Efficiency'.[63] Churchill, in short, though dubbed by contemporaries a 'Radical', was a Radical of a very distinctive type, since his main preoccupation was with using the machinery of the state for the purpose of social and political *integration* – in other words to *unite* people from a variety of different backgrounds, not to stir up animosity between them.

Such a 'national' perspective also coloured his private conduct. At about this time he formed a lifelong friendship with the swash-buckling Conservative backbencher, F.E.Smith, with whom he co-founded 'The Other Club', a forum for cross-party sociability. Blissfully unaware, it would seem, of the hatred which his 'apostasy' had earned him in the eyes of most Conservatives, Churchill also cherished the hope that the more unpleasant aspects of party strife could be eliminated. 'We ought to pursue a national and not a sectional policy', Churchill told Asquith in January 1910, '& to try to make our prolonged tenure of power as agreeable as possible to the other half of our fellow countrymen.'[64]

62 See Sykes, *Tariff Reform*, p. 71; Churchill to Harmsworth, 26 Aug. 1903, Addison, *Churchill*, p. 32.
63 Typical of his political approach in these years are his likening of the Board of Trade to the Intelligence Department of the Army and his calls for a 'Committee of National Organisation', along the lines of the Committee of Imperial Defence, for the co-ordination of home policy (Addison, *Churchill*, pp. 80–1).
64 Addison, *Churchill*, p. 104.

Lloyd George, on the other hand, stood, ostensibly at least, for a more traditional kind of Radicalism. Entering politics as a Welsh Dissenter with a deep instinctive hatred of the 'feudal' Establishment, he had gone on to make a name for himself by vituperative attacks on Chamberlain at the time of the Boer War. Indeed, to his enemies (inside as well as outside the party) the Welshman seemed to symbolise everything that was destructive about sectarian radicalism and divisive about two-party politics.

Yet appearances were deceptive. Even in the opening years of the century there were already signs of political inclinations which were shortly to redirect Lloyd George's career. For example, although a 'Pro-Boer', he admired Rosebery, whose Chesterfield Speech had indicated a willingness to pursue a negotiated settlement in South Africa which the other Liberal Imperialists, too heavily committed to Milner, were not even prepared to contemplate.

Lloyd George subsequently established his parliamentary credentials through his attacks on the 1902 Education Act. But, in hindsight, it seems significant that he was not content to rest his case on the grievances of his fellow Nonconformists or on the principle of 'popular control' but should also have sounded a note of warning about the economic 'struggle for existence': 'We are engaged in a series of wars more dangerous to our supremacy than the South African war . . . , an industrial war for commercial supremacy', he told a meeting of party workers in December 1902; British workmen should be trained to meet the struggle, just as on the Continent they trained 'every man in the use of arms', since only in this way could Britain avoid being 'beaten by better trained countries' and end the 'bitterness and strife' which was plunging Capital and Labour into a kind of 'civil war'.[65] This, of course, was the language of 'National Efficiency': it owed little to traditional Radicalism.

Lloyd George's political vistas widened still further during his years at the Board of Trade between 1905 and 1908 when he had ample opportunity for meeting with leading industrialists and merchants. In a surprising public outburst in January 1909 Lloyd George confessed that he had learned much from these encounters:

> After years of strife, politically, I found myself at peace with all my neighbours. I met men of all political parties and of no political parties – because there are a great many people who care very little about any

65 *Lincoln Leader*, 13 Dec. 1902, cited in Chris Wrigley, *Lloyd George* (Oxford, 1992), pp. 32–3.

political party in this country . . . . And . . . they all did their best to
help me to administer the affairs of the Board of Trade in the general
interest of the trade and commerce of the country; and it was quite a
delightful experience to be able, for two or three years, to work in a
department where there was really no political feeling, no political bias,
and no political prejudice'.[66]

It is certainly true that many of the businessmen who met Lloyd
George in an official capacity came to appreciate his quickness and
open-mindedness. Prominent Tariff Reformers, too, sensed that the
President of the Board of Trade was by no means a doctrinaire
Free Trader and admired many of his initiatives: for example, the
Industrial Census Bill and his patents legislation. Some even had a
premonition that the career trajectory of this Radical firebrand might
later follow that of one of his predecessors at the Board of Trade,
Joseph Chamberlain. Significantly, in his private conversation, Lloyd
George *himself* was soon drawing such parallels.[67]

A few years earlier, in 1903, inveighing against the 'hopelessness'
of the party system, Milner had complained that 'only one man in
a hundred dares give effect or utterance to the statesmanship that is
in him', before going on to prophesy: 'Perhaps a great *Charlatan* –
political scallywag, buffoon, liar, stump orator and in other respects
popular favourite – may some day arise, who is nevertheless a
statesman . . . and who, having attained and maintaining power
by popular art, may use it for national ends.'[68] It was during the
Constitutional Crisis that Lloyd George began to prepare himself for
such a role.

THE CONSTITUTIONAL CRISIS, 1909–11

The Constitutional Crisis began as a dispute about the proper relationship between the two Houses of Parliament. But it soon became
entangled with the Irish Question, not least because the first General

66 29 Jan. 1909, cited in Scally, *Lloyd George Coalition*, p. 144.

67 Riddell diary, 27 May 1912, Lord Riddell, *More Pages From My Diary,
1908–1914* (1934), p. 64. The Radical journalist A.G. Gardiner made much of Lloyd
George's resemblances with Chamberlain in his collection of essays, *Prophets, Priests,
and Kings* (1908).

68 Milner to Lady Edward Cecil, 24 April 1903, Cecil Headlam (ed.), *The Milner
Papers: South Africa, 1899–1905*, vol II (1933), p. 447.

Election of 1910 had produced a deadlocked Commons, with the Irish (and Labour) holding the balance of seats; this enabled the Irish to insist that the Liberals honour the promise which Gladstone had made a quarter of a century earlier by creating a Dublin Parliament. Moreover, as everyone realised, the abolition of the Lords' absolute Veto would at a stroke remove the main obstacle to the attainment of a Home Rule settlement.

However, the prospect of a bitter fight to the death over Home Rule filled most of the leaders of the two main parties with dismay. Liberal Ministers, for example, resented their dependence on the votes of Irish Members who were now setting out to 'dictate' policy to them. At the same time many Unionists, too, saw advantages in ending a dispute which threatened to damage British imperial and strategic interests by alienating both the United States and also 'Colonies of Settlement' like Australia, where there were large Irish communities. 'Federalism' or 'Home-Rule-All-Round' offered Unionists who were concerned at this situation a possible escape from the impasse.

One of the many merits of Federalism was that it seemed to have the *imprimatur* of Joseph Chamberlain, who had sketched out a scheme along these lines way back in 1886, a consideration that was bound to weigh heavily with his son, Austen. Since then the idea of Federalism had several times been given an airing. In October 1902, for example, Sidney Low had pointed out that National Councils or Home-Rule-All-Round might not only solve the Irish problem, but would have the additional advantage of freeing imperial affairs from domestic politics, so that both could be dealt with adequately and with the minimum of party rancour: 'It seems impossible to get rid of the party system altogether; but we might at least render it a little more logical and coherent', Low had concluded.[69] Such a reform could also be presented as a way of 'modernising' the Constitution so as to reduce 'congestion' in the Westminster Parliament – in the interests of legislative efficiency. The Colonies, for their part, would be far more willing to send representatives to an Imperial Parliament or Council once 'imperial' issues had become separated from 'parish pump' matters – at least this was what some Unionists claimed.

After the January 1910 General Election there was an added incentive for the Unionists to abandon their rigid defence of the status quo. For it seemed possible that 'Federalism', along with other concessions, might succeed in winning over to the Unionist

69 Low, 'Conservative Reform Programme', 685–8.

side the group of Irish MPs headed by William O'Brien and Tim Healy which had broken away from John Redmond's Irish Nationalist Party. In January 1910 Garvin was reminding fellow Unionists that such a deal would in any case be a logical one, since the O'Brienites broadly agreed with them on education, licensing, Tariff Reform and, above all, on food taxes. Even when the tactical benefits of launching an initiative of this kind had largely disappeared, some Unionists continued to press the party to give ground on Ireland in the interests of a wider settlement.[70] Garvin, in particular, feared that, without a 'federal solution' for Ireland, Britain would 'be stripped of the sympathy of the Dominions'.[71]

However, as Milner's young acolyte F.S. Oliver put it to Balfour in a private Memorandum in September, the Unionist Party alone could not offer federal Home Rule: 'To attempt anything of the kind would be to repeat the offence of Peel in '47 [*sic*] and Gladstone in '86', he observed. But Oliver went on to argue that what a party could 'not make political capital out of, [might] not adopt for the sake – real or apparent – of votes and power', it could 'accept without dishonour or demoralisation for patriotic reasons' as part of a 'settlement by consent and mutual compromise'.[72] Austen Chamberlain privately agreed, saying that much was 'possible and safe as a *national* settlement which would be disastrous if passed as a party measure under party conditions'.[73]

When Oliver penned his Memorandum there was, in fact, a forum already in existence at which such matters might conceivably have been discussed. For in June, following the death of Edward VII, the two sets of leaders had agreed to enter a Constitutional Conference in an attempt to resolve their differences, following the publication of a series of well-publicised letters in *The Times* by Oliver, under the pseudonym 'Pacificus'[74] and the appearance of a gushing editorial in Garvin's *Observer* calling for a 'Truce of God'.[75]

This is not the place to go through the complex negotiations of the Constitutional Conference, which met on and off from June

70 See Garvin to Balfour, 17 Oct. 1910, A.M. Gollin, *The Observer and J.L. Garvin, 1908–1914* (Oxford, 1960), pp. 213–15, especially p. 215.

71 Garvin to Northcliffe, 19 Oct. 1910, ibid., p. 210.

72 F.S. Oliver, Memorandum of 28 Sept. 1910, in John D. Fair, *British Interparty Conferences*, (Oxford, 1980), pp. 288–93.

73 Cited in David Dutton, *'His Majesty's Loyal Opposition': The Unionist Party in Opposition 1905–1915* (Liverpool, 1992), p. 84.

74 'Pacificus''s letters appeared in *The Times* on 23 May, 6 June, 8 June 1910.

75 *Observer*, 15 May 1910, cited in Gollin, *Garvin*, p. 191.

to November 1910. But two of its features merit attention. First, membership of the Conference was confined to the two main parties, each of which contributed four members: the Irish Nationalists and Labour were excluded. Second, the party leaders came quite close in these confidential discussions to a constitutional settlement based on a scheme for resolving deadlocks by 'joint sessions' of the two Houses of Parliament (the so-called Ripon Plan), even though this was a proposal quite unknown to most Liberal MPs and party activists, who had been campaigning during the recent election for the replacement of the Lords' absolute Veto by a temporary one. Thus the search was already on to find a 'middle path' which would allow the party leaders (the Liberals especially) to escape from their electoral pledges – and from the pressures being exerted on them by the minor parties. Well might partisans on both sides of the party divide worry over the possibility of a 'national settlement' being privately reached behind their backs.

In the event, the gap between the two sides on the constitutional issue proved to be unbridgeable. Realising that this was so, Garvin came out openly for a broadening of the Conference agenda in the hope that the Lords question and the related issue of Ireland might be made part of a wider national settlement. The 'Conference method' of establishing 'consensus' was recommended even more vigorously by Oliver, who had written a well-received biography of Alexander Hamilton, the Federalist who had helped draft the American Constitution. In the light of the recent success of the Conference which had created the Union of South Africa, this seemed a promising line of advance.

In mid-June Garvin had his first meeting with Lloyd George, by whom he was charmed;[76] presumably the two men discussed the merits of the 'Conference method'. But Lloyd George had even bolder ideas about how to achieve a national agreement. For in early October, in the interstices of the formal Constitutional Conference, he approached Balfour and dangled before his eyes the prospect of establishing a *Coalition Ministry*. According to the Memorandum which he had dictated at Criccieth two months earlier, Lloyd George seems to have believed that such a Coalition would enable the 'first-rate men' in both parties to embark on a great scheme of 'National reorganisation'.

A few of the main features of the complex and controversial Secret

76 Ibid., pp. 198–9.

Coalition talks must be emphasised. First, it is interesting to observe Lloyd George employing the language of business managerialism which had been so prominent in the rhetoric of 'National Efficiency' earlier in the decade. In his August Memorandum, for example, an elaborate analogy is drawn between the state and a business corporation. Although, claimed Lloyd George, the country had in the past 'gained a good deal from the conflict and rivalry of Parties', more would now be achieved by 'bringing the resources of the two Parties into joint stock in order to liquidate arrears which, if much longer neglected, may end in national impoverishment, if not insolvency'.

This managerial rhetoric is especially interesting, given the fact that earlier in the year, in the company of friends, Lloyd George had discussed 'the question of re-forming a Government in which he would be Prime Minister, playing with the idea of having it composed of business men, Sir Christopher Furness, Alfred Mond', and so on – an echo, deliberate or otherwise, of what Lord Rosebery had said at Edinburgh nearly a decade earlier. True, Lloyd George had gone on to observe: 'They are very simple people, these Captains of Industry. I can do what I like with them. I found that out at the Board of Trade.'[77] Shortly afterwards, in conversation with George Riddell, Lloyd George also showed a shrewd awareness of the *differences* between the work of politics and business and of why it was that so few businessmen managed to succeed in Parliament.[78] All the same, the idea of establishing a 'Business Government' seems to have deeply fascinated Lloyd George, as his later career testifies.

What would Lloyd George's proposed coalition have sought to accomplish? The basic notion seems to have been that the Liberals would make concessions to their opponents by introducing some measure of compulsory military training (on the model of the Swiss Militia system), strengthening the Navy, and setting up an inquiry into aspects of the fiscal question. As a quid pro quo, the Unionists would be asked to commit themselves to a number of advanced social reforms (including the National Insurance scheme upon which the Chancellor was currently working) and to accept a compromise solution of the Irish question involving some kind of Home-Rule-All-Round or Federalism. Lloyd George also broached the issue of personnel: for example, at one stage he hinted that,

[77] Lucy Masterman's diary, early April 1910, cited in Lucy Masterman, *C.F.G. Masterman* (1939), p. 160.
[78] Riddell diary, 14 June 1913, Riddell, *More Pages*, p. 161.

should the Coalition materialise, Asquith might be persuaded to take a peerage, leaving the Leadership of the Commons to Balfour.[79]

It is not perhaps surprising that Lloyd George tended to emphasise whichever item in this catalogue of proposals he thought to be most likely to attract the audience he was currently addressing.[80] Thus, he allowed some Liberals to come away with the belief that the main purpose of the initiative was the construction of a bi-partisan basis for the carrying of a comprehensive measure of National Insurance, including Widows and Orphans' Benefits, thereby circumventing the obstreperous industrial insurance companies. To Churchill, in particular, Coalition was presented as a device for enacting a bold and far-reaching scheme of social reconstruction.[81] By contrast, F.E. Smith, whom Lloyd George had initially employed to carry his overture to Balfour, felt that the Radical Chancellor had 'come over' to the *Unionist* side on all the issues which really counted.[82]

Despite all this confusion, some of it, one feels, deliberately manufactured by Lloyd George himself, negotiations with the Unionist leaders continued for over three weeks. This is surely because, on all sides, there was a feeling that party animosities were spinning dangerously out of control, with 'sensible' leaders at risk of being propelled into 'extreme' courses of actions by the fanatical forces in their rear. Thus, Lloyd George and other senior Liberals clearly hankered after an arrangement with their opposite numbers which would free them from dependence upon the troublesome Irish, who could be left 'to stew in their own juice'.[83]

In fact, far more than earlier in the century, one gets the impression that underlying all the talk about the 'national interest' lay frustration with the way in which sensible policy-making was being impeded by electoral pressure. The implication was that statesmen who 'knew the facts' could not act on their knowledge because no Opposition would be able to resist the temptation of exploiting an unpopular ministerial initiative. Compulsory military service, for example, might well

[79] This is ironic, given the fact that earlier in the century Balfour was being portrayed as the archetypal 'Mandarin'.

[80] Searle, *National Efficiency*, Chapter 6.

[81] Bentley B. Gilbert, *David Lloyd George: The Architect of Change 1863–1912*, (1987), pp. 421–2.

[82] Smith to Austen Chamberlain, 20, 21 Oct. 1910, in Earl of Birkenhead, *Frederick Edwin Earl of Birkenhead: The First Phase* (1933; 1936 edn), pp. 205–8.

[83] At least, so Smith reports him as saying. Austen Chamberlain to Cawdor, 21 Oct. 1910, Austen Chamberlain, *Politics From Inside: An Epistolary Chronicle 1906–1914* (1936), p. 287.

be desirable, but it would be so unpopular in the country that neither party dared promote it. Similarly, a comprehensive National Insurance Scheme made overwhelming sense, but neither party felt able to 'take on' the powerful insurance lobby and its army of collectors.

The same reasoning applied with a vengeance to Ireland. Most Liberal Ministers had lost confidence in Home Rule, but they dare not admit as much. Many Unionists knew that the status quo in Ireland, unsustainable in the long run, was already damaging Britain's reputation and influence in the world; but to retreat even by an inch from a rigid defence of the Union would leave them open to the charge of betrayal. The great advantage of 'fusion' was that it would spread the risks of taking unpopular, but necessary, decisions, thereby cutting out 'the least-responsible, the least well-informed and the most selfish amongst the Electorate', as Lloyd George had put it in his August Memorandum.

These considerations particularly influenced a number of senior politicians, who developed a sympathy for the idea of Coalition which long outlasted the 'Secret Coalition' episode. One such figure was Austen Chamberlain, who, though unwilling to behave disloyally towards the Unionist Party and its Leader, Balfour, also felt that in associating himself with 'Devolution' he would be discharging a filial duty and so was tempted by Lloyd George's offer. As for Churchill, the first senior Liberal (with the possible exception of Masterman) whom Lloyd George approached, he reacted with enthusiasm to the prospect of a National Government (though his wife expressed dismay).[84] His Conservative friend, 'FE', also became an ardent convert.

Perhaps the most wholehearted commitment to the Coalition idea came from Garvin, whom Lloyd George had let in on the secret with a view to his preparing the Unionist public for a possible volte-face through his famous *Observer* editorials.[85] Not surprisingly, Garvin was overwhelmed by a sense of the magnitude of the possibilities. 'Well, if this great thing comes off, I shall not care much what

84 Riddell diary, 2 July 1912, J.M. McEwen, *The Riddell Diaries 1908–1923* (1986), pp. 46–7.

85 See the *Observer* editorial of 16 Oct. 1910, cited in Gollin, *Garvin*, p. 209. However, Garvin's editorials gave the slightly misleading impression that what was afoot was the summoning of a second Conference to discuss a 'national' Irish settlement.

becomes of the rest of life', he wrote to his employer Northcliffe when the negotiations were entering their decisive phase.[86]

Lloyd George's role is more difficult to characterise. What he seems to have been groping his way towards was a strategy which combined Chamberlain's conception of 'national politics' (that is to say, a creative synthesis of social reform and imperialism) with Rosebery's understanding of the advantages of 'fusion'.

What is less clear is how seriously Lloyd George had committed himself to such a strategy in 1910. Indeed, precisely what *was* his strategy? In the *War Memoirs* the coalition talks are portrayed as a far-sighted attempt to achieve national unity under the imminent threat of a war with Germany. But this is not the impression conveyed by his two 'Secret Coalition' Memoranda. Nor did Lloyd George take a consistent line with the Opposition Leaders. For much of the time he gave the impression that his prime concern was to ditch the *Irish Nationalists*. Yet Balfour's own Memorandum on the affair suggests that the Chancellor's interest may have shifted during the course of October towards the idea of retaining the support of the Irish in an alliance mainly directed against *Labour*.[87] There is also some uncertainty over when Lloyd George took the Prime Minister into his confidence. If he only did so at a late stage, it would be tempting to see the Secret Coalition talks as an anti-Asquith intrigue, perhaps foreshadowing the drama of December 1916.

All this is speculation. For, largely because of the intractable nature of the Irish difficulty, Garvin's 'great thing' did *not*, in the event, 'come off'. During the first week of November Lloyd George and Balfour terminated their negotiations, and almost immediately afterwards the Conference itself was disbanded. With the end of the search for a 'national compromise', the two parties withdrew to battle stations, and the fight commenced that was to culminate in the following year with the 1911 Parliament Act and the crisis in the Unionist Party which cost Balfour his leadership.

CONFLICT AND CONSENSUS, 1911–14

In the years 1911–14, with Ireland hovering on the brink of civil war and violence threatening to spill over on to the British mainland,

86 Garvin to Northcliffe, 21 Oct. 1910, ibid., pp. 210–11.
87 Searle, *National Efficiency*, Chapter 6. G.R. Searle, 'Balfour's Coalition Memorandum of 1910', in *Historical Research*, 66 (1993), 222–9.

party hatreds reached a new level of intensity. And this process of political polarisation was expedited by the behaviour of many 'whole-hog' Tariff Reformers. We have already seen that, in the eyes of Chamberlain himself, 'fusion', involving a negotiated compromise with the Liberal enemy, had always been anathema. Many of his more fanatical acolytes felt likewise. Made uneasy by the rumours that some wider 'national compromise' was imminent, a group which included Lord Willoughby de Broke, Page Croft and Lord Winterton, backed by Maxse's *National Review*, had accordingly come together in the summer of 1910 to found the 'Reveille' Movement.[88] 'Beware of the men you are engaged with, . . . none of whom are to be trusted out of sight', wrote Maxse to Garvin in June. 'All they want is time that a regicide government may get itself forgotten.'[89]

But the 'Reveille' politicians were scarcely less suspicious of their *own* leaders, Balfour and Lansdowne, who seemed to be on the point of 'selling out' to the enemy. 'National interests', feared Maxse, were being sacrificed to the dishonesty of two-party politics centring around the sham battles between 'the Right Hon. A.J. Foozle and the Right Hon. H.H. Boozle'.[90] It was such dissatisfactions as these which lay behind the Diehard protests of 1911.

The eventual resignation of Balfour, 'the Champion Scuttler', led to a slight revival of confidence in the party leadership amongst these Radical Unionists, since, initially at least, Bonar Law, the new Leader, commanded much greater respect in their eyes. However, there was menace as well as encouragement in Willoughby's words of May 1912 about the need to 'create a strong permanent body of followers who will rely on you [Bonar Law] to vindicate National or Tory principles'.[91]

These members of the 'Radical Right', as they are sometimes called, continued to worry lest the Opposition Front Bench 'betray' them over Ireland, as it very quickly proceeded to do over the Tariff when food taxes were dropped from the party programme. Such was the level of anxiety that some longed for a breakdown of law and order in Ireland, even an outbreak of civil war, hoping that this might destroy the hated party system and provide the British people with

---

88 Sykes, *Tariff Reform*, pp. 218, 226–8.

89 Maxse to Garvin, 10 June 1910, Gollin, *Garvin*, p. 198.

90 Cited in G.R. Searle, 'The "Revolt from the Right" in Edwardian Britain', in Paul Kennedy and Anthony Nicholls (eds), *Nationalist and Racialist Movements in Britain and Germany Before 1914* (1981), p. 27.

91 Willoughby de Broke, 5 May 1912, cited in Sykes, *Tariff Reform*, p. 257.

the kind of salutary shock which could arouse it from its lethargy and torpor. A few of the Milnerites, disillusioned by the breakdown of the cross-party negotiations in 1910, felt similarly. '*Nothing* will save us except the sight of red blood running pretty freely', observed F.S. Oliver, adding: 'but whether British *and* German blood, or only British I don't know – nor do I think it much matters.'[92]

Such malcontents saw the entire political system as corrupt, with the 'Mandarins' of the Conservative Party at least partially implicated in the corruption. How else explain the failure of the Opposition Leaders to press home their attacks against Liberal Ministers during the Marconi Scandal? 'I am afraid that both Front Benches will be found on the side of the "Hush-Ups"', wrote Willoughby in August 1913: 'They do love one another so.'[93] These anxieties were further stimulated by revelations of the Government's 'honours trafficking'. Unionist officialdom had good reason to treat this issue with some circumspection, because their own Whips had traditionally indulged in not dissimilar practices. But the *National Review* boldly espoused the auditing of party funds, a device which it thought might not only end an intolerable abuse but also weaken the entire party system. This quest for 'clean' government had made considerable progress by the eve of the war, drawing in a miscellaneous group of mavericks, including Arnold White, Hilaire Belloc and the Chesterton brothers, as well as Maxse and his friends.

What were the real political convictions of men such as Maxse and Willoughby de Broke? Some historians see them as traditional Tories at heart, driven by the tensions of the day into sponsoring more 'extreme' courses of action than would normally have been thought compatible with either Conservatism or parliamentary political life.[94] But others take a different line. They note the enthusiasm of these Radical Unionists for the Referendum, a mechanism which, widely used, would have led to the establishment of a plebiscitary democracy and the complete bypassing of all political parties. The violent attacks on the 'Mandarins" traditional fund-raising methods may also suggest that the Radical Right felt itself to be alienated from normal two-party politics in a rather profound way.

92 Oliver to Milner, 3 March 1911, cited in Searle, 'Revolt from Right', p. 27.

93 Cited in Searle, 'Critics of Edwardian Society: The Case of the Radical Right', in Alan O'Day (ed.), *The Edwardian Age: Conflict and Stability 1900–1914* (1979), p. 89.

94 Alan Sykes, 'The Radical Right and the Crisis of Conservatism Before the First World War', *Historical Journal*, 26 (1983), 661–76.

Both interpretations are partially valid. For Maxse and Willoughby had a very ambivalent attitude towards the Unionist Party in particular and towards parliamentary politics more generally. This can be seen in the articles which Willoughby wrote for the *National Review* during these pre-war years. In them he called repeatedly for the establishment of a 'National Party'. But what did this mean? In places it seems as though Willoughby merely had in mind a purified form of Toryism, re-invigorated through contact with 'the matchless tradition of Chatham, Pitt, Burke, and Beaconsfield', behind whom allegedly stood Bolingbroke, the creator of the Tory creed. Such sentiments echo the earlier attempts of Disraeli to present the Conservative Party as the one truly 'National Party'. Willoughby's idealisation of the hierarchically ordered rural community also links him to an earlier 'Tory Democracy' tradition.[95]

Yet it is significant that when Willoughby writes about the Conservative and Unionist Party, he seldom gives the impression of describing the party as it had historically existed, still less the party of late Victorian and Edwardian times. It seems, rather, that he has in mind some imaginary party of his own invention, by comparison with which the shortcomings of all contemporary political organisations can be exposed.[96] Obviously, if forced to take sides, Willoughby (like Maxse) would not have hesitated to back the party of Balfour and Bonar Law, such was his contempt for Liberalism and his fear of socialism. He was also sufficient of a realist to recognise that 'nothing in this country [had] a real chance until it [was] adopted by one of the Party machines'.

But none of this made Willoughby an orthodox Conservative. 'No one who seriously considers the state of the nation will assert that the present situation can be dealt with by a process of party politics, as we know them', he claimed: on the contrary, it was 'this very system of party politics that ha[d] wrought so much havoc'. Willoughby's invocation of a 'National Party' thus carried with it an implied threat: that if the Conservative Party did not show itself to be true to its higher ideals, a new organisation might have to be brought into existence to shame it into better behaviour and to promote essential

---

95 In this respect Willoughby and Maxse, who both emanated from traditional landed society, differed from Joseph Chamberlain, the prophet of 'modernisation'.

96 The same, of course, could be said of the young Disraeli's depiction of the ·Tory Party in his 'Young England' phase. Willoughby, however, seems actually to have *believed* in his vision of the Tory Party.

'national' interests. Of this line of argument, too, much more was to be heard shortly.

Moreover, behind such rhetoric lay a more profound dilemma. During the Edwardian decade several 'patriotic leagues' (the Navy League, the Imperial Maritime League, the National Service League, etc.), had come into existence to combat the dangers facing the country. These causes, believed ardent nationalists, transcended party loyalty and so should be organised on a non-partisan basis.

Yet of the two parties it was the Unionists (whatever their short-comings) who showed the greater sympathy to these national causes. And so the members of the Leagues found that it made sense to try to capture official Unionism and 'permeate' it with their own beliefs.[97] Naturally, the Conservative Leadership initially welcomed such overtures. However, the activities of the 'radical nationalists' (the Tariff Reform Leaguers in particular) in seeking to dictate terms to the party inevitably created bad blood, since Unionists of a different stripe furiously resented the attempted 'take-over'.[98]

'For Party or Country?': this had emerged as a dilemma even before 1914. It was to become even sharper when Britain entered the Great War and the 'national crisis' of which there had recently so much rather loose talk erupted with a vengeance.

Yet even in these turbulent pre-war years the prospect of establishing a National Government never *totally* disappeared. Indeed, horrified by the escalation of partisan animosities, several participants in the Coalition talks were soon looking back upon them as a tragic 'lost opportunity'. For example, when Lloyd George later introduced his National Insurance Bill into Parliament, Garvin tried hard to create a bi-partisan agreement. 'In spirit', readers of the *Observer* were told, the Bill 'transcends all partisanship', drawing as it did upon the 'creative principles of State Insurance founded just thirty years ago by Bismarck', 'the constructive example set by Mr Chamberlain' and 'the idea of social order and progress foreshadowed by Lord Beaconsfield'. National Insurance, Garvin argued, could never 'be accomplished by Party means. But it may – and we believe it will – afford an opportunity for the first piece of constructive cooperation between parties that has yet been known in democratic politics'.[99]

97 Though, of course, they strenuously insisted that there was a complete identity of interests between party and nation.

98 See Frans Coetzee, *For Party or Country: Nationalism and the Dilemmas of Popular Conservatism in Edwardian England* (New York, 1990).

99 *Observer*, 7 May 1911, cited in Scally, *Lloyd George Coalition*, p. 216.

Naturally Lloyd George himself encouraged such talk,[100] and Garvin, in his excitable way, was soon regaling his readers with the advantages that would flow from the establishment of 'a real *national party*'.[101] All to no avail, for the Opposition was soon making Part I of the National Insurance Act the subject of a violent party attack – to the disquiet of those Unionists who took 'constructive' social reform seriously.

Amid the ensuing partisan uproar Churchill continued to dream his coalitionist dreams. In March 1913 Lord Riddell records him as putting forward a proposal for 'a national party', saying:

> Our national life requires more organisation and more discipline.
> There is a body of sensible men in both parties who are tired of the
> existing state of things. In both parties there are fools at one end and
> crackpots at the other, but the great body in the middle is sound and
> wise.[102]

Later in the year it seemed possible that these vague aspirations might lead to something concrete when Lord Loreburn, who had recently served as Asquith's Lord Chancellor, released a letter to the press on 11 September calling on all parties to compromise over Ireland before the country slid into civil war. Talks over Ulster between Asquith and Bonar Law began shortly afterwards, but Churchill decided to launch an initiative of his own. In November 1913 he entertained Austen Chamberlain on the Admiralty yacht, the *Enchantress*. 'Both sides had to make speeches full of party claptrap and no surrender and then insert a few sentences at the end for wise and discerning people on the other side to see and ponder . . .', Churchill disarmingly told his guest. Chamberlain responded by broaching the possibility of 'a Federal settlement by consent'. Winston then tried to take the discussion further. He referred back to the 1910 Secret Coalition talks and 'indicated very clearly that he would like to see them renewed now'. Although Chamberlain gave him little encouragement, Churchill returned several times to this theme. Chamberlain came away from the meeting convinced that 'the idea of fusion with an extreme wing left out on either side [was] obviously constantly in [Churchill's] mind and would be greatly liked by him'.[103] So once again the possibility of Coalition had become tied

---

100 See the revealing letter from Sandars to Balfour, 6 May 1911, ibid., p. 219.
101 *Observer*, 2 April 1911, ibid., p. 218.
102 Riddell diary, 21 March 1913, cited McEwen, *Riddell Diaries*, p. 58.
103 Chamberlain's Memorandum of Conversation with Churchill, 27 Nov. 1913, in Chamberlain, *Politics From Inside*, pp. 574–7. For Lansdowne's sceptical response, see Lansdowne to Chamberlain, 30 Nov.1913, ibid., pp. 577–8.

up with the issue of Federalism, about which there was considerable discussion in late 1913 and early 1914. In this discussion many of the Milnerites including Amery and Oliver, though not Milner himself,[104] took a prominent part.

What of Lloyd George? Although he spoke to the journalist Kennedy Jones and others in 1913 about his earlier Coalition plan, saying that the party differences of the day were 'unreal' compared with 'the German menace',[105] the Chancellor seems on the whole to have accepted that the time for a 'national settlement' had passed. True, he occasionally came out in public as a critic of party: 'There are many things which, if you could get a party truce for five years, you could get through and transform this land', he somewhat wistfully told an audience in Oxford in late 1913.[106] But in general he threw his very considerable energies into pursuing the party fight, in particular through his flamboyant 'Land Campaign'.

However, by late 1913 Lloyd George, too, was looking for a way out of the Irish impasse, and, like Churchill, came round to favouring some kind of federal arrangement, if one could be found that was acceptable to the Opposition. So, at about the same time as Churchill and Chamberlain were exchanging views, the Chancellor was in correspondence with F.E. Smith – who, incidentally, had recently acted as his counsel in the *Le Matin* case during the Marconi Scandal, to the fury of most Conservatives.

Smith seems to have made the first overture. In a letter to the Chancellor on 26 September, he suggested that the King be asked to preside over a Conference on Ireland, where, in defiance of the 'extremists' on both sides, the two sets of party leaders could discuss not only Ireland but also House of Lords reform and the land: 'From such a conference anything could follow'. To this Lloyd George responded: 'You know how anxious I have been for years to work with you and a few others on your side. I have always realized that our differences have been very artificial & do not reach the "realities".'[107] But the episode ended when an irritated Bonar Law stepped in to stop Smith involving the Opposition as a whole in an embarrassing entanglement.[108]

104 See Gollin, *Milner*, p. 210
105 Scally, *Lloyd George Coalition*, p. 234.
106 *Oxford Chronicle*, 28 Nov. 1913, cited in Wrigley, *Lloyd George*, p. 50.
107 Smith to Lloyd George, 26 Sept. 1913; Lloyd George to Smith, 6 Oct. 1913, in John Campbell, *F. E. Smith: First Earl of Birkenhead* (1983), pp. 340–1.
108 Robert Blake, *The Unknown Prime Minister: The Life and Times of Andrew Bonar Law 1858–1923* (1955), p. 159.

Meanwhile the *Observer* had returned to its old enthusiasm for a Conference on Federalism (14 September 1913), and early in the new year Garvin took part in discussions over Ireland with Lloyd George and some of the Milnerites.[109] Estranged over Marconi, Garvin and Lloyd George had since 'made it up' once more: 'Essentially [your ends] are mine and mine are yours', wrote Lloyd George on 31 December. 'Our quarrel is about methods and it is the fault of your leaders that those are not identical. *You know the story of their great refusal.*' Garvin excitedly signalled his agreement.[110]

Lloyd George was adept at telling his auditors exactly what they wanted to hear, so too much should not be read into these pleasantries. Indeed, much of the talk about 'National Parties' and 'Coalitions' tells us more about the temporary frustrations of leading politicians and their short-term tactics than it does about their inner beliefs.

Yet one cannot simply dismiss the torrent of speculation on the subject of Coalition, for it reflected a genuine dissatisfaction with the operation of the party system during a period when the fear of socialism was decidedly on the increase. Smith, in a private letter of October 1910, claimed that he could 'never in 20 years remember a time when so many men in England were sick of mere party cries and faction. A great sight of relief would go up over the whole of business England if a strong and stable government were formed'.[111] Such feelings were reinforced by the legalistic personality of the Prime Minister, Asquith, seen by his opponents as the epitome of everything that was wrong with the party system in that he seemed always to be arguing (often persuasively and eloquently) to a brief in which he may or may not have believed.

'Coalition fever' therefore mattered, not least because it acclimatised both MPs and the wider public to the idea that, should the 'national crisis' deepen in some unspecified way, the establishment of a Coalition Government might become a patriotic imperative. Here, in short, was a political expedient which stood waiting in the wings, ready to be summoned on to the stage when Destiny called.

109 Scally, *Lloyd George Coalition*, pp. 234–5, 242. Oliver, too, linked his hopes for Federalism to his belief in the suspension of party strife, along 1910 lines (F.S. Oliver, *What Federalism Is* Not (1914), especially pp. 112–13).

110 Lloyd George to Garvin, 31 Dec. 1913; Garvin to Lloyd George, 1 Jan. 1914, in ibid., p. 245.

111 Smith to Austen Chamberlain, 20 Oct. 1910, cited in Birkenhead, *Birkenhead*, p. 206.

CHAPTER FIVE
First World War and Coalition

FROM AUGUST 1914 TO THE FIRST COALITION GOVERNMENT, MAY 1915

In August 1914 Britain entered the Great War: the supreme national crisis, so long predicted, had finally arrived. Before long, enough 'red blood' was 'running freely' to satisfy the most sanguinary patriot. And yet, paradoxically perhaps, it took another nine months before a Coalition of National Unity was established. In the interim Asquith's Liberal Ministry remained in place (with Lord Kitchener occupying the War Office), while the Unionist leaders offered patriotic support from the Opposition Benches. Meanwhile an electoral truce put an end to contested by-elections, and all the parties combined in the recruiting campaign.

Why was there not more of an initial outcry in support of a Coalition, more of a recognition that, in Garvin's words, 'party Government as the organ of national unity is a contradiction in terms'?[1] In part it was because most well-informed opinion thought that the war would shortly come to a conclusion. Moreover, party animosities still ran deep. When in September 1914 the Government decided to defer the implementation of the Home Rule and Welsh Church Bills but to put them on the statute book, the Opposition walked out of the House in protest, Bonar Law having previously lodged a formal complaint to Asquith over an action which was bound 'to revive party controversy'.[2]

---

1 *Observer*, 23 May 1915.

2 Robert Blake, *The Unknown Prime Minister: The Life and Times of Andrew Bonar Law, 1858–1923* (1955), pp. 228–9. See Bridgeman diary, 29 Nov. 1914, in Philip Williamson (ed.), *The Modernisation of Conservative Politics: The Diaries and Letters of William Bridgeman, 1904–1935* (1988), p. 81.

To understand the situation during the first nine months of war, it is also necessary to go back to its very outbreak. Briefly it had seemed as though Asquith would be unable to maintain a united Cabinet and party. Indeed, Churchill, an enthusiastic proponent as ever of interparty co-operation, had approached the Unionist leaders on 31 July, through his friend Smith, to find out whether they would enter a coalition government to fill any vacancies caused by Liberal resignations.[3] Bonar Law's friend, the newspaper proprietor Max Aitken, who was in conclave with the Unionist leaders when the matter was broached, later portrayed this overture as 'the first attempt to form a Coalition Government'.[4] But Bonar Law, who profoundly mistrusted Churchill, offered no encouragement, and shortly afterwards Asquith was able to declare war on Germany without losing more than two of his Cabinet Ministers (Lord Morley and John Burns), neither of them crucial to its fate.

As Garvin realised, this put paid, temporarily, to all prospect of coalition, leaving patriots with no option but to support the Asquith regime: 'The war is being conducted by a Liberal Government, and it is essential that they should carry Liberals with them', the *Observer* told its readers on 30 August. Asquith, who anyway thought the Conservative leaders incompetent, believed that 'coalitions have hardly ever turned out well in our history'.[5] That did not stop him skilfully using its possibility to put pressure on the waverers inside his own party.

True, the former Conservative Leader, Balfour, attended the War Council on a regular basis and also had his own room at the Admiralty, where, according to Asquith, he exercised his 'superficial charm' over the First Lord, Churchill.[6] Indeed, as Asquith was clearly aware, Churchill himself still hankered 'after coalitions and odd re-groupings, mainly designed (as one thinks) to bring in F.E. Smith & perhaps the Duke of Marlborough'. But all this struck the Prime Minister as simply silly.[7]

Meanwhile Bonar Law kept his distance from the affairs of government. At the end of 1914 Dawson, the editor of *The Times*, found him

3 Blake, *Bonar Law*, pp. 220–1.

4 Lord Beaverbrook, *Politicians and the War, 1914–1916* (1928), p. 22.

5 Cameron Hazlehurst, *Politicians At War, July 1914 to May 1915* (1971), pp. 114–15.

6 See Asquith to Venetia Stanley, 25 March 1915, in M. and E. Brock (eds), *H.H. Asquith: Letters to Venetia Stanley* (Oxford, 1982), p. 508.

7 Asquith to Venetia Stanley, 9 Feb. 1915, ibid., p. 423.

'very much opposed at the present stage to anything like a Coalition Government' in which he would 'feel very uncomfortable', although Law admitted that the Liberals would eventually have to 'turn to [coalition] when they came to clearing up the mess at the end of the war . . . .'[8] As the Opposition Leader later explained to the Liberal politician, Sydney Buxton, he had 'always been against a Coalition and hoped that it would not become necessary', which was why, from the very outbreak of war, he had set his face 'against anything in the nature of party criticism'.[9]

Nor was Bonar Law alone in these views. In January 1915 all the Unionist leaders had reacted angrily to what they saw as an attempt on the part of Lord Crewe, the Liberal Leader in the Lords, to make them partly responsible for the conduct of the war.[10] In a Memorandum written later that month Curzon made clear the nature of their objections: 'A Coalition would tie our hands and close our lips even more effectively than at present. It would make us responsible for many things which we ought to criticise . . . . If the country were actually and seriously invaded a Coalition Government might become expedient and even necessary. But for the present it does not seem needful to discuss it.'[11] Moreover, as another prominent Conservative put it, should a coalition be formed, 'whatever was unpopular (e.g. a strong line on recruiting) would be ascribed to our agency and would cause a split among the Radicals, who might well accept conscription if passed by their own government'.[12]

This was the crux of the matter. It seemed as though national unity would best be promoted by having in power the party which had traditionally viewed war with aversion. The risk of dissentient Radicals coming out as open critics would certainly have increased had Asquith been toppled. A coalition would also have jeopardised the support for the war effort being given by most Irish Nationalist leaders and perhaps brought about a disruption of the industrial truce.

Did Lloyd George himself see the situation in this way? It may be significant that in early December the Welshman was regaling his friend George Riddell with an account of the Secret Coalition

8 Dawson, Memorandum of Conversation with Bonar Law, 29 Dec. 1914, in John Evelyn Wrench, *Geoffrey Dawson and Our Times* (1955), p. 115.

9 Martin D. Pugh, 'Asquith, Bonar Law and the First Coalition', *Historical Journal*, 17 (1974), 826.

10 Ibid., 821–2.

11 Ibid., 823. Walter Long wrote in the same sense.

12 Crawford diary, 2 Feb. 1915, in John Vincent (ed.), *The Crawford Papers* (Manchester, 1984), p. 347.

talks, an episode he also discussed with Austen Chamberlain the following month.[13] Indeed, by the spring of 1915 rumour had it that Lloyd George and Balfour were intriguing to establish a Coalition Government. But when Asquith confronted his Chancellor with the rumour, the latter tearfully denied the charge, blaming it upon his jealous mischief-making colleague, Reginald McKenna.[14]

Commenting on this interview in a letter to his mistress, Lloyd George bluntly declared that a Coalition 'was the last thing he would wish for'.[15] Yet there is evidence that he was already beginning to lose patience with Asquith's hesitant leadership, and this, plus his anger over Kitchener's mishandling of the provision of munitions supplies, may have prompted him to work up a press campaign against the War Secretary via the newspaper magnate, Lord Northcliffe. Whether encouraged or not, in early 1915 the Northcliffe press was calling for a new government comprising all the 'best' men, which could 'get on with the war'; Haldane and Churchill were singled out as targets in this campaign to 'Sack the Duds' – ironically, in view of Haldane's earlier commitment to 'National Efficiency' and Churchill's lifelong coalitionist enthusiasms.[16]

Yet Garvin's *Observer* would have nothing to do with such attacks, which it saw as unpatriotic; and Churchill, in particular, was stoutly defended in its pages ('Mr Churchill has not had fair play', it declared on 1 November). But, with the war continuing to go badly, even Garvin found it impossible to sustain this line. On 2 May 1915 the *Observer* was still berating those who 'think that there is party profit to be made from indiscriminate girding at Ministers', but it now admitted that 'the question of reconstruction' might become 'urgent' in two or three months' time. The following week Garvin

13 Riddell diary, 20 Dec. 1914, in *Lord Riddell's War Diary 1914–1918* (1933), pp. 46–7; Bentley Brinkerhoff Gilbert, *David Lloyd George: The Organizer of Victory 1912–16* (1992), p. 181. This was the occasion when Austen Chamberlain asked for a copy of the October Memorandum, which he had never previously seen: see G.R. Searle, *The Quest for National Efficiency: A Study in British Politics and Political Thought, 1899–1914* (Oxford, 1971; new edn, 1990), p. 184.

14 Earlier Lloyd George had suggested, as had others, that the chief plotter was Churchill. See Asquith to Venetia Stanley, 25, 29 March 1915, in Brock (eds), *Letters to Venetia Stanley*, pp. 508, 519. For McKenna's later version of how the first Coalition Government had come into being, see Charles Hobhouse's diary, 17 May, 17 June 1915, in Edward David (ed.), *Inside Asquith's Cabinet: From the Diaries of Charles Hobhouse* (1977), pp. 243, 247–8.

15 Frances Stevenson diary, 8 April 1915, in A.J.P. Taylor (ed.), *Lloyd George: A Diary by Frances Stevenson* (1971), p. 42.

16 *The History of the Times: Vol. 4: 1912–1920* (1952), Part I, p. 272.

went further, calling for 'A Government of Public Safety, such as exists in France'.

In fact, as John Burns complained, by the end of March 'Coalition [was] in the air', fanned by the newspapers but also encouraged by the Conservative Party Chairman, Arthur Steel-Maitland.[17] However, there were as yet few signs that *senior* politicians in either party took Coalition seriously. Thus, when on 12 May the backbench Liberal MP Handel Booth asked the Prime Minister whether 'in view of the steps necessary to be taken in order to grapple with the rearrangement of industry and social life consequent upon a prolonged struggle, he [would] consider the desirability of admitting into the ranks of Ministers leading Members of the various political parties in this House', Asquith replied with a crisp negative. Five days later, supported by two other Liberal backbenchers, Booth repeated his call for 'a Government which is above party'.[18] But by this time the moves towards the establishment of a Coalition were well under way. What had happened to produce the abrupt change of front?

The May 1915 reconstruction came about because of the convergence of two different crises: the shell shortage scandal and the quarrel between Churchill and the First Sea Lord, Admiral Fisher, leading to the latter's extraordinary resignation. But these events by themselves need not have brought down the government. Leaving aside a few mavericks like Booth, few Liberal MPs wanted a Coalition at all, and Asquith's later presentation of one as a *fait accompli* was greeted with fury.[19] In Martin Pugh's words, 'There can be no doubt that had Asquith attempted to consult his party beforehand he would have found them more ready to go down fighting in an election than to invite the Unionists into the Cabinet.'[20] Nor, even at this late stage, were most Conservatives particularly eager to share responsibility for running the war with their political adversaries, particularly since, as Bonar Law subsequently explained, there seemed to be a good chance of the Conservatives gaining office themselves 'and dispossessing those who had so long occupied it'.[21]

But although Churchill was able, with the minimum of delay, to replace Fisher as First Sea Lord, the troubles at the Admiralty

17 Pugh, 'Asquith, Bonar Law and First Coalition', 825.

18 Parl. Deb., 5th ser., 71, 1642: 12 May 1915; Hazlehurst, *Politicians At War*, p. 274.

19 Trevor Wilson, *The Downfall of the Liberal Party 1914–1935* (1966), pp. 40–1, 58–9.

20 Pugh, 'Asquith, Bonar Law and First Coalition', 818.

21 Ibid., 816.

convinced Lloyd George and Bonar Law that the status quo could no longer be sustained. Meeting at the Treasury, the two men agreed to push for a Coalition. Possibly to their surprise, Asquith quickly fell into line, and the whole matter was sewn up 'in less than a quarter of an hour'. Churchill later blamed Lloyd George for his 'Machiavellian cleverness' in devising and carrying through the Coalition, but the latter replied, reasonably enough, that he had 'had no design whatever. I saw things had reached a stage when we could not carry on and that a Coalition was the best way out.'[22]

Asquith later told his angry parliamentary party that he 'could not reveal the truth to us yet without imperilling national safety' but that he had acted out of dire national necessity. This was by no means the whole truth. In fact, what had actually happened was that both party leaders, anxious to avoid a Khaki Election, had united to impose a settlement upon their resentful followers – Bonar Law because he was fearful of losing control of his Party and Asquith because his Liberal Cabinet was threatened with disintegration.[23]

ASQUITH'S COALITION MINISTRY, MAY 1915–DECEMBER 1916

Asquith undoubtedly used his greater experience and stronger bargaining position in May 1915 to secure advantages for the Liberal Party – something which was to be crucial for the future of wartime politics. True, Balfour was brought into the Admiralty in place of an indignant Churchill, who was demoted to the office of Chancellor of the Duchy of Lancaster. But all the key Ministries concerned with the running of the War were kept in Liberal hands, except for the War Office which continued to be headed by the non-political Kitchener. Moreover, the Liberals would not countenance a Tariff Reformer as Chancellor of the Exchequer, so when Lloyd George moved out of the Treasury to take charge of the new Ministry of Munitions, his old berth passed to McKenna, a traditional Liberal and friend of Asquith, which meant that Bonar Law had to content himself with the minor post of Colonial Secretary. And although Haldane was dropped from the Woolsack, in deference to Tory prejudices, his

22 Riddell diary, 4 July 1915, *War Diary*, p. 109.
23 John Turner, *British Politics and the Great War: Coalition and Conflict 1915–1918* (New Haven, 1992), p. 61.

successor was another Liberal, Lord Buckmaster. In fact, though the Liberal and Unionist parliamentary parties were of approximately the same size, only eight Cabinet posts went to Unionists, as against the Liberals' twelve and Labour's one; a similar imbalance also existed at the lower levels of government.[24]

But although Asquith and the Liberals may have initially benefited from this situation, in the long run the dissatisfaction which it created in the Unionist ranks weakened the new Administration. It also allowed Unionists to feel that they did not bear full responsibility for the various mishaps which were shortly to occur. Nor did Asquith often bother to conceal the disdain which he felt for his former party opponents: 'to seem to welcome into the intimacy of the political household strange, alien, hitherto hostile figures, is a most intolerable test', he later wrote.[25] 'Asquith's 1915 government was only halfway to coalition', concludes John Ramsden judiciously; 'it was in fact a coalition of parties rather than a coalition of men, and it was run so as to maximise continuity'.[26]

Significantly enough, few newspapers approved of the new Coalition Ministry. True, the *Observer* (23 May 1915) tried to put a brave face on things. The country, it explained to its readers, had faced a choice between 'Coalition – Chaos – or Dictatorship', and in opting for Coalition, the party leaders had returned to the co-operation which had briefly flourished at the time of the 1910 Constitutional Conference. Indeed, according to Garvin, 'some thinkers on both sides' had 'never quite lost touch with each other'. Yet the *Observer*, while arguing that the Ministry of Munitions 'was sufficient, if temporary, justification for a faulty National Coalition', regretted the way in which the new Administration had come into existence and felt that it did 'not answer in all respects to the theoretical or even to the practical ideal of a Ministry of all the Talents, with every statesman among its members in his right place'.

Northcliffe was still more dissatisfied, because he wanted the exclusion, not just of Haldane, but also of Asquith, Grey and Kitchener as well.[27] Nor did Milner's friends feel much confidence in the new

24 There were six Conservative non-Cabinet Ministers (compared with eight Liberals and one Nationalist), and eleven Conservatives in junior posts, compared with fifteen Liberals and two Labour.

25 H.H. Asquith, *On Coalition* (1925), p. 40, cited in Keith Middlemas, *Politics in Industrial Society: The Experience of the British System Since 1911* (1979), pp. 309–10.

26 John Ramsden, *The Age of Balfour and Baldwin 1902–1940* (1978), p. 131.

27 *History of Times*, IV, Part I, p. 275.

regime: 'the old vat', wrote Oliver, 'had been half-emptied of its former contents and filled up with new wine; but it was the same vat, and the predominating flavour remained the same'.[28] Among this group there were other grounds for despondency. 'Democracy is not going to win this war or any other', Oliver had written in December 1914. 'If we win it will be because the spirit of the small remnant who hate and despise democracy and all its works will save the country in spite of its democratic government . . . .'[29] The Milnerites might have taken a more cheerful view of the events of May 1915 had Asquith agreed to Austen Chamberlain's public-spirited offer to serve as an under-secretary under Milner. But the offer was rejected, and Milner was left bewailing the conduct of a Ministry which drifted and toyed with half-measures and only took a strong lead when forced to do so by outside pressure.[30]

It can be argued that such criticism was in some respects unfair. Nothing is easier, with the wisdom of hindsight, than to criticise the Asquith Coalition Ministry by comparing it unfavourably with the later Lloyd George regime. However, many of the measures adopted by Lloyd George after December 1916 would have split the country had they been attempted earlier. Asquith's cautious step-by-step approach to extending controls over the economy should therefore not be seen as mere lethargy or lack of courage. Asquith may have underestimated the extent of the patriotic sacrifice that the organised working class was prepared to make, but those in 1915 who advocated far-reaching measures of national service (including even industrial conscription) were urging the Government to take a reckless gamble, the outcome of which might have been fatal to the war effort.[31]

Asquith also felt that national unity required that he should refrain from action which would split his own party by driving its Radical wing into outright opposition to the war. For these reasons Garvin, for one, always insisted that a Liberal must head any wartime administration: 'No Premier is possible but a Liberal Premier', declared the *Observer* on 3 December 1916. Yet such considerations

28 F.S. Oliver, *Ordeal by Battle* (1915; 1916 abridged edn), p. li.

29 Letter of 26 Dec. 1914, cited in A.M. Gollin, *Proconsul in Politics: A Study of Lord Milner in Opposition and in Power* (1964), p. 247.

30 Milner to Austen Chamberlain, 21 May 1915, Hazlehurst *Politicians at War*, p. 271.

31 On 'the depletion of industry' threatened by the adoption of conscription, see Turner, *British Politics*, pp. 74–5.

all too easily confirmed Asquith in his arrogant and complacent conviction that he was the 'indispensable' national leader. Meanwhile an increasing body of critics (not all of them Conservatives) came to see the Premier's stance as one which subordinated the national advantage to personal ambition and to the needs of party – Asquith's own party. Indeed, by 1915, his former association with Rosebery long forgotten, Asquith had become identified in the public mind as the very incarnation of the lawyer-Mandarin class produced by the party system: hence, Maxse's view of Asquith as a typical party hack who always gave the impression that he regarded the war as a tiresome interruption of normal political life, namely, the pursuit of the party game.

Amongst Conservative backbenchers, too, discontent grew. The ex-Chief Whip Crawford observed in June 1916: '. . . Our party is sore, querulous, and divided – our leaders blamed – not so much for the actual proposals now being put forward, but for having allowed themselves to be jockeyed by the Radicals. Everybody says that Bonar Law is hypnotised by Asquith, that our men acquiesce in all Squiff proposes . . . .'[32] There was also muttering about the way in which most of the leading Conservatives had availed themselves of the opportunity, now back in office, of exploiting the honours system. Particular offence was caused by the award of a baronetcy to Max Aitken in the summer of 1916, Bonar Law's friendship with this controversial Canadian financier and newspaper magnate having long been a subject of censorious comment. In all these ways the impression gained ground that the Coalition, far from *ending* the abuses of the party system, was simply *magnifying* them.[33]

Articulating these criticisms from the Back Benches was the Unionist War Committee, formed in January 1916, whose figurehead was the dangerous Edward Carson, who had resigned from the Government in the previous autumn in protest at the failure to reinforce the Serbian Front. Along with the Unionist Business Committee, this 'ginger group' provided vigorous criticism of the supine war effort.[34] But its main concern was less to promote Conservative Party interests in the face of Asquith's unscrupulous manoeuvring than to insist that the prosecution of the war should be placed before all other considerations – an objective which members shared with their opposite numbers in the Liberal War Committee.

32 Diary, 11 July 1916, in Vincent (ed.), *Crawford Papers*, pp. 355–6.
33 G.R. Searle, *Corruption in British Politics, 1895–1930* (Oxford, 1987), pp. 305–7.
34 Turner, *British Politics*, pp. 83–4.

For there was a mounting impatience with party squabbles, which contrasted so painfully with the camaraderie and shared sacrifices of the men in uniform. Moreover, as the *Observer* had put it in on the formation of the Asquith Coalition (23 May 1915), 'the irrelevance of the labels "Ministerialists" and "Opposition" to anything that is of practical consequence just now cries aloud to high Heaven'. It is indeed true that, at the level of policy, many of the great wartime debates produced alignments which cut clean across the boundaries of party. Significantly, the question of Salonika, which eventually provoked Carson's resignation, had seen a momentary alliance between Carson, Bonar Law and Lloyd George – the 'triumvirate' that later destroyed Asquith's Coalition in December 1916.

In other words, party cohesion itself was breaking down in the course of 1915. This seriously undermined the authority of Bonar Law, already disadvantaged by being marooned in the Colonial Office away from the main scene of action.[35] Yet at the same time it seemed as if the war effort was being hampered by the survival of archaic party prejudices and interests, particularly in respect of the efficient conduct of the government machine.

Asquith's unwillingness to abandon the old Cabinet system was perhaps his greatest single failure in office. True, smaller bodies were created to deal with the formulation of strategy: the War Council, followed by the Dardanelles Committee, followed by the War Committee. But all these new bodies suffered from the same defects: their membership tended steadily to expand, they lacked the support of a proper secretariat, and aggrieved Ministers who had been overruled could always seek a reversal of the offending decision at the full Cabinet. For it was the Cabinet, twenty-two members strong, which retained sovereignty. And Asquith preferred to rely upon this large organisation, partly because he was temperamentally a traditionalist, but also because he was still thinking in terms of political and party *balance*.[36]

Such an approach to policy-formation gravely hampered the activities of those who wanted to prioritise 'national service'. By 1916 this concept had come to mean, not just the adoption of compulsory military service but also planning for the mobilisation of the country's

35 That is why Ramsden is sceptical of the claim that the Conservative Party benefited from the war, arguing that what gains it did make were largely cancelled out by the damaging effects of Coalition (*Age of Balfour and Baldwin*, p. 110).

36 See Gollin's verdict, in Gollin, *Milner*, p. 229.

entire material and manpower resources – a drastic breach with peacetime administration which, by challenging 'individual liberties', on the one hand, and 'property rights', on the other, inevitably provoked collisions with the custodians of the party creeds.

On both counts the most fundamental challenge to the Asquith Coalition came from Milner and his friends. Barely had the new Government been formed than Milner dashed off a letter to *The Times*, calling for national service, firm leadership and organisation: 'To do this systematically and fairly requires a census and proper classification. It is a big work of national organisation. It will take time . . .'[37] In June Milner became chairman of the National Service League: 'All law, all order, all discipline, involves . . . compulsion', he now declared.[38]

Privately Milner was despondent about the likelihood of success. He feared that democracy was going to fail, '& the British Empire with it', unless his countrymen succeeded in emancipating themselves 'from machine-made caucus-ridden politics' and gave 'men of independence & character more of a chance . . .'[39] Later, only two days before the Nigerian debate which started the crisis that eventually destroyed the Asquith Coalition, Milner fulminated in another letter to *The Times* against those who thought 'that the principles of GO AS YOU PLEASE and the General Scramble, which may have been necessary and even appropriate during the inevitable break-up of the Old Order, could possibly be the permanent foundations of the New'.[40]

Nor did the Milnerites confine themselves to general exhortation. In August 1915 Amery urged his 'Chief' to assemble an 'effective board of conspirators' to prepare for the eradication of 'Asquith and Co', so that there would be a 'Milner policy or National Policy as distinct from the Party or Mandarin Policies', committed to national service, munitions, finance and the empire.[41] Four months later Milner emerged as the leader of a 'Forward Party', comprising Lords Midleton, Sydenham, Loreburn, Peel and Ancaster,[42] and in

---

37 27 May 1915, in Gollin, *Milner*, pp. 268–9.

38 Ibid., pp. 275–6.

39 Milner to Curtis, 27 Nov. 1915, ibid., p. 314.

40 6 Nov. 1916, Robert J. Scally, *The Origins of the Lloyd George Coalition: The Politics of Social Imperialism, 1900–1918* (Princeton, 1975), p. 314.

41 Amery to Milner, 2 Aug. 1915, Gollin, *Milner*, p. 277.

42 Ibid., p. 317.

mid-January 1916 Amery created the 'Monday Night Cabal', which included, among others, Astor, the proprietor of the *Observer*.[43]

So despondent had Milner become with the existing Government that by March 1916 he was seriously contemplating the creation of a new party which could fight for a 'national policy' in the forthcoming general election, whenever that might materialise. Milner saw only too clearly the irony of a situation in which 'the only way to get rid of an INCUBUS, the curse of which [was] due more than anything else to the Party system . . . should be the formation of a new Party'. But, as he privately conceded, it was hard to see how anything could be achieved without organisation: 'And organisation does mean something like a Party, if it be only an *ad hoc* Party, aiming at nothing more than *energy and forethought* in the conduct of the war', whether going under the name of 'an Organised Opposition, a National Party' or some other label.[44]

Meanwhile, of more immediate practicality were attempts by Milner's friends to link up with Lloyd George. In late September 1915 Lloyd George had visited Milner for luncheon at the latter's London house,[45] and soon afterwards most members of the 'Monday Night Cabal', Oliver dissenting, agreed that the Welshman was the best available replacement Premier.[46] Amery felt sure that, in the construction of a 'National Policy', Carson would almost certainly co-operate. 'So *will* Lloyd George, if he once felt certain that he has no chance of becoming Prime Minister . . .'[47] In March of the following year F.E. Smith made unsuccessful overtures to Lloyd George.[48] And two months later Astor took the plunge and approached Christopher Addison, Lloyd George's junior Liberal colleague, to find out what the latter thought of the idea of a government reconstruction in which Milner would be leader, perhaps Premier, with Lloyd George as his number two. Addison brusquely dismissed both proposals as 'absurd', saying that 'rightly or wrongly few men in the country were more distrusted than Milner'.[49] (In an unpublished part of the Diary Addison derisively called Milner 'a second-rate windbag'.)[50]

43 Ibid., pp. 323–4.
44 Milner's 'Notes on the Present War Situation', 12 March 1916, ibid., pp. 332–3.
45 Ibid., pp. 295–6.
46 Ibid., p. 330.
47 Ibid., p. 277.
48 Smith to Lloyd George, 20 March 1916, in Scally, *Lloyd George Coalition*, p. 287.
49 Addison diary, 1 May 1916, in *Four And A Half Years* (1934), I, p. 201.
50 Turner, *British Politics*, p. 113.

All the same, the Milnerites' new-found interest in Lloyd George merits discussion, if only as one of several manifestations of a growing body of feeling on the political Right that Lloyd George was the most appropriate leader of a truly National Government. What caused people to think in this way?

As early as May 1915 some Unionists had already begun to revise their earlier unfavourable attitude towards Lloyd George. Garvin, of course, had all along been an enthusiastic acolyte: 'you are practically my leader now', he told Lloyd George in the summer of 1915.

> I can't help wishing that Winston were your right hand man as in the great Conference days of 1910 and that you had him (with all that brain and stomach and physical vigour) in something better than a sinecure. Likewise I wish you had Haldane back in the Min. of Science, and that Milner, a big statesman with all his crochets, were in the War Council . . . .[51]

But Hewins' diary observations, penned shortly before the May Crisis, were more typical of Unionist opinion at this early stage of the war. Lloyd George, Hewins pondered, *might* give the Unionists national leadership, but only if he chose to risk his position with his own party: 'I doubt whether Lloyd George is man enough to do it', Hewins concluded.[52]

However, three things recommended Lloyd George to many of his former opponents. First, there was his record of achievement at the newly created Ministry of Munitions, which had been built up as a formidable 'businessman's organisation' into which dynamic industrialists had been co-opted from private industry. Of these the most interesting personality was the railway manager Eric Geddes, who, as we shall see, later had an important political career of his own. Ever since the time of the Boer War, there had been talk of the need to put government on to a business footing. Lloyd George, it seemed, was now translating rhetoric into deeds: and certainly his suspicion of 'red-tape' and established civil service routines, his eagerness to achieve quick production results at almost any cost, and his liking for the company of 'men of push and go', all chimed in with the popular mood. That there was both a financial and a moral cost to pay for these unorthodox methods only time would tell – and by then Lloyd George had moved on to other tasks. Meanwhile the Minister

---

51 Garvin to Lloyd George, 5 July 1915, Scally, *Lloyd George Coalition*, p. 259.
52 19 March 1915, W.A.S. Hewins, *The Apologia of an Imperialist* (1929), II, p. 21.

of Munitions was establishing precedents which, many argued, could be extended after the war into other areas of national life.

Secondly, Lloyd George gave the impression, as Asquith never did, that he desperately wanted to win the war and would shrink from nothing to achieve his ends. And, finally, it was soon being observed by friend and foe that, in his unconcern for party (for example, over the issue of conscription), Lloyd George seemed to have secured for himself a non-party position – one, in fact, where he commanded more admiration from his opponents than from his party colleagues. Comparisons with Joseph Chamberlain were often made. In June 1915 the Liberal journalist, J.A. Spender, told Riddell 'that the Liberals are very disgruntled with L.G. They believe he is going the way of Chamberlain . . . .'[53] A month later Beatrice Webb was reaching the same conclusion: 'From all we hear Lloyd George is going the way of Chamberlain – exchanging the leadership of the Radicals for the leadership of an Imperialist Nationalist Party . . . .'[54]

Did Lloyd George personally seek out such a role? On 12 October 1915, when Carson resigned from the Government, Lloyd George reassured him that he was 'doing absolutely the right thing'.[55] This exchange occurred at the time of the conscription crisis, when it was rumoured that Lloyd George and his Conservative supporters had designs on the premiership.[56] Certainly there were many, Garvin and Smith included, who urged the Welshman to break with Asquith. So, too, did Churchill, who, after his resignation in November 1915, became a formidable critic of the Coalition's military and administrative shortcomings.[57] Moreover, in March 1916 Addison learned that there was a movement among some Conservatives to make Lloyd George Prime Minister.[58] The Conservative politician, Arthur Lee, went further and made a direct appeal: 'The people are yearning for a leader – witness the pathetic quest for "The Man" . . .', wrote Lee to Lloyd George, in a letter in which he urged the formation

53 Riddell diary, 11 June 1915, J.M.McEwen, *The Riddell Diaries, 1908–1923* (1986), p. 122. See also 9 Nov. 1915, ibid., p. 138.

54 Beatrice Webb's diary, 8 July 1915, cited in Scally, *Lloyd George Coalition*, p. 261.

55 Ian Colvin, *Life of Lord Carson* (1936), III, p. 97.

56 Turner, *British Politics*, p. 70.

57 See Churchill to Lloyd George, 27 Dec. 1915, in Scally, *Lloyd George Coalition*, p. 266.

58 Addison diary, 17 March 1916, Christopher Addison, *Four and A Half Years*, I, p. 183.

of a new administration with 'a strong leaven of non-politicians, to which all parties would give loyal support'.[59]

Such appeals probably made some impression on Lloyd George, whose thoughts by the spring of 1916 were perhaps turning towards some kind of political realignment. In late April Riddell surmised that Lloyd George was contemplating 'a new party'.[60] Riddell was also present to record a discussion which occurred on 3 June 1916, following the recent disappointment of Jutland and the problems created by the Easter Rising. At this meeting Lloyd George once more referred to Chamberlain as someone who 'had always remained a Radical'; he also noted that no Radical could ever lead the Conservative Party, before adding the significant rider: 'That is, of course, if it remained the Conservative Party'.[61]

Soon afterwards, when on the point of becoming War Secretary, Lloyd George once more flirted with the idea of resigning in protest at the way the war was being conducted: 'If I went out I should at once form a great Party organization', he privately declared. 'I have promises of all the money necessary.'[62] Indeed, for some time Lloyd George had been causing anxiety among his friends by consorting with Northcliffe, who in October 1915 had advocated a 'Committee of Safety, comprising perhaps five leading men', to replace the existing Ministry.[63] 'It looks as if LG and Northcliffe are working to dethrone Mr A.', observed Riddell.[64] Yet Lloyd George's relationship with the Conservatives was by no means trouble-free, and the deterioration in his relations with the military High Command, which found expression in his attacks on Field Marshal Robertson, the Chief of the Imperial General Staff (CIGS), led to his being sharply criticised in the Conservative Press later that year – a prelude to the trouble which lay ahead.[65]

Nevertheless, as military disappointment followed disappointment, the feeling grew that the Asquith Coalition would have to be

59 Lee to Lloyd George, 2 April 1916, in Scally, *Lloyd George Coalition*, pp. 289–90.

60 Riddell diary, 28 April 1916, McEwen, *Riddell Diaries*, p. 154. Riddell thought this 'a dangerous experiment at such a time', given Lloyd George's unpopularity with the working classes.

61 Riddell, *War Diary*, pp. 186–7. Significantly, Lloyd George linked these remarks to the possibilities of achieving Imperial Federation.

62 Riddell diary, 11 June 1916, McEwen, *Riddell Diaries*, p. 159.

63 21 Oct. 1915, ibid., p. 133.

64 Diary, 21 May 1916, ibid., p. 156.

65 Turner, *British Politics*, pp. 123–4.

replaced by a real National Government. Recalling Dickens's attacks on administrative incompetence during the Crimean War, Garvin's *Observer* now portrayed the Ministry's efforts as an example of 'How Not To Do It' (16 April 1916). 'National unity', it proclaimed on 30 April, was being jeopardised by the government's disunity, something which made its total reconstruction unavoidable. In fact, it was to be dissatisfaction with the machinery of government which brought about the fall of the Asquith Ministry six months later – by which time even loyal Liberal newspapers like the *Westminster Gazette* had come out in open criticism of Asquith's handling of the war.

In the event, the Government's collapse in December 1916 – so long predicted and so often deferred – happened very quickly. The Asquith Coalition had only survived as long as it did because its many critics could not agree upon an alternative. But once Lloyd George, Carson and Bonar Law found themselves up against Asquith's obstinate refusal to reform the machinery of government in the interests of improved efficiency, and thus forced to fight their corner, the first Coalition Ministry was doomed.[66] Lloyd George then became Prime Minister, as John Turner shows, because those who most hated the Welshman also despised Asquith, while the Liberal Centre supported Asquith so tepidly that they were not prepared to make a stand on his behalf.[67]

LLOYD GEORGE'S COALITION MINISTRY

There are a number of points to be made about the new Coalition Government which Lloyd George formed in December 1916. The first is that Asquith effectively excluded himself from office by refusing to stay on as Lord Chancellor in a Ministry headed by Bonar Law. But this was not a purely personal decision, for it meant that nearly all the senior Liberal Ministers followed Asquith on to the Back Benches. This, in turn, had the largely unintended consequence of creating a *new* kind of party imbalance: in May 1915 Asquith had succeeded only too well in preserving the Liberal Party's predominant position, but after December 1916 the situation

---

66 Clearly no attempt can be made in this volume to retell the story of the 'Buckingham Palace Revolution' which led to Asquith's replacement by Lloyd George nor to allocate responsibility for its demise.

67 Turner, *British Politics*, p. 150.

was reversed. So much is apparent from a comparison of the share of offices which the Conservatives received during the first and second Coalition Ministries:[68]

	Cabinet Ministers	Unionists in Cabinet	Total Ministers	Total Unionists
May 1915	22	8	24	9
Dec 1916	23	13	32	14

The likes of Carson and Milner cannot have been displeased by such a state of affairs. But Garvin realised that the Liberal discomfiture militated against national unity; for, as the *Observer* presciently remarked on 10 December, there was the risk that the official Liberal Party, embittered over the circumstances in which it had been ejected from power, might drift into an oppositional role. There was also a danger of Lloyd George becoming the prisoner of the Conservative Party. The new Premier was well aware of this, and he partially redressed the balance in July 1917 when he brought two senior Liberals into his Ministry, Edwin Montagu, who became Indian Secretary, and Churchill who, much to the fury of most Conservatives, was made Minister of Munitions. But this move only succeeded in further deepening the divisions within the troubled Liberal Party – divisions which were hardly conducive to national unity.

A second weakness from which the new Coalition Ministry suffered was that in order to establish himself securely in power at all, Lloyd George had had to make concessions which later crucially limited his freedom of action. For example, although Montagu had been devising a plan of industrial compulsion in November 1916 (a plan in which Lloyd George firmly believed), he had to drop this item from his programme in order to win over Labour, just as, in order to propitiate Curzon, he found it necessary to give a pledge that he would not dismiss Haig from the military High Command – a pledge which he was to spend the next eighteen months trying to wriggle out of.[69] Indeed, the new Prime Minister actually installed Lord Derby, the 'Soldier's Friend', as the new War Secretary.

68 Ramsden, *Age of Balfour and Baldwin*, p. 134.
69 Turner, *British Politics*, pp. 153–4, 166.

Thus, despite Lloyd George's desire to pursue a 'national' strategy, the Government was constrained by party pressures from the very start. Milner, a major beneficiary from the change of Government, shrewdly recognised these limitations:

> Unfortunately, as I think, the *unexpected firmness* of B.L., while it certainly gave the *coup de grace* to Squiff, has resulted in the return of the old Unionist tail – A.J.B. and all the rest of them – so that the new Government is really the old Unionist hordes, L.G., and *some* new men – I don't know how many. So we have not, after all, completely sloughed off the party skin.[70]

Yet, on the positive side, Lloyd George *was* able to make a decisive change in the machinery of government through the institution of a small War Cabinet of five Ministers, all of whom (bar Bonar Law, the Chancellor of the Exchequer) were freed from departmental responsibilities so that they could concentrate on overall war strategy. Moreover, Law, the Conservative Leader, was the only member who owed his position primarily to party considerations. Arthur Henderson was included because of the pressing need for a senior and respected trade unionist with credibility on the factory floor. Curzon was valued for his deep knowledge of international affairs. And, most interestingly of all, the 'political Ishmaelite' Milner was brought in from the cold because he was a skilful administrator with a crucial contribution to make in the field of economic planning. Even though over time Lloyd George's War Cabinet grew in size and increasingly had to delegate work to sub-committees, the new machinery greatly increased the efficiency of government.

It is also significant that although Milner had played very little direct part in the downfall of the Asquith Coalition, he was able to introduce many of his friends into the new Government: Amery became a member of the Secretariat which Lloyd George had attached to the War Cabinet (headed by Maurice Hankey), two members of the 'Kindergarten', Philip Kerr and Lionel Curtis, became Private Secretaries to the Prime Minister, and later, on Garvin's insistence, Waldorf Astor also joined the 'Garden Suburb', as Lloyd George's extensive personal secretariat was known. John Buchan, the novelist, had meanwhile been appointed Director of Information.[71]

But, of course, the central role was played by Lloyd George himself. 'For the first time (since Cromwell) we have a dictatorship by one,

70 In private letter of 8 Dec. 1916, cited in Scally, *Lloyd George Coalition*, p. 341.
71 Gollin, *Milner*, pp. 376–9.

or possibly by three, men', thought Beatrice Webb.[72] Cromwell was also in the mind of Garvin, whose friendship with the Welshman had cooled during 1916,[73] but who greeted Lloyd George's advent to the premiership with enthusiasm, saluting him in the *Observer* (10 December 1916) as 'the man' for whom the country had long been waiting: 'If he succeeds he will rank with two leaders alone in our history – Cromwell and Chatham.' Initially, such admiration was quite widespread amongst Conservatives, testimony perhaps to the contempt which they had felt for Asquith. 'The extraordinary thing is the undisguised joy and relief which the fall of the Asquith ministry has produced in every quarter', wrote Oliver to his brother on 14 December. 'The country cheered and said, "Now we have a chance of winning the war" . . .'[74]

'CORPORATISM' AND RECONSTRUCTION

Moreover, there were two ways in which Lloyd George seemed intent on breaking free from the traditional party system and pursuing a new kind of 'national politics'. The first was the enhanced role assigned to businessmen. If Lloyd George found that he could not 'form a Cabinet from amongst the politicians, he [would] invoke the aid of business men to carry on the war', Riddell had noted in his diary on 6 December.[75]

In the event this proved unnecessary. But when Lloyd George assumed the premiership he brought businessmen into his Government in unprecedented numbers. 'Under the Lloyd George regimen, each department has been handed over to the "interest" with which it is concerned', noted Beatrice Webb sardonically. 'In that way, our little Welsh attorney thinks, you combine the least political opposition with the maximum technical knowledge.'[76] Thus, Devonport, a wholesale grocer, was made Food Controller, Albert Stanley, a railway director, became President of the Board of Trade, and Joseph

---

72 Beatrice Webb diary, 12 Dec. 1916, in Norman and Jeanne MacKenzie (eds), *The Diary of Beatrice Webb: Vol. 3 1905–1924: 'The Power to Alter Things'* (1984), p. 272.

73 Scally, *Lloyd George Coalition*, p. 287.

74 F.S. Oliver, *The Anvil of War: Letters between F.S. Oliver and His Brother 1914–1918* (ed. S. Gwynn) (1936), p. 163.

75 Riddell diary, 6 Dec. 1916, McEwen, *War Diaries*, p. 176.

76 Webb diary, 22 Feb. 1917, in *Beatrice Webb's Diary, III*, p. 276.

Maclay, a ship-owner, served as Director of Shipping (the latter did not even have a seat in either House of Parliament). Meanwhile, the Ministry of Labour was entrusted to a trade unionist (John Hodge), and a don, H.A.L. Fisher, was put in charge of Education. Lord Weir went to the Air Board, the coal-owner, Lord Rhondda, after succeeding Devonport as Food Controller, became President of the Local Government Board, and the newspaper magnate, Lord Beaverbrook (formerly Max Aitken), was made Minister of Information in early 1918. Perhaps the most spectacular of all such promotions was the elevation (in July 1917) of Geddes, the railway manager whose ability had earlier caught Lloyd George's attention, to the post of First Lord of the Admiralty.

The experiment enjoyed mixed fortunes. One historian has observed that it merely exposed the 'claptrap about the superiority of the modern business man',[77] and, even at the time, there was grumbling about the calibre of these 'outsiders'. The Conservative MP Willie Bridgeman, for one, felt sure that 'the large introduction of business men into the Govt. [had] not yet justified itself', instancing, among others, Devonport, Rhondda, Stanley and Geddes – though he admitted that Maclay seemed to have done well as shipping controller. 'They are narrow in their outlook, bad at working together, and generally ignorant of matters outside their own particular sphere', Bridgeman concluded.[78] Nor, it seems, were businessmen universally successful as *administrators*, despite the presumption (which Lloyd George himself certainly shared) that they possessed qualities of energetic initiative rarely to be found among the Whitehall Mandarins, with their bureaucratic habits and love of red-tape.

Some of the criticism of the businessman in government emanated from the jealousy of civil servants and politicians at the intrusion of 'aliens' into their particular domains. But there were more legitimate grounds for concern: for example, the fear that the impartiality of the state was being undermined by the activities of some temporary civil servants who used their official positions to promote their own private interests.[79] It would also seem as though the consequential

---

77 R.P.T. Davonport-Hines, *Dudley Docker: The Life and Times of A Trade Warrior* (Cambridge, 1984), p. 104.

78 Bridgeman diary, Feb. 1918, in Williamson (ed.), *Modernisation of Conservative Politics*, pp. 126–7.

79 See Davenport-Hines, *Docker*, pp. 100–1; Chris Wrigley, 'The Ministry of Munitions: an Innovatory Department', in K. Burk (ed.), *War and the State* (1982), pp. 41–2.

abandonment of Treasury control led to much extravagance and waste. Yet these were risks which perhaps the Government *had* to take, since the Great War required the state to mobilise the entire economy, a task which the pre-war officials had neither the numbers nor the training to perform.

There is, however, a dispute among historians as to what this importation of businessmen into Westminster and Whitehall really signified. Professor Middlemas has interpreted it as the start of 'corporatism'. The war years, he argues, saw

> the creation in Parliamentary politics of a *staatspartei*, composed of Liberals and mainstream Conservatives (leaving a fringe Right wing and a much larger, but powerless Labour Left); complemented in industrial politics by a triangular collaboration in which employers' organisations and TUC . . . [made] themselves representative of their members and in return receive[d] recognition as *estates* by government.[80]

In the pursuit of 'crisis avoidance', Middlemas claims, Lloyd George's Ministry preferred to deal directly with these 'peak organisations' (representing Capital and Labour), a method of transacting public business which largely bypassed Parliament and the political parties.

However, most historians question how far this process had really gone by 1918 or even by 1922, and they are still more sceptical about its *effectiveness*, in so far as it was attempted at all. Dudley Docker, a determined 'corporatist', may have wanted a Ministry of Commerce to promote business interests, but this proposal never won much support from the political elite and remained unimplemented.[81] Indeed, some historians stress the relative autonomy of the state, that it so say, its ability to *resist* being captured by either Organised Labour or by business interests.[82]

Nevertheless, for all his exaggerations, Middlemas is probably correct in pointing to ways in which a new kind of relationship was fashioned between government and economic interest groups in the final years of the War. The result was a diminution of the importance of *party*.

This development tied in with another important wartime innovation: the emergence of the idea of 'Reconstruction'. It had been Asquith,

80 Keith Middlemas, *Politics in Industrial Society: The Experience of the British System Since 1911* (1979), p. 151.
81 Turner, *British Politics*, pp. 388–9.
82 Ibid., pp. 336, 358.

while Prime Minister, who had set up the Reconstruction Committee, but in July 1917 Reconstruction became a full-blown Ministry under the direction of Christopher Addison, one of Lloyd George's most trusted Liberal supporters. Its brief was never very clearly defined. One obvious concern was planning for the transition to peace (demobilisation, for example). But, even more ambitiously, working through a myriad of sub-committees on to which the appropriate experts had been co-opted, the Ministry of Reconstruction soon began to devise ways in which the wartime machinery of state could be employed after the Armistice for the purpose of modernising industry and improving the living conditions of the British people.[83]

Reconstruction acquired a sharper urgency with the outbreak of strikes in the engineering industry in May. Coming hard upon the fall of the Russian Tsar, this development excited fears about the stability of the entire social order and gave a new twist to government policy. 'A coalition which had been set up merely to improve the execution of war policy now became a barrier against the corrosive effects of socialism', concludes Turner. 'Slowly and unselfconsciously the Lloyd George Coalition began to make itself a counter-revolutionary government.'[84] Social reforms were now partly brought forward with the intention of inserting a wedge between 'sane Labour' and the dangerous militantly class-conscious elements which the Government was determined to destroy.

Yet it would be a mistake to view Reconstruction *solely* in these cynical terms. For both Lloyd George and Addison seem to have retained much of the earlier utopian optimism. On 16 March 1917 the Prime Minister had made his famous observation to the Reconstruction Committee: 'The nation now was in a molten condition: it was malleable now, and would continue to be so for a short time after the war, but not for long.'[85] This vision was never entirely lost. For it really did seem that there was an opportunity for carrying out, on a consensual basis, a comprehensive reform scheme which would transform the social conditions of the British people and ensure that the unity that had been forged in war would continue into the years of peace. Out of this optimism came housing plans (the genesis of Addison's 1919 Housing Act) and the creation of the Ministry of

83 See the discussion in Scott Newton and Dilwyn Porter, *Modernization Frustrated: The Politics of Industrial Decline in Britain since 1900* (1988), pp. 45–55.

84 Turner, *British Politics*, pp. 194–5.

85 Scally, *Lloyd George Coalition*, p. 354.

Health, to which Parliament gave its assent even before the war had ended.

It has been argued that 'Reconstruction . . . helped to keep party identities alive within the Coalition' because most Liberals were enthusiastic about social reform, while most Unionists set greater store by Tariff Reform.[86] But one must not forget the contribution to Reconstruction made by Bismarckian paternalists like Milner and by technocrats and businessmen like Geddes, to whom the goal of a scientifically ordered society held a much greater appeal than did the prospect of a return to market competition. As Kenneth Morgan argues, such men 'were truly liberated from ideology, impatient with party politics, dedicated only to business efficiency and collective control within an increasingly corporate state'.[87] The advisers whom the Prime Minister had gathered around himself in the 'Garden Suburb' could be similarly described.[88] 'If there was a realistic supra-party basis for a post-war coalition government', comments Morgan, 'reconstruction would form the core of it.'[89] Bentley Gilbert agrees, calling the Ministry of Reconstruction 'a species of government-supported idea-factory for a postwar party that would evolve under the leadership of Lloyd George'.[90]

How seriously did senior politicians take that possibility in the later stages of the war? In October 1917 a group including Lloyd George, Addison, Milner and Kerr assembled to discuss the drafting of a War Cabinet Report, which would chronicle the Coalition's achievements and lay down guidelines for a future Reconstruction programme. There 'would probably be no great difficulty in arriving at an agreement' except on the tariff question, Addison felt.[91] Symptomatic of the changed political atmosphere was Addison's revision of his earlier slighting view of Milner, whom he now loved and reverenced 'for his serene greatness';[92] the two men were shortly to co-operate with one another in the battle to establish a Ministry of Health.

Little wonder, then, that Milner was again present when Lloyd George, Addison and Victor Fisher, the 'patriotic' Labour representa-

86 Turner, *British Politics*, p. 334.
87 Kenneth O. Morgan, *Consensus and Disunity: The Lloyd George Coalition Government 1918–1922* (Oxford, 1979), p. 16.
88 Ibid., pp. 16–17.
89 Ibid., p. 25.
90 Bentley B. Gilbert, *British Social Policy 1914–1939* (1970), p. 9.
91 Turner, *British Politics*, p. 241.
92 Addison diary, 8 June 1917, *Four and A Half Years*, II, p. 395.

tive, met in Astor's home for another policy discussion in December. The group agreed that 'L.G.'s chief weakness at present [was] that he ha[d] no organisation', but Addison felt that there would be 'no difficulty in having a really comprehensive programme which would carry a large mass of the Tory Party as well as of Labour and of Liberals' since 'a good many old distinctions are dim these days and the country is ready for a bold move forward under State inspiration'.[93] The search was thus on for the creation of a new 'National Party' under Lloyd George's leadership.

Lord Riddell's diary provides evidence that the Prime Minister himself took this enterprise very seriously. 'The old parties are moribund', Riddell records him as saying in October 1917: 'They stand for nothing. The problems which produced them have faded into insignificance.'[94] Next month the Premier was speaking of relying on the 'business classes' to provide him with bedrock support should the Liberals split, as he thought they would.[95] A few weeks later he dismissed 'the Liberal Party in its old form' as 'a thing of the past' which could not 'be galvanised into life' and declared that he was planning to form his own organisation.[96] Well might some of his Labour colleagues react nervously to Lloyd George's references to the 'necessity of a national party in the House and the country'.[97]

The Milnerite group, on the other hand, would obviously have welcomed an initiative of this sort. Writing to Oliver as early as 8 April 1917, Milner had predicted that scientific solutions to national problems would never materialise 'under our present party system, which is more or less in abeyance'; but he feared that this 'system' would revive once the war ended, unless we could 'get a lot of new men, unpledged to the old parties, *in to the next House of Commons*'. 'We want a group of independent "Nationalists"', Milner concluded: 'Where are they?'[98]

---

93 Addison diary, 28 Dec. 1917, ibid., II, p. 459. At this meeting alarm was expressed over Henderson and Labour – passages which Addison omitted when he published his diaries (he was then a member of the Labour Party!) (Turner, *British Politics*, pp. 254–5).

94 Riddell diary, 20 Oct. 1917, McEwen, *War Diaries*, p. 202.

95 24 Nov.1917, ibid., p. 207.

96 27 Jan. 1918, ibid., pp. 214–15. In fact, a rudimentary Coalition Liberal organisation had existed since May.

97 Fisher diary, 21 Nov. 1917, cited in Turner, *British Politics*, p. 242.

98 Chris Wrigley, '"In the Excess of their Patriotism": the National Party and Threats of Subversion', in Chris Wrigley (ed.), *Warfare, Diplomacy and Politics* (1986), p. 99.

THE NATIONAL PARTY

In fact, the autumn of 1917 saw the emergence of just such a patriotic grouping, when a number of right-wing Conservatives, led by Henry Page Croft, came together to form the 'National Party'. The manifesto of this new organisation blamed *all* the coalition parties for the failure to achieve a speedy military victory. 'For years past the old party system has been nothing better than an organized mockery of the true spirit of the nation', it declared. 'If we are to win victory in the war – *and after* – we must free ourselves, somehow or other, from the clutches of this octopus.' The manifesto went on to commit the new body to 'a National as against a class, sectional, or sectarian policy', 'the eradication of German influence', 'honest administration, a pure political system and no sale of honours', 'class unity and confidence between employer and employed', plus fair wages and fair profits, the safeguarding of British industries and agriculture, Empire unity, 'a National social policy' and demobilisation and reconstruction with special regard to the interests of sailors and soldiers. Finally, the National Party appealed for support from anyone who shared its impatience with the 'worn-out party system and its ruthless machines' and its belief 'that the old political associations [were] not merely inadequate for the work of national reconstruction, but [were] *obstacles in the way of it*'.[99]

Despite support from the *Morning Post*, the *National Review* and Dudley Docker's *Globe*, Page Croft's movement did not make much progress. This was partly because its strategy in 1917 and early 1918 was so confused. Did it aim to oust Lloyd George, or was it hoping to help him in his patriotic struggles to free himself from the 'Old Gangs'? No one, including the founders, seemed quite sure. To add to the confusion, it was rumoured at the time of the new organisation's launch that the Prime Minister himself was 'working away at forming a National Party'.[100]

However, the importance of the National Party is that it indicates how attitudes towards the Premier were beginning to change. Such had been the disgust with the Asquithian regime that many Tariff Reform enthusiasts had initially welcomed the Welshman's advent to power, some even managing to convince themselves that the new regime would launch a determined attack on the system of secret

99 *Morning Post*, 30 Aug. 1917, cited in Lord Croft, *My Life of Strife* (n.d.), pp. 131–2.
100 Wrigley, 'Excess of Patriotism', p. 100.

party funding and on those abuses in the honours system which had been causing disquiet for many years past.

But such hopes were quickly to be dashed. For, denied access to the Liberal Party Fund, which remained under Asquithian control, Lloyd George quickly started exploiting his powers of patronage so as to create a new party fund of his own. This resulted in swollen honours lists and in ugly rumours circulating in London clubland about the unscrupulous intrigues of several of the Prime Minister's intimates, notably his personal secretary, William Sutherland, and the Chief Coalition Liberal Whip, Freddie Guest. Little wonder that the National Party manifesto spoke of the importance of fostering 'the honesty and capacity of our public men'. 'Politics is a matter of national life or death', claimed the manifesto: 'Should it continue to be played as a game of party interests and personal ambition, served by two machines which are kept in funds by the Sale of Honours, the end can only be disaster'.[101]

Another expression of this distaste for conventional party activities took the form of a renewed campaign to make the political system more responsive to the needs of industry by sending an increased number of businessmen into Parliament. In this campaign a leading role was played by a new pressure group called the British Commonwealth Union, whose Council was joined in the spring of 1918 by Docker and Maxse, both otherwise associated with the National Party.[102] In fact, after the 1918 Election, an 'Industrial Group' was formed at Westminster, though it never came remotely close to realising Docker's ideal of a 'manufacturer's party'.[103] The main political parties, therefore, continued to hold centre stage; but their leaders knew that they would only survive into the post-war world by adapting their strategies to take account of the changed circumstances.

TOWARDS THE 'COUPON ELECTION', DECEMBER 1918

The politics of 1918 are extremely complicated, but three of their features need to be emphasised. First, there was, if anything, a growth

101 Croft, *Life of Strife*, p. 131. On the 'honours scandals' of this period, see Searle, *Corruption*, pp. 309–13.

102 Davenport-Hines, *Docker*, pp. 122–5; J.A. Turner, 'The British Commonwealth Union and the General Election of 1918', *English Historical Review*, 93 (1978), 528–59.

103 Davenport-Hines, *Docker*, pp. 129–31.

in the feelings of hostility towards traditional party politics. Nowhere
was the indictment of party more powerfully made than by Lloyd
George's journalistic friend, Harold Spender, in the February number
of the *Contemporary Review*:

> No one, indeed, who visits the constituencies can doubt that both the
> great parties are deep in coma; and that the outside public recks little
> whether that coma passes into death. There is everywhere a friendliness
> between party leaders fatal to party warfare or to the renewal of it. We
> have seen at the Front how fatal is fraternisation to the fury necessary
> for real warfare. Well, there has been a fraternisation between the great
> political parties throughout Great Britain for nearly four years. Is this
> fraternisation going to count for nothing? The party swords have been
> beaten into ploughshares. Is it going to be easy to beat them back into
> swords? . . . Coalition . . . is becoming a vested interest.[104]

Secondly, it is important to remember that, from the start of 1918,
all the political leaders were preparing for the general election which
they expected would be held once the new electoral register had been
prepared on the basis of the recently enacted Representation of the
People Act. Moreover, until the very end of the year, it was also
generally assumed that the purpose of this election would be to
return a government that could defeat the Central Powers. Even
when Lloyd George asked the King for a dissolution on 5 November,
he still thought that the election would take place *before* the end of
hostilities.[105]

But, thirdly, political debate was complicated throughout most of
1918 by the fact that Lloyd George's own future remained shrouded
in uncertainty. As the year opened, the Premier still had little idea of
how much support he really commanded in the House of Commons,
something that would only be clarified when Asquith challenged
him over the Maurice Affair in May. But even in the aftermath
of Maurice the Coalition Liberals hesitated between three distinct
strategies: to make preparations for fighting an election in alliance
with the Conservatives, to reunite with the official Liberal Party, or
to create some kind of new 'National Party'.

Unsure of which way to turn, the Prime Minister kept his options
open almost until the last moment. His Liberal friends were equally
uncertain and divided. Addison, who had no confidence in the

104 Harold Spender, 'The War and the Parties', *Contemporary Review*, 113 (Feb.
1918), 137–8.
105 Turner, *British Politics*, p. 317. Admittedly, Lloyd George by now envisaged
an 'early prospect of a termination of the War'.

Asquithians ('They have the pre-war mind unchanged'), discussed with Beaverbrook 'the formation of a strong L.G. Party'.[106] 'Future progress', he felt, depended 'either upon the co-operative action of a group of men who [were] prepared to apply the lessons of the war sensibly and courageously' or else upon a reconstructed Labour Party.[107]

But could Conservatives be persuaded to join up with Lloyd George, so turning his following into a genuinely 'national' party? That this might be feasible was suggested by the re-emergence of 'Federalism' as a way of resolving the endless Irish difficulty. In February discussions took place within the government about the possibility of federating the entire United Kingdom, or at least devolving powers on to an Irish Parliament in such a way that a fully federal system might eventually result. During the crisis weeks of April 1918, at the time of the so-called 'German plot', Guest was actually in touch with Conservative Federalists like Amery to discuss this possibility. And when Austen Chamberlain re-entered the Government in mid-April he made his acceptance of office conditional on a promise to make any Irish settlement compatible with a later federal arrangement. But the Southern Unionists were split, the Ulster Loyalists suspicious, and Conservative opinion outside Parliament hostile to all such heterodoxies.[108] Once again Federalism had proved to be a will-o'-the-wisp, and the wider projects associated with it likewise foundered.

However, at the time none of this was so clear to the circle directly surrounding the Prime Minister as it seems in retrospect, and the rhetoric of 'national politics' continued to flourish. Thus in early March 1918 Riddell remarked that 'just now a National Party with national aims would be the most popular. The old-fashioned badges have ceased to have any meaning.' Lloyd George replied: 'Yes, I agree that would be a good title – "The National Party" to enforce a national policy.'[109] Moreover, on 16 March Guest actually wrote to the Conservative Chairman, Younger, advocating 'a completely new organisation, both in name and premises' and suggesting the names '"Government Coalition", "National", or "National Reform"'.[110]

106 Addison diary, 16 May 1918, *Four and A Half Years*, II, p. 528.
107 Addison diary, 17 May 1918, ibid.
108 Turner, *British Politics*, pp. 282–92. On Federalism, see also J.E. Kendle, 'Federalism and the Irish Problem in 1918', *History*, 56 (1971), 207–30.
109 'We overlooked that the title has already been appropriated by Page-Croft and Co.', Riddell added: 2 March 1918, *War Diary*, p. 317.
110 Turner, *British Politics*, p. 301.

But the Premier hesitated. On the one hand, he saw the attractions, of placing himself 'at the head of a definite Party and a definite organisation', as he put it in June, and he was confident that 'many of the younger members of the Conservative Party' favoured such an arrangement. On the other hand, he knew that such a step 'would bring about an absolute and definite split' in the Liberal ranks.[111]

Most members of the Coalition Liberal group felt an even deeper reluctance to make a decisive break with their old party friends. Some, like Edwin Montagu, still hankered after reunion. Even Guest did not want to go down to posterity as the man who had wrecked the historic Liberal Party: as late as August 1918 he was advising Lloyd George to 'pause before committing [himself] to any alliance with the Unionists, except for the purpose of the War'.[112]

Because of these reservations, even after Lloyd George's friends had become drawn into detailed negotiations with the Conservatives about the allocation of seats in preparation for the coming election, it was not clear which political groups would benefit most. Indeed, the Prime Minister sent an emissary to Asquith in late September with the offer of the Woolsack, ministerial offices for other Liberals whom Asquith would nominate, and assurances about policy. And Guest not only wanted this particular door to be kept open, but, in his negotiations, also assumed that some seats would be allocated to Labour.

In the end, events made Lloyd George's mind up for him. First, the German Army suddenly collapsed, with the result that the election that had been planned for war actually took place shortly after the signing of the Armistice. Secondly, Asquith turned down Lloyd George's offer, a fateful decision which virtually *forced* the Coalition Liberals to go into the election as the allies of the Conservative Party in opposition to their one-time Liberal colleagues. Thirdly, the Conservative leaders, who attached little importance to the support of the Coalition Liberals but were very anxious to capture Lloyd George, eventually agreed upon a deal with the Prime Minister which guaranteed their own organisational independence (way back

---

111 Riddell diary, 30 June 1918, McEwen, *Riddell Diaries*, p. 230.
112 But he thought that Lloyd George would return from an election 'with greatly enhanced authority to lead a Coalition Government' if he simply concentrated on the winning of the war. This would give him 'complete freedom, at a later date, to announce a Democratic Domestic Programme, which would be entirely [his] own' (Guest to Lloyd George, 3 Aug. 1918, in Barry McGill, 'Lloyd George's Timing of the 1918 Election', in *Journal of British Studies*, 14 (1974), 115–16).

,in March Bonar Law had privately ruled out the idea of 'a new joint party').[113] Bonar Law was thus able to tell his followers that they would be fighting the election 'as a Unionist Party forming a portion of a coalition'. In Ramsden's words, 'what was proposed was not the submersion of party in a wider unit, but a parliament of collaboration between independent groups'.[114]

Finally, at a specially convened Conference on 14 November, Labour voted by nearly three to one to withdraw from the Coalition, a decision which most, though not all, Labour Ministers obeyed. This was obviously a development of enormous significance since it meant that the post-war 'National Government' was one containing no genuine representatives of the organised working class. As the Independent Liberal, Pringle, later commented, the Prime Minister had retained 'the respectable figure of Mr Barnes with the transient phantoms of Messrs. Parker, Roberts and Wardle' but, as a result of losing all the other major Labour personalities, a situation had been created in which 'more than half of the electors who [took] any interest in politics [were] opposed to the government which claim[ed] to represent a united nation'.[115]

Garvin was one of the few critics of party who immediately recognised the seriousness of this predicament. The *Observer* had already regretted the exclusion of Asquith from the governing Coalition, and it now expressed even greater concern over the departure from the Government of a 'moderate' trade unionist like Clynes: 'Those who care for the future of the country must ask why' this had happened 'and whether there is no remedy', ran the editorial of 24 November.

Enthused by Lloyd George's earlier Manchester speech of 12 September, a high-water mark of Reconstruction idealism with its promises of social reconstruction aimed at the returning troops, Garvin urged the adoption of a 'national' policy that embraced far-reaching and radical changes. But he saw the corollary of this position: 'If the National Coalition is to be worthy of its name or equal for long to its tasks every effort must be made to broaden its basis.' Once the election was out of the way, he suggested, the Prime Minister should open talks with Labour as he had done in December 1916.[116] But of course, nothing of the kind was to happen.

113 Sanders diary, 24 March 1918, John Ramsden (ed.), *Real Old Tory Politics: The Political Diaries of Lord Bayford 1910–1935* (1984), p. 102.

114 Ramsden, *Age of Balfour and Baldwin*, pp. 139–40.

115 W.M.R. Pringle, 'Against a Permanent Coalition Party', *Review of Reviews*, 61 (Jan. 1920), 35.

116 *Observer*, 24 Nov. 1918.

The rest of the story can be briefly told. Coupons were duly distributed to supporters of the government: 364 went to Conservative candidates, 159 to Lloyd George Liberals, and eighteen to the National Democratic Party, the mouthpiece of 'patriotic Labour'. Lloyd George and Bonar Law agreed upon a joint manifesto strong on uplift if short on detail, which deferred contentious party issues like the tariff. But 'every section of the electorate, without distinction of party' was invited 'to support the Coalition Government in the execution of a policy devised in the interest of no particular class or section', and, as in Lloyd George's earlier Manchester speech, the two Leaders pulled every string in an attempt to perpetuate the wartime spirit of patriotic co-operation: 'Well and truly have rich and poor, castle and cottage, stood the ordeal of fire. Right earnestly do we trust that the united temper, the quiet fortitude, the high and resolute patriotism of our nation may be long preserved into the golden times of peace.'[117]

This struck the right note in the sense that during the actual election campaign it was generally assumed that 'national' co-operation would and should continue. On mainland Britain only the Labour Party, for the first time fielding enough candidates to be taken seriously as a possible party of government, broke free from this consensus.

Even the official Liberal Party, though understandably objecting to the Coupon, still offered support to the Government – it certainly did not operate as a normal Opposition. The Asquithian Herbert Samuel, for example, presented himself to his constituents as a slightly detached ally of Lloyd George's Coalition Government who wanted to support the Prime Minister in a continuation of 'the union of parties which happily prevailed during the war'.[118] In fact, the confusions enveloping the entire Asquithian campaign can be traced back to an earlier speech which Asquith himself made at Glasgow on 1 November, when he deprecated 'the artificial turmoil of a general election', but went on to say that, having personally advised the formation of the first Coalition Government, he did 'not intend in the least degree or for a moment' to apologise for Coalition, all the more so given the delicacy of the peace negotiations, in which it was 'all-important – as important as it

117 F.W.S. Craig, *British General Election Manifestos 1900–1974* (London and Basingstoke, 1970), pp. 28, 30.
118 Turner, *British Politics*, pp. 325–6.

has been at any stage in the prosecution of the war – that we should continue, until it is over, to preserve an unbroken national front'.[119]

As a Minister, Churchill could afford to make a more open avowal of the merits of Coalition. 'Why should peace have nothing but the squabbles and the selfishness and the pettiness of daily life?', he asked in an election speech of 26 November:

> Why if men and women, all classes, all parties, are able to work together for five years like a mighty machine to produce *destruction*, can they not work together for another five years to produce *abundance*? . . . But surely we have a common purpose? Surely this period of reconstruction may be looked upon as if it were a part of the war? . . . Five years of faction, of bickering, of class jealousies and Party froth, will not merely not give us prosperity, it will land us in utter and universal privation.[120]

These were indeed noble sentiments. It remained to be seen whether such patriotic idealism would long survive the onset of peacetime realities.

---

119 *The Times*, 2 Nov. 1918. Of course, these words were later quoted against Asquith when he came out as a fierce critic of the Lloyd George Coalition.
120 Martin Gilbert, *Winston S. Churchill, Vol. IV: 1916–1922* (1975), pp. 171–2.

CHAPTER SIX

The Post-War Coalition, 1918–1922

MOSLEY AND THE NEW MEMBERS GROUP

'There is a widespread universal desire to maintain and to extend in peace that sense of comradeship which has been won in war . . .':[1] so much had been said by the National Party in its opening manifesto, and it certainly encapsulated the mood of much of the country in 1918. Despite the bitterness felt by that section of the Liberal Party which had been the victims of the 'Coupon' arrangement, most people, outside the ranks of Labour supporters, seem to have endorsed the concept of a broad-based 'National Government' that could see the country through the perilous transition from war to peace.

Humdrum party politics anyhow seemed out of place in the atmosphere following the Armistice, when expectations ran high, with millions sustained by the hope that they were living on the threshold of a new and better age. The Labour Movement was not the only section of the community gripped by this sort of Utopianism. In 1918 there were also many people from middle- and upper-class families who, in their own different way, sincerely wanted radical changes in the social order, even though they felt cut off by class or conviction (or both) from the Labour Movement with its new socialist objective. This was what lay behind the appeal of 'Reconstruction', embodied in the person of Christopher Addison. To such 'idealists' the post-war Lloyd George Coalition therefore stood for collectivist social reform, organised by an expanded and modernised bureaucracy; but, more than that, it also promised a break from the sterility of

---

1 *Morning Post*, 30 Aug. 1917, cited in Lord Croft, *My Life of Strife* (n.d.), p. 132.

party strife. Thus, the Lloyd George Government, as K.O. Morgan has argued, can be seriously viewed as a *National* Government, 'the only plausible inter-party government of national unity that Britain has known, other than during times of war'.[2]

It was this latter aspect of the post-war Coalition which particularly appealed to the young – those young people, at least, who could not or would not attach themselves to Labour. One of the significant features of 1918 was the election to Parliament, as Lloyd George supporters, of a group of young officers, fresh from the trenches, hoping to articulate the wishes and needs of the returning soldiers. Not surprisingly, these new recruits to parliamentary life instinctively embraced the Coalition. After all, most of them had been mere schoolboys when the political battles of Edwardian Britain were being fought. It was the Great War which had brought them to political awareness and shaped their still somewhat undeveloped views. How could these new MPs be expected to show respectful attention to a politician like Asquith, who struck them as a quaint survivor from a vanished world? These young officers wanted action, but, while having total confidence in Lloyd George, 'the Little Man Who Had Won The War', they did not, initially at least, care much about *party*. One thinks of Captain Walter Elliot who, while still in uniform, received through the post an invitation to stand for Parliament in the 1918 Election. 'Yes', replied Elliot; 'which side?'[3] In the end it was on the Conservative ticket that Elliot became an MP, but party labels did not greatly matter to him at this stage of his career. In fact, Elliot was soon writing for the *Lloyd George Magazine*, and Oscar Guest (on whom, see below) even had him mistakenly classified as a Liberal![4]

Party certainly did not matter to the newly elected MP for Harrow, Oswald Mosley, an ex-officer who had only just passed his twenty-second birthday. Mosley had stood as a Conservative but he was really a 'national' supporter of Lloyd George and the self-proclaimed spokesman for the 'lost generation' which had gone through hell in France and Flanders.

Like other politicians of his generation, Mosley brought to politics from his experience of war a number of attitudes which he was never to lose. One was a sense of having been spared by Providence – in

2 Kenneth O. Morgan, *Consensus and Disunity: The Lloyd George Coalition Government 1918–1922* (Oxford, 1979), p. 1.

3 Colin Coote, *A Companion of Honour* (1965), p. 48, where the story is said to be 'apocryphal', but *ben trovato*.

4 See list in Guest to Lloyd George, 10 May 1919, *Lloyd George Papers*, F/21/3/21.

Mosley's case by the good fortune of having been mildly injured in a flying accident. This mishap probably saved him from the death which overtook so many of his friends and contemporaries, for the survival-chances of a young airman or junior army officer were very low. Gratitude at having been spared was coupled with a strong sense of obligation to those who had not been so lucky. To such men as Mosley, slogans like 'Homes Fit For Heroes' were not simply popular vote-catching phrases. Social progress, they believed, *must* take place, if only to demonstrate that the appalling sacrifices of the Great War had not been in vain. For the events of 1914–18 had awakened these men's social conscience and given them a sense of mission.

This leads on to a second point. From their experience of the trenches, from their participation in the society of the mess-room and the air squadron, politicians like Mosley brought a vision of life as it might be: purged of the horror of war but a world where, as in the trenches, there was a sense of shared purpose uniting people of widely different temperaments and backgrounds: where men were held together by discipline and fraternity and a sense of collective endeavour which overrode all thoughts of personal comfort and self-interest. Needless to say, this was *not* the prevailing ethos of Westminster, with its party squabbles, class animosities and petty personal ambitions.

The third characteristic marking out these young politicians was indeed their youth: their self-identity as representatives of the war generation, and their barely concealed hostility towards middle-aged and elderly civilian politicians who had so unfeelingly despatched young men in their hundreds of thousands to a pointless death – feelings common among young officers, as First World War poetry testifies. So in Mosley's case contempt for the middle-aged and elderly and contempt for party combined in a distaste for 'the Old Gangs', the senior party politicians of all persuasions who had botched the war and now seemed about to botch the peace. Significantly, however, Lloyd George himself was still exempted from the indictment, and, to start with, the post-war Coalition experiment could even be seen as a valiant attempt to break the power of these 'Old Gangs' and all that they represented. Lloyd George was well aware of such considerations, and in the difficult months that lay ahead he was to be buoyed up by the thought that the younger Conservatives supported him and the 'new' politics which he was trying to pioneer.[5]

5 Riddell diary, 7 Sept. 1919, J.M. McEwen (ed.), *The Riddell Diaries, 1908–1923* (1986), p. 290; 1 Feb. 1920, ibid., p. 304.

Shortly after arriving at Westminster, Mosley and Elliot formed what became known as the 'New Members Group'. This was an informal association of about a hundred Coalition Liberal and Conservative MPs, parliamentary novices who lacked strong party loyalties and would have liked the Coalition to become a permanency, buttressed perhaps by some sort of 'Centre Party' fusing Liberalism and Conservatism. Under the chairmanship of Oscar Montague Guest, Freddie Guest's brother, this 'Group', in conjunction with the National Democratic Party (a splinter right-wing Labour organisation) provided the hard-core supporters for 'fusion': a cause which even had its own magazine, *Popular View*, jointly produced by Conservatives and Coalition Liberals.[6] The 'movement was initiated by New Members', Freddie Guest explained to the Premier, 'as it was felt that they were not restricted by past political associations and preconceptions or prejudiced by the memories of past controversies, and therefore were in a better position than old Members to promote a clearer and more effective understanding between the various component elements of the present coalition'.[7]

THE CASE FOR 'FUSION'

But the 'New Members Group' would have been of little significance had not so many senior Ministers from both main Coalition parties had similar aspirations. As it was, Freddie Guest provided the Group with quiet encouragement and kept his 'Chief' informed of its doings, while even Younger, the Conservative Party Chairman, was initially not unfriendly.[8] Nor was Guest alone in his sympathies, since scarcely had the 'Coupon' Election been concluded than a group of ardent 'fusionists' emerged from within the government, many of them old proponents of 'national politics' like Addison, Churchill and Birkenhead (the former F.E. Smith). (Incidentally,

6 Though it was abandoned in September 1921. See Younger to R. Sanders, 23 Sept. 1921, in John Ramsden (ed.), *Real Old Tory Politics: The Political Diaries of Robert Sanders, Lord Bayford 1910–1935* (1984), p. 160. In these early years the dominant figure was Elliot rather than Mosley.

7 F.E. Guest to Lloyd George, 10 May 1919, *Lloyd George Papers*, F/21/3/21. The New Members later toned down their demands. See Oscar Guest to Lloyd George (n.d.) in ibid., F/95/1/38.

8 F.E. Guest to Lloyd George, 10 May 1919, ibid., F/21/3/21.

both Churchill and Birkenhead went to the trouble of addressing the New Members Group, as did two other Ministers, Auckland Geddes and Worthington-Evans.)[9]

Of course, the 'fusion' project depended crucially upon the enormous popularity of Lloyd George. Garvin had hailed him during the 1918 Election as 'the greatest fighting leader that this country has known since Chatham'.[10] In the period following the Armistice none of the other party leaders came anywhere close to rivalling him. Yet, though dominating the political scene, Lloyd George lacked a secure base, as did his 132 fellow Coalition Liberal MPs. One former sympathiser privately called him 'a great Liberal in an impasse' and likened him to Richard Coeur-de-Lion, captured on his return from a Crusade.[11]

Essentially Lloyd George was faced with a choice between three strategies: he could continue to lead the Coalition on an *ad hoc* basis; or, once he had secured a viable international settlement, he could return to the Liberal fold; or, finally, he could try and perpetuate his own premiership by attaching to himself his 'moderate' Conservative admirers. The third of these strategies had an obvious attraction: having split his own party, his personal long-term survival perhaps depended on his engineering a split within the *Conservative* ranks as well.

But the interesting thing is that in the spring of 1920 many Conservative politicians, both Ministers and backbenchers, had their own reasons for thinking 'fusion' to be a desirable objective. In particular, the idea came to exercise a strong fascination over senior Conservative Ministers such as Austen Chamberlain, Balfour and Robert Horne.

Indeed, those who favoured 'fusion' could mount a formidable case. In the circumstances of 1918 and 1919 it was difficult to see what the traditional political parties stood for. The Tariff issue was in abeyance; and though the Irish problem was still very much alive, its character had changed so dramatically since 1914 that the old party positions on the subject no longer seemed relevant; finally, former bones of contention between the parties like Welsh Disestablishment were on the point of settlement on a bipartisan basis.

Lloyd George told a doubtful C.P. Scott in late 1919 that 'any government at present must be a Coalition, since the alternative to

9 F.E. Guest to Lloyd George, 8 July 1919, ibid., F/21/4/1. Guest hoped that later in the Session Bonar Law and the Prime Minister would also attend.

10 *Observer*, 17 Nov. 1918.

11 Harry Barnes to F.E. Guest, 21 Nov. 1919, *Lloyd George Papers*, F/21/4/6.

the present Coalition was a Labour and "Asquithian" Coalition'.[12] In 1920 and 1921 even critics of the Coalition like Lord Robert Cecil were plotting to replace it with a more morally elevated kind of 'centre combination', not thinking of a return to traditional party strife.[13] It is significant that Asquith ran into difficulties when he later tried to attack the *principle* of Coalition, given his own responsibility for originating the Coalition Ministry in May 1915. 'If Coalition is a sin against Liberalism', mocked Lloyd George, 'Mr Asquith is a Jehoshaphat.'[14]

As C.F.G. Masterman put it, it was widely believed that 'the old parties, with all their ancient loyalties' had 'fulfilled their purpose in their generation' but were out of place in the 'changed world' of post-war Britain.[15] Birkenhead certainly took this view: 'For twenty or perhaps for fifty years our statesmen must busy themselves with entirely new problems, and the new electors will wave impatiently aside, as if they belonged to the Victorian age, those who try to marshal the dying forces of extinct controversies.'[16]

These arguments for Coalition were buttressed by emotional invocation of the camaraderie generated during the War, coupled with warnings about the dangers of returning to the rancorous partisanship of the past. Both points were made with great eloquence by Churchill when he addressed the New Members Group at the Criterion Restaurant in July 1919: 'Why are we to plunge into faction and set our batteries firing at each other with poison-gas shells?', he asked. After revealing (for the first time publicly) the existence of the 1910 Secret Coalition talks, he described how Britain subsequently 'slid headlong into the most bitter, dangerous political period' of modern times, a period when the country had trembled on 'the very verge of civil war' before being 'rescued by Armageddon!'.

12 Scott diary, 30 Nov.–1 Dec. 1919, in Trevor Wilson (ed.), *The Political Diaries of C.P. Scott 1911–1928* (1970), p. 379.

13 For the 'Grey Conspiracy', see Michael Bentley, 'Liberal Politics and the Grey Conspiracy of 1921', *Historical Journal*, 20 (1977), 461–78. The point was also made by the Attorney-General, Gordon Hewart: *Sunday Times*, 7 Aug. 1921.

14 Lloyd George to Welsh Liberal Federation at Llandudno, *The Times*, 9 Oct. 1920.

15 C.F.G. Masterman, 'The New Democratic Party', *Contemporary Review*, 117 (Feb. 1920), 153.

16 Article in *Weekly Dispatch*, 25 Jan. 1920, cited in Viscount Birkenhead, *Points of View* (1922), II, p. 199. At about the same time Elliot was writing: 'The galvanic twitching of the respective party corpses elicited by the *Manchester Guardian* and the *Morning Post* have now but a pathological significance' (Captain Walter E. Elliot MP, 'For a Permanent Coalition Party', *Review of Reviews*, 61 (Jan. 1920), 32).

'The great war, with all its horrors, at any rate rescued us from the disasters of that epoch', concluded Churchill. 'We must not get back to it again.'[17] Walter Elliot, too, claimed that 'the first seed of the Coalition Party was sowed' in 1910, and said that it was 'the greatest tragedy of the century so far that [the talks in that year] failed . . . to come to fruition'.[18]

Some proponents of Coalition clothed their ideals in a utopian religious language. The 'Old Dispensation', wrote the Coalition Conservative MP Ernest Wild, was about to be replaced by the 'New Commandment'. As a result of 'the Great Awakening', all classes and sects had learned that they were 'members one of another'. This meant that 'if either wing revert[ed] to pre-war methods, to pre-war trivialities', it would 'be sinning against the light', and committing what the Psalmist called 'the presumptuous sin'. Wild called upon the citizenry to 'sink' their own 'partisan differences' as a mark of respect for the much greater sacrifices that had been made by the war-dead.[19] More common was O.F. MacLagan's claim that Coalition was 'the natural corollary to the League of Nations' and an embodiment of the true principles of Christianity: 'it is almost, I think, an essential of religion, whether it be Christian, Jewish or any other, because it is the working out in a practical fashion of charity towards one's neighbour'.[20]

Guest's successor as Coalition Liberal Whip, Charles McCurdy, put forward a similar argument, according to which coalition government involved 'co-operation' and, as such, was recommended by both Christianity and common sense. But he linked this to an abusive attack on the 'caucus', 'a machine which live[d] upon artificially nurtured hatred and distrust'. Himself a Liberal, McCurdy portrayed the current Coalition Ministry as the direct heir to the great Victorian reform movements which, long before the 'caucus' had been invented, had triumphantly carried 'the great Reform Act, the emancipation of religion, the emancipation of the slave, and the repeal of the Corn Laws'. 'English Radicalism has always stood for something nobler than mere automatic loyalty to party dogmas', argued McCurdy. 'It

17 Speech at Criterion Restaurant, 15 July 1919, Robert Rhodes James (ed.), *Churchill Speaks* (1981), pp. 380–1.

18 Elliot, 'Permanent Coalition Party', 31.

19 Ernest E. Wild, 'The Coalition', *Nineteenth Century*, 87 (March 1920), 397–408.

20 O.F. MacLagan, *Coalition Government: A League of Parties as an efficient Method of Government* (1922?), pp. 6, 12. This seems to align him more with Lord Robert Cecil than with members of the Coalition Government itself.

is, then, a singular misrepresentation to say that there is something inconsistent with Radical traditions in that political co-operation of which a Coalition Government is the expression.' In McCurdy's view, what Lloyd George was therefore doing was rescuing Liberalism from 'the soulless machine that was made in Birmingham in 1867' and returning it to its true roots.[21]

This line of argument, though interesting, can only have had minority appeal. Proponents of coalition usually employed arguments of a more mundane kind. They drew attention, for example, to the unprecedented crisis facing the British Government at home and abroad after 1918, a crisis with which only experienced statesmen from major parties could cope. 'We really cannot afford such indulgences' as a return to party strife, declared Churchill. 'The times are too solemn, the margin is too small, our risks are too high, our hopes are too bright for us to involve ourselves in strife for mere sport': 'to indulge in faction for the sake of faction would, indeed, be a criminal enterprise'.[22] In a speech to the Commons, Lloyd George made an additional point: Ministers, he suggested, now had no *time* to spare for party organisation, given the immensity of their tasks.[23]

Of the pressing dangers confronting the nation, the greatest seemed to be the challenge of 'Bolshevism' at home and abroad. The 'Bolshevik' threat clearly played a major part in the thinking of Winston Churchill who, as War Secretary, was organising military intervention against Lenin's regime. 'National unity does not mean national unanimity', he declared at Sunderland on 3 January 1920, but then went on to attack 'thin-blooded defeatists', with their cosmopolitan views and 'their naggings and carpings'; let us resist 'the subversive and morbid doctrines of Bolshevism and Communism', he urged.[24]

This approach also had implications for domestic affairs, since it implied the existence of an 'enemy within' as well as an external threat to essential British interests. Such fears lay at the heart of the commitment to the Coalition of Birkenhead, who, as his biographer notes, had abandoned, in the face of the socialist threat, his old Bismarckian Toryism in favour of a more liberal *laissez-faire* set of

21 C.A. McCurdy, 'Coalition, Caucus, and Common Sense', *Fortnightly Review*, 109 (March 1921), 353–61; *Lloyd George Liberal Magazine*, Aug. 1921, 667–8. But no reference was made to Chamberlain, the 'caucus' being described as the invention of Schnadhorst, who sounded suitably foreign!

22 Speech at Criterion Restaurant, 15 July 1919, James (ed.), *Churchill Speaks*, pp. 380–2.

23 Hansard, 5th ser., vol. 125, 35–6: 10 Feb. 1920.

24 James (ed.), *Churchill Speaks*, pp. 384–8.

policies.[25] (Note how far this concept of Coalition diverged from that of Addison, with his ambitions for Reconstruction.)

In a major speech at Manchester on 6 December 1919 the Prime Minister did, it is true, concede that there were many moderate men in the Labour Party, but he went on to warn of the existence of 'Syndicalists', 'Direct Actionists', 'Sovietists' and 'Bolshevists' to reinforce his message that 'National unity alone can save Britain, can save Europe, can save the world'.[26] In his heart of hearts Lloyd George did not perhaps take his own rhetoric entirely seriously. But he publicly played up the 'Bolshevik threat' in order to present himself as the saviour of the nation, the one man who could uphold the constitution from the forces of subversion.[27] Nor is it coincidental that the moves towards coalition in early 1920 should have occurred at just the moment when the Cabinet was most fearful of revolutionary disturbances precipitating a breakdown of law and order in Britain.[28]

In any case, even the mainstream Labour Party, with its new commitment to socialism enshrined in Clause 4 of its Constitution, was bound to strike fear into the hearts of many opponents. The post-war Labour Party appeared to be a 'class party', and stopping it at almost any price became for many politicians a national imperative. This, in turn, furnished arguments for the perpetuation of the Coalition, since Churchill believed its break-up could only result in pushing the Labour Party into power at a period in development when it was quite unfitted for the responsibility of government.[29]

These possibilities seemed very real in the wake of Labour's spectacular advances in the 1919 municipal elections and its success in the Spen Valley by-election the following month. Already, particularly at the level of local politics, anti-Labour pacts were being formed, notably in Clydeside, Liverpool, Bristol and Birmingham. In Liverpool, one of the centres of Coalitionist enthusiasm, Max

25 John Campbell, *F.E. Smith: First Earl of Birkenhead* (1983), pp. 536–7.

26 Cited in Morgan, *Consensus and Disunity*, p. 180; Bentley B. Gilbert, *British Social Policy, 1914–1939* (1970), p. 40.

27 See Michael Bentley, *The Liberal Mind, 1914–1929* (Cambridge, 1977), pp. 134–5. Lloyd George's anxieties about Labour are taken far more seriously in Chris Wrigley, *Lloyd George and the Challenge of Labour: The Post-War Coalition 1918–1922* (Hemel Hempstead, 1990).

28 See Hankey to Thomas Jones, 17 Jan. 1920, in Keith Middlemas (ed.), *Thomas Jones, Whitehall Diary* (Oxford, 1969), I, p. 97.

29 See his speech of 4 March 1922, James (ed.), *Churchill Speaks*, pp. 411–12.

Muspratt, the Liberal chemicals manufacturer, wanted to go further and advocated the formation of 'a new party combining all the constitutional forces', although he thought it would be 'a mistake to rush it'.[30]

Liverpool was a city in which the Conservatives had traditionally been very strong. Where the dominant party before 1914 had been the Liberal Party, or even the Liberal Unionist Party, anti-Labour pacts made still better sense. Austen Chamberlain felt, with some justification, that the MPs and constituency activists who wanted a return to 'independence' tended to come from London and the Home Counties and were thus not representative of Conservative opinion in the great industrial centres, where local leaders were urging him 'to remain united. They realise that disintegration means Labour victories'.[31]

Moreover, it is important to remember that the Conservative Party had not won a straight electoral victory since 1900, so it is hardly surprising that, in the dangerous new situation, its leaders lacked confidence in their ability, unaided, to make a successful appeal to voters. It was felt that Conservatives stood in sore need of Lloyd George's personal popularity as well as of assistance from their Coalition Liberal allies. Birkenhead, for example, denied that there was 'the slightest chance of an independent Unionist Government obtaining an adequate working majority'.[32] And Austen Chamberlain made what in retrospect looks like a succession of reckless predictions along the same lines.[33]

But many felt that the Coalition's existence would not be enough, by itself, to keep Labour at bay. So long as Conservatives and Coalition Liberals maintained their separate organisations, there would inevitably be quarrels over who should have the succession to a parliamentary seat when it fell vacant. Conservative Central Office also disliked having to stand down for their Coalition partners in constituencies where this threatened to let Labour in. To some Conservatives such difficulties constituted a good argument for bringing the Coalition to a speedy end.

But others drew the opposite conclusion, namely, that the Coalition

30 Riddell diary, 15 Feb. 1920, *Intimate Diary of the Peace Conference and After, 1918–1923* (1933), p. 170.

31 Riddell diary, 23 March 1922, ibid., p. 367.

32 Campbell, *Smith*, p. 591.

33 Chamberlain to Fraser, 6 Oct. 1922, in David Dutton, *Austen Chamberlain: Gentleman in Politics* (Bolton, 1985), p. 193.

parties needed to *fuse*. This was particularly the view of Birkenhead, who fretted at the inability of Lloyd George's Government to hit back effectively at its Labour opponents. Far from subscribing to a wishy-washy consensual view of politics, Birkenhead, as ever, took a combative approach. In an article in the *Weekly Dispatch* in January 1920 he proclaimed the need for a 'National Party' that was 'organised and disciplined', saying that for parties, as for armies, this was what made for success. He also insisted that 'every Government, Coalition or not', had constantly to compromise: 'but where a unified Government compromises, little or no adverse comment follows. When a Coalition compromises it is accused of bad faith'.[34]

The proponents of 'fusion' could also employ more positive arguments. Addison and his friends, for example, still clung to the old wartime idealism about Reconstruction. In their eyes, welfare reforms were intrinsically worth pursuing, but a Coalition had the advantage that it might protect their progressive advocates against *Conservative* obstruction. In fact, some Conservative Ministers, primarily motivated by anti-socialism, were prepared to go along with Reconstruction because they saw this as a moderate programme that would drive a wedge between 'sane' Labour and the revolutionary elements.

Lloyd George brought together all these different arguments in his appeals for 'fair play'. Starting off from a belief in the identity of interests between Capital and Labour, the Premier vowed to fight for a 'national' policy which would avoid the extremes of Revolution and Reaction. 'I shall not be for the "haves" or the "have-nots"', he told Riddell. 'My policy is to endeavour to hold an even balance between the two. I intend to advocate reforms which will remove gross inequalities and grave abuses. On the other hand, I am convinced that the world cannot be carried on without the aid of the skilled managerial class', the 'leaders and captains of industry' upon whom industrial progress ultimately depended. Yet, said the Prime Minister, one had to ensure that the capitalists did not 'get too much' and did not 'grind the other classes under their heel'.[35] Thus, to Lloyd George, the national interest involved striking a *balance* between different classes.

34 *Weekly Dispatch*, 11 Jan. 1920; Campbell, *Smith*, pp. 530–2; Birkenhead, *Points of View*, II, pp. 196–7.

35 Riddell, 20 Sept. 1919, *Intimate Diary*, p. 128. For a public statement of the same argument, see Lloyd George's speech at the inaugural dinner of the 1920 Club, *Daily Chronicle*, 18 March 1921, cited in *Lloyd George Liberal Magazine*, April 1921, 429.

THE QUEST FOR A CENTRE PARTY, 1919–20

So much for the arguments in favour of 'fusion'; what progress was made towards their implementation? No sooner had the 'Coupon Election' ended than some Ministers' minds turned to the possibility of a major political realignment. 'A Central party probable', noted Fisher in his diary in February.[36] But the plotting began in earnest in the summer after the Prime Minister had returned from Versailles. In mid-July Churchill visited Lloyd George at his Criccieth home, where the issue was discussed,[37] following which Churchill was entertained at the Criterion Restaurant by the New Members Group, to whom he gave his speech alluding to the lost opportunity for a national settlement in 1910.[38] The press, which had received a partial account of the meeting, became very excited: the *Daily Mail* declared that 'a political sensation of the first importance' had been created by 'the attempted inauguration of a new political party' which aimed to embrace 'the moderate men of both' parties. 'The formation of a new Centre Party . . . in place of the existing Coalition', it said, was now regarded by those involved 'as a certainty in the very near future'.[39]

The Prime Minister then probably lost interest in the idea, as his attention became absorbed by the railway strike at home and European problems abroad. But at the end of 1919, entertaining a sceptical Scott, he again 'sang the praises of Coalitions'.[40] And as the New Year dawned, it was widely felt that unless speedy steps were taken to bring the two main Coalition parties closer together, circumstances would before long drive them further apart.

Motives varied from one person to another. The Prime Minister had become worried over Asquith's imminent return to Parliament. His mistress noted in her diary: 'D. very busy on the political situation. Asquith is standing for Paisley, & if he gets in, it will be a great blow to the Coalition.' She added that though the Prime

---

36 Fisher diary, 21 Feb. 1919, in Bentley, *Liberal Mind*, p. 133.

37 Wrigley, *Lloyd George and Labour*, pp. 201–2.

38 Masterman thought this speech had weakened the cause, 'with its obvious indifference to political principle, with its unfortunate allusions to the attempt at a Coalition in 1910, concerning which all involved had hitherto kept silent': Masterman, 'New Democratic Party', p. 155.

39 *Daily Mail*, 16 July 1919. The *Evening Standard* (16 July 1919) welcomed such a development as a protection against 'sectionalism, class war, direct action, and an economic profligacy which could only be the ruin of any nation which adopted it'.

40 Scott diary, 30 Nov.–1 Dec. 1919, Wilson (ed.), *C.P. Scott*, p. 379.

Minister could not 'quite see his way', she understood that some of his friends wanted him 'to come out & lead a party of his own'.[41]

However, a few weeks earlier, at a secret meeting at Birkenhead's house attended by Coalition Liberals and senior Conservatives (including Bonar Law), the talk was rather of 'fusion in order to strengthen resistance to Labour', with Lloyd George suggesting a programme that might last five or ten years. Nearly all thought it advisable to move 'in the course of the next few months'.[42] Birkenhead then floated the idea of a 'National Party' in the first of his well-publicised letters to the *Weekly Dispatch* on 11 January.[43]

The next few weeks saw a flurry of activity: Fisher was asked to draft the Liberal section of the programme of the new party, Horne and Birkenhead the Unionist part, and discussion even extended to the name of the new merged organisation – 'United Reform Party' was Lloyd George's own choice.[44] By late February Macnamara had put together the new Centre Party manifesto.[45] This would have relieved Freddie Guest, who had concluded from Asquith's victory at Paisley earlier in the month that 'the Coalition must either fuse or disintegrate' and now favoured 'an early definite statement of the policy of the "New" Party'.[46] Some patchy evidence exists to suggest that such a denouement would indeed have had significant electoral appeal.[47]

However, the crucial decision rested in the hands of the Conservative leadership. Writing to Balfour on 5 October 1919 Bonar Law predicted that Lloyd George was likely to follow Chamberlain's example, which he felt would 'not be a bad thing for our Party and a good thing for the Nation' since he shared the quite widespread

41 Frances Stevenson diary, 23 Jan. 1920, A.J.P. Taylor (ed.), *Lloyd George: A Diary by Frances Stevenson* (1971), p. 199. This diary entry has led one historian to the conclusion that 'at this time Lloyd George's prime concern was not with the rise of the Labour Party but to realign policies on Centre versus Labour lines before the Asquithian Liberals revived' (Wrigley, *Lloyd George and Labour*, p. 243).

42 Sanders diary, 8 Jan. 1920, Ramsden (ed.), *Real Old Tory Politics*, p. 134.

43 Not all reactions were favourable. Birkenhead's reference to the existing Coalition being 'invertebrate', thought one well-placed observer (Dalziel), had 'depreciated our stock for the moment by 20%' (F. Guest to Lloyd George, 16 January 1920, *Lloyd George Papers*, F/22/1/4).

44 Morgan, *Consensus and Disunity*, p. 180.

45 Bentley, *Liberal Mind*, p. 136.

46 Guest to Lloyd George, 25 Feb. 1920, *Lloyd George Papers*, F/22/1/13.

47 See material in ibid., especially Lewis J. Grant's Report on the North of England, 24 Sept. 1919 (F/21/4/6); Croydon Marks to F. Guest, 21 Jan. 1920 (F/22/1/4); A. Moreing to F. Guest, 31 March 1920 (F/22/1/25).

conviction that the Conservative Party 'on the old lines [would] never have any future again in this country'.[48] The Conservative Leader then began to take steps to prepare his followers for the new departure; addressing Conservative Party workers shortly afterwards, he spoke about the creation of 'a permanently fused party'.[49]

By January 1920 Bonar Law showed signs of retreating: both Sanders and Frances Stevenson thought his attitude towards 'fusion' was now 'hesitant'.[50] But Lloyd George remained confident: '"I think I am forming my party, Pussy"', he told his mistress in mid–February.[51] Finally, on 10 March, after the sympathetic Balfour had put pressure upon him, the Conservative Leader grudgingly gave his consent to further steps being taken.[52] The plan was now speedily finalised: Lloyd George, it was agreed, would secure the support of the Liberal Coalition Ministers on the 16 March and then explain his plans to the Liberal MPs two days later, after which Bonar Law would put the scheme before his own party.

Meanwhile the press, already excited by Birkenhead's overtures at the start of the year, had been well prepared for dramatic political changes. In February Masterman produced an obviously inspired article for the *Contemporary Review*, and Beaverbrook, approached by Lloyd George, 'half promised his support'.[53] Moreover, needless to say, Garvin (who had been on bad terms with the Premier earlier in the year)[54] had been recruited to the side of the 'fusionists'. 'It has happened', shrieked the *Observer* on 14 March: 'As regards main matters, the thing is done . . . . There has been nothing like it since Mr Chamberlain separated from Mr Gladstone.' Garvin's jubilation was premature.

Oddly enough, it was the Coalition Liberals, who apparently had most to gain from 'fusion', who eventually sabotaged the entire venture. From the start there had been Liberal Ministers who had had their doubts about the propriety of making a decisive break with

48 Bonar Law to Balfour, 5 Oct. 1919, in Morgan, *Consensus and Disunity*, p. 31.

49 *The Times*, 15 Oct. 1919.

50 Sanders diary, 8 Jan. 1920, Ramsden (ed.), *Real Old Tory Politics*, p. 134; Frances Stevenson diary, 23 Jan. 1920, in Taylor (ed.), *Frances Stevenson*, p. 199.

51 Stevenson diary, 11 Feb. 1920, Taylor (ed.), *Frances Stevenson*, p. 200.

52 John Ramsden, *The Age of Balfour and Baldwin 1902–1940* (1978), p. 143.

53 However, Lloyd George was not sure that he could trust Beaverbrook: Riddell diary, 15 Feb. 1920, in McEwen, *Riddell Diaries*, p. 306.

54 The *Observer* had suggested that the creation of a 'National Party' might mean Lloyd George had to leave office for a time!

their Asquithian colleagues. Guest seems by now to have accepted the inevitability of 'fusion', albeit without enthusiasm.[55] But only Addison and Churchill, for very different reasons, showed consistent enthusiasm for the idea.[56]

And so the situation was quite finely balanced when Lloyd George addressed his Liberal Ministers on 16 March. But the Prime Minister, whose stance towards the Labour movement had been hardening over previous months, struck the wrong note in presenting 'fusion' in largely negative terms. 'It was incumbent on Liberals to fight the Labour Party', Lloyd George declared. He asked his Coalie Liberal audience to 'face facts' by acknowledging the impossibility of creating a purely Liberal Administration.

Few supported him, bar Addison and Churchill, the latter calling in a 'vigorous speech' for 'a definite stand against the Labour Party on the lines of his recent speeches in the country' (though the following day he denied having used these words). But Fisher argued that it would be better to go for *temporary working arrangements* with the Conservatives – for example, by setting up a common fund for propaganda purposes. The Scottish Ministers were even more hostile: they pointed out that many of their local parties were divided in their sympathies, others sided with Asquith and none of them wanted to discard the name of 'Liberal'.

In reply, Lloyd George agreed that 'fusion' 'was a bad word, and announced that he never intended to use it'. He now spoke of a closer association with the Conservatives, and ended up by suggesting the creation of a 'National Democratic' or 'National Reform' Party to which the existing Coalition Liberal and Unionist associations could *affiliate*. Well might *The Times* conclude that 'the new party had had a serious setback'.[57] To make matters worse, someone present (Lloyd George suspected Macpherson, the Irish Chief Secretary) then leaked what had happened to the press, despite the fact that all had been enjoined to secrecy.[58]

---

55 See Guest to Lloyd George, 12 July 1919, *Lloyd George Papers*, F/21/4/3. Should the Coalition fail, he urged the Premier to consolidate 'under his Leadership a new Centre Party which would be made up of the bulk of the Liberal Party, together with the progressive wing of the Unionist Party and the moderate sections of Labour' (Bentley, *Liberal Mind*, p. 133).

56 See Riddell diary, 15 Feb. 1920, McEwen, *Riddell Diaries*, pp. 305–6.

57 *The Times*, 17 March 1920.

58 See Lloyd George's furious letter to the Liberal Ministers of 23 March, asking them whether they were responsible for the leak (*Lloyd George Papers*, F/22/1/17).

Not surprisingly, the Prime Minister, as Frances Stevenson notes in her diary, was tense and highly excited when he met the Coalition Liberal MPs two days later. By now it was obvious that the local Liberal activists were divided on the matter. In many northern constituencies the feeling was running strongly for Asquith and reunion – a sentiment checked only by respect for their sitting Coalie Liberal MP. Recognising that this was so, Lloyd George now took care to stress 'unity' rather than 'fusion'. The time 'was not yet ripe for fusion', he had earlier told Frances, and there was 'still some work to be done before that was tackled'.[59]

Bonar Law, speaking later at Worthing, followed Lloyd George's lead. He stoutly defended the Coalition, but, arguing that what needed to be abandoned was not party 'principle' but 'prejudice', he went on to call for nothing more than a better co-ordination between Conservatives and Coalition Liberals at constituency level, specifically denying that this 'meant sinking the old party organizations on either side'.[60]

Despite everything, *The Times* still thought that the plan for a new party had merely been postponed, not destroyed, since it thought that 'the men who count in the Coalition [would] not be happy till they get it'.[61] But 'fusion' had clearly run into a formidable obstacle. At both meetings Lloyd George's attacks on Labour had simply had the effect of goading many members of his audience into re-emphasising their own Liberalism.[62] True, some of the businessmen must have found Lloyd George's crude anti-Bolshevism attractive, but the majority view within the party was that 'revolution should be forestalled by a rapid programme of industrial and economic reforms'.[63] Ironically, in view of his own later behaviour, Sir John Simon publicly rebuked Lloyd George for setting the 'haves' against the 'have-nots',[64] a line of attack also pursued by *The Times*.[65] Garvin, in his editorial of 21 March, therefore missed the point completely

59 Frances Stevenson diary, 18 March 1920, Taylor (ed.), *Frances Stevenson*, p. 206).

60 *The Times*, 20 March 1920.

61 Ibid., 19 March 1920.

62 Morgan, *Consensus and Disunity*, pp. 185–6; Trevor Wilson, *The Downfall of the Liberal Party 1914–1935* (1966), p. 195.

63 *The Times*, 17 March 1920.

64 Ibid., 22 March 1920.

65 Ibid., 19 March 1920. An editorial accused the Prime Minister of waging a class war. The people, it thought, simply wanted 'honest government', and most Labour members were anyhow patriotic.

when he wrote of the Rubicon having been crossed. On the contrary, though this was not quite so obvious at the time, the decisive moment for fusion had passed, never to return.

The outcome was to extricate Bonar Law from a very difficult dilemma. On the morning of the 16 March Lloyd George had come away from a meeting with the Conservative Leader 'very bad-tempered', saying 'Bonar is funking it now.'[66] The outcome of the Coalition Liberal meeting thus clearly took a weight off Bonar Law's mind. Writing to Balfour on 24 March, he confessed that he was 'not sorry at the turn events [had] taken' since although he had come to think 'fusion' inevitable if the Coalition were to continue, it was something he would prefer to avoid. That Bonar Law was still thinking primarily in party terms is further shown by his concluding reflection: fusion, he opined, had 'always seemed to me more important from L.G.'s point of view than from ours'.[67]

As Ramsden notes, Bonar Law's position on fusion was indeed 'enigmatic, for he promoted fusion and yet was glad to see it fail. He was never an ideological coalitionist and never fell under Lloyd George's spell, for all their good personal relations.' Had his colleagues backed fusion in 1920, the Conservative Leader would have done so too, but although a majority of Conservative MPs, given a strong steer from the Front Bench, might then have fallen into line, there would almost certainly have been a party crisis, with the danger of a split in the wider organisation.[68]

COALITION POLITICS: THE FINAL PHASE, 1921–22

Yet there was to be a further ironic development in the story of 'fusion'. In June 1921 Bonar Law's poor health forced him into retirement, to be succeeded by Austen Chamberlain.[69] In his acceptance speech the new Leader made no secret of his continued

---

66 Frances Stevenson diary, 16 March 1920, Taylor (ed.), *Frances Stevenson*, p. 205.

67 Ramsden, *Age of Balfour and Baldwin*, p. 143.

68 Ibid., pp. 143–4.

69 Three Conservative MPs, G. Hamilton, Norton-Griffiths and Grattan-Doyle, actually suggested that the Leadership should pass to Lloyd George, as the prelude to the creation of a National Party! (Maurice Cowling, *The Impact of Labour 1920–1924* (Cambridge, 1971), p. 118).

commitment to closer alliance with his Coalition partners. As he told his audience:

> There are moments when the insistence upon party is as unforgiveable as insistence upon personal things, when the difficulties which the nation has to confront call for a wider outlook and a broader union than can be found even within the limits of a single party and when the traditions of more than one party, the ideas of more than one party need to be put into the common stock.[70]

Did his devotion to his father's memory perhaps play some part in this anxiety to work more closely with his Coalition Liberal colleagues?

Be that as it may, a further possible opening came the way of the 'coalitionists' later in 1921 when, once again, a 'national' settlement of the Irish Question seemed to offer the prospect of a major party realignment. Significantly, the team which had negotiated the Irish Treaty in December included, among others, Lloyd George, Chamberlain, Birkenhead and Churchill; indeed, the last two may well have been involved in the British Government team with a view to renewing the quest for 'fusion'. Certainly Lloyd George, Birkenhead and Chamberlain all made fusionist speeches at about this time.

But the attempt to perpetuate the Coalition by rushing the country into a premature general election was foiled by a press leak, followed by the publication of Younger's hostile party circular. In fact, Chamberlain himself had never wanted a quick dissolution at all, because he would have preferred to consolidate the Coalition into a single party *before* going to the country.[71] All the same, as he wrote in his Memorandum of 6 January, he still wanted 'to lead the Unionist party to accept merger in a new Party under the leadership of the present Prime Minister and including the great bulk of the old Unionists and old Liberals so as to secure the widest and closest possible union of all men and women of constitutional and progressive views'.[72] Perhaps, unlike Churchill and Balfour, Chamberlain did not favour *immediate* 'fusion',[73] but neither did he have any sympathy with those within his own party who were clamouring for 'independence'.

---

70 Dutton, *Chamberlain*, p. 164.

71 Ibid., p. 172.

72 Ibid., p. 175.

73 Michael Kinnear, *The Fall of Lloyd George: The Political Crisis of 1922* (1973), p. 108.

Another striking political development in early 1922 was the wholehearted conversion of Guest, previously a hesitant 'fusionist', to the idea of a final breach with the party system. Writing to Lloyd George on 16 January, he appealed to him to take a lead: 'this is the supreme opportunity for the formation of the Central Party and for the establishment of the great triumvirate' of Birkenhead, Churchill and Lloyd George. If 'FE' had the courage to 'test his strength with the Tory Party', Guest contended, 'at least one half of the Tory Members of the House of Commons would listen to a Fusionist appeal against Labour'.[74] Birkenhead, who had by now invested so heavily in the Prime Minister that he could not realistically contemplate a serious career except as one of his lieutenants, was delighted by the suggestion, and he proceeded to make a series of hectoring speeches on the subject, one to the New Members Group on 1 February.[75]

But the Liberal backbencher MacCallum Scott was not the only person to see that, from Lloyd George's point of view, the main purpose of the exercise was 'to split the Tory Party and to use a general election for the purpose of wiping out the Diehards as a Parliamentary force' and then to 'build up a central Party of his own'.[76] By 1922 there were formidable impediments to the achievement of this objective since Chamberlain's belief that only 'Coalition' stood between the country and socialism was now held by only a minority of his followers, while many of the Coalition Liberals, including some senior Ministers, were becoming increasingly restless with Coalition politics and tempted to opt for reunion with the Asquithians.[77]

And so 'fusion' was defeated: a defeat which prefigured the collapse of the Coalition itself later in the year. Over the next few months the Government experienced a succession of disappointments, failures and humiliations: for example, the breakdown of the Genoa Conference, the Honours Scandal, and the assassination of Field-Marshal Henry Wilson. Dissatisfaction mounted within the Conservative Party at Austen Chamberlain's leadership. Hence, when the latter tried to drive his critics into a corner at the Carlton Club in October 1922, they successfully fought him off. By 185 votes to 88, Conservative MPs resolved that their party, 'whilst willing to co-operate with the

74 Campbell, *Smith*, pp. 588–9.
75 Ibid., pp. 589–90.
76 MacCallum Scott's diary, 23 Jan. 1922, in Bentley, *Liberal Mind*, p. 138.
77 See Riddell diary, *Intimate Diary*, 4 March 1922, pp. 364–5.

Coalition Liberals, [should fight] the election as an independent party, with its own leader and its own programme'. Thus, ironically, as Ramsden has observed, the advent of a convinced Coalitionist to the leadership of the largest of the Coalition parties had contributed to the *collapse* of the Coalition.[78]

COALITION AND SOCIAL REALIGNMENT?

But 'fusion', and its failure, was about much more than the fate of a party leader and the future of Conservatism. To understand its wider significance it is necessary to look at the changing social face of British politics after 1918.

The exigencies of war had propelled into the Coalition Government quite a few social outsiders, men with the kinds of background which would probably have disqualified them from office even in a pre-war Liberal Government and which would certainly have been a serious handicap had they attempted to pursue a career through the Conservative Party. Of course, leaving aside a few renegade socialists, the working class was unrepresented in the post-war Coalition. However, by British standards, the Lloyd George Government contained an unusually large number of businessmen. Interestingly, these businessmen, Bonar Law, Eric Geddes and Lord Inverforth, were all members of the *Conservative* Party, though to men like Geddes party labels mattered very little. There were also more Scottish, Welsh and Jewish Ministers than was customary in British public life. Lloyd George, a man without the educational credentials normally to be found in a Prime Minister, symbolised this new situation.

The contrast with pre-war years is even more apparent if one looks at the social and educational backgrounds of Conservative MPs. A new breed of politician, it seems, had secured election to the Commons for the first time in 1918: only 15 per cent of Conservative MPs were from landed backgrounds, but 39 per cent were businessmen (most of the others came from the professions). Moreover, over 43 per cent of the 'new' intake (compared with under 30 per cent of the older cohorts) were businessmen, of whom only a minority had received an elite education. Though there were

---

78 Ramsden, *Age of Balfour and Baldwin*, p. 151.

still social differences between the Liberals and the Conservatives (particularly in religious backgrounds, since only a tiny number of Conservative MPs were Nonconformists), comparatively little separated the *new* Conservative members from the Coalition Liberals. Thus, 19.2 per cent of the Coalition Liberals and 26 per cent of the 'new' Conservative MPs had attended 'Oxbridge', as against 51 per cent of the 'old' Tory MPs.

These changes in the composition of Parliament almost certainly affected the quest for 'fusion' in 1919 and 1920. Clearly the Tory Right was going to oppose the creation of a Centre Party with all its might and main, because in the reorganised political system for which Lloyd George was hankering, the Tory Diehards would be, at best, ineffectual, and, at worst, driven out of the mainstream of British politics altogether. But this was not simply a dispute over personalities and political tactics.

It would, of course, be idle to look for a neat tie-up between a man's opinions and his social background. There were two brothers on the Conservative backbenches, Oliver and Godfrey Locker-Lampson; the former was a committed believer in Coalition Government, while Godfrey was the Conservative MP who moved the motion attacking Lloyd George and honours trafficking in the Commons debate of July 1922, before predictably voting for the ending of the Coalition at the Carlton Club meeting.[79]

Moreover, political opinion was in a constant state of flux in these years. Many Conservatives who had arrived at Westminster in 1918, full of admiration for the Prime Minister and anxious to declare themselves his supporters, soon became disillusioned. Mosley, for example, actually crossed the floor of the House in October 1920. And of the eight-five Conservative MPs in the original New Members Group in 1920 only twenty-one voted with Austen Chamberlain at the Carlton Club in October 1922, while thirty-six actually voted against![80] The hope of preferment and resentment at being passed over for office often affected a politician's stance, as also did personal friendships and animosities, pressure from constituency activists, hopes for re-election and many other considerations.

79 On Samuel Roberts, father and son, see Ramsden (ed.), *Real Old Tory Politics*, p. 196.

80 The rest were either dead, ill, absent or had left the Party. But Kinnear's study of the voting shows that many Conservative MPs were in a confused or ambiguous state of mind: for example, three of the Conservative MPs who voted to end the Coalition later attended the dinner held in Chamberlain's honour.

Nevertheless, when all such qualifications have been made, it is clear that most Conservative MPs from business backgrounds were disposed to view the Coalition favourably, while the Diehard Opposition centred around the traditional aristocratic and landed families. One analysis shows that, of the Conservative MPs from 'traditional' backgrounds, 61.9 per cent were Diehards and only 20.9 per cent strong supporters of the Coalition. But 43 per cent of the Conservative businessmen supported the Coalition and only 11.9 per cent were Diehards. (Professional men fell between these two extremes.)[81]

Once again, there were cross-currents at work. Two considerations drove *some* Conservative businessmen into hostility to Lloyd George and to the idea of a continued Coalition Government. The first was Tariff Reform. Many Conservative business MPs believed that the economy would only revive (and with it their own careers) if the Government introduced protective tariffs, something that was clearly out of the question so long as the Conservatives were sharing power with the Free Trade Liberals.

The second complicating factor was resentment at high levels of government spending, for which reforming Liberals in Lloyd George's Cabinet like Addison took most of the blame. In 1921 and 1922 the press-lord Rothermere ran a great campaign for economy and put up 'Anti-Waste' candidates, some of whom were returned at by-elections. This issue was quickly taken up by the Diehards, who promised that a truly independent Conservative Administration of the kind that they favoured would end this wild extravagance – 'Squandermania', as they called it – a promise which undoubtedly seduced some Conservative business MPs. (It was also exploited by the Independent Parliamentary Group, led by the swindler, Horatio Bottomley.)[82]

Conversely, Lloyd George did not entirely lack support from within the traditional ruling class. Ambition kept elder statesmen like Balfour and Curzon loyal to the man who had the disposal of the great offices of state, while, initially at least, there was enthusiasm for Lloyd George's political innovations from many young newly elected

81 Kinnear, *Lloyd George*, p. 77.

82 Bottomley had been elected in 1918 on a programme combining xenophobia and radicalism. One of his declared objectives was 'the introduction of Business principles into the Government of the Country – including the issue of Premium Bonds' (Julian Symons, *Horatio Bottomley*, 1955, p. 223).

Conservative MPs from landed backgrounds, of whom Mosley was only one.

Yet Conservative support for 'fusion' remained significantly higher amongst recently elected MPs, many of whom were not old enough to have been involved in the rancorous struggle with the Liberals in the years before 1914. Moreover, about a third of these young MPs were businessmen who must have felt a considerable affinity for their opposite numbers on the Liberal benches. Thus, the *idea* of a National Government was now much less divisive than it had been in 1910, when there had been a sharper difference between the social catchment areas of the two main parties.

The corollary to this is that one would expect to find the most intense hostility to the Coalition concentrated among middle-aged and elderly Tory MPs of the traditional kind, resentful of the penetration of their party by 'hard-faced businessmen who looked as though they had done well out of the War' (as Baldwin memorably put it). Writing in February 1920, Masterman predicted that 'the old-fashioned Tory of the *Morning Post* type [would] stand aside, lamenting over a lost world', but this, he added, mattered little since 'the old Tory landed aristocracy and tradition seem[ed] likely soon to be as extinct as the Dodo', as the 'new Toryism' moved to embrace the 'new wealth'.[83] Masterman was right, in the sense that most, though not all, of the Diehards who called for a restoration of the old party system and the re-establishment of 'independent Conservatism' exactly fit his description. Who, after all, was the leader of the Diehards in 1922? The Marquess of Salisbury, son of the former Prime Minister.

As Morgan argues, 'independent Conservatism' can thus be seen, at one level, as an aristocratic response to 'the passing of ancient patterns of deference, control and stability' and so as an angry protest at the occupation of high office by such men as the vulgar *arrivistes*, Lloyd George, Birkenhead and Robert Horne.[84] Considered against this background, it is perfectly logical that one of the issues with which the Diehards tried to discredit the Lloyd George Coalition was honours trafficking. Politicians like Salisbury realised, of course, that the Coalition was especially vulnerable to attack on this score. But both Salisbury and the main body of the Diehards also felt genuine fury as they contemplated the 'adulteration of the peerage':

83 Masterman, 'New Democratic Party', pp. 156–7.
84 Morgan, *Consensus and Disunity*, p. 160.

the Crown was being insulted, they believed, and the House of Lords degraded every time some unsavoury businessman without breeding or the education of a gentleman was allowed to buy himself a title.

If this analysis be true, the failure of 'fusion' and the eventual collapse of the Coalition in October 1922 was an absolutely crucial turning-point in British political history. Had things turned out differently, the Conservative Party as we know it would have disappeared – or, rather, would have been swallowed up in a different kind of party of property, a more overtly capitalist party perhaps. As it was, the traditional ruling class was able to stage a limited comeback in the mid 1920s. Admittedly, Bonar Law, who followed Lloyd George as Prime Minister, was himself a symbol of the *embourgeoisement* of the Conservative Party, but the Cabinet which he headed was a decidedly aristocratic body and included many of the more level-headed Diehards, including Salisbury. And if one goes on to look at the Administration formed by Baldwin in late 1924 one can see that the great aristocratic dynasties had recovered their old domination: twelve of the Cabinet can be categorised as 'gentlemen' (as distinct from seven in 1919), twelve had attended Oxford or Cambridge Universities (as distinct from four in 1919), and so on. It had only one obvious businessman: Neville Chamberlain. Moreover, many of the 'new' MPs, first elected during the War, at the 'Coupon' Election or during the course of the 1918 Parliament, dropped out of public life thereafter. No fewer than thirty-seven of the Coalition Liberals fall into this category.

Yet this did not mean that businessmen disappeared in large numbers from parliamentary politics after 1922. On the contrary, by the late 1930s over 40 per cent of MPs in Neville Chamberlain's Conservative Party were businessmen, a higher proportion even than in 1918 (though, of course, by the 1930s the distinction between businessmen and aristocracy was becoming ever more difficult to draw). Thus, if the Diehards thought that by ousting Lloyd George from office they would succeed in turning the clock back and reviving the fortunes of landed society, they were soon to be disappointed.

What had happened was that Lloyd George had paid the price for trying to move *too quickly*: in his honours lists, as in his plans for 'fusion', the Welshman had aroused anxiety by breaking too abruptly with established traditions and by threatening national institutions which still commanded respect – a mistake which was to be avoided by Stanley Baldwin, the dominant figure in British politics for the fifteen years following Lloyd George's political demise.

WHY DID THE COALITION FAIL?

But the failure of 'fusion' also had more immediate causes. For a start, not everyone was convinced by the 'anti-Bolshevik' rhetoric so insistently employed by Churchill and Birkenhead. Most Liberals still liked to think of themselves as 'progressives' and disapproved of the class prejudice underlying much of the 'fusionist' case. The *Manchester Guardian*, for example, called the 'socialist menace' 'a political bogy by which we decline to be terrified', and observed that Lloyd George had unintentionally shown how essential it was to keep a progressive and independent Liberal Party in being.[85] C.P. Scott, in other words, still hankered after a re-creation of the pre-war Progressive Alliance, as did many other orthodox Liberals.

More surprising, perhaps, is the way in which some Conservatives, especially those on the Diehard wing of the Party, rejected 'anti-Bolshevism' as a political strategy. Rather than trying to whip up fear of the working class, they said, it would make better long-term sense to appeal to the working man's patriotism. Thus the *National Review* shared Simon's disapproval of actions that would create a division between the 'Haves' and the 'Have-nots',[86] and Page Croft's National Party rejected Birkenhead's contention that politics should be organised around a struggle between 'Lloyd George and Labour' by insisting that 'the forces of disruption and Labour extremists' could only be defeated by an appeal based, not on the personality of an individual, but on 'national principles' which transcended class.[87]

There is also a sense in which the Coalition was on a 'hiding to nothing'. For when Labour performed well in by-elections, the government's critics would claim that 'anti-Bolshevism' had failed as a strategy – indeed, was even stimulating the very political developments it was trying to thwart. But as the prospect of a dramatic Labour breakthrough receded and the chances of an outright Conservative victory correspondingly improved, anti-Bolshevism lost much of its relevance.[88] Similarly Labour's poor performance in the municipal elections of 1922 could not but weaken Conservative apprehension at the 'grave extension of socialistic doctrines', upon

85 Wilson, *Liberal Party*.

86 *National Review*, 75 (April 1920), 166–7, 169.

87 Croft, *My Life of Strife*, p. 147.

88 For example, see Sanders diary, 1 Nov. 1921, Ramsden (ed.), *Real Old Tory Politics*, p. 163.

which, as Crawford noted, Austen Chamberlain had been 'so emphatic in supporting a coalition'.[89]

For this, and other reasons, party feeling steadily revived after 1919. But it must also be said that party considerations had never been quite as unimportant as the more sanguine advocates of coalition government had initially believed. The fundamental difficulty was that the 'Coupon' Election had produced an unbalanced Parliament. The Coalition Unionists accounted for 335 of the 707 MPs (another twenty-three were independent Conservatives and twenty-five Irish Unionists), which, given the refusal of the seventy-three Sinn Feiners to take their seats, gave them a clear majority over *all other parties*. Yet although they constituted 70 per cent of all the Coalition MPs, the Conservatives held only twelve of the twenty-one Cabinet seats, as against the eight occupied by the Coalition Liberals and the one by Coalition Labour. When the Coalition crumbled, the thoughts of one of its Ministers, Crawford, turned uneasily to 'the number of competent and hungry Conservatives who [had] no part in the Coalition'.[90] No wonder that Conservative Central Office and its Chairman, Younger, should have resented the disproportionate sacrifices being demanded of the dominant group at government level.

Conservatives also resented having to stand down at by-elections in favour of Coalition Liberals with weak or non-existent organisations when this carried a clear risk of the seat being captured by Labour. And, naturally enough, Austen Chamberlain's conception of his responsibilities as Conservative Leader offended many of the faithful: Younger was not alone in believing that the first duty of a Leader was 'to try to preserve party unity'.[91]

So long as Lloyd George was able to mesmerise his Conservative allies with his reputation and personality, all went reasonably well with the Coalition. The scepticism of Younger, however, became increasingly significant. True, the Conservative Chairman, at the rally of the New Members in July 1919, had argued strongly for the 'necessity of the permanence of the Coalition', under Lloyd George's leadership.[92] But Younger had never confused the survival of the Coalition with actual 'fusion'.

89 Crawford diary, 2 Nov. 1922, John Vincent (ed.), *The Crawford Papers* (Manchester, 1984), p. 463.

90 Crawford diary, 20 Oct. 1922, ibid., p. 456.

91 Younger to Sanders, 25 Sept. 1922, Ramsden (ed.), *Real Old Tory Politics*, p. 184.

92 See Morgan, *Consensus and Disunity*, p. 183; F. Guest to Lloyd George, *Lloyd George Papers*, F/21/4/6).

In any case, the oft-repeated claim that the older political parties had ceased to stand for distinctive principles and policies had never been entirely convincing. Over India, for example, the differences were acute – as the Liberal Indian Secretary, Edwin Montagu, the butt of Diehard hostility, found to his cost. Ireland also continued to be a source of discord, with the Prime Minister being accused by one Coalition Liberal of having 'sold the pass to the Tories'.[93] Many Conservatives were equally furious with the 'treachery' of Birkenhead and Austen Chamberlain. Finally, as the economy deteriorated, Tory backbenchers predictably began to fret at the dropping of tariffs and tried to revive the old protectionist campaign – in the process making demands which, equally predictably, the Liberals resisted.

There were also more profound reasons for tension between the two parties. The Coalition Liberals, taunted for 'apostasy' by the Asquithians, felt driven into public demonstrations of the authentically Liberal nature of many of the Coalition's policies, for example, in social reconstruction. But the more vociferously and plausibly they made this claim, the more resentful and suspicious the Conservative Party tended to become.[94] Finally, at all levels of the Conservative Party, there was anger at the Government's failure to honour its promise to institute reform of the House of Lords – an issue particularly exploited by those avowed enemies of Coalition, the Diehards.[95]

As these policy divisions intensified, the Coalition increasingly resembled a dishonest combination whose sole aim was the retention of power. *Punch*'s cartoon on the 'fusion' episode summed up these sentiments: Lloyd George, depicted as the captain of a ship that was undergoing a refit, is asked by the mate whether she should be given a new name: '"Fusion" Or "Confusion" – It's All One To Me So Long As I'm Skipper', he replies.[96]

It was a sign of the times that by January 1920 Maxse had come round to the view that it might be better if *Labour* formed a short-lived administration. At least this might enable the Conservatives to recover their soul: 'What does the Unionist Party of Mr Bonar Law and Earl Curzon of Kedleston signify?', asked the *National Review*. 'Who knows? Least of all its leaders, who apparently regard

93 See the division between Arthur Murray and Ian Macpherson, the late Chief Secretary for Ireland (Wrigley, *Lloyd George and Labour*, pp. 327–8).

94 Cowling, *Impact of Labour*, p. 114.

95 Ibid., pp. 116–17.

96 *Punch*, 24 March 1920, 223.

place-at-any-price as the whole duty of Mandarins.'[97] The Diehards suspected that those who joined the 'fusion' cry were simply out for personal advancement. For, claimed Maxse, 'in the absence of principles, convictions, enthusiasms, patronage becomes the decisive factor in politics; it is the only thing that counts'.[98]

Thus, by a strange inversion of position, the one-time disparagers of party (Page Croft included) now wanted a return to the decencies of party rivalry, in order to purify public life. Invoking the famous sentiments of Burke, they argued that parties acted as a barrier to unprincipled careerists by committing those who entered public life to the espousal of clear principles and policies on which they would have to stand or fall. But it was not just the Diehards or the incumbents of Conservative Central Office who took up this position, for by 1922 similar views were also being expressed by middle-of-the-road loyalist Conservative MPs – and, indeed, by the Independent Liberals.

Moreover, as the war receded, the interest in 'strong' government somewhat faded. Such recent innovations as the Cabinet Secretariat and, still more, Lloyd George's swollen Secretariat at 10 Downing Street came under attack as manifestation of a new 'Prime Ministerial Dictatorship'. The easy access to power of the great press-lords was also thought to be a deplorable departure from the better traditions of British public life. For all these reasons, there were calls for a return to 'normalcy', which, it seemed, presupposed the dissolution of the Coalition and the restoration of traditional two-party politics.

It is against this background that the Honours Scandal of the summer of 1922 should be viewed. Disquiet over Lloyd George's cynical abuse of his powers of patronage went back many years. In 1919 the issue had been debated in the House of Commons, largely at the insistence of Page Croft, the leader of the National Party, which, backed by the *National Review*, agitated strenuously for a fundamental overhaul of the system of secret party funds which it thought to be the source of so much of the corruption in public life.

Naturally the issue was viewed from a somewhat different perspective in Conservative Central Office. Younger and his officials did not want a fundamental overhaul of the honours system since they were themselves

---

97 *National Review*, 74 (Jan. 1920), 604. Bewilderingly, Birkenhead himself, in his speech at the Criterion Restaurant in July 1919, spoke of the desirability of Labour being 'educated' through experience of office (*Daily Mail*, 16 July 1919).

98 *National Review*, 75 (April 1920), 167.

implicated in some of its seamier aspects. *Their* complaint was that, through his recklessness, Lloyd George and his friends were bringing the system into disrepute, thereby playing into the hands of 'extremists' of both Left and Right. It also rankled with Younger that Lloyd George was 'poaching' Conservative Party subscribers through his unscrupulous distribution of honours. These were the grievances which helped destabilise Lloyd George's Ministry and played a significant part in its eventual downfall.[99] Equally important, the Honours Scandal helped to associate Coalition Government itself with chicanery and corruption – an association persistently emphasised by Baldwin, who was to emerge as the main beneficiary of the collapse of the Coalition.[100]

On a quite different level, the Coalition experiment had perhaps already been seriously weakened by the onset of the recession which by the end of 1920 had effectively put paid to Addison's attempted reform programme. 'Reconstruction' fell victim to the Treasury's insistence on the need to cut back on public expenditure in order to retain London's position as an international financial centre. It was clear, at least in retrospect, that Addison's brand of welfare capitalism could not be sustained through a depression in the face of the Treasury's deflationary policies.

This mattered because the fate of Reconstruction was so closely bound up with the idea of Coalition. In consequence, both suffered a fatal blow in the summer of 1921 when Addison, largely at Conservative insistence, was moved from the Ministry of Health before resigning shortly afterwards. Eventually Geddes wielded his famous Axe and buried Reconstruction as a political cause – which was poignantly ironical since, as Morgan says, 'far from being a symbol of "hard-faced" reaction', initially Geddes had been 'an index of the government's commitment to retain the planning structure that had carried the nation through after 1916'.[101]

But, even before the onset of the Slump, the mood of national harmony engendered by the war had started to evaporate. The railway companies, for example, were soon sabotaging Eric Geddes's attempt to create a 'national' integrated transport policy. Similarly, the failure of the National Industrial Conference in 1919, which most of the big unions did not even bother to attend, signalled an early

99 G.R. Searle, *Corruption in British Politics, 1895–1930* (Oxford, 1987), Chapter 15.
100 Ibid., Chapter 16.
101 Morgan, *Consensus and Disunity*, p. 44.

end to the 'industrial truce'. This destroyed the ideal of 'industrial self-government': the hope that Whitehall could safely withdraw from economic life, leaving the two sides of industry to reach a 'national settlement' that would secure high profits, high wages and social peace.

Moreover, in the dangerous confrontations between Capital and Labour which soon broke out, the wartime ideal of 'incorporating' Labour and Capital into the machinery of the state was also lost. Increasingly government saw its main task as involving the reining-in of public expenditure, on the one hand, and resistance to the pretensions of the working class, on the other. Mosley was one of the first politicians to appreciate the incompatibility of such practices with the idea of 'national politics'.

Finally, there was perhaps a tendency for the critics of the party political system to confuse three somewhat separate things: the maintenance of the Coalition, 'fusion', and the creation of a 'National Party'. Following Birkenhead's article in the *Weekly Dispatch*, *The Times* pertinently asked what the Lord Chancellor meant by calling for a 'National Party': 'Can it be that he is merely clothing the skeleton of "fusion" which Mr BONAR LAW has cautiously exposed to the view of more than one audience in the country?', wondered *The Times*. 'That would be no new party; it would be the old Coalition writ large.'[102] Similarly the outside world was left unsure in the spring of 1922 what 'Coalition-minded' Ministers actually wanted to achieve: Churchill and Balfour both made public speeches in which the objective was said to be the creation of 'a national party', but Austen Chamberlain, who had recently been talking about 'fusion', seemed now to be advocating 'a form of symbiotic non-alliance' which would allow the Lloyd George Ministry to go to the country 'as a government', which presumably involved a new 'Coupon' Election fought by separate Conservative and National Liberal Parties.[103]

However, to write off, as foredoomed to failure, the whole enterprise of trying to break away from party politics would be an abuse of 'wisdom of hindsight'. In the spring of 1920 the chances of success were still good. Unfortunately, Lloyd George badly botched his meeting with Coalition Liberal Ministers on 16 March. Nor, as Frances Stevenson observed in her diary, was the project (or the Prime

102 *The Times*, 13 Jan. 1920, cited in Campbell, *Smith*, p. 532.
103 Kinnear, *Lloyd George*, p. 108.

Minister's standing) helped through its association with Churchill and Birkenhead, two of the most mistrusted of all senior politicians: 'They may be brilliant, but they don't do him any good.'[104]

By 1922 the odds were heavily on a return to party political strife. Even then, however, all was not lost. The Carlton Club motion did not actually express hostility to coalitions as such: it simply stipulated that the Conservatives should not go into another election bound to the Coalition Liberals while Lloyd George was still Prime Minister. If Chamberlain had made it clear to the meeting that, following the election, he would insist that his position as Leader of the largest Coalition party entitled him to take the premiership, he might have made a much greater impression on the meeting. But he did not do so, and paid for his ineptitude by finally destroying all prospects of coalition government for the foreseeable future – along with his own leadership. Birkenhead's drunken harangue to the Conservative Under-Secretaries in August 1922 was, in its own way, equally disastrous. It is difficult to resist the conclusion that the coalition cause was killed off by the ineptitude of its own supporters, as well as by the open hostility of the 'sound party men'.

104 Frances Stevenson diary, 23 Jan. 1920, Taylor (ed.), *Frances Stevenson*, p. 199.

CHAPTER SEVEN

Towards the National Government, 1922–1931

THE AFTERMATH OF THE LLOYD GEORGE COALITION

The sort of coalitionism associated with Lloyd George's post-war Administration did not completely die out in October 1922. On the contrary, its ghost continued to haunt Baldwin and Asquith for many years to come. After his ejection from office, Lloyd George began 'working like a little dynamo to break up the Conservative Party by bringing the more advanced section to his flag, to join up with the "Wee Frees", and to detach the more moderate members of the Labour Party – this with the object of forming a Central Party of which he will be a leader'.[1] As Lloyd George told his wife shortly afterwards, he did not care who won office, since he was 'working for a break 2 or 3 years hence after we have formed a Centre party with a strong progressive bias'.[2]

In March 1923 Asquith was still very suspicious of Lloyd George's intentions, construing a recent speech by the latter as part of a renewed attempt to conjure up 'the illusory phantom of a Centre or Middle Party – in fact, a Coalition under an *alias*'; had the idea of a Centre Party been definitely abandoned?, Asquith asked anxiously.[3] It was

---

1 Riddell diary, 18 Nov. 1922, J.M. McEwen, *The Riddell Diaries, 1908–1923* (1986), p. 382.

2 Kenneth O. Morgan (ed.), *Lloyd George Family Letters 1885–1936* (Cardiff, 1973), p. 200.

3 1 March 1923, in Trevor Wilson, *The Downfall of the Liberal Party 1914–1935* (1966), p. 246.

a question constantly on the lips of official Liberals, mainstream Conservatives and Diehards alike throughout the mid 1920s.[4]

In particular, Baldwin's closest allies in the Conservative Party were on edge for the rest of the decade lest Lloyd George join up once more with his one-time Conservative colleagues and try to recreate the Coalition. Alarm bells again rang when Churchill, after a period of silence, spoke out in May 1923 at the Aldwych Club luncheon about the need for Liberals and Conservatives to resist socialism.[5] It is even possible that Baldwin's adoption of protection in late 1923 was intended as a means of scotching a new Lloyd George-dominated Centre Party.

One might have thought that by the end of 1924 the spectre of Coalition had finally been laid. After all, a year earlier the two wings of the Liberal Party had formally reunited, the Coalitionist Conservatives had been reabsorbed into the mainstream of their party, and Churchill, after a period of dangerous 'floating', had seemingly been anchored when he finally accepted the post of Chancellor of the Exchequer in Baldwin's Second Ministry. Yet *still* the orthodox party men feared that the 'Coalition gang' (in loose alliance with the press-lords Beaverbrook and Rothermere) were up to their old tricks.

Nor could 'sound' Liberals be sure that Lloyd George was fully committed once more to the Liberal Party, even after he had been elected Chairman of the Parliamentary Party. And those who entertained these fears would have been confirmed in their paranoia had they known that from time to time Churchill and Lloyd George were still in contact. Indeed, in August 1925, at the time of 'Red Friday', Lloyd George made an unsuccessful overture to the Conservatives via the inveterate Coalitionist Garvin, offering them his support at a time of social and industrial peril.[6] Later, with the approach of the 1929 General Election, Lloyd George realised that his best bet was the achievement of a hung Parliament in which he could bargain with both the main parties, Conservatives as well as Labour.[7]

In truth, there was nothing of great substance in these rather amateurish plots and feverish rumours, though they do testify to

4 Gretton felt sure that the '"Brains", as they like to think themselves . . . still hanker after a Centre Party' (1 Nov. 1924, cited in Michael Bentley, *The Liberal Mind, 1914–1929*, Cambridge, 1977, p. 139).

5 Paul Addison, *Churchill on the Home Front 1900–1955* (1992), p. 227.

6 Bentley, *Liberal Mind*, pp. 98–9.

7 John Campbell, *Lloyd George: The Goat in the Wilderness 1922–1931* (1977), p. 182.

the fact that the *idea* of Coalition was still capable of inspiring both devotion and hatred. But 'national politics' was shortly to enter a dramatically new phase – and to take on a rather different character from what it had had during the years of Lloyd George's ascendancy.

INTER-WAR COALITIONISM

'I am just off to the Kingsway Hall where S. Baldwin is about to explain to the Party why he has formed the Coalition of Coalitions', wrote Walter Elliot to a friend on 28 August 1931. 'Although a hardened Coalitionist, I must admit that a Coalition of Snowden, myself and Archie Sinclair had not entered my calculations.'[8] Well might Elliot have registered astonishment, for this was not at all the sort of 'national government' which had been envisaged by the proponents of 'fusion' in the early 1920s. Politics were indeed in a topsy-turvy state when a Coalition could be formed headed by MacDonald and Baldwin, the leaders of the 'old gangs', but excluding both Lloyd George and Churchill, along with that other persistent advocate of 'national' politics, L.S. Amery.

To understand how this came about it is first necessary to realise that by the late 1920s the meaning of 'national politics' had changed. As we have seen, long before the end of Lloyd George's Coalition Ministry the emphasis had switched from a major party realignment in pursuit of radical policies of Reconstruction to anti-socialism pure and simple. In particular, Austen Chamberlain had staked his career on two predictions: first, that the Conservatives could never win a future election unaided; and, second, that a return to party politics would simply split the anti-Labour vote, allowing Labour to form a government – an eventuality which he and other convinced 'Coalitionists' thought would be a national catastrophe.

On the first count Chamberlain was shortly to be proved totally wrong. In the 1922 General Election Bonar Law won an outright Conservative majority, albeit on only 38.2 per cent of the total vote, and later in October 1924 Baldwin swept back to office in one of the most spectacular landslide victories of modern times. On the second count, Chamberlain was both right and wrong.

8 Cited in Colin Coote, *A Companion of Honour: The Story of Walter Elliot* (1965), p. 124.

In 1923, and again in 1929, triangular electoral contests did lead to a hung Parliament and a minority Labour Ministry. However, although Labour hardly distinguished itself in office, neither did it justify the alarmist predictions that Churchill and Birkenhead had made at the time of the 1920 fusion talks. As many mainstream Conservatives and some Diehards had sensed all along, experience soon taught Labour leaders the difference between the rhetoric of opposition and the responsibilities of government. Indeed, as Lloyd George privately complained within weeks of Labour's first taste of office, MacDonald and his so-called socialist colleagues seemed to be mainly bent on proving their *respectability*.[9]

Despite the anxieties occasioned by the short-lived General Strike, even the fear of trade union power had very considerably subsided by the late 1920s. The number of days lost in strike action fell away sharply after 1921 (1926 was, of course, an exception). The more lurid anti-Bolshevik rhetoric of the Coalition years seemed rather foolish in 1928 or 1929, when the economy was in recession and no sensible person really believed that the leaders of the big trade unions were harbouring revolutionary designs.

But it was precisely the depression which now gave rise to a new set of concerns. The human waste and misery consequent upon mass unemployment obviously became a political issue; so too did lost markets and falling profit margins. Ministers and Treasury officials watched with dismay the steady rise of social expenditure, up sevenfold since pre-war days; by the end of the decade the cost of unemployment benefit alone was threatening to unbalance the budget. As a result, tariffs, changes in monetary policy and 'rationalisation', all highly contentious solutions, now forced their way on to the political agenda.[10]

More fundamentally still, there was a return to the feverish atmosphere of 'crisis' in which the old rhetoric of abuse directed against party politics once more resounded throughout the land. Now, one can broadly place the advocates of a 'national' strategy for dealing with the crisis into one of two camps. Taking a 'positive' view of the situation, there were those who started off from the premise that recent events had dramatised the bankruptcy of the political system: the old party creeds and nostrums, they argued, had failed

9 Lloyd George to Megan Lloyd George, 4 Feb. 1924, in Morgan (ed.), *Lloyd George Family Letters*, p. 202.

10 Philip Williamson, *National Crisis and National Government: British Politics, the Economy and Empire, 1926–1932* (Cambridge, 1992), p. 59.

to provide answers to a predicament which was without historical precedent, while 'socialism', effective enough as a storehouse of protest slogans, had nothing 'constructive' to offer the country either. Hence the need for some fundamental party realignment which would allow 'dynamic' and 'creative' thinkers to rally behind a programme of national recovery, without reference to their former party background.

But running parallel with this movement of opinion there was a much more 'negative' response to the crisis. This blamed the country's economic difficulties on the unwillingness of government to cut back drastically on public expenditure. Since, said these critics, no single party dared embark on a serious programme of Retrenchment embracing substantial savings on the vast sums being 'wasted' on social security benefits, the situation called for the formation of an all-party coalition which could 'spread the electoral risks'.

In practice, as we will see, these two strategies frequently inter-meshed, and not all politicians can easily be assigned to one camp or the other. Nevertheless, it may make the confused events of 1930–32 more intelligible if one starts off by looking at the 'positive', and then goes on to examine the 'negative', conception of the requirements of 'national politics'.

TOWARDS A 'NATIONAL PLAN'

In the preceding chapter we saw how a young generation of middle- and upper-class politicians, including Mosley, arrived at Westminster anxious to turn Lloyd George's rhetoric about 'homes fit for heroes' into concrete action. But 'Reconstruction' had collapsed by 1921, partly because of the revival of party feeling, but also because, in response to the recession, the Treasury took its axe to all ambitious spending programmes.

Disillusionment led most of these young idealists to scale down their expectations, so that aspirations would fit current economic 'realities'. Oswald Mosley, by contrast, set out to alter reality so that it would fit the earlier expectations. Between about 1921 and 1924 he took a number of momentous decisions. First, in October 1920 he withdrew his support from the Lloyd George Coalition and crossed the floor of the House – ostensibly in protest against Black and Tan atrocities in Ireland. Soon afterwards he announced his conversion to socialism, joined the ILP and became a Labour MP, emerging as a spokesman for a kind of 'Soldier's Socialism'. It was also at about this time that Mosley began his study of economics in an attempt to discover some way by which governments might lift the country out of the recession and reduce the high unemployment which was destroying all possibility of social improvement.

When Mosley joined the Labour Party, he obviously did so in the expectation that, sharing his own eagerness to create a New Social Order, Labour would be highly receptive to the kind of radical economic analysis upon which, together with John Strachey and Alan Young, he had begun to work. For Mosley's active mind was already playing creatively with novel ways of reducing mass unemployment. Surely the Labour Party would welcome such an intelligent and public-spirited new recruit. So, initially, it did. When MacDonald formed his second Minority Administration in 1929 he made Mosley Chancellor of the Duchy of Lancaster, a sinecure post which left the latter free to work on his plan for economic recovery. A year later Mosley presented the Cabinet with his famous Memorandum, which urged the country to jettison Free Trade and write off Britain's traditional export markets, in the hope that such losses could be compensated for by a strengthened *home* market insulated from the fluctuations of world trade by tariff barriers and commodity agreements with empire countries.

Mosley's unorthodox ideas predictably flew in the face of Treasury and City opinion. But the Mosley Memorandum also fell foul of MacDonald's Cabinet, which rejected it so decisively that its author resigned soon afterwards and took his case to the Parliamentary Party, where he was defeated, and then to Annual Conference, where (this time narrowly) he again failed to carry his case. In disgust Mosley left the Labour Party altogether and declared war on the party political system itself. By the end of 1930, as the junior Labour minister Hugh Dalton learned, Mosley was planning to form 'a National Party' which would draw its members from all three parties and, backed by two national newspapers and a fighting fund of £250,000, would have the resources to field up to 400 candidates at the next election.[11] This was the origin of Mosley's 'New Party', which, at its flotation in February 1931, was presented to the world as a sort of anti-party – a natural resting place for all who were disgusted with the party system and wanted to break free from what a later generation would call 'adversary politics'.

11 Dalton's diary, 24 Nov. 1930, Ben Pimlott (ed.), *The Political Diary of Hugh Dalton* (1986), p. 131.

Most of the New Party's original members came from the ILP, though these began to fall away when they realised where Mosley was leading them. At the same time, Mosley soon became the idol of many young Conservative MPs, like Harold Macmillan, Bob Boothby, Walter Elliot and Oliver Stanley, who all flirted with the idea of joining the New Party.[12] Macmillan was typical of the group. As he explained to Harold Nicolson, one of Mosley's closest colleagues, his 'heart [was] entirely with the New Party', but he felt that he could 'help us better by remaining in the Conservative ranks'. Macmillan added, with apparent sincerity, that if the New Party succeeded in obtaining 'a certain number of seats in Parliament, most of the young Tories, all the Liberals and a large proportion of the youngish Labour people would come over to us', in which case 'five years from now, the New Party [would] have its great opportunity'.[13]

By the end of 1930 Mosley had also started to attract disgruntled *elder statesmen* exasperated by the current stalemate and looking for some new departure. L.S. Amery, for example, had a high regard for Sir Oswald and greeted his Memorandum with rapturous enthusiasm.[14] Restless spirits like Garvin and Churchill and the press-lords Beaverbrook and Rothermere were all in touch with him, as was Lloyd George. (The 'Other Club' to which, at the instigation of Churchill, Mosley was elected in November 1930 provided a useful meeting place.)[15]

Why did the relatively inexperienced Mosley arouse so much interest when he resigned from the Government in May 1930? The economic ideas contained within the Mosley Memorandum constituted part of the attraction, since several of his contemporaries were thinking along broadly the same lines. This is particularly true of Lloyd George and the Liberals, who had gone into the 1929 General Election advocating a 'policy of National Development' as drawn up by the Executive Committee of the 'Liberal Summer School', a group

12 Mosley was in touch with O. Stanley, Elliot, Moore-Brabazon, Terence O'Connor and Boothby (Robert Skidelsky, *Oswald Mosley*, 1975, p. 224).

13 Diary, 30 May 1931, Nigel Nicolson (ed.), *Harold Nicolson: Diaries and Letters 1930–1939* (1966), p. 76. See also Skidelsky, *Mosley*, pp. 228, 240.

14 John Barnes and David Nicholson (eds), *The Empire At Bay: The Leo Amery Diaries 1929–1945* (1988), p. 100.

15 Williamson, *National Crisis*, p. 146; Skidelsky, *Mosley*, p. 236, note. Boothby feared that the public might conceivably react to such developments by saying 'By God, now all the shits have climbed into the same basket . . .' (Nicholas Mosley, *Rules of the Game* (1982; Fontana 1983 edn), pp. 150–3).

of intellectuals which included Keynes. The result had been a Liberal programme which tried to reach out to disillusioned social groups unable to identify either with Organised Labour or Big Business, such as technicians and managers. Significantly, in the *Yellow Book* (as the Report of the Liberal Industrial Inquiry was called) the Liberals had mocked as 'obsolete' the ancient controversy between individualism and collectivism, *laissez-faire* and socialism, offering instead a national basis for a reformed, managed capitalism; even the Edwardian slogan of 'National Efficiency' was resurrected in support of the cause.[16]

Indeed, it was once thought that the Mosley Memorandum reflected the new economic analysis of Keynes, with whom for several years Mosley had kept up a friendly correspondence. Mosley certainly believed that Keynes would sign his 'Manifesto'.[17] This is readily comprehensible, since both men shared a commitment to raising the level of demand by monetary reform and to using the budget as an instrument of economic policy, then a relatively new idea and one rejected by both the Labour and Conservative Front Benches.

However, it is now generally accepted that Mosley never really understood Keynes, and perhaps had not even read him seriously. Keynes might have been shown the Memorandum prior to its publication, but it owed little to his influence.[18] Co-operation between Mosley and Lloyd George would also have been difficult, given the latter's commitment to a Liberal Party which by 1930 was retreating from the bold programme on which it had fought the previous election and falling back instead on the ultra-orthodox dogmas of Retrenchment and Free Trade.[19]

Nevertheless, there were important *political* affinities linking Mosley to his contemporary admirers. For example, what helped to make Mosley an attractive figure was his appeal to 'Youth', of which the obverse was his attack on the party 'Old Gangs', men supposedly out-of-touch with the demands of the 'modern age'. What the country needed, Mosley told the Commons in October 1930, was the application of 'modern minds' to 'modern problems' – a very characteristic phrase.[20] Similarly, in an earlier article published in the

16 *Britain's Industrial Future, being the Report of the Liberal Industrial Inquiry* (1928), xx and *passim*.

17 Nicolson diary, 30 Nov. 1930, Nicolson (ed.), *Diaries and Letters*, p. 61. See also 29 April 1931, ibid., pp. 71–2.

18 Skidelsky, *Mosley*, pp. 145, 193. See also ibid., pp. 202, 218.

19 Williamson, *National Crisis*, p. 525.

20 Hansard, 5th ser., vol. 244, 80: 29 Oct. 1930.

Sunday Express, Mosley proclaimed himself as the spokesman, not of a class or party creed, but of a *generation* – a politician in tune with the 'dynamic' present age, which differed so greatly from the softer and 'static' pre-war world.[21]

In the autumn of 1930 Garvin, an open admirer of Mosley, was himself encouraging the revolt of the young men. 'The rising generation in every party', he wrote, 'feels that if things are not put right in the next few years by a mighty and sustained effort of peace-energy on a war scale, it is going to be their funeral.'[22] Garvin linked this conviction to his premonition that the old party alliances were doomed to disappear:

> No one remembers a time when discontents were so rife in all parties together and when movements were so kaleidoscopic. The whole country feels that fundamental changes are required . . . . Amongst the younger generation in all parties the strongest sentiment is in favour of 'clearing out all the Old Gangs'.[23]

Macmillan, a self-conscious member of the post-war era, agreed: 'The old party machines are worn out', he thought, and 'the economic situation is so serious that it will lead to a breakdown of the whole party system.' Macmillan predicted that the Tories would return from the next election with a majority of twenty and then be swept away on a snap vote: 'no other single party will form a Government and then there will be a Cabinet of young men'.[24] If Lloyd George failed to come forward as the 'national saviour', which was perhaps Macmillan's preferred option, Mosley seemed to be the natural leader of such a hypothetical grouping. On 18 May 1930 Boothby, too, could hail Mosley as 'the ONLY one of my generation – of the post-war school of thought – who is capable of translating into action any of the ideas in which I genuinely believe'.[25]

Mosley's appeal was strengthened by his constant invocations of the Great War and of the methods which his hero Lloyd George had earlier adopted to lead the country from disaster to victory. Thus Mosley proposed a fundamental reform of the machinery of government, involving the creation of a small Cabinet, based on Lloyd George's War Cabinet. Indeed, it was Mosley's contention

---

21 Cited in Skidelsky, *Mosley*, p. 225.
22 *Observer*, 19 Oct. 1930.
23 Ibid., 2 Nov. 1930.
24 Nicolson diary, 2 July 1930, Nicolson (ed.), *Diaries and Letters*, p. 51.
25 Boothby to Mosley, 18 May 1930, Mosley, *Rules of the Game*, p. 144.

that Britain faced in 1930 an emergency comparable to that of the war years, since, despite the lack of an *external* enemy, she was locked in a struggle for national survival no less acute. Mosley also wanted to downgrade local government by centralising his road-building programme in the hands of the Ministry of Transport. This meant bypassing the local authorities, many of which, Mosley believed, were behaving obstructively. No wonder that at this time Mosley should have been seeing so much of Lloyd George, who had recently been arguing a similar case in his *We Can Conquer Unemployment*.

Finally, Mosley won converts through his attempts to mobilise people of different social and political backgrounds behind a 'national plan'. For although not everyone found his particular economic programme either practical or desirable, *planning* was all the rage in 1930–31.

In February 1931 the *Week-End Review*, a periodical edited by Gerald Barry, took a prominent part in the popularisation of this concept when it published a pioneering article by Max Nicholson entitled 'A National Plan for Great Britain'. 'The old Gang is still fairly generally in power, both in politics and in industry', Nicholson announced, 'but its prestige has gone for good . . . . The post-war generation, which will soon outnumber the more elderly electorate, is ready to respond to a realistic lead.' Nicholson's Plan provided a sketch of a new kind of 'modern' government, headed by ten ministers presiding over a 'Planning Commission', an Industrial Court, and a Bureau of Statistics, which would modernise the economy and public administration through the utilisation of science. It thus looked backwards to some of the 'National Efficiency' literature of Edwardian times as well as forward to 'Political and Economic Planning' (PEP), a 'think-tank' which shortly emerged from the discussion which Nicholson had stimulated.[26]

Behind all this enthusiasm for 'national plans' there lay an impatience with party politics and a belief that, at the very least, economic policy should be taken out of the party arena since it was far too important to be treated in a 'partisan' way. Keynes, for example, wanted to inject into government 'the scientific spirit as distinct from the sterility of the purely party attitude'.[27] True, the authors of the *Week-End Review*

---

26 *Week-End Review*, 14 Feb. 1931, v–xii. See also Paul Addison, *The Road to 1945: British Politics and the Second World War* (1975), pp. 38–9; Williamson, *National Crisis*, pp. 139–40.

27 Cited in Williamson, *National Crisis*, p. 66.

'Plan' saw little merit in coalition, but they hoped to 'rope in all progressive elements in industry, trade unions, commerce, banking, and so on, regardless of whether in the confused post-war politics, with no grand dividing issue, they may have labelled themselves Conservative, Liberal, or Labour'.[28]

Garvin, of course, wanted to go further. In language which recalled Walter Elliot's in 1920, he proclaimed: 'The old age of mere politics is dead. We live in an age of economics.' Garvin went on to call for the adoption of a revenue tariff under the aegis of the sort of comprehensive National Government last seen during the war: his list of possible participants included Lloyd George, Reading (the former Liberal Viceroy of India), Simon, Churchill, Baldwin, Beaverbrook and Mosley, and his preferred Premier, perhaps surprisingly, was Ramsay MacDonald.[29]

Mosley took an even more extreme line. Long before his final drift into Fascism, he had developed a withering critique of parliamentary institutions. In place of a system which elevated 'talkers' over 'men of action', Mosley hoped to create a 'modern' political movement which could 'hold the ring', so allowing economists and scientists to proceed unhindered with the work of national reconstruction. His October Memorandum accordingly called for the establishment of an authoritarian regime which would, for example, apply 'Caesarism' to the task of governing India. Mosley also advocated a General Powers Bill which would confine Parliament to a right of veto, cheerfully admitting that this would involve 'a certain surrender of political liberty'.[30]

RETRENCHMENT

Meanwhile, a less excited response to the country's troubles was developing apace among those closer to the centre of government. A good starting-point for an examination of *their* attitudes would be the entry which Maurice Hankey, the Cabinet Secretary, wrote in his diary on 6 September 1931. 'We are living just now through the most serious crisis since the war and the future outlook is black', thought

28 *Week-End Review*, 14 Feb. 1931, p. v.
29 *Observer*, 22 Feb. 1931.
30 See Williamson, *National Crisis*, pp. 147–8.

Hankey. 'After the war we failed to adopt the measures of economy necessary to a nation that had dissipated a large part of its wealth in smoke and explosions.' Lloyd George had made irresponsible election speeches about 'homes fit for heroes'. Thereafter, Hankey continued, it had 'been a "rake's progress" for which each successive Government ha[d] its share of responsibility . . .', in particular through their protection of the extravagant 'dole'. Self-evidently, he argued, all classes should have been making sacrifices in order to restore the economy's lost competitiveness, yet 'the exigencies of party politics ha[d] compelled each party leader to declare repeatedly, and right up to the present time, that the standard of living must be maintained'.[31]

A similar case was argued, with important long-term consequences, in the Majority Report of the May Committee on Public Expenditure, which documented the growing costs of unemployment benefit and demanded that they be cut. 'After the heavy sacrifices of the war', the Committee asserted, 'large sections of the nation looked to the post-war period with the natural expectation of a general improvement in the old conditions of life', with the result that '*all* [my emphasis] parties ha[d] felt the insistent pressure for promises of "reforms" as the price of support, such "reforms" being in fact mostly of the nature of privileges or benefits for particular classes at the cost of the general taxpayer'. The process was difficult to stop, since those desiring increased expenditure for particular purposes were 'usually far better organized, far more active and vocal than those who favour[ed] the vague and uninspiring course of strict economy'. As a result, many MPs found themselves returned to Parliament pledged, 'on a one-sided presentation of the case, to a course which on fuller knowledge they [saw] to be opposed to the national interests'. In short, the businessmen who dominated the May Committee took a very gloomy view of the country's prospects because they believed that 'the mass of the electorate still d[id] not appreciate the true economic position of the country and its problems'.[32]

Such a diagnosis was generally accepted within the business community, and the winter of 1930–31 saw the proliferation of commercial organisations advocating 'economy' and berating the

31 Diary, 6 Sept. 1931, in Stephen Roskill, *Hankey Man of Secrets*, *Vol. II 1919–1931* (1972), pp. 544–5.
32 Cited in J.R. Hay, *The Development of the British Welfare State 1880–1975* (1978), 92–3.

political parties for their cowardice. For example, the motor-car manufacturer William Morris announced that could he but have his way, he would happily give all the politicians 'the sack'! Despairing of the competence and good faith of Conservative MPs, Morris joined up with like-minded associates in December 1930 to found the 'League of Industry', which planned to run candidates at the next election with a view to creating a 'businessman's government'. Meanwhile, a group of old-fashioned Liberal businessmen, most of them staunch Free Traders, had earlier produced a 'Manifesto on Economy', which *The Times* printed on 16 July 1930: 'no present party' took 'any serious interest in economy', they complained, since party leaders preferred to pursue the foolish ploy of 'bribing the people with their own money'. Surely, the Manifesto plaintively concluded, *one* of the parties would have the sense to emblazon retrenchment on its banner.[33]

What connection did such appeals have with the anti-Bolshevik propaganda of the post-Armistice years? With Labour in office, the old 'Coalitionists' had by no means given up their earlier attempts to create an anti-socialist bloc. Before and after the 1929 Election, for example, Garvin came forward with a plan to get Conservatives and Liberals to unite in a 'National Party',[34] while later, in the summer of 1929, Lloyd George, acting through Churchill as an intermediary, offered to help the Conservatives back to office in return for an Electoral Reform Bill – an offer which met with the approval of Austen Chamberlain, who continued to favour 'co-operation and ultimate fusion with the Liberal Party'.[35] Indeed, Chamberlain, along with his loyal follower Warden Chilcott, was now able to argue that recent events had vindicated those who had attempted to resist the 'dissolution of the old Coalition and foretold some of the consequences of its disruption'.[36] Another prominent advocate of this kind of 'fusion' was Edward Grigg, a former Liberal MP, who had recently returned to domestic politics after a spell as Governor of Kenya.[37]

33 Williamson, *National Crisis*, pp. 138–9.

34 Ibid., pp. 140–1.

35 Amery diary, 11 July 1929, Barnes and Nicholson (eds), *Empire At Bay*, pp. 42–3.

36 Foreword to Warden Chilcott, *Political Salvation* (1932), p. 10. Chilcott claims to have been an 'unrepentant Coalitionist' in 1929 but one who was so disillusioned that he gave up his seat rather than stand as a Baldwinite candidate, thinking that he could thus better serve his country (ibid., p. 19).

37 Williamson, *National Crisis*, p. 116.

But it is important to note that the *prime* worry of those calling for a 'National Government' was no longer the spread of 'socialism'. For by the end of the 1920s it was hardly possible to blame all the country's woes on 'Labour'; after all, it was evident that the Conservatives, the dominant party of government, also had a major responsibility for the high expenditure which was allegedly bankrupting the state. If there was now a villain to be blamed at all, it was the 'democracy' itself and the readiness of all parties to humour its whims. This was also the position taken by *The Times*, which, once the National Government had actually been created, welcomed the 'reversal of a policy of extravagance to which all parties have pandered in the past'.[38] Such a diagnosis pointed, therefore, to the desirability, not of constructing an anti-Labour confederation, but, on the contrary, of *involving* Labour in some sort of 'national settlement', so that all parties would share the electoral risks of necessary, but unpopular, measures.

There were even some *Labour* Ministers who wanted to be rescued in this way from the temptations to which they felt themselves exposed. For example, when Snowden (the Chancellor) set up the May Committee, he did so hoping thereby to overcome resistance within his own party to drastic cutbacks in public expenditure. All-party co-operation also made an appeal to leading figures in the other parties, as General Seely, a former Liberal Cabinet Minister, well understood. 'Economy is vitally necessary but extremely unpopular', he declared in *The Times*. 'Any single party who propounded it would very soon come down to the ground, and the evil would continue.'[39] No one understood this better than Neville Chamberlain, who privately took the view that the cost of 'transitional' benefit should be transferred to the Poor Law authorities and made the subject of a means test but refrained from saying so publicly after being told by a group of Conservative MPs and candidates that such an admission would 'lose . . . the election' for the party.[40] Hence Chamberlain's eagerness that the minority Labour Administration should 'grasp the nettle' and 'face up to its responsibility' by initiating 'economies' which the other parties could support from the Opposition Benches. But, failing this denouement, Chamberlain eventually came to see that the next best solution might be the creation of an all-party Coalition,

38 *The Times*, 25 Aug. 1931.
39 Ibid., 2 Dec. 1930.
40 Williamson, *National Crisis*, p. 246.

with Labour's full involvement. The problem was how to devise a way of achieving such an outcome.

NATIONAL CRISIS

In the autumn of 1930 events started to drive the 'positive' and the 'negative' critics of party politics into a loose alliance. Spurring both of them onwards was the marked deterioration of the economy, which had shown signs of improvement twelve months earlier. Disturbances in India intensified the prevailing sense of crisis and provided further ammunition for those who felt that the country's problems were too intractable to be dealt with on conventional party lines. In any case, all three parties seemed in deep disarray. Morale on the Labour side of the House was low; Lloyd George was struggling to keep his Liberal followers united behind his devious manoeuvring; meanwhile, assailed by the press-lords Beaverbrook and Rothermere, Baldwin faced an uncertain future as Conservative Leader. The entire system of parliamentary government seemed on the verge of total breakdown: by February 1931 Garvin was not alone in believing that the party leaders were 'making British politics the laughing stock of the world'.[41]

Mosley, from the Back Benches, now worked energetically to produce some kind of 'creative' political realignment. But in his October Memorandum he also set out to woo the more 'negative' economists with the promise of income tax cuts and the recasting of the unemployment system on an actuarial basis. Morris, who later became the main paymaster of the New Party, was one of several disgruntled businessmen who rose to the bait. Indeed, Mosley's December Memorandum won the endorsement of *most* leading critics of Britain's traditional political system.[42]

But the event which more than any other made the idea of a 'National Government' a major talking point was the letter which Seely sent to *The Times*, where it was published on 2 December 1930. 'It is clear that Britain is confronted with a grave emergency', Seely began. 'It is equally clear that an election on party lines will not help us to meet it.' Speaking as Chairman of the National Savings Commission, Seely disclosed that he had met 'not hundreds,

41 *Observer*, 22 Feb. 1931.
42 Williamson, *National Crisis*, p. 148.

but thousands, of men and women of every class and shade of opinion . . . . They all say, if the right man were to appeal to the people of Britain to abandon party strife and come together and pull together until this emergency is over, he would receive overwhelming support from the whole mass of the people.'[43]

Seely's letter formed only one episode in the flurry of speculation on the subject of 'National Government'. In the pages of the *Whitehall Gazette*, Chilcott's attacks on the mischief being wreaked by the party system grew ever more frantic.[44] In November Garvin devoted some of his most impassioned *Observer* editorials to the subject, calling on a 'national government' to 'heave the country clean out of the ruts'.[45] Keynes, in more measured language, conveyed a similar message in *The Economist*. Businessmen drafted manifestos for the newspapers, demanding that the parliamentary talking shop give way to a 'business government'. In addition, Dawson of *The Times* and Gwynne of the *Morning Post* warned that time was rapidly running out. In fact, as 1930 drew to an end, the language employed by leading politicians and journalists to describe the country's situation became positively apocalyptic – although not everyone took his own rhetoric entirely seriously.[46]

London clubland and Westminster were awash with rumours and vague panaceas. John Buchan, who had broached the topic of a National Government with Lloyd George in September 1930, raised the matter in Parliament the following month.[47] Soon afterwards a Liberal MP, Morris-Jones, tabled a Commons motion, drawing attention to 'the Need of Better Co-operation among the Parties', though this excited some mirth among the worldly-wise.[48]

Meanwhile Buchan, Stanley and Elliot were persuading the ex-Chancellor, Sir Robert Horne, to launch his own appeal.[49]

---

43 General J.B. Seely, letter to *The Times*, 2 Dec. 1930. However, in its editorial comment *The Times* showed little sympathy with the idea of attempting to create 'a mixed Cabinet, a brilliant miscellany glowing with all the talents and with the nebular heat of principles in combustion'.

44 See Chilcott, *Political Salvation*.

45 Cited in Williamson, *National Crisis*, p. 149.

46 Ibid., pp. 134–5.

47 Hansard, 5th ser., vol. 244, 122–3: 29 Oct. 1930.

48 Ibid., vol. 245, 439: 19 Nov. 1930. Earlier he had publicly advocated a National Government as the only way of resolving the economic crisis (Henry Morris-Jones, *Doctor in the Whips' Room*, 1955, pp. 85–6).

49 Williamson, *National Crisis*, pp. 150–1. The businessmen, Henry Mond, Sir Arthur Balfour and Abe Bailey were among the many active conspirators (David Marquand, *Ramsay MacDonald* (1977), p. 574).

More significantly, George V was given a Memorandum written by the industrialist, Sir Arthur Balfour, arguing that 'the time has come when even emergency measures may be necessary to avert a calamity which . . . is not altogether incomparable with the Great War'. Suitably impressed, George V persuaded the Cabinet to include in the King's Speech an appeal to 'all sections of Parliament' to 'unite' in treating unemployment 'on national as distinct from Party lines'. Moreover, not only did the King later see Seely's appeal before its publication, but his secretary, Stamfordham, wished the General 'every success',[50] while another royal official, Clive Wigram, also became drawn into these intrigues – evidence of how deeply Buckingham Palace had committed itself to the notion of establishing a National Government.

Meanwhile the first exploratory discussions were taking place between the leading figures of all parties. Six weeks before composing his piece for *The Times*, Seely had joined with Lord Reading in organising a dinner at the Athenaeum, at which a paper advocating a National Government was read out to a select audience which included MacDonald, Churchill, Lloyd George, Reading and Horne.[51] In fact, it was Reading (Garvin's current favourite to head a National Government) who persuaded Dawson to print Seely's letter in *The Times*.[52] Later, on the eve of its publication, Seely held a second dinner (3 December 1930), this time attended by MacDonald, Reading, Churchill, Horne and Lloyd George's son, Gwilym.[53]

What significance did these gatherings have? Lloyd George was too ill to attend the second dinner (hence the presence of his son), but he was known to be having informal talks with Churchill, Mosley and the younger Conservatives,[54] while publicly he spoke out in favour of a 'pooling' of the 'best brains of all Parties' to 'extricate the nation from its emergency'.[55]

On the other hand, although peripherally involved in the National Government discussions in late 1930, MacDonald does not seem to have taken them very seriously. Thus, when Buchan told the Prime Minister that Lloyd George had been busily canvassing the idea, he

50 Williamson, *National Crisis*, pp. 152–3.

51 Andrew Thorpe, *The British General Election of 1931* (Oxford, 1991), p. 55; Marquand, *MacDonald*, p. 576.

52 Williamson, *National Crisis*, pp. 155–6.

53 Ibid., p. 151.

54 Thorpe, *General Election of 1931*, p. 55.

55 See *Manchester Guardian*, 4, 6 December.

returned a vague reply, and, after Sir Arthur Balfour had written to him in October to advocate 'some form of Coalition Government', he categorically turned down the suggestion.[56] Indeed, in the privacy of his diary, MacDonald confessed that his own inclination was to 'go out altogether' so that he could freely express his views from the Back Benches.[57] Moreover, when he attended the first Seely dinner, the Premier did not know what was the purpose of the occasion.[58] True, MacDonald tentatively raised the prospect of a National Government on 1 December in private conversations with Baldwin, but when the latter responded discouragingly, he did not seek to pursue the matter, and his biographer thinks that he soon forgot all about it until the long-awaited 'crisis' broke in earnest nine months later.[59] Still less can any significance be read into MacDonald's earlier remarks about the desirability of the Commons behaving like a 'Council of State'; this, after all, was an obvious appeal for the Leader of a minority administration to make.

At this stage the *Conservative* leadership was equally disinclined to view the prospect of a 'National Government' sympathetically. Baldwin, in particular, took a consistently sceptical line, partly no doubt because having brought down one Coalition, he had no wish to establish another – least of all a coalition in which Lloyd George would play a prominent role.[60] In December 1930 Baldwin was, instead, using the time-hallowed argument that Conservatism alone formed the basis for a 'national party'.[61] Neville Chamberlain kept a rather more open mind, but, like other Conservatives in the summer of 1931, he was looking forward confidently to the collapse of the Labour Ministry, followed by a Conservative electoral landslide which would at last give his party a mandate to introduce tariffs. Such an outcome seemed very likely following Labour's catastrophic showing in the Shipley by-election of 6 November.

Nevertheless, as Philip Williamson argues, the coalition talk of late 1930 cannot simply be dismissed as idle chatter. 'Rather it was an idea which might possibly have service if economic or imperial

56 Marquand, *MacDonald*, pp. 575–6.

57 Ibid., p. 577.

58 Williamson, *National Crisis*, p. 159.

59 Ibid., pp. 160–1. Marquand, *MacDonald*, pp. 578–80.

60 Robert Rhodes James (ed.), *Memoirs of a Conservative: J.C.C. Davidson's Memoirs and Papers 1910–37* (1969), p. 368.

61 Stuart Ball, 'The Conservative Party and the Formation of the National Government: August 1931, *Historical Journal*, 29 (1986), 161.

conditions deteriorated further and if party conditions continued to frustrate effective action: it might then provide either an escape from a political *impasse* or else an arrangement for coping with a real emergency.' Even so, '"national government" remained only one, extreme, possibility'.[62]

Indeed, the crisis mood of late 1930 fairly quickly evaporated. This was partly the result of the Labour Government's success in presiding over the Irwin–Gandhi Pact, but the enhanced credibility of the Administration also owed much to Lloyd George's decision in January 1931 to keep Labour in office in return for the promise of certain concessions, notably electoral reform – a development which infuriated Churchill, Austen Chamberlain and Horne.[63] In fact, by the middle of 1931 it seemed as though a new kind of two-party system was about to take root, with a 'progressive' Labour-Lloyd George alliance confronting a right-wing bloc comprising the Conservative Party and the Liberal followers of Sir John Simon.[64]

Nevertheless, both the New Party and certain business pressure groups continued to push the idea of a National Government.[65] In January 1931 rumours reached the Conservative backbencher Headlam to the effect that 'the discontented ones', Churchill included, were 'busily scheming to form a "National Party"'.[66] But even Garvin, still starstruck by Lloyd George, now took more interest in a party realignment produced by the coming-together of Conservatives and Simonites.[67] Moreover, when in June 1931 the South African financier Abe Bailey held a dinner of celebrities to promote the idea of a MacDonald-led National Government, Baldwin and the Conservative Party organisers were adamant that their followers 'would not stand it for a moment'.[68]

---

62 Williamson, *National Crisis*, pp. 154–5.

63 Ibid., p. 176.

64 The right-wing Simonites, who deeply mistrusted Lloyd George, already constituted the nucleus of a breakaway Liberal group, but they hesitated to form a separate party because they could not bring themselves to endorse the tariff. Simon himself behaved ultra-cautiously (Williamson, *National Crisis*, p. 248). See also Robert Skidelsky, *Politicians and the Slump: The Labour Government of 1929–1931* (1967), pp. 330–3.

65 Williamson, *National Crisis*, pp. 229–31.

66 Headlam diary, 21 Jan. 1931, in Stuart Ball (ed.), *Parliament and Politics in the Age of Baldwin and MacDonald: The Headlam Diaries 1923–1935* (1992), p. 201.

67 Williamson, *National Crisis*, p. 232.

68 Ibid., pp. 232–3.

CHAPTER EIGHT

The National Government and its Critics, 1931–39

FORMATION OF THE NATIONAL GOVERNMENT, AUGUST 1931

The 'crisis', when it did finally come, caught almost all politicians, Ministers and Opposition alike, by surprise. Only a few key points need be selected from the complex story of the August Crisis which destroyed the Labour Minority Administration and led to the creation of the 'National Government'.

First of all, it is important to realise that, for all his much-discussed self-pity, MacDonald's own instinct was to try and put together a package of measures which would reassure the markets, receive the endorsement of the Opposition parties and hold the Labour Party together, an objective in pursuit of which he showed considerable tenacity and ingenuity. Even when MacDonald later asked the Conservative and Liberal leaders jocularly whether they were 'prepared to join the Board of Directors',[1] he seems to have had in mind an arrangement in which a temporary Coalition was formed under Baldwin's leadership. The Dominions Secretary, J.H. Thomas, may have taken a long-term interest in the idea of a National Government:[2] MacDonald certainly did not.

However, with the onset of the sterling crisis in the summer of 1931, some senior Liberals quickly saw that a Coalition might now be

---

1 Philip Williamson, *National Crisis and National Government: British Politics, the Economy and Empire, 1926–1932* (Cambridge, 1992), p. 320.

2 See A. Thorpe, '"I am in the Cabinet": J.H. Thomas's Decision to Join the National Government in 1931', *Historical Research*, 64 (1991), 391.

imminent. On 30 July Donald Maclean, for example, spoke publicly of the need for 'a Committee of Public National Financial Safety'.[3] On the other hand, Baldwin was still so hostile to the idea that, in discussion with Neville Chamberlain, he even denied that MacDonald had ever broached the subject with him.[4] Amery may have favoured an emergency government on the lines of the one formed during the Great War, but most Front-Bench Conservatives clung to their earlier strategy of forcing Labour to take responsibility for the situation by imposing spending cuts.[5] As late as 18 July, *The Times*, too, was still against a Coalition, saying that it wanted a national basis for a tariff policy but, given that there were 'no inverted Peels in either party', it simply recommended the Conservatives to turn themselves into 'a national party pursuing a national policy'.

It was the hitherto sceptical Neville Chamberlain who now emerged as the one prominent Conservative sympathetic to the establishment of a National Government, perhaps because he feared that his bugbear, Lloyd George, would appropriate the leadership of such a combination if the Conservatives held back. Admittedly, in mid-August Chamberlain, like other Conservatives, was still pointing to the desirability from the party point of view of getting 'economy' out of the way before a general election.[6] But a week later he reacted irritably to Baldwin's declaration that he still 'hoped and prayed that he might not have to join a National Government'.[7]

Meanwhile, within the party at large, the feeling was gaining ground that circumstances might shortly make a coalition unavoidable, and several Conservative leaders were prepared to countenance such an arrangement if it were to accept tariffs and if Baldwin were to head it.[8] Yet, along with such fervent advocates of National Government as Garvin and Seely, Conservatives continued to assume, almost to the end, that, should a coalition ever be formed, a major Labour figure like Arthur Henderson would be among its members.

What totally transformed the situation was Henderson's belated recognition of the disastrous consequences which would befall the Labour Movement if its leadership became committed to an economic

3 Williamson, *National Crisis*, p. 277. However, Maclean had in mind an all-party group of MPs, not a National Government.

4 Ibid., pp. 277–8.

5 Ibid., pp. 277–9.

6 Chamberlain to Gwynne, 17 Aug. 1931, cited in Williamson, *National Crisis*, p. 285.

7 Ibid., p. 336.

8 Andrew Thorpe, *The British General Election of 1931* (Oxford, 1991), p. 46.

programme which ran flat counter to the wishes of the trade unions. Of course, it was Henderson's abandonment of the strategy of Retrenchment which eventually brought down the Labour Government. But this development, happening so suddenly, created a dilemma for all the party leaders. Theoretically, it could have resulted in the formation of a Conservative–Liberal Administration. But Chamberlain saw how dangerous it would be, from the Conservative point of view, were a united Labour Party to go into Opposition. Nor did such a denouement appeal to MacDonald. On the contrary, contemptuous of Henderson's submission to the 'dictation' of a mere pressure group, the Prime Minister was now open to the suggestion that he might have a 'national duty' to stay in office – a consideration forcefully pressed upon him by Buckingham Palace.

Even this need not have led to a lasting schism within the Labour Movement. For when the 'National Government' was set up, the party leaders thought that it would last for no more than about six weeks. 'The specific object for which the new Government is being formed', said the official communiqué, 'is to deal with the national emergency that now exists. It will not be a Coalition Government in the usual sense of the term, but a Government of Cooperation for this one purpose. When that purpose is achieved the political parties will resume their respective positions.' The party leaders went on to promise that when the election took place, following the end of the emergency period, there would be 'no "coupons", pacts or other arrangements'.[9] A similar version of events was being promulgated by *The Times* as late as 25 August. For the time being MacDonald could thus flatter himself that he had *saved* the Labour Party from another 'Coupon' election.

TOWARDS THE GENERAL ELECTION OF OCTOBER 1931

But at this point the relationship between the party leaders was changed by two new developments. In September the Bank of England, 'while disclaiming any right to an opinion on political events', declared 'that a general election in which the three parties were acting independently would not be regarded as providing sufficient certainty for the establishment of a stable government . . .'.

9 Thorpe, *General Election of 1931*, pp. 91–2.

'An appeal to the electorate by a National Government on a national policy devised to rectify the financial situation', it argued, 'was more likely to be regarded favourably abroad.'[10]

Secondly, and even more significantly, the Labour Party reacted to the formation of the National Government with a violent hostility which MacDonald could not have expected. True, in the confused situation created by the dramatic events of 24 August, it seemed initially as though many of his followers would give him some sympathy and support. Herbert Morrison was probably not the only junior Minister to have been briefly tempted to follow MacDonald's lead.[11] But in the end only five backbench MPs publicly endorsed the actions of MacDonald, Snowden, Thomas and Sankey, the quartet of ex-Labour Ministers who took office in the National Government.

What is more, the Labour Party quickly adopted a position of total opposition to the policy of cuts to which most of its leaders had been committed only a few weeks earlier. Instead, at the behest of the General Council of the TUC, Labour formulated its own 'socialist' alternative, including the funding of unemployment insurance by means of a graduated levy on the whole community, war-debt conversion, the suspension of the Sinking Fund, and a rentier tax.[12] Such a programme may or may not have been feasible: it certainly bore little relationship to what Labour had recently been doing in office.

These policy changes were accompanied by a sharply accentuated class rhetoric. For example, Labour's 27 August manifesto laid the blame for the crisis on 'international and national financial interests', and belief in the existence of a 'banker's ramp' and a Buckingham Palace plot soon became an item of party faith. Indeed, many Labour MPs now proclaimed that the capacity of capitalism to reform itself had become exhausted, so that working-class interests could only be protected by a revolutionary assault on capitalist power. An equally sharp break with the recent past was the attempt to turn the Parliamentary Party into an adjunct of the Trade Union movement – a development which particularly horrified Snowden.[13]

The 'extremism' of the new Labour programme, from which

10 Cited in Vernon Bogdanor, *Multi-party politics and the Constitution* (Cambridge, 1983), p. 176. This was in total opposition to what it had earlier argued.

11 See Bernard Donoughue and George Jones, *Herbert Morrison: Professional Politician* (1973), pp. 162–7.

12 Williamson, *National Crisis*, pp. 312–13.

13 Ibid., pp. 315–16, 378.

Henderson tried in vain to dissociate himself, destroyed any possibility of a Labour reunion and left MacDonald and his 'National Labour' followers angry and contemptuous at the 'cowards who had run away'. It also revived the fears of socialism which had been so prevalent a decade earlier. Even non-socialist politicians like Reading and Grey who had previously wanted the entire Labour Party included in a government of 'national co-operation' now changed their minds. The view grew that Parliament should be dissolved, so that in the ensuing election there would be an opportunity to *punish* Labour for its irresponsibility.[14] Most Conservatives soon began pressing the National Government to break its earlier pledges by seeking a 'doctor's mandate'.

Paradoxically, then, the two capitalist parties found themselves being drawn into the very situation which a 'national government' was originally supposed to *avoid*. Some Conservatives looked on with dismay as their leaders fell into the 'trap': 'Had Ramsay brought in the bulk of his party with him, there might have been something in a temporary coalition – but except on paper this is not a coalition', observed Headlam. 'It is a collection of people collected together to save the situation – most of them are Conservatives and Liberals.' As events unfolded, Headlam became increasingly 'scared': 'I don't like this direct cleavage between the "Haves" and the "Have nots"', he wrote: the conflict was simply playing into Labour's hands.[15]

Nor were such fears groundless, since, released from the constraints of office, the newly militant Labour Party started to attack the necessity for *any* retrenchment (except cuts in the salaries of Cabinet Ministers and judges!), thereby thrusting the onus and the odium for introducing the economies on to its political opponents. Initially, therefore, the general election seemed to be a risky gamble, though perhaps one that could no longer be avoided.

In the event, to the astonishment of its leaders who had been misled by the enthusiasm of their hardcore supporters, Labour was routed in the General Election of November 1931: only forty-six of its candidates were successful. What had happened was that the National Government's appeal for 'sacrifice' and 'national unity' had largely swamped Labour's socialist propaganda. This particularly benefited the Conservatives, who felt that they could legitimately ask others

---

14 Ibid., pp. 387–8.

15 Headlam diary, 24, 27, 28 Aug. 1931, in Stuart Ball (ed.), *Parliament and Politics in the Age of Baldwin and MacDonald: The Headlam Diaries 1923–1935* (1992), pp. 213–14.

for sacrifice because, in entering the National Government, they had sacrificed the almost certain prospect of forming a Ministry of their own.[16]

From the viewpoint of most of the Labour Party's opponents, the electoral triumph of the National Government was, of course, a highly gratifying event. The most anti-socialist of all the major political groupings, the 'Liberal Nationals' (as the Simonites were now called) had particular cause for celebration. Yet from the very start some Government supporters felt differently. For example, 'National Labour' and the official Liberal Party, led by Samuel, which had both been dragged reluctantly into the election, watched with foreboding as the huge Conservative majority piled up: unhappy memories of how Lloyd George's post-war Coalition had been weakened by the party imbalance in the Commons must have returned to haunt them.

Nor did all the earlier proponents of a 'National Government' find the sort of Ministry resulting from the political crisis of 1931 at all to their liking. Amery, denied office, grumbled in his diary about how a chance to create 'a real national coalition, including the Trade Unions', had been missed.[17] And once the election results had come in, he went to bed, sore at heart, brooding over the prospect of the country being governed by 'a coalition of old gangs and old gangsters with no policy and probably incapable of finding one'. 'I disliked the whole humbug about National Government', he confided to his diary.[18] The Government, Amery later observed, was an 'absurd dishonest Coalition of old gangs'.[19] Page Croft agreed.

Another erstwhile Coalitionist, Churchill, felt duty-bound to support the National Government, but he, too, was one of the 'losers' of 1931, having recently resigned from the Conservative Shadow Cabinet in protest at the party's moderate Indian policy – a critical decision which ensured his exclusion from office after 1931. Adapting to the new situation, Churchill belatedly embraced the tariff. But he continued to hammer away over India – even though it was obvious that MacDonald and Baldwin, together in government, had a virtually free hand in pursuing the sort of 'liberal' policy he loathed.

Lloyd George, out of action because of a prostate operation, was also excluded from the National Government. Indeed, once

16 Thorpe, *General Election of 1931*, pp. 95–6, 237.

17 Williamson, *National Crisis*, p. 357.

18 Amery diary, 27 Oct. 1931, John Barnes and David Nicholson (eds), *The Empire At Bay: The Leo Amery Diaries 1929–1945* (1988), p. 212.

19 Amery diary, 22 Jan. 1932, ibid., p. 227.

returned to health and vigour, the Welshman soon emerged as one of its most caustic critics. This saddened Austen Chamberlain, who, despite his disappointment at being dropped from office following the 1931 Election, continued to salute the National Government as a continuation of the Coalition whose break-up he had been unable to prevent nine years earlier.[20]

Most pathetic of all the 'losers' of 1931 was Oswald Mosley, who had initially greeted the formation of the National Government with some optimism, as a vindication of his own political analysis. But, true to his deeply held convictions, Mosley argued that, although the country faced a grave 'national emergency', the real problem was not so much the budgetary crisis as the need for industrial regeneration, a stance which drew him into opposition to the Government's emphasis on economy.[21]

For Mosley the turning-point came with his failure to negotiate an electoral pact with Neville Chamberlain. Isolated, he began attacking the National Government openly as a 'mere combination of the older politicians' who had failed the country in the past. But Mosley's campaign received little press coverage, his New Party organisation was still too weak to cope with the strains of an election, and most of his important allies quickly melted away. In the 1931 Election all the New Party candidates, Mosley included, lost their seats.

From this debacle Mosley came away with the conviction that 'a new movement [could] not be made within the frame of a parliamentary party',[22] and, feeling betrayed by the 'Old Gangs' who ran these parties, he set off down the fateful path which was to lead him to the creation of the British Union of Fascists (BUF). Unconsciously or otherwise, Mosley had always drawn heavily on the writings of the turn-of-the-century 'National Efficiency' advocates and he did not abandon these ideas now. An impatience with the party system, an eagerness to create a 'modern' 'dynamic' synthesis of Left and Right, a vision of a 'Greater Britain' that transcended sectional and class interests, the celebration of the heroic man of action ('Caesarism'), and a belief in science's potential to find solutions to the country's social and economic problems: such concerns as these continued to make Mosley a sympathetic figure in Lloyd George's eyes.

But by breaking entirely with the established political system

20 Warden Chilcott, *Political Salvation* (1932), pp. 10, 14–15.
21 Williamson, *National Crisis*, pp. 369–70.
22 Ibid., p. 469.

and deriding parliamentary institutions themselves, Mosley had cut himself off completely from mainstream political life. Almost overnight he lost his importance as a magnet for the malcontents. Nor was there any future for a self-proclaimed national saviour whose creed seemed to align him with foreign dictatorships which threatened essential British interests. Most of Mosley's sympathisers in the older parties soon lost patience with him, while a colleague from New Party days, Harold Nicolson, always a moderate at heart, found a 'respectable' outlet for his dissatisfaction with conventional party politics by getting elected to Parliament at the 1935 Election on the National Labour ticket.

THE NATIONAL GOVERNMENT: A PIOUS FRAUD?

It is often said that the National Government stood for little that was distinctively 'national', especially once the Samuelite Liberals had withdrawn from it in September 1932. As early as September 1931 a Conservative like Cuthbert Headlam could privately ask: 'what earthly difference, except in name, is there between the Nationalists and the Conservatives?'[23] Shortly afterwards the Conservative MP for Smethwick, A.R. Wise, was even calling publicly for an end to 'this monstrous hybrid coalition'.[24]

Naturally the Labour Party was disposed to take the same line: during the election campaign Henderson, for example, bluntly declared that the only purpose of the Tories' 'National' allies was 'to give the so-called National Government a cloak of respectability under which the country could be stampeded into tariffs'.[25] And Lansbury spoke for the entire Labour Party when he later called the National Government 'a national humbug'.[26]

To what extent are these scathing indictments borne out by the conduct of the Conservative and Liberal Parties during the 1931 election campaign? The evidence is susceptible to more than one interpretation. In some parts of the country a warm camaraderie developed as the 'Coalition partners' drew together to fight a common campaign. The West Dorset Conservative Association, for example,

---

23 Headlam diary, 14 Sept. 1931, in Ball (ed.), *Parliament and Politics*, p. 216.

24 Cited in Neville Thompson, *The Anti-Appeasers: Conservative Opposition to Appeasement in the 1930s* (Oxford, 1971), p. 9.

25 Thorpe, *General Election of 1931*, p. 236.

26 Bernard Wasserstein, *Herbert Samuel: A Political Life* (Oxford, 1992), p. 344.

expressed a wish to contest the election 'as a National Party, avoiding as far as possible the use of the word Conservative so as to make it easier for members of other Parties to support the national cause'.[27]

In the main, the official party manifestos echoed this appeal. The Conservative document spoke of the country needing 'a stable government with a large majority backed by the resolution of a great majority of the electors' if it were to cope with the economic crisis.[28] The Liberal Nationals, too, urged the electorate to rally behind 'THE COMMON CAUSE'.[29] But the most fervent patriotic rhetoric emanated from the National Labour Party. 'WE MUST ALL PULL TOGETHER', it proclaimed.

> NATIONAL UNITY ESSENTIAL. Whilst our present conditions last [remedial action cannot be taken] by political parties fighting partisan battles on platforms and in Parliament . . . THE WORLD IS WATCHING. In August we won the admiration of the world by our instant subordination of party politics to national interests. Let us now prove that we are determined to see the matter through until we have brought the country out beyond these cloudy days into clearer and more tranquil times.[30]

Yet, at constituency level, a spirit of harmony and brotherly love did not always prevail. Many Conservative associations felt cheated of the electoral victory which was their due; believing that Conservatism was anyhow the 'national' creed, they did not see the need of working with Liberal and Labour allies at all. Some local parties paid lip service to the 'National' campaign, but this amounted to little more than stamping 'National' on to the Conservative pamphlets which were already in stock![31]

In any case, although united in hostility to 'socialism', the old differences of opinion over the tariff continued to make for bad blood between 'official' (Samuelite) Liberals and Conservatives. Indeed, an ancillary reason why many Conservatives favoured an election in November 1931, as Henderson rightly noted, was because they saw this as a way of using the 'national emergency' to crush the Free Trade obstruction and to split the Liberal Party.

The official Liberals, in fact, found themselves in a very difficult

---

27 Thorpe, *General Election of 1931*, p. 110.

28 F.W.S. Craig, *British General Election Manifestos 1900–1974* (London and Basingstoke, 1970), p. 90.

29 Ibid., p. 93.

30 Ibid., pp. 92–3.

31 Thorpe, *General Election of 1931*, p. 188.

situation. They announced that they felt it to be 'their duty to co-operate with the Prime Minister in maintaining a strong and stable Government composed of men of all parties', but they made no bones about their reluctance to follow MacDonald into a general election. In fact, the Liberals presented themselves to the electorate 'as an independent party, standing with undiminished conviction for those causes of individual and national liberty and social progress with which Liberalism has always been identified'. This was coded language which signified a continuing determination to uphold Free Trade, a policy which most Conservatives were clearly anxious to destroy.[32]

Little wonder that, whereas Conservative Central Office had little difficulty in reaching electoral agreements with Simonite Liberals and National Labour, in many parts of the country Conservative and Samuelite Liberal candidates clashed. Only four Simonites encountered Conservative opposition, but no fewer than twenty-six Samuelites did so. Among the latter was Samuel himself, whose opponent at Darwen was personally supported by Page Croft.[33] When Baldwin tried to quash such rebellions, he risked being rebuffed.

The 1931 Election was a precursor to the trouble which erupted the following year, when in September the Conservatives finally goaded the Samuelites into leaving the National Government over the issue of the Ottawa negotiations (which instituted a system of Imperial Preference). In vain did MacDonald work to protect Samuel: the notorious 'agreement to differ' merely delayed his departure for a few more months.[34] A leading Samuelite, Lord Lothian, explained what had happened. Lothian personally favoured continuing the policy of 'national unity', but he noted that most orthodox Liberals felt that the choice which faced them was 'between submerging Liberalism in another 1885 Liberal Unionist combination leaving the "classes" naked and facing one another', or 'trying to infuse the Liberal spirit of reason and tolerance into the left parties'.[35] The official Liberals eventually took the latter option.

32 Craig, *General Election Manifestos*, pp. 99–100. On Samuel's defiant assertion of his Liberal faith, see Wasserstein, *Samuel*, p. 319.

33 Wasserstein, *Samuel*, pp. 330–1. Ninety Conservative candidates faced Liberal or, less frequently, National Labour opposition, and it was from them that much of the hostility to the 'National' label came (Tom Stannage, *Baldwin Thwarts the Opposition: The British General Election of 1935*, 1980, p. 24).

34 On the origin of the 'agreement to differ', see Wasserstein, *Samuel*, pp. 343–4.

35 Lothian to Jones, 9 Sept. 1932, in Thomas Jones, *A Diary with Letters, 1931–1950* (Oxford, 1954), p. 54.

For MacDonald the dilemma was no less cruel. From the very start he had seen the danger of becoming a 'Tory slave'.[36] Aware of his exposed position, he pleaded with Samuel not to resign: 'Whatever use I may have rests on the fact that I represent a combination', he wrote. 'If you go, I am no longer the head of a combination . . . . I should be regarded as a limpet in office.'[37] As 'a Prime Minister who [did] not belong to the party in power', MacDonald explained to the King, his personal position was likely to become 'more and more degrading'.[38]

The Samuelite defection, when it occurred, did indeed damage MacDonald, for, as his biographer argues, the official Liberals, for all their shortcomings, were a genuine party, with principles, organisation and a tradition – things lacking among National Labour and the Simonite Liberals.[39] Despite all of this, the Prime Minister allowed himself to be persuaded that the resignation of the Free Traders (Snowden, as well as the Samuelites) made his own position as the guarantor of national unity all the more important.

Thereafter, the Prime Minister became pathetically dependent on Sir John Simon who was widely thought to be a failure as Foreign Secretary but who, as David Dutton says, did at least have three merits: 'He was safely 'National', safely anti-Lloyd George . . . and at least not a Conservative.'[40] But within the sea of Conservative backbenchers the thirty-five Simonite Liberals were little more than token guarantors of the Government's 'national' status, their importance steadily diminishing as the crisis of 1931 receded into the past. Thus, however skilfully Simon exploited MacDonald's need of him to protect his own followers, by the middle of the decade little seemed to distinguish the Liberal Nationals from the Conservatives.[41]

In his diary the hapless Prime Minister bemoaned his fate. 'What strange lands I have been pushed into!', he observed in November 1931.[42] Nor, he discovered, did the Conservatives improve on further

---

36 Williamson, *National Crisis*, p. 438.

37 MacDonald to Samuel, 10 Sept. 1932, in Wasserstein, *Samuel*, p. 357.

38 Ibid., p. 358.

39 David Marquand, *Ramsay MacDonald* (1977), p. 731. Henry Morris-Jones, later its Whip, concedes that 'the Liberal National Party was never intended to be permanent' (Henry Morris-Jones, *Doctor in the Whips' Room*, 1955, p. 87).

40 David Dutton, *Simon: A political biography of Sir John Simon* (1992), p. 118.

41 Ibid., p. 162, pp. 222–4.

42 MacDonald diary, 10 Nov. 1931, Marquant, *MacDonald* p. 672. Also, 5 Oct. 1931, ibid., p. 666.

acquaintance. Admittedly, Baldwin treated him considerately enough, but the Government was 'nae my oon hoose'.

It could therefore be argued that long before 7 June 1935, when MacDonald swapped offices with Baldwin, the National Government had become a mere shell. Certainly, the Prime Minister's own party lacked substance. As Marquand says, 'it had no distinctive policies, no identifiable grass roots support, and, apart from personal loyalty to MacDonald, no obvious *raison d'être*'.[43] MacDonald's talk of resigning to form his own Centre Party or, alternatively, bringing Lloyd George into the Government, testifies to his growing desperation.[44] Yet, feeling a personal responsibility for having given the Conservatives their majority, the Prime Minister concluded that he had a duty to soldier on.[45]

Despite all this, the National Government differed from a pure Conservative Ministry in several significant respects. Take, first of all, the issue of the distribution of offices. In 1931 the Conservatives comprised only just over one half of the Cabinet. Even after the Samuelite secession, they held no more than thirteen of the nineteen Cabinet posts: after 1935 sixteen out of twenty-two. And when Neville Chamberlain became Prime Minister in 1937, he still found room for four Liberal Nationals and two National Labour Ministers in his Cabinet of twenty-one – to the considerable annoyance of many Conservative backbenchers.[46]

The continuing importance of 'national politics' is even more vividly illustrated by the appointment of Sir John Anderson to Cabinet office as Lord Privy Seal in October 1938. Anderson, a former senior civil servant, had recently been elected on the 'Nationalist' ticket as MP for the Scottish Universities, having declared himself a severely practical man, who had had no time for frivolous political questions and so had 'studiously avoided any Party affiliation': 'I could not now, without a tinge of hypocrisy, assume any Party label even if I did not feel that by doing so I should be, to a considerable extent, undermining the basis of the only claim I can legitimately make to the confidence of any electorate – that of a public servant'.[47] Such a

43 Ibid., p. 677.

44 Ibid., pp. 743, 764–5.

45 Ibid., p. 728.

46 R.J. Minney, *The Private Papers of Hore-Belisha* (1960), pp. 17–18. They also disliked the fact that a Jew (the Liberal National, Hore-Belisha) had been made War Secretary.

47 John W. Wheeler-Bennett, *John Anderson, Viscount Waverley* (1962), p. 185.

frank disavowal of interest in the activities of the Conservative Party did nothing to hamper Anderson's subsequent political career.

However, the National Government meant very much more than a widening of the ministerial catchment area. For Baldwin almost certainly took the 'National' label seriously enough to modify official policies on India and disarmament with a view to conciliating his Coalition partners. As one historian has noted, the National Government 'continued to operate unlike a party government until at least 1934–35', evoking a response in the country which no ordinary Ministry could have done.[48] Women, who now comprised 52 per cent of the electorate, were thought to have been particularly attracted to the National Government by Baldwin's 'wholesome, non-political appeal'.[49]

It also seems highly probable that the National Government both won and retained the allegiance of significant numbers of former Liberals (and perhaps a few former Labour supporters, too). This point can be tellingly illustrated by the case of G.M. Trevelyan, who had been a partisan Radical before 1914 but who became during the inter-war years the expositor of a Liberalism that was truly 'national'. As his biographer shows, Trevelyan's concern was now 'to evoke and to explain – and perhaps to reinforce – the continuity and community of British national life and British national identity, and to celebrate "the fundamentally kind and tolerant nature of our English world"'.[50] In the mid-1930s Trevelyan privately confessed that he was 'not any longer political', but he added that, 'insofar as every citizen has some politics', he liked and admired Baldwin, Simon, Runciman and Halifax, and supported the National Government in the belief that it had 'done more for this country than any since the war'.[51] Trevelyan had by this stage in his career become increasingly conservative in his general outlook, but this distinguished proponent of progressive Whiggery would surely never have identified himself so wholeheartedly with a purely Conservative Administration.

Such a freedom from the constraints of conventional party loyalties also benefited the National Government in other ways. For example, it perhaps allowed statesmen like Baldwin to consider contentious

---

48 John Ramsden, *The Age of Balfour and Baldwin, 1902–1940* (1978), p. 325.

49 Ibid., p. 327; Martin Pugh, *The Making of Modern British Politics, 1867–1939* (Oxford, 1982), p. 276.

50 David Cannadine, *G.M. Trevelyan: A Life in History* (1992), pp. 113–14.

51 In letters of Nov. 1935 and Feb. 1936: ibid., pp. 132–3.

issues like the tariff on their administrative merits.[52] Indeed, it can be argued that the Conservative Leader used 'Coalition' rather in the way that Salisbury had relied upon the Liberal Unionists after 1886 – in order to get his more obdurate backbenchers to make the concessions which he regarded as the price that Conservatives needed to pay if they were to survive in a democratic age. In particular, as Ramsden says, these arrangements gave Baldwin a 'a chance to work out many of the ideas that he had always stood for, in the creation of harmony, moderate policies, and consistency along a middle course'.[53] Well might Simon, writing in March 1932 to a fellow Liberal National MP, Geoffrey Shakespeare, describe the Conservative Leader as 'the embodiment, from the Conservative side, of the spirit of national co-operation which we seek to promote'.[54]

This liberal, conciliatory approach was particularly applied to India. Indeed, the Government's concessionary Indian policy excited Diehard fears that Baldwin had surrendered to his socialist and Liberal colleagues in the name of 'national unity', and there were calls for a return to party politics, or, failing that, the Government's reconstitution with a stronger Conservative element.[55] The *Morning Post*, for example, complained in October 1935 that the National Government had 'departed from some very good Tory principles in the past four years'.[56]

Paradoxically, it was the one-time advocate of 'national politics', Churchill, who now put himself at the head of the malcontents. 'Winston is out to make the maximum of trouble', observed Samuel Hoare. 'He is determined to smash the National Government and believes that India is a good battering ram as he has a large section of the Conservative Party behind him.'[57] But Churchill's assault proved to be counterproductive, especially when his son, Randolph, campaigning on the Indian issue, intervened against the official Conservative candidate in the Wavertree by-election of early 1935, securing enough votes to hand a safe Conservative seat over to the Labour Party.

52 Williamson, *National Crisis*, p. 485.

53 Ramsden, *Age of Balfour and Baldwin*, p. 330; Pugh, *Making of Modern British Politics*, pp. 274–5.

54 Simon to Shakespeare, 7 March 1932, *Simon Papers* (Bodleian Library), SP 71, f. 127.

55 Stannage, *Baldwin*, p. 41.

56 Ibid., p. 201.

57 Hoare to Willingdon, 10 March 1933, cited in John Charmley, *Lord Lloyd and the Decline of the British Empire* (1987), p. 185.

In any case, the Churchillian stance was rather at variance with the dominant mood of contemporary Conservatism, many of whose prominent spokesmen now openly avowed their impatience with party. For example, Lord Eustace Percy, Minister without Portfolio between June 1935 and March 1936, wrote a political tract, *Government in Transition* (1934), in which he described how the National Government had been brought about by an 'alliance between different schools of political thought'. 'The allies at first regarded the emergency which brought them together as a mere interruption of normal conditions', argued Percy, but they were 'beginning to recognise it now as the end of an era', since even the Government's sternest critics recognised that no alternative could be based on 'any of the old political parties acting on the old lines'.[58]

A similar rhetoric was employed by Walter Elliot, who held a succession of offices in the National Government. Speaking on the Import Duties Bill in February 1932, he invoked 'the rising spirit of the young generation' and deprecated the way in which great issues of national reorganisation were 'being "cribbed, cabin'd and confined" by [the] dusty and fusty remnants of nineteenth-century problems'[59] – language reminiscent of his utterances ten years earlier when he had been a leading light of the New Members Group. Elliot further displayed his ecumenical spirit by accepting election to the Other Club in 1932 and two years later, more daringly, by marrying a 'robust Liberal', Katharine Tennant, the half-sister of Asquith's widow![60] At the level of official work, first as Minister of Agriculture and Fisheries and then as Minister of Health, Elliot showed himself to be the kind of reforming, interventionist Conservative who was far more at home in a broad-based Administration than he could ever have been in an orthodox party government.

REACTION AGAINST PARTY IN THE 1930s

In fact, in the early 1930s there was even some discussion of 'fusion', which, perhaps surprisingly, found favour with Neville Chamberlain,

---

58 Cited in Maurice Cowling, *The Impact of Hitler: British Politics and British Policy 1933–1940* (Cambridge, 1975), p. 52; see also ibid., p. 52.

59 Cited in Bogdanor, *Multi-party politics*, p. 179.

60 Colin Coote, *A Companion of Honour: The Story of Walter Elliot* (1965), pp. 131, 148.

who was possibly influenced by his family's earlier involvement in Liberal Unionism.[61] 'A National Party', wrote Chamberlain in a family letter of late 1931, would 'get rid of that odious title of Conservative which has kept so many from joining us in the past.'[62] Indeed, the Samuelite resignations of the following year prompted the thought that this might hasten the moves 'towards that fused Party under a National name which I regard as certain to come'.[63] Baldwin, too, hoped that, in time, it might prove possible 'to change the title of our Party to National', a logical move since it seemed that soon little would 'really [divide] us from the great bulk of the Liberals'.[64]

One reason why this did not happen was that National Labour and the Liberal Nationals both opposed the establishment of a new organisation which they felt would weaken the small influence they were still able to wield 'in a coalition of equals'.[65] In addition, alarmed at the way events were shaping, Tory rightwingers threatened to secede. Lord Stonehaven, the Conservative Chairman, therefore compromised. He urged the party to go on collaborating with its allies for as long as possible by cultivating 'a National rather than a Party spirit in politics', but, at the same time, he discouraged anything that would jeopardise the integrity of the Conservative organisation.[66]

For some supporters of the National Government this was not enough. Austen Chamberlain and Chilcott, for example, called for the creation of a 'National' Party. The names of socialist, conservative and liberal were 'obsolete', Chamberlain declared, and simply perpetuated 'prejudices and differences which ha[d] no present basis in fact and reason'. 'Has not the time come for all men of good-will to proclaim themselves "Nationals" and thus secure the permanent triumph of the National cause?', he asked.[67] Chilcott, as ever, echoed His Master's Voice, though in more strident tones:

61 In fact, Chamberlain had never had much sympathy with 'the old fogies who can't get away from the old habit of regarding the [Conservative] party as an end in itself, instead of an instrument for attaining ends of national importance', as he had put it towards the end of the Great War (Keith Feiling, *The Life of Neville Chamberlain*, 1946, p. 81).

62 Neville Chamberlain to I. and H. Chamberlain, 19 Sept., 24 Oct. 1931, cited in Williamson, *National Crisis*, p. 484.

63 Iain Macleod, *Neville Chamberlain* (1961), p. 161.

64 Jones's diary, 28 Jan. 1932, Jones, *Diary With Letters*, pp. 25–6.

65 Cowling, *Impact of Hitler*, p. 51; Williamson, *National Crisis*, p. 485; Stannage, *Baldwin*, pp. 26, 39.

66 At a practical level, this led to the establishment in March 1933 of the National Coordinating Committee (Stannage, *Baldwin*, pp. 27, 29, 37–8).

67 Chilcott, *Political Salvation*, p. 14.

FINAL WARNING. THE NATION MUST STAND FAST BY THE
NATIONAL GOVERNMENT. One scarcely dare contemplate such
an alternative as a second return of the old Party political Farce . . . .
Should it fall, this country as a first-class Power must fall with it.[68]

Although few politicians took so apocalyptic a view of the world,
many Conservative MPs favoured the systematic elimination of the
old party slogans. For example, the Attorney-General, Sir Thomas
Inskip, made a speech on 24 April 1934 in which he broached the
possibility of 'the permanent constitution of a National Party'.[69]
The idea was taken up on 17 May by *The Times*, which estimated
that three-quarters of all Conservative MPs had been elected on
the National label. Such men, it argued, 'deeply resent attempts to
turn them into party hacks and to make them swallow a version
of Conservative principles and traditions with which they have
not the slightest sympathy'. But though *The Times* thought that
changing conditions had made the former differences between parties
'irrelevant', it advised against hurrying people into 'fusion', simply
insisting that 'the prefix "National" be emphasised by all parties'.

More significant than this cautious editorial, however, was the
response which it elicited. Published in *The Times* on 14 June
over the names of a hundred Conservative MPs, this took the
form of a manifesto which called for closer co-operation between
the parties and regretted that it was not possible to drop 'the
sub-labels of Conservative, Liberal and Labour, which distinguish
persons but have ceased to differentiate between the policies of
supporters of the Government'. 'A National Party, without prefix
or suffix, must grow', it concluded. Meanwhile there must be
no Liberal/Conservative divisions in face of the socialist challenge,
and disparaging remarks about the National Government in the
Conservative press must cease. 'While we recognise the value that
the old party traditions had in the past', the MPs declared, 'we feel
that they have small bearing on the problems of the present day.'

The background of these hundred Conservative MPs merits attention.
Seventy had been returned to the Commons for the first time in 1931
or at subsequent by-elections. Moreover, no fewer than sixty-nine of
them had been elected for a seat which had returned a Labour MP in
1929; indeed, an astonishing 57 per cent represented working-class
constituencies in the urban and mining areas of the country, most

68 Ibid., p. 159.
69 Stannage, *Baldwin*, p. 47.

of them located in the Midlands and the North of England. What this suggests is that the events of 1931 had brought into Parliament a new generation of MPs whose survival, as one historian puts it, 'was dependent on the continuation of "National" government and Baldwin as leader of the party'.[70] As the *Spectator* noted at the time, there was thus a sense in which support for the 'National Government' quickly became self-perpetuating.[71]

Moreover, although by 1934 the acute 'crisis' which had produced the National Government had largely evaporated, Baldwin soon discovered another reason for keeping such a broad-based Administration in being: it provided a secure underpinning for 'democracy' in a dangerous world by offering protection against foreign dictatorships of both Right and Left, just as it could also act as a buffer against the domestic challenge being mounted from opposite ends of the political spectrum by Mosley and Stafford Cripps, the prominent left-wing socialist.[72] For the National Government stood for peace, social harmony and stability – in short, for a distinctively *British* set of values. In a later speech of 1936 Baldwin spelled out what these phrases meant:

> I think that we must all be full of a sense of profound thankfulness
> that we are living in this country, under a system of National
> Government . . . . True to our traditions, we have avoided all
> extremes. We have steered clear of fascism, communism, dictatorship,
> and we have shown the world that democratic government, constitu-
> tional methods and ordered liberty are not inconsistent with progress
> and prosperity.[73]

In a way, then, 'National Government' now seemed to be a way of *preserving the old political system from extremism* – a total reversal of Mosley's coalitionist rhetoric.

All these themes were emphasised in October 1934 at a luncheon which the National Labour Committee organised at the Trocadero Restaurant in honour of Baldwin and Simon. MacDonald made a

---

70 Ibid., p. 13.

71 In its number of 2 Jan. 1932 it noted the significance of the influx of new Conservative MPs, who 'intend to emphasize the national character of the Government, being very clear about the basis on which they were elected'. These MPs, it continued, 'seem more apathetic about Party in the ordinary sense, therein no doubt, reflecting the feeling of the nation that returned them' (cited in Thompson, *Anti-Appeasers*, p. 10).

72 On Cripps, see Chapter 9.

73 Ramsden, *Age of Balfour and Baldwin*, p. 331.

speech about the government's peace-loving credentials and foreign policy successes. He also deprecated 'sharp breaks and revolutions' which threatened stability and class harmony, and invited 'Youth' to join in the great work, out of respect for the war dead. The Prime Minister was followed by Baldwin, who gently mocked the doctrinaires in his own party who regarded him as a 'backslider' and 'more than half a Socialist', ending with a strong plea for the continuation of the National Government which provided, he claimed, the greatest possible 'guarantee of peace, the greatest guarantee of social and democratic stability'. Simon echoed this appeal: the party system, he declared, was 'a luxury which could be afforded when times were good', but, with democracy locked in a life-and-death struggle with dictatorship, it now had to give way to all-party co-operation.[74]

As the 1935 General Election approached, the Government set up a committee to devise an election manifesto: only five of its nine members were Conservatives, though it did not work on party lines in any case.[75] Once the campaign got under way, Baldwin, the new Prime Minister, was careful to reassure his followers that he would consult them before making any further commitments to an all-party grouping.[76] However, this did not prevent the National Government, under the supervision of a 'National Publicity Bureau', from making a joint appeal to the electorate. Only a 'united' British government, it proclaimed, was capable of embodying that 'spirit of national co-operation which [would] best secure the confidence and respect of the world'.[77]

Once again the electorate endorsed the Government's stance. Even though the 'national' parties fell back slightly, they nevertheless returned 432 MPs strong, compared with Labour's 154 and the Liberals' twenty-one. Indeed, so crushing was this victory that when disillusionment with the National Government later set in, it tended to take a 'national' form. For, as we shall see, by the end of the decade it was ruefully acknowledged by many members of the Left that Labour could not win office unaided.

Another manifestation of this flight from party was the proliferation of 'centrist' groupings dedicated to the task of national planning, of which the most important was the all-party 'Next

74 *The Times*, 30 Oct. 1934.
75 Ramsden, *Age of Balfour and Baldwin*, p. 326.
76 Ibid., p. 343.
77 Craig, *General Election Manifestos*, p. 107.

Five Years Group', which produced a collective manifesto in 1935 bearing the significant subtitle, *An Essay in Political Agreement*. Harold Macmillan, one of the group's leading members, had a year earlier written a tract of his own, *Reconstruction: A Plea for a National Policy*, in which, once again, the call went out for the 'mobilisation of all the moderate and intelligent elements in the country . . . to ensure that the drastic changes which are seen to be essential when the real nature of the crisis is understood, are carried out with courage and with conviction'.[78] This was also the message conveyed by Macmillan's next book, *The Middle Way* (1938).

Yet another committed 'centrist' was Keynes. By the early 1930s, Keynes no longer had much to do with the Liberal Party, which had once looked as though it might develop into a serious Centre Party but which had virtually disintegrated since 1932. As we have seen, his brief flirtation with Mosley had also come to a speedy end. This left the great economist free, perhaps for the first time, to propound his 'centrist' panaceas, unfettered by party ties, to any political group which cared to listen to him.

Now, it is true, as Skidelsky observes, that a distinction needs to be drawn between those, including Macmillan, who 'were obsessed with developing a machinery of planning to replace failed market forces', and Keynes, who 'wanted to supply the market system with enough demand to maintain full employment'.[79] All the same, there were important affinities between the two groups, in that both were offering, to quote Macmillan's words, 'a reasonable compromise between the rival claims of individualist and collectivist conceptions of society', a national synthesis of hitherto conflicting schools of political thought.[80] And to Keynes and Macmillan alike planning now seemed necessary, not so much to save capitalism from the assault of socialism (as centrists had earlier argued) but rather to save *freedom* from the challenge of *dictatorship*.

As for the 'National Government' itself: what kind of regime did it provide? Initially, its advocates had envisaged a risk-sharing ministry which would encompass all the major parties, Labour included. As we have seen, the events of August 1931 destroyed that strategy and instead brought about a return to an earlier view of National Government as an anti-socialist bloc.

---

78 Harold Macmillan, *Reconstruction: A Plea for National Policy* (1933), p. 128.
79 Robert Skidelsky, *John Maynard Keynes: The Economist as Saviour 1920–1937* (1992), p. 438.
80 Macmillan, *Reconstruction*, pp. 128–9.

In the process, a strange reversal of roles had taken place. Baldwin, the opponent of Coalition in 1922, became a key figure in the National Governments of the 1930s, from which the old anti-Labour 'fusionists' were absent. By this time Birkenhead was dead; Horne had withdrawn into the shadows; the ageing Austen Chamberlain served as First Lord of the Admiralty in August 1931, but, to his great indignation, was dropped from the Government after the 1931 Election; finally, most paradoxical of all, Winston Churchill, omitted from office, put himself at the head of the 'Diehards' to whom the 'National Government' seemed to be a betrayal of national interests. Similar role reversals occurred inside Liberalism, with Lloyd George emerging (perhaps to his own surprise) as a fierce critic of a National Government in which the former Asquithian, Simon, held the Foreign Secretaryship.[81]

What about policy? The National Government certainly did not degenerate into the sterile, anti-Bolshevist, 'do-nothing' regime of Amery's foreboding. Indeed, some of its activities bore a close resemblance to what Keynes and Mosley had earlier advocated. This is perhaps not altogether surprising since the National Government contained several former admirers of Mosley, notably Oliver Stanley and Walter Elliot (the creator of the Milk Marketing Board). It has even been argued that the new interest in planning and interventionism displayed by the National Governments of the 1930s foreshadowed the 'mixed economy' and 'Butskellism' of the 1950s.[82]

EMERGENCE OF A 'NATIONAL OPPOSITION'?

In name at least the country was still being ruled by a 'National Government' as the decade drew to an end. But Labour never accepted the 'national' credentials of this Administration, and there seemed to be something unsatisfactory about a 'National Government' whose supporting parties had won only 53.7 per cent of the vote in the 1935 General Election. Baldwin himself was troubled on

81 One should in fairness add that there were also *some* continuities between the two Coalition Ministries, as the case of Walter Elliot shows – a theme explored in Chapter 12.

82 Williamson, *National Crisis*, p. 530. On the relationship between the National Governments and 'industrial modernisation', see Scott Newton and Dilwyn Porter, *Modernization Frustrated: The Politics of Industrial Decline in Britain since 1900* (1988), pp. 76–89.

this score: as early as February 1934 we find him toying with the idea of a reconstructed government containing 'a strong Labour leader like Bevin'.[83] Similarly, in November 1936 Thomas Jones recorded 'a growing opinion in many quarters in favour of a *genuine* National Government which would bring in Herbert Morrison, etc.'[84]

The issue became more sharply focused when Neville Chamberlain succeeded Baldwin as Prime Minister in 1937. Admittedly, Chamberlain can be portrayed as a 'moderniser', a politician whose 'liberal' views on a range of policy issues made for an easy working alliance with Simon. In some respects, too, he attached little importance to party allegiance, as his promotion of Sir John Anderson shows. The fact is that Chamberlain, who valued Anderson's administrative skills highly, was in no way troubled by his lack of a party base. Another 'non-political' figure whom Chamberlain raised to high office because of his expertise was an admiral, Lord Chatfield, made Minister for the Co-ordination of Defence in January 1939.[85]

At the same time, nothing did more to destroy the Government's 'national' aura than Chamberlain's own personality. Politics is often about mood as much as about policy, and Chamberlain, in total contrast to Baldwin, had the sort of combative temperament which prevented him from making any effort to conceal his contempt for the Labour Party – a contempt which Labour heartily reciprocated. By the autumn of 1939 the Prime Minister was a deeply divisive figure who 'engendered personal dislike among his opponents to an extent almost unbelievable . . .', as the Chief Whip, David Margesson, later put it to Baldwin.[86]

Chamberlain knew that this was so. In a revealing letter of April 1938 to his sister he said that the Conservative Chairman had told him that 'he'd never known the Party so united, but on the other hand that my outspokenness and precision had probably frightened the weak-kneed Liberals who felt safe with S.B.' Chamberlain admitted the broad truth of this assessment, but commented: 'I can't change my nature and must hope to make up for Liberal defections by greater enthusiasm in our own Party.'[87]

But the Prime Minister's style worried some of his fellow Ministers,

83 Jones, *Diary With Letters*, p. 123.

84 Ibid., p. 280.

85 Maurice Cowling emphasises Chamberlain's respect for ministerial 'expertise', *Impact of Hitler*, pp. 263–4.

86 Cited in Keith Middlemas, *Politics in Industrial Society* (1979), p. 269.

87 Neville to Hilda Chamberlain, 9 April 1938, cited in John Charmley, *Chamberlain and the Lost Peace* (1989), p. 59.

like Butler and Halifax, and it also angered some of his backbenchers. 'The long years of Lord Baldwin's leadership have taught people to expect a different attitude from a Prime Minister than that of party champion', the young Conservative MP, Ronald Cartland, explained to his sister in early 1939.[88] Later in the year Cartland gave public expression to these convictions: 'it is much more important . . . to get the whole country behind you than make jeering pettifogging party speeches which divide the nation', he exploded.[89]

Indeed, such was the abrasiveness of Chamberlain's approach that it soon threatened to create a 'National Opposition' – the very eventuality envisaged by Lloyd George at the start of the decade when he had discussed a possible combination including Mosley, Churchill and himself.[90] Mosley, and to a lesser extent Churchill, may through gross errors of judgment have excluded *themselves* from office. But Lloyd George and Amery, though spending the entire decade on the back benches, still retained considerable influence, and they were joined in due course by former Ministers like Anthony Eden and Duff Cooper, who had fallen out with Chamberlain over the conduct of foreign policy. Also alienated from the government was the eccentric young 'progressive' Tory Harold Macmillan, who for a time entertained the hope that the 'Next Five Years Group' might develop into a kind of party of the Centre Left, under the leadership of Herbert Morrison![91] Meanwhile Macmillan kept in touch with his boyhood hero, Lloyd George, who continued to work hard to cultivate the middle ground.

There was certainly plenty of discontent with the prevailing political dispensation for critics to exploit. In the midst of the Munich Crisis the Foreign Office clerk, Oliver Harvey wrote in his diary:

I have an uneasy feeling that the present Party system is effete and cannot rid itself of its own waste and that unless we go outside and straight back to the country, somebody else quite fresh, a sort of English Mussolini, may arise and kick over the old parties and sweep in. Who knows what such a Boanerges might stand for?[92]

88 Barbara Cartland, *Ronald Cartland* (n.d.), p. 129.

89 Thompson, *Anti-Appeasers*, p. 218. The *Spectator* (11 Aug. 1939) took a similar line: 'The long years of Mr Baldwin's leadership taught people to expect a different attitude from a Prime Minister than that of party champion.'

90 Harold Nicolson diary, 21 July 1931, Nigel Nicolson (ed.), *Harold Nicolson: Diaries and Letters 1930–1939* (1966), pp. 81–2.

91 Ben Pimlott, *Labour and the Left in the 1930s* (Cambridge, 1977), p. 147.

92 Harvey diary, 8 Oct. 1938, John Harvey (ed.), *The Diplomatic Diaries of Oliver Harvey 1937–1940* (1970), p. 211.

In fact, by this time Chamberlain's policy of 'Appeasement' was troubling critics on both the Left and the Right. The former believed that a more determined opposition should be shown to Fascism, while the latter were angry over what they saw as the neglect of British imperial interests in a futile attempt to propitiate Germany. Had Chamberlain's opponents succeeded in joining forces with the 'respectable' wing of the Labour Party, a 'national combination', at once patriotic and progressive, might well have been created.

In the spring of 1938 there was indeed talk of a possible *rapprochement* between Labour and the Tory rebels, after the *Reynolds' News* had launched a new popular front campaign, later backed by the *New Statesman* and the *News Chronicle*.[93] At Westminster, too, an attempt was made to combine elements from different parties. In the middle of the Munich Crisis Macmillan actually approached Hugh Dalton, the Labour Party's foreign affairs spokesman, with the suggestion that the Labour leadership should concert parliamentary opposition to the Government with Churchill and his friends. This overture led to an inconclusive exchange of views between Dalton, Churchill and Eden at Brendan Bracken's house. What Macmillan was hankering after, Dalton sensed, was a '1931 in reverse'.[94]

Churchill's role in such a combination would have been highly controversial. In 1938 he was still widely mistrusted, especially on the Left, where he had never been entirely forgiven for his earlier 'anti-Bolshevism' and his more recent 'reactionary' stance over India. When Churchill joined Beaverbrook in a quixotic defence of Edward VIII during the Abdication Crisis, he confirmed the prevalent impression that he lacked the judgement and stability of character required in a national leader.

Yet later, as the international situation deteriorated, Churchill's reputation began to revive. To a backbench rebel like Cartland, Churchill was 'the personification, not only of youth itself but of all that youth wants'.[95] And so by the summer of 1939 voices were raised for Churchill to be brought back into government; such a development, wrote Garvin in the *Observer* on 22 July, 'would be accepted as the conclusive proof of national efficiency and resolution'.[96] Churchill played up to these preconceptions by presenting himself as a unifying 'national figure'. He called for the

93 Pimlott, *Labour and the Left*, pp. 152–3.
94 Ibid., pp. 163–4, 166.
95 Cartland, *Cartland*, p. 130.
96 Martin Gilbert, *Winston Churchill: Volume 5 1922–1939* (1976), pp. 1090–1.

establishment of a Ministry of Supply, insisting that this was 'no party question'.[97] Indeed, Churchill was one of thirty MPs (along with Eden and Duff Cooper) who signed a motion in March 1939 advocating a truly National Government. And as war approached, he urged the Prime Minister to bring senior Liberals into his administration,[98] though Labour, as he well knew, was implacably hostile to Chamberlain's leadership.

However, in the manoeuvring of 1938–39 it was Anthony Eden who emerged as the main magnet for the malcontents. Eden, after all, had the ear of 'liberal' opinion in a way that Churchill did not. Whether or not Eden could have offered a viable foreign policy in place of Chamberlain's personal diplomacy is a moot point. What is indisputable is that after his resignation in February 1938 Eden seemed to stand for an alternative *kind* of politics from Chamberlain's – more liberal, consensual and 'national'.

Baldwin, now out of office, proffered encouragement. Eden's former Parliamentary Private Secretary (PPS), Jim Thomas (no relation to J.H. Thomas), wrote back to his friend describing Baldwin's 'fury at what Neville C. had done – "all my work in keeping politics national instead of party undone"'.[99] There was even some desultory talk of Baldwin emerging from retirement to re-create a truly National Government once again. This was unlikely to happen, but a momentous future seemed to await Eden, Baldwin's natural heir.

That was certainly the viewpoint of Harold Nicolson, who, believing that Eden had been jockeyed out of office by the party wire-pullers, wanted him to 'clearly indicate that he stands for postwar England against the old men'.[100] Churchill, too, publicly encouraged such notions when he drew parallels between Eden's career and that of his own father, Lord Randolph, both of whom, he argued, had been 'crushed' by the party machine.[101]

97 Ibid., p. 1021.

98 In fact, Chamberlain had vainly offered Samuel (who had supported Munich) a place in his Government the previous October (Wasserstein, *Samuel*, p. 392.)

99 Oliver Harvey's diary, 12 March 1938, *Harvey Diaries*, p. 115. Also, see Harvey's diary, 13 April 1938, ibid., p. 126.

100 Nicolson diary, 11 April 1938, *Nicolson Diaries*, p. 334. 'Every party today is crushed by its own old men; out of all this there may emerge a party which young men can join with fervour', Nicolson later reflected (Nicolson diary, 19 July 1939, ibid., p. 406).

101 Robert Rhodes James, *Anthony Eden* (1986), p. 216.

Privately Eden spoke of the need for a National Party and a National Government to deal with the current crisis, contemptuously rejecting Chamberlain as 'essentially a party man'.[102] More to the point, before and after Munich he went to some trouble to portray himself as a national saviour, following Harvey's advice that he should appeal to 'liberal' opinion in the country, where his main support lay. For example, in April 1938 Eden delivered a St George's Day oration in which he called for a 'sustained national effort' to counter the dangerous competition emanating from the 'autocratic states'.[103] He followed this up with a letter to his constituents in which he sounded the note that he was to repeat insistently until war finally broke out: 'We live in most anxious times', and 'the sooner we realize[d] true national unity the stronger [would] be the democracies and the less the risk of war'.[104]

Moreover, in the summer and autumn of 1938 Eden made a series of speeches in different parts of the country in which he consciously strove to shake off his reputation as merely a 'foreign affairs expert' by talking about the country's 'national traditions' and by linking social improvement at home to the well-being of the empire abroad. In September 1938 Harvey found him 'full of impressions of industrial conditions and [the] need for revival of Disraeli Tory democracy'.[105] It was such convictions as these that underlay Eden's public warning that there was 'a real danger that matters may so drift that England may become a nation where one half does not know how the other half lives' and his proclamation that the empire's safety depended upon an enhanced sense of national identity.[106]

In the House of Commons in November 1938 Eden made a well-received speech in which the rhetoric of 'Tory Democracy' was more directly combined with the language of 'National Efficiency': 'Health is man-power and man-power is strength', he now announced. Interestingly, Eden then went on to question 'whether under the present party system, as we work it, an effort commensurate with our needs can be made at all'. He ended by calling for 'real unity' and an 'ordered plan'. 'My appeal', Eden said, 'is not merely for a Government of all the parties – that is mere machinery. What is far more important is the spirit behind such unity.'[107]

102 Ibid., p. 206.
103 *The Times*, 27 April 1938.
104 Ibid., 6 June 1938.
105 8 Sept. 1938, *Harvey's Diaries*, p. 172.
106 Cited in James, *Eden*, p. 212.
107 Hansard, 5th ser., 341, 374–81: 10 Nov. 1938.

Previously Amery had shown little sympathy with Eden's 'liberal' approach to international problems. However, by late 1938 he sensed that the latter might be enlisted in his favourite cause, that of 'national service': 'the time may soon be coming', Amery felt, 'when some form of reconstruction on a basis embracing all Parties ought to be seriously considered'.[108] Amery was therefore impressed by Eden's Commons speech, though he noted that it had 'created much speculation as to exactly what he meant, whether he was angling for Socialist and Liberal support for a new coalition, or not'.[109]

What Eden probably wanted was for Chamberlain to broaden his Government by taking back into office 'rebels' like himself, along with a handful of Opposition figures. Within the Cabinet, Halifax, Eden's successor at the Foreign Office, emerged as an ally. But Chamberlain adamantly refused to listen to advice. Indeed, by August 1939 Eden had become so desperate that he was privately hazarding the view that, in the event of the Government calling a snap election, he might have to stand as an Independent Conservative or even create a new party of his own.[110]

Yet when it came to public action, Eden's behaviour was ultra-cautious. For example, whereas Macmillan (helped by the young Reginald Maudling) intervened in the Oxford by-election in October 1938 in support of Lindsay, the non-party anti-Munich candidate, Eden was not prepared to challenge the Conservative organisation in so open a way.[111] Well might the *New Statesman* conclude that Eden was 'playing not for a Tory split and a new Coalition, but for the leadership of the Conservative Party on a policy which he hopes will win Labour and Liberal support'.[112] Attlee later grumbled about how impossible it had been to 'get the revolting Tories up to scratch'.[113] Some members of the 'Eden Group', like Harold Nicolson, became almost as irritated. 'Anthony does not wish to defy the Tory Party', Nicolson wearily observed in July 1939, 'and is in fact missing every boat with exquisite elegance'.[114] Nicolson, a National Labour man,

108 *The Times*, 7 Oct. 1938.

109 Amery diary, 10 Nov. 1938, Barnes and Nicholson (eds), *Empire at Bay*, p. 535.

110 James, *Eden*, pp. 219–20.

111 See Iain McLean, 'Oxford and Bridgwater', in Chris Cook and John Ramsden (eds), *By-Elections in British Politics* (1973), pp. 144–9.

112 *New Statesman*, 19 Nov. 1938, cited in Thompson, *Anti-Appeasers*, p. 196.

113 Pimlott, *Labour and the Left*, p. 168.

114 Diary, 18 July 1939, Nicolson (ed.), *Nicolson Diaries*, p. 406.

privately confessed to *hating* the Conservatives.[115] But, however out of sympathy he might have been with its current Leader, Eden was, in the last analysis, a Conservative, and this restricted his room for manoeuvre.

Meanwhile there was also resistance to the idea of a 'national opposition' on the *Labour* side of the House. This became apparent when Stafford Cripps came forward in October 1938 with the recommendation that Labour should 'put Socialism aside for the present' in order to organise support for a 'programme to preserve our democratic liberties, to rebuild collective security, and for national control of our economic life'.[116] Three months later Cripps launched a new 'Popular Front' agitation by issuing a personal Memorandum: 'present times are not normal', it proclaimed, 'indeed they are absolutely unprecedented in their seriousness for democratic and working-class institutions of every kind'. At this stage in his career Cripps was still denouncing Churchill as a 'warmonger and an Imperialist' but he *was* prepared to work with the Liberals, the Communist Party and the ILP.[117]

All to no avail. True, some very prominent Liberals, among them the Party Leader, Archibald Sinclair, Lloyd George, Keynes and Sir Richard Acland (of whom more in the next chapter), came out in Cripps's support.[118] It is also interesting to find an opinion poll taken in March 1939 showing that 56 per cent of respondents approved of Cripps's efforts to get the Opposition parties to act together to defeat the Government at the next election, as against only 21 per cent who disapproved.[119]

Unfortunately, Cripps fatally damaged his own case by making too much depend on his prediction that, unaided, Labour could not for the foreseeable future win power through the ballot box. Only a cross-party alliance, Cripps felt, could prevent the 'certain use by the National Government of the call for National Unity against a foreign enemy'.[120] But politicians win no plaudits from their colleagues by

115 13 March 1938, ibid., p. 331.

116 Pimlott, *Labour and the Left*, p. 165. See also Thompson, *Anti-Appeasers*, p. 195.

117 Pimlott, *Labour and the Left*, pp. 170–1.

118 Ibid., p. 176. For an interpretation which emphasises the links between the Popular Front and the pre-war 'Progressive Alliance', see David Blaazer, *The Popular Front and the Progressive Tradition: Socialists, Liberals, and the Quest for Unity, 1884–1939* (Cambridge, 1992).

119 Hadley Cantril, *Public Opinion, 1935–1946* (Princeton, 1951), p. 195.

120 Cowling, *Impact of Labour*, p. 217.

casting doubt on their party's chances of electoral success. In any case, Labour had reacted to the 'Great Betrayal' of 1931 by resolving that never again would it compromise its independence by deals with other parties, except in the direst of national emergencies – and neither the Munich Settlement nor even Germany's occupation of Prague could quite be described in those terms. In January 1939 Labour's National Executive Committee had Cripps expelled.

This action further distanced Cripps from mainstream political life. 'I don't think that "party politics" in the old sense will have any meaning in this country for a very long time to come', he told his aunt, Beatrice Webb, in June 1939: 'They are discredited and useless as a means of directing policies in times like these'.[121]

Beatrice Webb agreed with this assessment, believing, as she did, that her nephew would eventually find himself 'on the Front Bench of a National government composed mainly of the old governing class, converted by the course of events, to a compromise with the new social order'.[122] This was a shrewd prediction. For even though there was no chance of a collapse of party during normal peacetime conditions, new possibilities of cross-party combination were about to open up with Britain's entry into the Second World War.

121 Paul Addison, *The Road to 1945* (1975), p. 193.
122 Beatrice Webb's diary, 9 July 1939, Norman and Jeanne MacKenzie (eds), *The Diary of Beatrice Webb: Vol. 4: 1924–1943: 'The Wheel of Life'* (1985), p. 437.

CHAPTER NINE

The Second World War

THE NATIONAL GOVERNMENT AND ITS CRITICS ON THE EVE OF WAR

Everyone knew in 1939 how a total war should be fought, if only because there were so many figures in public life who had participated, as Ministers, administrators and experts, during the Great War. All could agree that, above all else, total war required 'national unity'. And, as Arthur Greenwood said on 2 August 1939, this in turn meant 'that reasonable sacrifice of party opinions, personal opinion and party interest should be made to contribute to the national security'.[1] Only by such means could the government carry necessary, but unpopular, measures like the commandeering of property, food rationing and the conscription of labour. Yet the history of the First World War uncannily repeated itself, in the sense that it again took almost three-quarters of a year before the country acquired a Coalition Government.

This delay may in part have reflected the reluctance of several senior Ministers to accept that Britain was locked in a life-and-death struggle with the German Reich. Neville Chamberlain, in particular, was gambling on there being a limited war, which would preclude the need for a Coalition at all.[2] But, quite apart from these considerations, the state of British politics when war broke out in September 1939 was decidedly strange: the government had critics aplenty, but they seemed totally unable to combine in order to turn Chamberlain out.

1 Cited in Neville Thompson, *The Anti-Appeasers* (Oxford, 1971), p. 217.
2 Paul Addison, *The Road to 1945* (1975), p. 63.

ORIGINS OF THE CHURCHILL COALITION

In fact, when war broke out in September 1939 no alternative 'National Government' was remotely in prospect. On the contrary, if anything the commencement of hostilities set back the chances of a fundamental political realignment. For while Eden and Churchill accepted office in Chamberlain's Administration, Labour's Parliamentary Party Executive unanimously resolved that members of the party would never join a Ministry of which Chamberlain and Simon were two of the leading Ministers.[3] True, the Acting Leader, Greenwood, had responded to Amery's appeal that he 'speak for England', when the Government was still hesitating over whether or not to declare war. But Labour had, as yet, no wish to exchange its place on the Opposition Benches for the responsibility of office. Paradoxically, then, the end of 1939 saw the country experiencing something nearer to a straightforward party administration than it had had since Baldwin's departure from 10 Downing Street in 1929!

It was difficult to see whence 'national salvation' was to come, since the elderly Lloyd George now exuded an air of defeatism, while Mosley's plans to save the empire by doing a deal with Germany hardly endeared him to his contemporaries.[4] For want of an alternative, opposition to the Government devolved upon Clement Davies's All-Party Parliamentary Action Group, which, through one of its founder members, Boothby, maintained regular contact with Lloyd George.[5] This pressure group was joined in April 1940 by Lord Salisbury's 'Watching Committee', composed of some twenty-six critical Conservative MPs. Meanwhile the 'Eden Group' (minus Eden, now a Cabinet Member) continued to retain a shadowy existence.[6]

Interestingly enough, providing a modicum of cohesion to these opposition forces was L.S. Amery, dismissed by some as a 'tariff bore', but undoubtedly the most energetic and distinguished of the proponents of 'national politics' still untrammelled by the responsibilities of office. Indeed, Beaverbrook briefly entertained the notion that Amery might become Prime Minister as part of 'a clean sweep

---

3 Ibid., p. 60.

4 Indeed, it was shortly to lead to his incarceration under Regulation 18B. Thus Mosley became the victim of the 'emergency powers' of which he had long been the advocate.

5 Addison, *1945*, p. 67.

6 Thompson, *Anti-Appeasers*, pp. 222–3.

eliminating the old Conservative gang as far as possible'. Amery quickly rejected this not very realistic idea, but persuaded the parliamentary rebels that, together, they should 'support any Prime Minister who would form a truly National Government appointing its men by merit and not on Whips' lines and making a real War Cabinet' – an important resolution.[7] In fact, when Amery made his famous 'In the name of God, go' speech in the Commons on 7 May, he explicitly demanded the replacement of the National Government (which he called 'a coalition based upon no clear political principles') by a new Administration representing 'all the elements of real political power in this country, whether in this House or not'.[8]

Of course, it could be argued that what really brought the Churchill Coalition into existence was the crisis which broke when the German Armies overran the Low Countries and invaded France. Dalton and Attlee, who would otherwise have preferred Halifax as Premier, privately agreed that 'now it *must* be Churchill'.[9] Yet of equal importance was the *manner* in which Churchill, brushing Halifax aside, came to be installed as Prime Minister in May 1940.[10] In particular, Labour's role in the destruction of Chamberlain's National Government was to prove crucial for the future trajectory of British politics. For whereas Labour *might* have been admitted as a junior partner in a Coalition government several months earlier, in the event, as Addison says, they were not really given office at all: instead, 'they broke in and took it, on terms of moral equality'.[11]

NATURE OF THE CHURCHILL COALITION

Despite this, Labour was initially at a numerical disadvantage in the Coalition, especially in the lower ministerial ranks, holding only sixteen posts, as against the Conservatives' fifty-two, an imbalance which was rectified over the following months, but only slightly. Nevertheless, from the very start, Churchill's Coalition was an

7 Amery diary, 9 May 1940, John Barnes and David Nicholson (eds), *The Empire At Bay: The Leo Amery Diaries 1929–1945* (1988), pp. 611–12.

8 Parl. Deb., 5th ser., vol. 360, 1149–50: 7 May 1940.

9 Hugh Dalton, *The Fateful Years: Memoirs 1931–1945* (1957), p. 312.

10 For a recent account of Churchill's ascent to power, see Robert Blake, 'How Churchill Became Prime Minister', in Robert Blake and William Roger Louis (eds), *Churchill* (Oxford, 1993), Chapter 15.

11 Addison, *1945*, p. 62.

authentic National Government, with power genuinely shared between the two main parties: Labour, for example, occupied several of the key positions on the Cabinet committees dealing with social and economic policy.[12] Churchill boasted (and with good reason) that he had formed the broadest administration known to history: there was even room in it for the former leader of the National Party, Page Croft (now Lord Croft). But he never lost sight of his crucial dependence upon Labour, whose new-found importance was symbolised by the presence at the Ministry of Labour of Ernest Bevin, equipped with wide-ranging authority, a 'clear recognition of trade union power to determine, either way, supply, production, manpower and morale', as Keith Middlemas puts it.[13] Thus, Labour, whose exclusion from office had been a dominant concern in 'national' politics for decades, was now called upon to come forward as national saviour – a role which Bevin, for one, enormously relished.[14]

In any case, Churchill was not really a party figure at all, if indeed he had *ever* been. 'Like you I have no party of my own', he wrote with only slight exaggeration when attempting to lure Lloyd George into his Administration in late May 1940.[15] Churchill saw himself, rather, as the 'father of his people', and, as one historian puts it, 'the coalition was part of his personal dialogue with the nation'.[16] The Commons may have laughed when Churchill told it in October 1944 that he had never previously seen any Government to which he had 'been able to give a more loyal, confident, and consistent support'.[17] But the Premier's affection for his Ministry was deep and genuine; as it drew to its end in 1945, he wanted to strike a medal which he could award to those who had served it.[18]

Admittedly, in the early days of his premiership Churchill had to tread warily. His memories of the closing stages of the Great War must have alerted him to the possibility that Chamberlain might later

12 Ibid., p. 106, for further details. At the start of 1944 Labour held eight of forty-two ministerial posts (Cripps not included), but three of the eight War Cabinet seats.

13 Keith Middlemas, *Politics in Industrial Society* (1979), p. 271.

14 See, for example, Bevin's famous address to the trade unionists on 25 May 1940.

15 Churchill to Lloyd George (n.d.), in Colin Cross (ed.), *Life with Lloyd George: The Diary of A.J. Sylvester 1931–45* (1975), p. 266.

16 J.M. Lee, *The Churchill Coalition 1940–1945* (1980), p. 15.

17 Winston S. Churchill, *The Second World War: Vol. VI: Triumph and Tragedy* (1954), p. 510.

18 Lee, *Churchill Coalition*, p. 17.

threaten him, as Asquith had once threatened Lloyd George. Churchill guarded against this eventuality by keeping Chamberlain on as Lord President of the Council and treating him with consideration and courtesy – magnanimous behaviour that the other man reciprocated. For the same reason Halifax remained at the Foreign Office until December 1940, while Simon was moved to the Woolsack. Nor would Churchill countenance any general vendetta against the so-called 'Guilty Men'. For although the hapless Elliot (who had actually contemplated resignation over the Munich Settlement) was dropped, Margesson, Chamberlain's Chief Whip, was in fact promoted to War Secretary in December 1940.[19]

Lloyd George summed up the situation succinctly: Churchill, he opined, would 'not smash the Tory Party to save the country, as I smashed the Liberal Party'.[20] This refusal, on the Premier's part, to attempt a clear-out of the 'Old Gangs' particularly annoyed two of his junior Ministers, Amery (who had been fobbed off with the India Office) and Macmillan: 'Winston has not been nearly bold enough in his changes', fumed Amery in his diary in mid-May 1940, 'and [was] much too afraid of the Party which he feels has never really quite readmitted him into the fold.' Although a distinct improvement on 'the unholy and essentially dishonest coalition of 1931', Amery felt that Churchill's Administration was 'still only a political coalition and not a real national government of efficiency' – and thus much inferior to the Ministry which Lloyd George had headed after December 1916.[21]

In fact, Churchill's original War Cabinet[22] bore a closer resemblance to the former Asquith Coalition, being largely a *combination* of party leaders, not, as Amery and his friends had earlier demanded, a 'genuine National Government' in which the Premier chose 'his colleagues on merit, and not on the recommendation of any party

19 However, Margesson was sacked from the War Office in 1942, to be replaced by G.P.J. Grigg.

20 Jones to Violet Markham, 13 July 1940, Thomas Jones, *A Diary With Letters 1931–1950* (1954), p. 465.

21 Amery diary, 12, 13 May 1940, Barnes and Nicholson (eds), *Empire At Bay*, pp. 616–18; William Roger Louis, *In The Name of God Go! Leo Amery and the British Empire in the Age of Churchill* (New York, 1992), p. 125. A persistent criticism was that Churchill behaved like a dictator, ignoring his War Cabinet.

22 Chamberlain had created a War Cabinet on the outbreak of war, but it was nine members strong: Chamberlain, Hoare, Simon, Halifax, Churchill, Kingsley Wood, Chatfield, Hankey and Hore-Belisha.

manager'.[23] After all, its membership comprised, in addition to Churchill himself, four Ministers: Attlee and Greenwood, Leader and Deputy Leader of the Labour Party, Chamberlain and Halifax – hardly the most dynamic quartet imaginable. Party balance, of a kind, was also secured by alloting the three Service Ministries to each of the three political parties.[24] For at this stage of the war Churchill still intended to work *through* these parties. But this did not necessarily mean 'the right man in the right place'. Macmillan's observation to Beaverbrook in October 1941 was therefore acute: 'All the symptoms are developing which marked the end of the *Asquith* coalition (a coalition of parties) and the formation of the *Lloyd George* coalition (a coalition of personalities). But in this case the second coalition must be under the same leadership.'[25]

It was in the hope of speeding up such a transition that Amery spearheaded the 'Under-Secretaries' Plot' of June 1940 (Boothby and Macmillan were also involved), in which the rebels called, in lieu of the existing War Cabinet, for the establishment of a Committee of Public Safety dominated by the Prime Minister, Lloyd George and Bevin.[26] But Churchill had easily squashed this intrigue. What is more, in his anxiety to placate important sectors of political opinion, he actually allowed the size of the War Cabinet to *grow*, the reshuffle of October 1940 bringing an enlargement of its membership to eight, which many contemporaries saw as a regrettable departure from the principles of 1916.[27] Admittedly, Bevin's promotion to the War Cabinet made considerable sense; but was it necessary to bring in Kingsley Wood as well? Such developments confirmed Beveridge, impatiently awaiting the call to public service, in his belief that the war effort was being far less efficiently conducted by Churchill than it had been under Lloyd George, an episode now bathed in a nostalgic glow.[28]

When Chamberlain retired from the Government, terminally ill,

23 *The Times*, 10 May 1940.

24 The War Office to Eden (Conservative), the Admiralty to Alexander (Labour) and the Air Ministry to Sinclair (Liberal).

25 Addison, *1945*, p. 197.

26 Ibid., pp. 109–10; Kevin Jefferys, *The Churchill Coalition and Wartime Politics, 1940–1945* (Manchester, 1991), p. 46.

27 Jefferys, *Churchill Coalition*, p. 51.

28 Beveridge wanted the Government to control all national resources, and in a series of articles and letters at the start of the war called for a small War Cabinet whose members would be freed from departmental duties, aided by an Economic General Staff.

in October 1940, Churchill, in defiance of his wife's advice, had himself elected as Conservative Leader. However, as the Prime Minister became more securely seated, his regime began to acquire more obviously 'national' features. For example, in February 1942 the ineffectual Greenwood was sacked, and, though Attlee, 'a real lightweight', had to be kept on simply because he was head of the Labour Party,[29] it was now possible to give important positions to more competent Labour figures like Herbert Morrison, who entered the War Cabinet as Home Secretary in November 1942.

In addition, following the precedent of the Great War, non-party administrators and 'technocrats' were promoted to high office. To be fair, Neville Chamberlain, who always put 'business capacity' before political correctness, had taken the first steps in this direction. Thus, Sir Andrew Duncan, the Chairman of the Iron and Steel Federation (who had twice in the past stood for Parliament as a National Liberal candidate), was brought into the Government as President of the Board of Trade in January 1940,[30] and Lord Hankey and Lord Reith also became Ministers. Furthermore, in April 1940 Chamberlain persuaded a reluctant Lord Woolton, a successful businessman in the Lewis' retail chain, then aged fifty-eight, to become Minister of Food.

But Churchill took the process much further. He recruited the businessman Lord Leathers to the post of Minister of War Transport in 1941, and in 1943 made Woolton the first Minister of Reconstruction, with a seat in the Cabinet. At the time Woolton was still an Independent: indeed he delayed joining the Conservative Party until after Churchill's election defeat in 1945. Moreover, a series of important official positions, including Minister of Production with a seat in the War Cabinet, were assigned to Oliver Lyttelton, formerly Managing Director of the British Metal Corporation – though, unlike the other businessmen brought into government, Lyttelton, as Churchill later observed, had been 'running in and out of the purlieus of politics since he was in knickerbockers'.[31]

Professional civil servants also found themselves performing a

---

29 See the grumbling of the circle surrounding Eden, in Oliver Harvey's diary, 18 Feb. 1942 (John Harvey, ed., *The War Diaries of Oliver Harvey*, 1978, p. 99).

30 For the rest of the war he alternated between that post and the Ministry of Supply. On first becoming a Minister, he sought election for the City of London as a 'National'. As secretary of the Shipbuilders' Employers Federation, Duncan had been an expert adviser during the First World War to first Maclay and then Geddes.

31 Earl of Woolton, *Memoirs* (1959) p. 177.

ministerial role. In February 1942 the War Office was entrusted to its former Permanent Under-Secretary, P.J. Grigg. That even more distinguished civil servant, Sir John Anderson, whom Chamberlain had made Home Secretary on the outbreak of war, was raised still higher up the ministerial pecking order when Churchill sent him to the Treasury in September 1943. Indeed, in early 1945 Churchill wrote a confidential letter to the King, recommending that, in the event of the sudden death of himself and Eden, the premiership should go to Anderson, a man who still had no party affiliations of any kind – a revealing commentary on the politics of war.

Rather more controversial was the prominence achieved by 'court favourites' like Lord Cherwell (Paymaster-General), Brendan Bracken (Minister of Information) and Beaverbrook (Minister of Aircraft Production and then Minister of Supply, with a seat in the War Cabinet). 'The gangsters will shortly be in complete control', grumbled the straightlaced Halifax.[32] But at least the 'Old Gangs' had been cut down to size, which was what the proponents of 'national politics' had all along demanded. Indeed, by the end of the war, as A.J.P. Taylor has observed, Attlee 'was the only party wheel-horse in the Cabinet', all the others being 'outsiders or former rebels', with a notable absence of reliable Conservatives.[33]

COALITION: TEMPORARY EXPEDIENT OR PERMANENCY?

Churchill's wartime Administration has been the subject of two important historical debates. First, was it a mere government of emergency or did it seem likely to have a more extended life? Secondly, what did the existence of this coalition really *signify*?

Churchill's own position on the question of coalition is not in doubt: he wanted it to continue into the years of peace, if this could be arranged. So much was apparent from the Premier's address to Conservative Central Council in March 1941, when he outlined his plans for the post-war world. Churchill hoped that there would

32 Jefferys, *Churchill Coalition*, pp. 39–40. Baldwin's old friend, Davidson, agreed: 'the crooks are on top, as they were in the last war – we must keep our powder dry!' (cited in Andrew Roberts, '*The Holy Fox*', 1991, p. 208).

33 A.J.P. Taylor, '1932–1945', in David Butler (ed.), *Coalitions in British Politics* (1978), p. 90.

'be national unity in certain measures of reconstruction and social advance to enable this country to recover from the war and, as one great family, to get into its stride again'. Failure to achieve this, he warned, would be 'a misfortune, because we should then have to ask the nation to decide upon the outstanding issues, and a party government would be the result'.[34] In a radio broadcast two years later the Prime Minister, more explicitly still, called upon 'the best men in all parties' to serve in a 'National' government that would implement his Four-Year Plan.[35]

Even as late as 1945 Churchill was promising in his speech to Conservative Conference that, if the Coalition broke up, he would want a Conservative government broadened by the inclusion of men of 'every party and no party'.[36] In private Churchill used similar language: 'The social and economic problems are immensely urgent', he argued. 'That is why the parties should continue to work together as they have done since 1940. We have been good colleagues and happy to co-operate. The partnership has been a successful one. Why dissolve it now?[37] Thus Churchill's PPS, Harvie Watt, was probably reflecting his master's views when he told Dalton in September 1944 that it would be 'political damnation for either Party to run the Government alone in the post-war years'.[38]

This sort of language has been interpreted by some historians as an attempt to secure party advantage: either by 'placing the onus for leaving the coalition on Labour Ministers or by embarrassing those such as Bevin still rumoured to favour continued co-operation'. It has also been claimed that when on 18 May 1945 Churchill urged the leaders of the Labour and Liberal Parties to carry on with the Coalition until the defeat of Japan, he anyhow knew that Labour would reject the offer.[39] Colville's diary suggests that Macmillan and Randolph Churchill may indeed have been thinking in this way.[40]

But to attribute such cynicism to Churchill himself is surely to ignore all the evidence of his lifelong yearning to escape from

34 Paul Addison, *Churchill on the Home Front 1900–1955* (1992), p. 361.

35 Angus Calder, *The People's War: Britain 1939–45* (1969; 1971 edn), p. 616.

36 Jefferys, *Churchill Coalition*, pp. 182–3.

37 In a private conversation during March 1945: G.S. Harvie-Watt, *Most of My Life* (1980), pp. 185–6.

38 Addison, *1945*, p. 235.

39 Jefferys, *Churchill Coalition*, pp. 182–4.

40 Colville's diary, 21 May 1945, John Colville, *The Fringes of Power: Downing Street Diaries 1939–1955* (1985), p. 601.

The Second World War

adversarial politics. For in Churchill's eyes, Coalition was actually
the best possible government, not simply a necessary device for
winning the war. Indeed, Churchill's wartime Coalition in a way
represented the culmination of a lifelong pursuit of a 'National'
government, unfettered by party traditions and restraints. Something
of the intensity of emotion with which Churchill regarded the
Coalition can be seen in his conduct at a farewell party held at
Downing Street when, 'with tears running down his cheeks', he
saluted his former colleagues, saying that 'the light of history will
shine on all your helmets.'[41]

Moreover, as Lee shows, other senior Ministers shared Churchill's
disquiet at the prospect of their party being left, unaided, to tackle
necessary but unpopular tasks once the war was over: 'Coalition by
1943–44 came to be seen partly as a protection against the unrealistic
demands of popular expectation', he writes. In addition, many civil
servants, 'feared the ideological arguments and suspicions which they
thought would be engendered' if unpopular measures were introduced
by a single-party government.[42] Such anxieties help explain why until
1943 it was commonly assumed, both in Westminster and Whitehall,
that the Coalition would last for three years after the end of the
war.[43] The Tory Reform Committee and *The Times* had similar
expectations.[44]

Nor was this mere wishful thinking since until late in the war
Churchill had good grounds for supposing that many of his senior
Labour colleagues, Bevin especially, agreed with him on the importance
of postponing a return to two-party politics. In fact, in May 1943
Bevin and Churchill, backed by Lord Cherwell, specifically discussed
the possibility of a post-war Coalition.[45] According to Eden's *Reckoning*,
Bevin still appeared to think in June 1944 that 'it might be necessary
to continue the National Government into the immediate post-war
period', though Bevin insisted as a precondition that the Government
must commit itself to the nationalisation of the coal mines. It was
only in the autumn of that year that he finally changed his mind.[46]

41 Dalton diary, 26 May 1945, Ben Pimlott (ed.), *The Second World War Diary of
Hugh Dalton, 1940–1945* (1986), p. 864.
    42 Lee, *Churchill Coalition*, pp. 138–9.
    43 See, for example, Harold Nicolson's diary, 31 Oct. 1944, Nigel Nicolson (ed.),
Diaries and Letters 1939–1945 (1967), p. 409.
    44 Addison, *1945*, p. 235.
    45 Addison, *Churchill on Home Front*, pp. 370–1.
    46 Earl of Avon, *The Eden Memoirs: The Reckoning* (1965), pp. 453–4.

Dalton and Morrison (the latter had long been admired by 'progressive' Tories) were the other two Labour Ministers who felt considerable sympathy with the idea of a continued Coalition arrangement. In 1943 Morrison even devised an ingenious plan whereby the three major parties should agree upon a minimum programme but go to the country as separate organisations stressing the priorities they would give to particular items of the programme and the additions they would like to make to it. True, from 1944 onwards he retreated from such a position, but Labour activists had good cause to worry in 1943 and 1944 about where Morrison was trying to lead the party – anxieties which would have been strengthened had they known more about his earlier prevarications in August 1931.

Dalton, too, was alarmed by the prospect of an abrupt return to party strife. For a while he favoured an agreement between the three main parties which would allow them to contest the post-war election as independent organisations; but Ministers would be returned unopposed, and, once the results were declared, a new Coalition would be formed, probably under Churchill's leadership. Moreover, Dalton also wanted the general election deferred until the war in the Far East had been brought to a conclusion. As he told Churchill in late 1944, he was also keen to avoid an election, immediately following the signing of an Armistice, if Parliament was in mid-session and 'engaged in passing good Bills'.[47]

In fact, at official level, the reluctance to return to party warfare persisted until the end. In September 1944 the National Executive Committee (NEC) tried to reassure the Labour faithful by announcing that 'despite malicious whisperings to the contrary, no responsible leader of Labour has ever toyed with the idea of a Coupon election'.[48] But this was clearly disingenuous, and Harold Laski and backbenchers like Aneurin Bevan were right to view the behaviour of some of their ministerial leaders with suspicion. For while Laski would have preferred to risk a Labour withdrawal from the Coalition rather than jeopardise 'socialism',[49] Attlee and Bevin, even as late as the Blackpool Conference in mid May 1945, were recommending that Labour stay

---

47 Ben Pimlott, *Hugh Dalton* (1985), pp. 363–5.

48 Stephen Brooke, *Labour's War: The Labour Party during the Second World War* (Oxford, 1992), p. 305.

49 Michael Newman, *Harold Laski: A Political Biography* (1993), p. 239.

in office till Japan be defeated – though all other senior Labour figures, Morrison included, now opposed this view.[50]

Why did some Labour leaders, in defiance of the overwhelming sentiment inside their party, continue to flirt with coalition in this way? The reasons are many. First, like their Conservative and Liberal opposite numbers, Labour Ministers were impressed by the appalling problems which the peace would bring. Some, for example, were worried over the prospect of unrest occasioned by demobilisation. Morrison's attitudes, too, are revealing. 'The bulk of our fellows don't in the least understand the political position', he told the editor of the *Manchester Guardian*. 'They have the idea that the country is waiting to hand them the reins of Government on a platter and that eventually they will do the country the kindness of taking office . . . '[51]

It was not so much that Labour Ministers had lost confidence in their distinctive political creed. Pimlott has shown, for example, how adroitly Dalton 'played the Labour card' in fighting inside the Coalition for social and industrial reform – to the frequent anger of Conservative backbenchers. It was rather that Dalton believed that Labour could achieve far more of its programme as a constituent element in a multi-party administration than would be possible once the Coalition broke up.

Underlying such opinions, of course, was the belief that Labour would lose the next election – or, rather, would lose an election should it find itself opposing a Churchill still flushed with military victory and at the height of his popularity. As Dalton admitted in a speech to a *New Statesman* lunch in September 1943, he wanted to avoid an election on party lines while the Prime Minister 'stood at or near the highest pinnacle of his fame'.[52]

What about public opinion? Asked in January 1943 whether 'after the war we shall go back to the party system we had before the war?', 20 per cent of respondents answered 'no', while 32 per cent did not know. However, faced ten months later with the question – 'At the end of the war, would you like to see a coalition government continue, or a party government with the other parties in opposition' – 41 per cent opted for a coalition government, as against 46 per cent who wanted a return to the party system (13 per cent did not know). And in August of the following year 35 per cent said they wanted

50 Alan Bullock, *The Life and Times of Ernest Bevin: Vol. 2: Minister of Labour 1940–1945* (1967), pp. 375–6.
51 Addison, *1945*, p. 235.
52 Dalton diary, 27 Sept. 1944, Pimlott (ed.), *Second World War Diary*, p. 645.

an all-party government to lead the country in the post-war period, as against 9 per cent who wanted a multi-party government and 42 per cent who wanted a single party government.[53]

Such figures are not easy to interpret, but they do suggest that there was a sizeable sector of the British population that neither expected nor wanted a return to old-style adversarial politics. True, it would seem that Churchill's popularity as a war leader did not make him a universal favourite as a prospective *peacetime* Premier: in February 1944, 62 per cent of respondents did not want him to assume such a position.[54] On the other hand, Churchill's main rival for the filling of this role was Anthony Eden, whose appeal had always transcended the boundaries of party. Indeed, in January 1941 Eden privately confessed that he 'had little sympathy with [the Conservative Party] or the men who composed it', although he admired Bevin, Cripps and Attlee, just as these senior Labour figures admired him.[55]

What makes the situation somewhat confusing, however, is the evidence furnished by a set of highly ambiguous by-election results. For the latter stages of the war witnessed the success of a number of 'independent' candidates standing in order to *protest* at the electoral truce. The most dramatic of these victories occurred in Rugby in April 1942 when W.J. Brown defeated a Conservative in a straight fight. Brown, who had briefly been a member of Mosley's New Party, made an assault on the party system the centre of his campaign. Indeed, as he later boasted in his Memoirs, he 'had, without a machine, stood up to and beaten a combination of all the machines'.[56] Brown's quarrel was not with Churchill as a person. His complaint was rather that the Prime Minister had 'sinned against his light' by basing his Ministry on 'the premises of the "pseudo-democratic Parliamentary compromise"', even though this meant retaining in power 'men for whose political judgment, and sometimes moral character, he could have entertained nothing but a lively contempt'.[57]

Once in Parliament Brown joined up with another 'rebel', Dennis

53 See Hadley Cantril, *Public Opinion, 1935–1946* (Princeton, 1951), p. 277. In August 1944 57 per cent wanted a general election to be deferred until Japan was defeated, as against 28 per cent who wanted one as soon as Germany surrendered (ibid., p. 195).

54 Addison, *1945*, p. 251.

55 Robert Rhodes James, *Anthony Eden* (1986), pp. 245–6.

56 W.J. Brown, *So Far . . .* (1943), p. 249.

57 Ibid., p. 244.

Kendall,[58] to form a 'People's Movement', which also attracted the crusty 'independent', Josiah Wedgwood.[59] Believing that the suspension of electoral competition was threatening Britain with its own kind of 'fascist' rule, in September 1942 Brown moved in Parliament for a general election to be held to decide whether the political truce should continue.[60] His own electoral success, he was sure, proved that the population at large was strongly disenchanted with the whole party political system.[61] The seeming paradox now becomes clear: Brown and his friends wanted to end the coalition, not because they *believed* in party, but because they had a fundamental *quarrel* to pick with it!

A similar, and even more successful, manifestation of the disapproval of Coalition was provided by Common Wealth, founded in 1942 under the leadership of Richard Acland, a former Liberal MP who had recently experienced a Pauline conversion to a kind of 'ethical socialism'. Common Wealth set out to intervene in by-elections and, according to its organiser, R.W.G. Mackay, hoped to turn itself into an effective Opposition by 'carrying on electoral organisation against the Coalition or Tory Government in preparation for the General Election when it comes'.[62] As for the candidates which it fielded in wartime by-elections, many of these (for example, Hugh Lawson, the victorious candidate at Skipton in January 1944) were clearly mobilising would-be Labour voters exasperated by their leaders' entanglement in the Churchill Coalition.[63] Common Wealth therefore functioned, at one level, as a 'stand-in' for Labour: by taking advantage of the mood of reviving party animosities in the later stages of the war, it was able to tap into left-wing dissatisfaction with the constraints of Coalition.

On the other hand, Common Wealth also seems to have attracted electoral support from social groups to which neither of the existing major parties made an overwhelming appeal. An examination of its membership, which peaked at around 15,000, reveals a high

58 One of Kendall's leaflets ran: 'Dennis Kendall is another Stafford Cripps. Independent yet Churchillian' (Paul Addison, 'By-Elections of the Second World War', C. Cook and J. Ramsden (eds), *By-Elections in British Politics*, 1973, p. 173).

59 Jefferys, *Churchill Coalition*, p. 147.

60 R.B. McCallum and Alison Readman, *The British General Election of 1945* (Oxford 1947), p. 6 and footnote.

61 Brown, *So Far*, p. 249.

62 Calder, *People's War*, pp. 634–5; Addison, 'By-Elections', *By-Elections*, p. 181.

63 Jefferys ,*Churchill Coalition*, pp. 154–5.

proportion of professional men and women (called 'the active middle classes' in party literature), many of whom had had little previous political involvement.[64] Calder says that the organisation's base was composed of 'solicitors, doctors and clergymen on the one hand, local government officers, salaried scientists in industry, schoolteachers and journalists on the other'. This fitted in well with the party's proclamation of the benevolence of the new managerial class. Moreover, most of the national and local leaders were still only in their thirties – a situation not unconnected to the fact that, like Mosley's New Party a decade earlier, Common Wealth tried to pitch its appeal at young voters.[65]

An undercurrent of impatience with traditional two-party politics is also revealed by the remarkable, if transient, popularity of Stafford Cripps, who had served as British Ambassador in Moscow since June 1940, returning in early 1942 to a seat in the War Cabinet, along with the office of Leader of the Commons. It was not until 1945 that Cripps was readmitted to the Labour Party. Meanwhile, as an Independent, he was able to advance a personal programme of his own for winning the war: a programme which embraced the establishment of a General Planning Staff to take charge of strategy and an increase of authority for the Minister of Production, who would be aided by a new 'Scientific Planning Staff'. Shortly afterwards, Cripps came out in favour of a Lloyd George-style War Cabinet and an independent War Planning Directorate, while also shrewdly associating himself with the popular Beveridge Report and with Keynes. He threatened resignation if his demands were not met.[66]

Writing in her diary on 22 February 1942, Beatrice Webb correctly identified the principal reason for her nephew's significance: 'He belongs to *no political party* and shows no sign of joining one that already exists or of creating a new one.'[67] A month later Harold Laski elaborated on this point in the *New Statesman*. Political parties, he sensed, had fallen into lower esteem than at any time since the reign of George III: 'The man in the street finds nothing so dull as an attempt to create interest in the future character of our party system.' And that, in Laski's view, was why Cripps felt 'much stronger in his

---

64 Ibid., p. 152; D.L. Prynn, 'Common Wealth – a British "Third Party" of the 1940s', *Journal of Contemporary History*, 7 (1972), 169–79.

65 Calder, *People's War*, pp. 633–4.

66 Addison, *1945*, pp. 205–9.

67 Norman and Jeanne MacKenzie (eds), *The Diary of Beatrice Webb: Vol. 4: 1924–1943: 'The Wheel of Life'* (1985), p. 479.

aloofness from parties than if he had the massed strength of Labour behind him'.[68]

In July 1942 Cripps was toying with the idea that the end of the war might see the emergence of a new 'Centre' party, under his own leadership, encompassing 'progressive' elements from all parties, which, backed by Conservative as well as by Labour MPs, would set itself the task of establishing a new efficient planned economy.[69] Nor did Cripps's ambitions stop there. The previous month he had actually asked Malcolm MacDonald to sound out other Cabinet Ministers about the acceptability of his own succession to the premiership.

Fortunately for Churchill, the victory of El Alamein, plus Cripps's own miscalculations (and conceit), enabled him to puncture the pretensions of his rival: in November 1942 Cripps was dropped from the War Cabinet and moved to the post of Minister of Aircraft Production. He never recovered his former importance.[70] But earlier in the year, as Orwell noted, Cripps had enjoyed 'a considerable personal reputation', which was part and parcel of the population's 'obvious loss of . . . faith in the old parties'.[71] In February Eden, too, took quite seriously Cripps's position as a possible Prime Minister.[72] For a while, then, Sir Stafford really had been a credible alternative to Churchill: only Eden rivalled him in popularity.[73]

WAS THERE A WARTIME 'CONSENSUS'?

Does all this mean that it is valid to talk, as some historians have done, about the existence of a wartime 'consensus'? Ever since the appearance in 1975 of Addison's acclaimed book, *The Road to 1945*, this is a term which has become central to academic discussions about

68 *New Statesman*, 21 March 1942, 188.

69 Addison, *1945*, p. 205.

70 Ibid., p. 210; Jefferys, *Churchill Coalition*, pp. 103–4. Eden became Leader of the Commons, and Morrison was brought into the War Cabinet for the first time.

71 'The British Crisis', 8 May 1942, in Sonia Orwell and Ian Angus (eds), *The Collected Essays, Journalism and Letters of George Orwell: Volume 2* (1968; 1970 edn), pp. 243–5.

72 Oliver Harvey's diary, 27 Feb. 1942, in *War Diaries of Oliver Harvey*, p. 102. So, too, did the wily Tom Jones six months later (Taylor, in Butler (ed.), *Coalitions*, p. 90).

73 Addison, *1945*, p. 200.

the politics of the Second World War.[74] Addison's thesis is that during the war years the Conservatives 'were obliged to integrate some of Labour's most important demands into their own philosophy', something which they were able to do 'without too much pain because Labour's demands had largely been cast in a mould of thought provided by the non-socialist intelligentsia between the wars and during World War II'.[75] All three parties which went to the polls in 1945 were thus 'committed to principles of social and economic reconstruction which their leaders had endorsed as members of the Coalition. A massive new middle ground had arisen in politics.' Although there were obviously differences of emphasis between Conservatives and Labour, especially over nationalisation, in practice the two sets of leaders had 'bypassed' such doctrinal issues 'in favour of "pragmatic" reform in a mixed economy'.[76] This 'consensus' involved a planned capitalism, the welfare state and the maintenance of full employment, all to be achieved through the instrumentality of the 'humane technocrat'.[77] Thus, in Addison's view, 'the Attlee governments of 1945 to 1951 [merely] completed and consolidated the work of the Coalition by establishing a peacetime managed economy, and the expanded welfare state envisaged by Beveridge'.[78]

Angus Calder, from the Left,[79] and Correlli Barnett from the Right,[80] have subsequently commented more critically on 'consensus politics', while broadly accepting the existence of such a phenomenon. Calder, for example, sees the development of a middle ground in politics which encompassed 'Cripps and Eden, Herbert Morrison and R.A. Butler, the Liberal Action Group and the Tory Reformers, William Beveridge and William Temple and many members of the Fabian Society'. He concedes that 'a distinction between the major parties was maintained by their different social bases': 'Labour's working-class base made it emphasize nationalization, whereas the Tory reformers emphasized "rationalization".' But, comments Calder, 'in practice the two would be little different'. That, in his opinion,

74 It perhaps originated in the official history of the war economy: see Middlemas, *Politics in Industrial Society*, p. 274.

75 Addison, *1945*, p. 278.

76 Ibid., p. 14.

77 Ibid., p. 277.

78 Ibid., p. 273.

79 Calder, *People's War*.

80 Writing of 1945, Barnett writes: 'New Jerusalem had indeed become the political consensus' (Correlli Barnett, *The Audit of War*, 1986, p. 37).

is why the talk of the creation of a new 'Centre Party' finally came to nothing: 'it was really much better for business to maintain two centre parties, as post-war history has shown'.[81]

Recently such interpretations have been much attacked. Criticism of the view that a 'consensus' developed during the Second World War has assumed many forms, but the main complaint is that Addison takes too sentimental a view of national unity and gives insufficient emphasis to the continuance of the sharp party animosities which characterised the years of the Churchill Coalition. Indeed, Stephen Brooke argues that 'Coalition itself created pressures against political consensus', because its existence caused unease among the Labour Left, which 'barracked all who would listen with a message of independence and reinvigorated socialism'.[82]

That there was such discontent no one would deny. Dalton himself wrote in his diary on 6 February 1942: 'We just don't deserve to win the war. We are all fighting each other instead of the enemy, and with such zest.'[83] Party animosities manifested themselves in a variety of ways. For example, throughout the war years many Conservatives keenly resented what they saw as the machinations of Labour Ministers trying to pursue their socialist policies under cover of 'national unity'. 'There is of course a "party truce"', grumbled Headlam, 'but it is only observed by one side. Every speech made by the Labour people in the H. of C. is a party speech and is propaganda.'[84] Churchill, too, had occasional anxieties on this score. In an unsent letter to Attlee of 20 November 1944, he complained about the way in which Labour Ministers dominated the government committees dealing with domestic affairs; 'you have a theme, which is Socialism, on which everything is directed', Churchill complained.[85]

It is therefore hardly surprising that the two main wings of the Coalition clashed from time to time. This happened, for example, over the issue of fuel rationing,[86] when the Conservatives succeeded

81 Calder, *People's War*, pp. 614–15.
82 Brooke, *Labour's War*, p. 341.
83 Ben Pimlott (ed.), *The Second World War Diary of Hugh Dalton 1940–45* (1986), p. 363.
84 Cited in Addison, *1945*, p. 115.
85 Brooke, *Labour's War*, pp. 168, 230. On Addison's admission that Churchill distrusted the 'creeping bureaucracy' which he associated with the Labour Party, see Paul Addison, 'Churchill in British Politics, 1940–55', in J.M.W. Bean (ed.), *The Political Culture of Modern Britain* (1987), p. 248.
86 Pimlott, *Dalton*, pp. 351–9.

in blocking Dalton's plans. Later 116 Conservative MPs voted against Bevin's Catering Wages Bill.[87] Labour, for its part, particularly disliked the compulsion of workers instituted by the Emergency Powers Act, for which it demanded a *quid pro quo*.[88] There were also marked differences of approach to social policy and Reconstruction, which the appearance of the Beveridge Report brought into sharp relief.[89] For although Butler encouraged Eden to try to make a pro-Beveridge stand with a view to seizing the issue for the Conservative Party, Kingsley Wood, the chief representative of the 'Old Gang', would have none of it. Difficulties of this kind tended to intensify in the latter stages of the war, as each party began to prepare for peacetime politics. 'I happen to be a Socialist', Bevin reminded the Commons in October 1944, 'and I am still a Socialist in spite of the chains that join me to the Coalition'.[90]

Yet attacks on the 'consensus thesis' have recently been taken to unreasonable lengths. For example, Addison's case is hardly undermined by a demonstration of how unpopular Coalition was with Bevan, Laski and Labour's constituency activists – rather the contrary, since the ferocity of such condemnation indicates the alarm of the Labour Left at what it saw as the leadership's abandonment of traditional party goals. In any case, as Kavanagh and Morris argue, each party obviously had its dissenting *wing*, but the people whose views really counted were 'the *governmentalists* in both political parties' who are the principal subject of Addison's concern.[91]

At ministerial level, Addison's case may need modifying somewhat, but it remains substantially sound since, despite some friction between leading Conservatives and socialists, the members of Churchill's Coalition Ministry broadly co-operated with one another across a wide range of issues. Lord Woolton has written of the 'shandy-gaff' of Conservatism and socialism which was formed during the war years.[92] And Attlee, revealingly, told Laski in May 1944 that he had found, in discussion with colleagues of other parties, 'on many matters

87 Lee, *Churchill Coalition*, p. 50.

88 Jefferys, *Churchill Coalition*, pp. 75–6.

89 Kevin Jefferys, in 'British Politics and Social Policy During the Second World War', *Historical Journal*, 30 (1987), 123–44, shows how untypical of Conservative opinion the Tory Reform Committee actually was.

90 Bullock, *Bevin*, II, p. 326.

91 D. Kavanagh and P. Morris, *Consensus Politics From Attlee to Thatcher* (1989), p. 14.

92 Woolton, *Memoirs*, p. 276.

more agreement than you would expect'. He added that there were anyhow 'limits to the extent to which the clock can be put forward or back'. The Labour Leader protested that he had 'never suggested that we should drop our principles and programme', but he insisted that it was 'better to argue from what has been done to what may be done rather than to suggest that very little has been accomplished'.[93]

Ministers who took such a line enjoyed considerable support from their own backbenchers – in particular, from the Tory Reform Committee, on one side, and from Labour MPs like Frederick Bellenger, on the other. In the later stages of the War Manny Shinwell became drawn into a cross-party group dedicated to post-war reform: 'On general political issues we were poles apart', he writes in his memoirs, 'but on the need for economic planning, Commonwealth development, the rehabilitation of industry, and on social welfare we were largely in agreement.'[94] As for foreign policy, this, of course, did lead to disagreements, but these did not follow straight party lines.[95] Thus, when Laski declared in March 1942 that, in the absence of 'common ground' between the parties, the British people might 'lose the habit which makes men prefer the debating chamber to the concentration camp',[96] he was ludicrously misreading the political mood.

In addition, the war years saw an administrative revolution in Whitehall, with the emergence of what Addison calls 'the collectivist state'.[97] As Lee puts it, 'the coalition loosened the rules of parliamentary government and facilitated the inevitable expansion of executive control', leading to the recruitment into the public service of a wide range of outsiders, journalists, dons, technicians and businessmen, who found that a coalition government made it much easier for them to 'apply their intelligence to the practical problems of government'.[98]

This was the environment in which Beveridge came to win so much importance, as well as public acclaim. In *Full Employment in a Free Society*, he felt able to recommend state management of aggregate demand by claiming: 'The policy outlined in the Report

93 Attlee to Laski, 1 May 1944, quoted in Kingsley Martin, *Harold Laski: A Biography* (1953: 1969 edn), pp. 150–3.

94 Emanuel Shinwell, *Conflict Without Malice* (1955), p. 161.

95 Taylor, in Butler (ed.), *Coalitions*, p. 93.

96 *New Statesman*, 21 March 1942, 189.

97 Paul Addison, 'The Road from 1945', in Peter Hennessy and Anthony Seldon (eds), *Ruling Performance: British Governments from Attlee to Thatcher* (Oxford, 1987), pp. 6–7.

98 Lee, *Churchill Coalition*, p. 16.

by-passes the socialist–capitalist controversy. It can be accepted by persons holding many different views on that controversy . . . . It could be done in a United States which remained capitalist as in a Soviet Union which was wholly collectivised or in a Britain which took the middle course.'[99] His biographer thinks that only the fear of alienating Churchill prevented Beveridge from joining Common Wealth, which 'bore all the marks of his spiritual home'.[100] But Beveridge, by his own later admission, had earlier toyed with the idea of standing as a Liberal, Labour, or Independent candidate, or else seeking one of the University seats, before eventually plumping for the Liberals.[101] Nor is this surprising since, in a sense, Beveridge, like Keynes, was a bureaucrat prepared to serve whatever ministry happened to be in power, and thus stood above party. This wartime spirit of consensus was also embodied in Common Wealth, with its cult of the benevolent technocrat and its faith in the new managerial class. Such an ideology was further promoted in the articles and editorials in *The Times* written by E.H. Carr and Barrington-Ward.

Finally, at the level of popular feeling there developed in the years after 1940 a 'radical patriotism' which cut clean across party. It had many traits. There was the emphasis on social solidarity, which perhaps derived from the broadcasts of J.B. Priestley but which achieved its purest expression in the literature of Common Wealth. 'Morality in Politics' was one of the party's slogans, and its leader, Acland, heralded the dawning of a new age, talking of the 'the emergence of a new kind of man, with a new kind of mind, new values, a new outlook on life, and, perhaps most important of all, new motives'.[102]

Even the traditional Left became caught up in this movement of thought and feeling, many socialists replacing the class rhetoric of the 1930s with a fashionable concern for 'community'. Orwell, in a famous phrase, may have defined England as 'a family with the wrong members in control'; but at least he still felt it appropriate to describe it as a family.[103] Nor was he alone, for, as Brooke shows, many socialists, like Evan Durbin, now presented 'socialism'

99 William Beveridge, *Full Employment in a Free Society* (1944), pp. 190–2.
100 Jose Harris, *William Beveridge: A Biography* (Oxford, 1977), p. 443.
101 Lord Beveridge, *Power and Influence* (1953), pp. 336–8.
102 Calder, *People's War*, pp. 632–3.
103 'The Lion and the Unicorn', in Orwell and Angus (eds), *Collected Essays*, II, p. 88.

as both an indigenous tradition and the ultimate expression of national identity.[104]

Finally, there was the vogue for planning which extended all the way from the socialist Left to the *National Policy for Industry*, written in 1942 by 120 industrialists. For all this, there were, as we have seen, precedents, the cult of planning having originated in the 1930s: but it flourished, as never before, in the peculiar environment created by total war. True, disagreement still raged over what form planning should take. But a belief in consensus does not require one to deny the importance of conflict, social tensions and partisan rivalries, which are endemic in all societies. Consensus, write Kavanagh and Morris, should rather be seen as 'a set of parameters which bounded the set of policy options regarded by senior politicians and civil servants as administratively practicable, economically affordable and politically acceptable'.[105]

Yet it is important to grasp that, however much common ground there may have been between them, the two main parties supporting the Churchill Coalition showed *absolutely no disposition to 'fuse'*. As we have seen, attempts were made to reach a bipartisan settlement, but these amounted to little more than discussions about the timing of the dissolution and about the exact circumstances in which the Coalition would be formally terminated: there was no question of a major party realignment. Churchill, for all his prestige, was not a potential leader of a new national party in 1944–45, as Lloyd George had been during the First World War; nor did Labour entertain any ambition of 'capturing' him!

For this reason the two main parties were able to extricate themselves from the Coalition in 1945 with their morale basically undamaged.[106] This suggests that, paradoxically, 'imperfect' coalitions, such as those formed during the Great War, cause far more disruption to the party system than a real coalition such as the one presided over by Churchill, post 1945.

THE 1945 GENERAL ELECTION

On 23 May 1945 the Coalition Government came to an end, after Attlee had formally rejected Churchill's offer of continued national

104 Brooke, *Labour's War*, pp. 273–5.
105 Kavanagh and Morris, *Consensus Politics*, p. 13.
106 See Taylor, in Butler (ed.), *Coalitions*, p. 93.

co-operation, made five days earlier. Attlee's decision disconcerted the Independent Liberals, who had been quite prepared, under their Leader, Archie Sinclair, to discuss 'the possibility of preserving the structure of the National Government under [Churchill's] leadership until the end of the Japanese War'. Churchill, too, publicly expressed his disappointment. However, in the circumstances he saw no purpose in postponing the general election until the autumn, as Labour would have preferred. Instead he secured the King's agreement to dissolve Parliament on 15 June, with polling due to take place on 5 July.

All the same, Churchill could not totally hide his reluctance to return to 'orthodox' party politics. For example, when on 25 May he formed his 'Caretaker' government to tide the country over until the election could take place, he was careful to insist, both publicly and privately, that it was a 'National', not a Conservative Party Administration.[107] This was partly a public relations exercise, but not entirely so since only twelve members of his sixteen–strong Cabinet were Conservatives; the rest consisted of a Liberal National, Lord Rosebery (son of the former Premier), and three non-party men, Anderson, Grigg and Woolton. As for the twenty-four junior Ministers, these comprised fourteen Conservatives, five non-party men, three Liberal Nationals (including Simon, who still occupied the Woolsack), one Liberal (Gwilym Lloyd George, acting in defiance of his party) and a law officer, Sir Walter Monckton, who did not get elected to the Commons until February 1951. Nor was Churchill yet reconciled to the loss of some of his former colleagues. He wrote a reproachful private letter to Sinclair on 26 May, and even sent a message to Bevin the following day, expressing his 'hope for re-union when Party passions [were] less strong'.[108] It was also with a view to maintaining co-operation between the parties that Churchill took Attlee with him to the Potsdam Conference, a move against which Laski complained in vain.[109]

When the 1945 General Election campaign got under way, it was, by a nice symbolism, Lord Rosebery, as Liberal National President, who in a party pamphlet most forcibly made out the case for continued national co-operation: 'There has been formed together from all Parties a Government which has been welded into

107 For example in his broadcast of 21 June, Martin Gilbert, *'Never Despair': Winston S. Churchill 1945–65* (1988), p. 48.

108 Ibid., pp. 23–4.

109 Newman, *Laski*, pp. 261–3.

a magnificent team, which has been the admiration of the world. It seems fantastic that this team at this critical stage should be disbanded.'[110] The Conservatives, too, intermittently tried to sound a 'National' note, one of their posters bearing the legend: 'HELP HIM finish the Job: VOTE NATIONAL'. But this merely goaded the Labour Party into responding with a poster of its own, headed: 'NATIONAL EYEWASH'.[111]

In the testy atmosphere of the election campaign, Churchill then made the error of drifting into intemperate tirades against socialism, of which the 'Gestapo' radio speech is the most notorious. This did not help the Conservative Party at all. On the contrary, the election saw the return of 393 Labour MPs, as against only 213 for the Conservatives and their allies.[112] There were many reasons why Labour should have won by such a landslide, but undoubtedly part of the reason is that Labour caught the wartime mood of consensual reconstruction better than did the Conservative Party, where Churchill's 'progressive' instincts were neutralised at fateful moments by Bracken and Beaverbrook.[113] Although no great ideological chasm separated the parties in the matter of reconstruction, the Conservatives were intolerably handicapped by being associated with the interwar Depression, while Labour benefited by showing, for example, much greater *commitment* in its advocacy of Beveridge. The fact that both Churchill and Eden had recently taken little interest in the fate of the Tory Party or in its management must also have contributed to the electoral outcome.

For the foreseeable future, then, Coalition was 'off' and adversarial two-party politics had returned. But this did not mean that 'consensus' was dead: on the contrary, the stability of the post–war years owed much to the common ground which had grown up between the main parties of government during the period of Churchill's premiership.

110 From Rosebery's *Don't Swap Horses in Mid-stream*, quoted in McCallum and Readman, *General Election of 1945*, p. 65, note 2.

111 Ibid., opposite pp. 82, 83.

112 To be precise, 189 Conservatives, nine Ulster Unionists, thirteen Liberal Nationals, and two 'Nationals'.

113 Scott Newton and Dilwyn Porter, *Modernization Frustrated: The Politics of Industrial Decline in Britain since 1900* (1988), p. 101.

CHAPTER TEN

The Postwar Labour–Conservative 'Duopoly', 1945–74

ESTABLISHMENT OF THE 'DUOPOLY'

The 1945 General Election marked a watershed in British politics, ushering in, as it did, a new stable two-party system that was to last for over a quarter of a century, characterised by a Labour–Conservative duopoly. The duopoly largely came about as a result of Labour's emergence during the Second World War as a credible rival to the Conservative Party.

At the same time, the likelihood of 'Independents' or members of small parties being returned to Westminster was greatly reduced by changes to the electoral system. In 1948 the six University constituencies, three of which had employed a form of the Single Transferable Vote (STV), were abolished. The redistribution of the following year also saw the disappearance of the remaining two-member boroughs.[1] The multi-member seat was a well-tried mechanism for securing co-operation between a major and a minor party, and so this was a change which further ossified the two-party system and decreased the likelihood of small parties securing parliamentary representation.

The strength of this Labour–Conservative duopoly can be seen in the statistics of the share of votes cast in general elections. In 1945 Labour and the Conservative Party (including the Liberal Nationals) secured 87.6 per cent of the total vote. Following the Liberal collapse of 1951, this proportion rose to an astonishing 96.8% per cent. Thereafter it fell back slightly. But even as late as 1966 the two

---

1 Twenty-three had survived after 1885 and twelve after 1918.

main parties still obtained nearly 90 per cent of all votes cast. As a result, between 1950 and 1970 there were never more than fourteen MPs from the minor parties – and in 1959 a mere six.

Moreover, in contrast to previous decades, there was now an approximate *balance* between the two main parties at Westminster. Admittedly, the Conservatives, partly through good luck and partly through the fractiousness of their opponents, had decidedly the better of the contest, winning three general elections in a row during the 1950s. However, the 1951 Election, which inaugurated the long thirteen-year run of Conservative Administrations still saw Labour polling a record number of votes – more votes, in fact, than the Conservatives. Even during the 1950s Labour's imminent return to power always looked entirely possible – something which had not been the case during the 1930s. So well matched was this contest that neither party won less than 40 per cent of the total vote in any of the seven elections between 1950 and 1970.

For this and other reasons, the late 1940s and the 1950s constituted, as Roy Jenkins observes, 'a classical period, as much so as the age of Gladstone and Disraeli, for the working of the British two-party system'.[2] Indeed, that system probably came closer to the realisation of its ideals in these years than at any other period in British history. 'Britain's experience of a stable two-party politics has . . . been both recent and relatively short-lived; it is only since the Second World War that two parties – Conservative and Labour – have alternated in exclusive incumbency of government office on the basis of an evenly balanced duopoly of electoral support and parliamentary seats'.[3] No wonder that when political scientists turn to analysing two-party politics, it is mainly this post-war phenomenon that they choose to examine.

Another curious feature of the post-war years was the *rigidity* of the party system. The Liberal Nationals (who, confusingly, changed their name to National Liberals in 1948) continued to operate an electoral pact with the Conservative Party, the Woolton–Teviot agreement of May 1947, which perpetuated the anti-Labour politics of the 1930s.[4] But though the National Liberals did not finally wind up

2 Lord Jenkins, 'Churchill: The Government of 1951–1955', in Robert Blake and William Roger Louis, *Churchill* (Oxford, 1993), p. 501.

3 Ivor Crewe, Bo Sarlvik and James Alt, 'Partisan Dealignment in Britain 1964–1974', *British Journal of Political Science*, 7 (1977), 129.

4 On the latter days of the National Liberal Party, see David Dutton, 'John Simon and the Post-War National Liberal Party: An Historical Postscript', *Historical Journal*, 32 (1989), 357–67.

their organisation until 1968, their party had long ceased to stand for anything particularly distinctive.

In his capacity as Opposition Leader after 1945, Churchill did make intermittent attempts to woo the *Independent* Liberals. In October 1951 he intervened vigorously on behalf of Asquith's daughter, Lady Violet Bonham Carter, who was contesting Colne Valley as a Liberal – the local Conservative association having been prevailed upon not to run a candidate of its own.[5] That this was more than a sentimental gesture on behalf of an old friend is shown by the fact that, on returning to 10 Downing Street in October 1951, Churchill tried to form a Coalition with the Liberals.[6] But, again, nothing came of this. Nor does great significance attach to the few constituencies where the Conservatives stood down to allow the official Liberal candidate a straight fight against Labour, as happened at Bolton West between 1951 and 1964 and at Huddersfield West between 1950 and 1964.

From time to time there was talk of a realignment involving the Liberal Party and *Labour*. A day after the 1959 General Election the Liberal Leader, Jo Grimond, spoke publicly about 'the creation of a new progressive movement'; but though a few right-wing Labour MPs like Woodrow Wyatt supported him, Gaitskell, the Labour Leader, held the Liberals in contempt, and the proposal came to nothing.[7] As always, a few individual MPs crossed the floor of the House, but otherwise the two-party duopoly survived intact. Indeed, it can be argued, retrospectively, that 'the absence of any . . . realignment in the years since 1945 . . . prevented the parties from modernising themselves, and . . . led to the ossification of the British political system'.[8] Yet at the time most people so took two-party politics for granted that it was difficult to envisage anything different.

Nor does it seem as though this limited choice was unacceptable to voters. Opinion polls showed that in 1964 almost half of Labour and Conservative electors identified strongly with their preferred party.[9] This loyal partisanship, in turn, led to a remarkable electoral stability. The swing between the two parties never rose above 2.2 per cent

5 Martin Gilbert, *'Never Despair': Winston S. Churchill 1945–1965* (1988), pp. 646–7.

6 See below.

7 Philip M. Williams, *Hugh Gaitskell* (1979), pp. 696–8.

8 Vernon Bogdanor (ed.), *Coalition Government in Western Europe* (1983), p. 12.

9 Dennis Kavanagh, *Thatcherism and British Politics: The End of Consensus?* (Oxford, 1987), p. 144.

at any general election in the 1950s.[10] Even more remarkable is the post-war *by-election* record.[11] The first seat to change hands from one major party to another was Sunderland South in May 1953, when, oddly enough, the switch occurred at the expense of Labour, the Opposition party. No government lost a by-election until Labour picked up Lewisham North from the Conservatives in February 1957, eleven and a half years after the termination of the war! Nor in these years were the Liberals able to perform their later role of channelling anti-government discontent: the Liberals won no by-elections until they captured Torrington from the Conservatives in March 1958. Indeed, their repetition of this feat at Orpington in March 1962 seemed so momentous that it helped panic Macmillan into sacking one-third of his Cabinet.[12] Such electoral stability had not been seen earlier in the century when government by-election losses to the main Opposition parties averaged out at about three a year;[13] nor was it to be seen subsequently. It must indicate a broad satisfaction with the political system.

THE POST-WAR CONSENSUS

Looking back at this phase of Britain's political history, Ian Gilmour was struck by the paradox that the stability of the two–party system had been caused by 'the closeness' of the two main parties to one another: 'If the parties are close together, they will necessarily be moderate. To be close together, they both have to be centrist, and centrism entails moderation. Similarly, they both have to be relatively

10 Percentage swings were as follows: 2.2 (1950): 1.4 (1951): 2.05 (1955): 1.15 (1959): 3.15 (1964): 2.65 (1966): 4.7 (1970): 1.2 (Feb. 1974): 2.25 (Oct.1974).

11 On this, see Chris Cook: 'Note: 1945 to 1960', Chris Cook and John Ramsden (eds), *By-Elections in British Politics* (1973), p. 196.

12 The reshuffle, however, took place four months later, after the Conservatives had been forced into third place at the Leicester North-East by-election (Ken Young, 'Orpington and the "Liberal Revival"', Cook and Ramsden (eds), *By-Elections*, pp. 214–15).

13 For example, the Liberals lost twelve seats to the Unionists between the 1906 and the Jan. 1910 elections, and another fourteen between December 1910 and the outbreak of the war. Between the 1924 and 1929 Elections the Conservatives lost eleven seats to Labour, five to the Liberals. And between 1935 and the start of the Second World War the supporters of the National Government lost thirteen seats to Labour, as well as other seats to Independent candidates.

free of ideology.'[14] This broadly describes the state of British politics between 1945 and 1970.

Undoubtedly, the Second World War had contributed to this situation. Whatever the party tensions after 1945, it was difficult for Conservatives to brand as 'enemies of the state' respected Labour Ministers who had helped run the war. Churchill found this out to his cost in the 1945 Election when his coarse attacks on Labour badly backfired. And even Churchill's main criticism was not of the Labour leaders themselves but of their organisation, whose constitution, he alleged, subordinated a Labour Prime Minister to the malign influence of a socialist professor. In addition, as we saw in the last chapter, the war years had generated a considerable measure of agreement about what needed to be done in the field of Reconstruction.

Other historians, sceptical of the extent of this wartime consensus, prefer to emphasise the changes which took place within both major parties in the *late* 1940s. Up until 1947, they insist, Labour continued to favour physical planning, rather than Keynesian demand-management, which only became the bedrock of Treasury policy after Cripps had replaced Dalton at the Exchequer in November 1947.[15] It is also claimed that, despite lip-service to Beveridge and reconstruction, the Conservative Party had gone into the 1945 General Election advocating a crude policy of 'de-control'; it was thus 'the profound shock of Labour's overwhelming victory' which 'was to be of greater importance than the experience of war in shifting the Tories towards a more fundamental reassessment of domestic policy'.[16] And even that shift took time, since it was the old-guard Conservatives representing safe Tory constituencies who had been most successful in holding on to their seats in 1945. In other words, there is a case for saying that the 'modern' version of Conservatism associated with Eden, Butler and Macmillan was very much a *post*-war phenomenon.[17]

14 Ian Gilmour, *Britain Can Work* (Oxford, 1983), p. 197.

15 Stephen Brooke, 'The Labour Party and the Second World War', in L. Johnman (ed.), *Contemporary British History, 1931–61* (1991), p. 12. However, Dalton's fourth budget of 1948 in some ways marked the crucial breakthrough (Ben Pimlott, *Hugh Dalton* (1985), p. 522). Oliver Stanley called it 'the end of an era of socialist policy and socialist propaganda' (Kenneth Harris, *Attlee* (1982), p. 429).

16 Kevin Jefferys, *The Churchill Coalition and Wartime Politics, 1940–1945* (Manchester, 1991), p. 205.

17 Not that Addison denies the importance of the events of the late 1940s in producing a convergence of policy between the two parties. See Paul Addison, *The Road to 1945* (1975), pp. 274–5.

Yet, whichever of these two explanations of the convergence of views between Conservatives and Labour is adopted, the fact is that by the late 1940s, and perhaps earlier, a new two-party system had come into existence, characterised by the competition for office between parties that were differentiated from one another by class and creed yet broadly shared many policy goals both at home and abroad. In particular, the two Front Benches were united in their broad objectives, which embraced commitment to NATO, the preservation of the mixed economy and the welfare state, and the use of techniques of Keynesian demand management in the interests of full employment.

In fact, very real disagreements between Labour and the Conservatives did still exist, with the former putting the main emphasis on equality, the latter on freedom. The two parties were also very different types of organisation, both in terms of structure and composition, and they spoke a different class language, which appealed to different social constituencies. Even in the 1950s, these tensions and policy disagreements led to many acrimonious clashes.[18]

But such conflicts, by giving meaning to the two-party system, also strengthened it. In any case, as during the war, *uncompromising* dissent was largely confined to groups of party members remote from power. True, had a Conservative ministry been returned by the electorate in 1945, it would almost certainly have pursued different policies from those sponsored by Attlee, notably in the matter of the institution of a national health service.[19] Yet even the differences between the two parties over nationalisation were not totally irreconcilable. Each accepted the inevitability of the mixed economy. And despite being in office continuously for thirteen years, the Conservative Governments did not embark upon *de-nationalisation*, except in respect of iron and steel and road-haulage.

This new consensus was most obvious during the 1950s and early 1960s when the Conservatives were lucky enough to be in power at a time of rising living standards when there was a general relaxation of social and political tension. 'The general election of May 1955',

18 Ben Pimlott, 'The Myth of Consensus', in L.M. Smith (ed.), *The Making of Britain: Echoes of Greatness* (1988), pp. 138–9.

19 Addison himself agrees with this view in so far as he admits that the War Cabinet finally broke up because 'Labour and Conservative ministers gradually exhausted the subjects on which they could agree, and were left with those on which they differed' (*1945*, p. 252).

opens the account of the Nuffield study, 'was, by universal consent, unprecedently quiet. The ritual of electioneering was performed passionlessly by the politicians and endured tranquilly by the voters'[20] – a far cry from the testy contest four years earlier, which had followed the convertibility crisis of 1947 and the 1949 devaluation. 'Issues? Issues? There are no issues. This is just a national census to see who's Labour and who's Conservative', one party agent is reported as saying twards the end of the 1955 campaign.[21]

No wonder that the Liberals claimed that little separated the two main parties: 'Which twin is the Toni?', they asked. Indeed, according to one political scientist, the distance between Conservatives and Labour in 1964 was only one-fifth of what it had been in 1931, findings which seemed to confirm the theory that two evenly matched parties, in their quest for the crucial floating voter, would tend to converge in their policies.[22]

The tone of politics was set by the Conservative leaders. Churchill, Prime Minister for a second time between 1951 and 1955, in many ways did not behave as though he were the leader of a party administration at all. During the 1951 General Election he had declared that what the country needed was 'a period of steady, stable administration by a broadly-based government, wielding the national power and content to serve the nation's interests rather than give party satisfaction'.[23]

On returning to 10 Downing Street, Churchill tried to realise this ambition by forming a Coalition with the Liberals, offering the Ministry of Education to the Liberal Leader, Clement Davies. A Simonite in the early 1930s before crossing back into opposition to rejoin the official party, Davies was tempted by the offer. But his followers would not allow him to take it up.[24] Despite this setback, Churchill was once again able to appoint to high office a number of men not originally from politics (Cherwell, Ismay, Leathers) and

20 D.E. Butler, *The British General Election of 1955* (1955), p. 1.

21 Ibid., p. 164.

22 David Robertson, *A Theory of Party Competition* (1976), Anthony Down, *An Economic Theory of Democracy* (1957), cited in Kavanagh, *Thatcherism*, p. 36.

23 Paul Addison, *Churchill on the Home Front 1900–1955* (1992), p. 406. In his political broadcast of 8 Oct., he declared that Britain's 'very existence' would be endangered 'if we go on consuming our strength in bitter party or class conflicts' (Gilbert, *'Never Despair'*, p. 643).

24 Gilbert, *'Never Despair'*, p. 655.

others from non–Conservative backgrounds (De La Warr, Simonds, Reading, Gwilym Lloyd George, Monckton, John Maclay, Arthur Salter).[25] Significantly, too, most members of Churchill's new Cabinet were 'moderates': neither Beaverbrook nor Bracken was given office.[26] By contrast, the key post of Chancellor of the Exchequer went to R. A. Butler, the inspirer of the recent 'Industrial Charter', an attempt to give a more modern, progressive face to post-war Conservatism. As Richard Crossman noted in his diary in October 1951: 'Just as Attlee was running what was virtually a coalition policy on a Party basis so Churchill may well do the same.'[27]

Churchill was succeeded as Conservative Leader by Anthony Eden, who had revealed his political priorities in a diary entry on the eve of the 1945 Election: 'I am afraid that I am not really much use as a party man. I dislike our extreme right more than somewhat & I seem for ever to be seeing the other feller's point of view. In other words I am not a political warrior like Winston but only a civil servant.' Eden added that he sincerely wanted to 'build a better England', but wondered 'how to do this thro' the sordid medium of Tory party politics & how else to do it?' Eden was suffering from illness and depression when he penned these words, but his biographer thinks that they convey his fundamental political beliefs.[28] Eden now came forward as a confident moderniser who even wanted to drop the name 'Conservative', which he thought a liability, especially with former Liberals.[29] Firmly anti-socialist Eden might have been, but he also deplored 'doctrinaire anti-socialism'.

Finally Harold Macmillan, the one-time rebel (he had had the whip taken away from him between June 1936 and July 1937) was able during his long premiership (January 1957 to October 1963) to stamp his personality on to an entire era. And although Macmillan had retreated from the rather impractical belief in economic planning which had informed *The Middle Way*, he still retained many aspects

25 Anthony Seldon, *Churchill's Indian Summer: the Conservative Government, 1951–55* (1981), pp. 76–7.

26 Addison, *Churchill on Home Front*, pp. 408–9. In fact, Bracken was offered the Colonial Office, but declined on the grounds of ill-health.

27 Cited in ibid., p. 409.

28 Robert Rhodes James, *Anthony Eden* (1986), p. 304. 'I dislike speaking to the Conservative Party. That is not where my supporters come from. The Conservative Party only has me because it must!, he had earlier remarked (John Harvey, ed., *The War Diaries of Oliver Harvey* (1978), p. 258).

29 James, *Eden*, pp. 326–7.

of his old creed, not least his horror of unemployment and his anxiety to represent the interests of all social classes. It may also be significant that his most successful Chancellor of the Exchequer, Derek Heathcote Amory (1958–60), had started life as a Liberal before being converted to the Conservative Party through reading *The Middle Way*.[30]

But perhaps the dominant political figure of the 1950s was Butler, a politician who had developed his conciliatory brand of politics as a junior member of the National Governments of the 1930s, as well as during his years as Education Minister in Churchill's wartime Coalition.[31] The growing bipartisanship between the two Front Benches caused *The Economist* to coin the phrase 'Butskellism' to describe the common Keynesian features of the policies pursued by Butler and his Labour predecessor, Hugh Gaitskell. This phrase annoyed the two men (and their biographers), and both may have suffered career-wise because of its wide circulation,[32] but this does not invalidate the concept.

The importance of 'Keynesianism', of course, was that its adoption seemed to be a way of bypassing, to some extent, the old controversy between socialism and market capitalism. Indeed, in the 1950s both parties took it as axiomatic that economic growth would continue, and assumed that political conflict involved a struggle to share out the resultant wealth. This, for example, was one of the central themes in *The Future of Socialism* (1956), written by the clever Gaiskellite economist Anthony Crosland.

A similar consensualism was displayed by most of the other leading Conservative Ministers of the 1950s: one thinks of Monckton's 'appeasement' of the trade unions at the Ministry of Labour (1951–55), Iain Macleod's pursuit of decolonisation at the Colonial Office (1959–61) or, later, Edward Boyle's launching of the new universities while at the Ministry of Education and Science (1962–64). The general thrust of Conservative policies during these years was a 'left of centre', 'One Nation' approach, which was unprovocative, interventionist and deliberately aimed at the securing of the political middle ground.

Meanwhile Labour's leaders were experiencing greater difficulties in edging their party away from traditional ideological goals towards

---

30 Alistair Horne, *Macmillan 1957–1986* (1989), p. 139.

31 See Anthony Howard, *RAB: The Life of R.A. Butler* (1987: 1988 edn).

32 Though it has been pointed out that the two men differed 'on the role of monetary policy; on the distribution of budgetary burdens and benefits; and on convertibility of sterling' (Williams, *Gaitskell*, p. 313).

a more consensual, managerial kind of approach. But even during the years of the Attlee Government a new kind of Labour politics was emerging: one which paid scant attention to the socialist goals inscribed on the party's constitution. For example, in 1947 the first truly Keynesian Chancellor, Stafford Cripps, began preaching the virtues of 'austerity' as a precondition of economic recovery – to the delight of the City and Conservative opinion and the unease of some socialists who saw the new Chancellor 'as a potential coalitionist, whose repeated national appeals would lead him to ally with Tories and Liberals'.[33] In any case, most of the leading Labour Ministers were, temperamentally, themselves 'men of the Centre': Herbert Morrison, for example, had long been a favourite with Tory social reformers, while Ernest Bevin, the Foreign Secretary, was trusted and admired on the Conservative Front Bench, especially by his opposite number, Eden.

On succeeding Attlee as Labour Leader in 1955, Hugh Gaitskell set about the modernisation of the party in an even more self-conscious way. Admittedly, this was to land him in bitter internal disputes, notably with the followers of Aneurin Bevan, who had resigned from Attlee's Government in January 1951 in protest at the adoption of charges for dental and ophthalmic treatment. In 1959 Gaitskell suffered a serious setback at the hands of his many 'Bevanite' enemies when he attempted to abandon the commitment to public ownership enshrined in Clause 4 of the Labour Party constitution, and, later, it was only after a protracted struggle that he was able to 'rescue' Labour from committing itself to the objectives of the Campaign for Nuclear Disarmament (CND). Significantly, in many ways there was greater ideological animosity *within* the Labour Party than *between* the two Front Benches – a situation somewhat reminiscent of the Palmerstonian era.

Ironically enough, the abandonment of traditional socialist goals made rather swifter progress after Gaitskell's premature death in January 1963, when the Leadership passed to the ex-Bevanite, Harold Wilson (Bevan himself had died in July 1960). As Ben Pimlott says, 'where Gaitskell had seemed to offer a regime based on welfare-minded paternalism, Wilson called for a sensible, gradualist social revolution', to be achieved through 'the centralized planning of science and technology'.[34] In a series of well-publicised speeches, which caught the mood of the times, Wilson redefined the meaning

33 Pimlott, *Dalton*, p. 552.
34 Ben Pimlott, *Harold Wilson* (1992), p. 272.

of socialism by making it synonymous with the purposive planning of national resources. Declaring war, not so much on capitalism as on the prevailing 'amateurism' of British public life, the new Labour Leader declared his commitment to a meritocratic society in which people would be recruited to public positions on the basis of their professionalism and brain-power: 'Socialism . . . means applying a sense of purpose to our national life . . . . Purpose means technical skill . . . . Ability must be the test, and ability is not to be measured by upper-class accents.'[35]

Wilson's achievement was to subordinate socialism to the proposition that Labour was better equipped than its rival to modernise the country's political institutions and to preside over economic growth. This can be seen from the party manifesto on which Labour returned to power in 1964, a manifesto which made no specific reference either to socialism or to the working class. Instead it promised that Labour would create 'A New Britain' by 'mobilising the resources of technology under a national plan'. 'As the tasks of government grow more numerous and more complex', it claimed, 'the machinery of government must be modernised', so that 'national regeneration' could be achieved through the adoption of 'new techniques, new kinds of skill and experience'. 'Only a major change of attitude to the scientific revolution, including an acceptance of the need for purposive planning, will enable us to mobilise the new resources technology is creating and harness them to human needs.'

Whereas Gaitskell's guru had been Keynes, Wilson had always owed a greater intellectual debt to Beveridge, for whom he had once acted as a research assistant. But in the early 1960s Wilson also started to pay attention to the advice being pressed upon him by a group of prominent scientists, led by Patrick Blackett.[36] Significantly, one of his first acts on becoming Prime Minister was to create a Ministry of Technology, and the first few months of his Administration were dominated by the formulation of the 'National Plan', under George Brown, installed at the newly created Department of Economic Affairs.

But, once again, there was no sharp contrast between the panaceas offered by the two Front Benches. For when in the early 1960s what has been called 'arm's-length' Keynesian Social Democracy broke down and the 'hands-on' variety took its place (involving a prices

35 Ibid., p. 307.
36 Ibid., p. 274.

and incomes policy, an industrial strategy, and so on), the two Front Benches again followed a somewhat similar policy trajectory. These were the years which saw the consolidation of what a later generation was to call 'Corporatism', the forging of regular links between Whitehall, on the one hand, and representatives of Capital and Labour, on the other. The Conservative Government's establishment of the National Economic Development Council ('Neddy') in early 1962 marked a decisive move in this direction – for which the apparent success of French 'indicative planning' provided the inspiration. And it was upon these foundations that Labour built when it returned to office in October 1964.

In countering Labour's propaganda the Conservatives were undoubtedly handicapped by having as their Leader Sir Alec Douglas-Home (the 14th Earl of Home as he had been before renouncing his peerage), a man whose background laid him open to the charge of being an archaic aristocrat, the very epitome of the sort of 'Establishment' figure that Labour held responsible for the country's economic decline. 'A group of obsolete Edwardians', was how Harold Wilson had described the Tories in November 1957.[37] This charge now took on an added plausibility.

Nevertheless, despite placing greater emphasis on individual freedom and competition (together with warnings that Labour's talk of a 'New Britain' was merely cosmetic), the Conservatives went into the 1964 Election with a programme which employed a rhetoric not dissimilar from that of their opponents. For example, they, too, advocated 'planning by partnership', the modernisation of industry, and the promotion of civil scientific research and development.

No wonder that there were those who believed that they were witnessing 'the end of ideology' (the title of a book by the American sociologist, Daniel Bell, published in 1960). The country faced a choice between two different kinds of technocratic 'managerialism', sufficiently distinct to arouse the voters' interest, but, for all that, variations on the same theme. In other words, whereas in earlier periods of British history the idea of scientific planning had usually formed the starting-point for an external *assault* on the party system, as had happened during the Edwardian quest for 'National Efficiency', a technocratic approach now became incorporated *within both major parties*.

The significant extension of public ownership after the war also

37 Cited in Pimlott, *Wilson*, p. 217.

meant the establishment of large corporations, most of which were now being run by successful businessmen recruited from the private sector, notably Dr Beeching, the chairman of British Rail. This convinced many politicians of both party persuasions that the old division between socialism and capitalism was becoming obsolete and that the main requirement in public life was an injection of managerial efficiency. In particular, this was the message conveyed by the Transport Secretary, Ernest Marples, himself an ex-business tycoon.

THE COLLAPSE OF CONSENSUS

What, then, went wrong with this post-war consensus?[38] Its troubles can be traced back to the period shortly following Macmillan's electoral triumph in 1959. Kenneth Morgan identifies 1961 as the turning-point: the moment when 'Britain embarked on a traumatic process of self-examination, self-doubt, and declining morale, a perception of external weakness and internal decay from which it had yet fully to recover in the late 1980s.'[39]

In the view of David Marquand, the root cause of the difficulty was the inability of successive governments to reconcile the pursuit of 'full employment' with wage stability and economic growth. 'Arm's-length Keynesianism', which dominated policy-making between 1947 and the early 1960s, soon led to sharp fluctuations in economic activity.[40] 'Full employment' and prosperity stimulated imports, which in turn created the acute balance of payments problems which plagued all governments in the late 1950s and 1960s. To this difficulty, the appropriate Keynesian response was the raising of interest rates. But this, in turn, meant a contraction of industrial activity and mounting unemployment until the Treasury relaxed credit once more, whereupon the cycle was resumed. This policy of 'stop–go', as it became known, proved debilitating to manufacturing industry, and led to low annual rates of economic growth – at 2.6 per cent a year, lower than any other developed country in the Western world

38 For a general discussion, see Kavanagh, *Thatcherism*, Chapter 5.
39 Kenneth O. Morgan, *The People's Peace: British History 1945–1989* (Oxford, 1990), p. 197.
40 David Marquand, *The Unprincipled Society* (1988), Chapter 2.

except Ireland, and significantly below that being achieved by the six members of the European Economic Community (EEC).[41]

It was this failure which explains why first the Conservative Ministries of Macmillan and Home, and then Wilson's Labour Government, started intervening in the economy with the object of stimulating production. Unable to do this directly, they tried instead to cajole producer interests (the CBI, the trade union leadership, etc.) into going for higher levels of investment and efficiency. But these interventions failed more often than not. Whitehall was often defied by the very groups it had publicly set out to influence, and even when the leaders of producer interests set out to be helpful, they could not always carry their own constituencies with them. As a consequence Ministers and their officials were exposed to humiliating and open rebuffs. In Kavanagh's words, 'The difficulty for government was that the range of problems for which it accepted responsibility grew while its capacity to deal with them decreased.'[42]

Economic difficulties also contributed to a corrosive loss of self-confidence, a sense that Britain's position was slipping in relation to other countries – expressed in a spate of books and articles from the early 1960s onwards. Among the classic works in this genre were Michael Shanks's *The Stagnant Society*, a collection of essays edited by Arthur Koestler entitled *Suicide of a Nation?* (1963), and a famous number of *Encounter* (July 1963), devoted to an analysis of the country's decline.[43] One did not need to be an economic expert to grasp what was happening, for, as David Owen later wrote, an ever-increasing number of British people, by travelling and taking their holidays abroad, could observe for themselves how their country's standard of living was steadily falling behind that of its European neighbours.[44]

A further consequence of economic decline was 'imperial over-stretch'. The British people were given a succession of savage reminders that their country lacked the means to maintain the Great Power status to which it aspired, something which should have been obvious from the earlier Suez Crisis (1956), but which had subsequently been

41 Ibid.; Morgan, *People's Peace*, pp. 209–10.

42 Kavanagh, *Thatcherism*, p. 124.

43 The articles bore such revealing titles as 'The Lion and the Ostrich' (Koestler), 'Taboo on Expertise' (Austen Albu), and 'Amateurs and Gentlemen' (Goronwy Rees).

44 David Owen and David Steel, *The Time Has Come: Partnership for Progress* (1987), p. 1.

half-forgotten. On top of all this, the outbreak of the 'Troubles' in Northern Ireland in 1968–69 produced a disintegration of law-and-order in Ulster, followed by the extension of the IRA's bombing campaign to mainland Britain. These events added appreciably to a crisis of morale more severe and very much more protracted than anything that the country had experienced since the dark days of the Boer War. In 1974 the Chancellor of the Exchequer, James Callaghan, was privately saying that he 'thought Britain was going down hill so fast that we might well lose our seat on the Security Council, then go on sliding down' and that 'there was no solution, that he could see, to our problems'.[45]

From the early 1960s through to the late 1970s all governments suffered embarrassing blows to their prestige. In December 1962 Macmillan was damaged by the American Administration's cancellation of 'Skybolt' (a long-range ballistic missile system which the British had planned to purchase to maintain the credibility of their own nuclear deterrent), followed a month later by de Gaulle's veto of Britain's belated application to join the EEC. Harold Wilson had to endure the pain of the 1967 devaluation and his government's failure to reform the trade union movement in the teeth of the latter's resistance. Heath never quite recovered from his 'U-Turn' over industrial strategy, and was finally brought down by the second of the two miners' strikes in 1974. Later came the indignity endured by the Callaghan Government, when the International Monetary Fund effectively imposed an economic policy on it in 1976. The twin pillars of post-war economic policy (Keynesian demand-management and 'corporatism') had apparently broken down, yet nothing viable had been put in their place:[46] a development which was to have a profound impact on the two-party system.

45 Benn diary, 17 Nov. 1974, Tony Benn, *Against the Tide: Diaries 1973–76* (1989; 1990 edn), p. 266.
46 See the discussion between Benn and William Rees-Mogg, in ibid., 5 Oct. 1976, p. 619.

CHAPTER ELEVEN
'Alliance Politics', 1967–87

THE KING–ROBENS 'CONSPIRACY'

Talk about coalition government, of course, is always likely to materialise during periods when governments are in dire straits. For example, Attlee had felt obliged to issue a public statement denouncing as 'utter nonsense' newspaper rumours concerning an impending coalition during the fuel crisis of 1947.[1]

But a much more acute sense of malaise spread in the late 1960s, when the Labour Government, which had been formed amid such high hopes in October 1964, seemed quite incapable of grappling with the various challenges, domestic and international, it was obliged to face. Harold Wilson gave the appearance of being a Prime Minister under siege. More to the point, the man who only a few years earlier had plausibly passed himself off as a modern technocrat now seemed to be the party politician incarnate, with all the faults of the breed. Yet the Leader of the Opposition, Edward Heath, consistently lagged behind him in the opinion poll ratings. It was against this background that the young academic, Robert Skidelsky (who, significantly, had already embarked upon his biography of Mosley) could write in January 1969 about a widespread revulsion against politics as such.[2]

In the crisis period before and after Labour's humiliating devaluation (November 1967) this discontent found outlet in talk about the desirability of forming a 'National Government'. For example, Professor Beloff, in a long letter which appeared in *The Times* on 7 December,

---

1 Kenneth Harris, *Attlee* (1982), p. 337.
2 'Politics Is Not Enough', *Encounter*, Jan. 1969, 25–35.

235

argued strongly for an end to what he called 'pendulum government' and called for 'major structural changes in our society' which no party government would ever attempt. 'Short of a straight descent into some form of authoritarianism', Beloff saw no other way in which Britain could be saved: 'Coalition is not just desirable; it is inevitable.'[3]

There was also renewed speculation at this time about the possibility of a 'businessman's government', much of it originating with Lord Robens, a former Labour MP, now Chairman of the National Coal Board (NCB), who, impatient with what he saw as the incompetence of his political masters, regaled all who were prepared to listen (including TV audiences) with the message that, to get out of its economic mess, 'Great Britain Limited' needed 'a damned good chairman and managing director and a damned good board'.[4]

Opinion polls showed that the concept of a 'businessman's government' (or BMG) met with widespread popular approval.[5] The organ of the Institute of Directors, *The Director*, even carried an article in February 1968 listing the members of a hypothetical 'Business Cabinet', headed by Robens, and including leading captains of industry like Lord Beeching and Sir Paul Chambers of ICI, Sir Frank Kearton of Courtaulds, and Sir Donald Stokes of Leylands. The allocation of the post of Home Secretary to the leisure impresario Sir Billy Butlin indicates that the piece was not meant to be taken entirely seriously! But slightly less farcical was its suggestion that Education and Science might usefully be entrusted to Cecil King, of International Publishing Company (IPC), the proprietors of the *Daily Mirror*.[6]

At this time King, a part-time director of the NCB, was in frequent contact with Robens. Both men were also meeting as members of the Court of the Bank of England, where, as Roy Jenkins later wrote,

---

3 His letter elicited a sympathetic response from Max Nicholson, the proponent of 'Planning' in the 1930s (*The Times*, 9 Dec. 1967).

4 Cited in *The Director*, Jan. 1968, 3.

5 In March 1968 Gallup recorded that 58 per cent approved, and only 23 per cent disapproved, of the proposition that the party which was successful at the next election should feel free 'to appoint leading men from successful private and nationalised industries to run the country's economic and political affairs' (George H. Gallup, *The Gallup International Public Opinion Polls: Great Britain, 1937–1975* (New York, n.d.), II, p. 975). There was also considerable support for a coalition government embracing the three parties, an option which in December 1967 attracted 32 per cent of respondents, as against 10 per cent who backed Labour and 34 per cent the Conservatives (ibid., II, p. 962).

6 *The Director*, Feb. 1968, 162.

King clearly found 'a natural affinity with Maurice Parsons, the sour and unbalanced deputy Governor'.[7] (Parsons, in fact, was telling King in January 1968 that he thought the country's plight 'as grave as that of 1940 – with no Winston Churchill waiting to take over'.)[8] King soon saw that Robens's idea of a 'businessman's government' was impractical,[9] but the two men shared a sense of outrage at the Labour Government's managerial incompetence. Indeed, though once an extravagant admirer of Wilson, King had now come to view the Prime Minister with total contempt. From his access to Bank of England statistics he was also convinced that the 1967 devaluation had failed to 'solve' the financial crisis and that sterling would shortly collapse, bringing the government down with it.

In a series of luncheons to which various celebrities from the political and business world were invited, King eagerly discussed how to set up a 'National Government'. Possessing much of the megalomania of his uncles, Northcliffe and Rothermere, he took it as axiomatic that destiny would assign *him* a pivotal role in the momentous events about to unfold. But who else would participate in the work of national salvation? Initially King's candidate for the premiership was the Defence Secretary, Dennis Healey.[10] But leading Conservatives, Macleod,[11] Whitelaw and Boyle, also attended King's luncheons and seem to have given him at least some encouragement. In addition, King had high hopes of utilising the 'business talents' of City friends, like Lord Cromer, and of such 'captains of industry' as Arnold Weinstock and Joe Hyman of Viyella. As the *Mirror*'s editor, Hugh Cudlipp, later wrote, 'Cecil's world in the last half of 1967 and the first half of 1968 was sincere, patriotic, exciting, but also whimsical and hallucinatory.'[12]

Inevitably this feverish plotting leaked out. King was foolish enough to discuss his plans with Tony Benn, who promptly passed them on to the Prime Minister.[13] Cudlipp had also (perhaps by way

7 Roy Jenkins, *A Life at the Centre* (1991), p. 253.

8 King diary, 4 Jan. 1968, *The Cecil King Diary, 1965–1970* (1972), p. 170.

9 Hugh Cudlipp, *Walking on the Water* (1976), pp. 318–19.

10 In his memoirs, Healey declares himself to be innocent of encouraging King, though Benn and Crossman thought otherwise (Benn diary, 17 Feb.1968, Tony Benn, *Office Without Power: Diaries 1968–72*, 1988, p. 37).

11 Macleod told King that he thought 'a coalition government quite a possibility but only after a crash' (King diary, 22 April 1968, *King Diary, 1965–70*, p. 190).

12 Cudlipp, *Walking on the Water*, p. 304.

13 King told Benn that 'the great British public wants a coalition and he pointed to a recent Gallup Poll', with Wilson being replaced by Healey (6 Feb. 1968, *Office Without Power*, p. 29).

237

of a warning) spoken about what was afoot to Richard Crossman, the Lord President of the Council.[14] The Prime Minister's office tipped off the *Guardian*, which on 19 February carried a front page story on the affair. King, it reported, was carrying out 'soundings' to bypass both Wilson and Heath, in the quest for a 'National Government' which would include established political figures from all three parties, such as Healey, Macleod and Jo Grimond.[15] The *Guardian* also suggested that King wanted to follow 'President Kennedy's practice of using in government efficient and intelligent people from outside party boundaries', a category to which Robens and King himself presumably belonged.[16]

An embarrassed King, abroad in Paris, put out a disingenuous denial. But he did not suspend his activities on behalf of what he now liked to call an '*Emergency* Government',[17] and on 8 May, accompanied by Cudlipp, he held a notorious interview with Lord Mountbatten, at which he spoke melodramatically about the possibility of bloody street rioting, so laying himself open to the probably unjust accusation that he was trying to foment a *coup d'état*.[18] Then two days later, in the wake of Labour's disastrous losses in the municipal elections, King 'went public' with his famous signed article in the *Daily Mirror*, 'Enough is Enough'. Britain, he declared, had failed during the last quarter of a century under Labour and Conservatives alike to make 'the recovery or the progress made by others, notably the defeated Japanese, Germans and Italians'. As a result, we were 'threatened with the greatest financial crisis in our history'. The article ended with a strident appeal to the PLP to replace Wilson with a new Prime Minister, who could give the country 'a fresh start'.

Precisely what King hoped his flamboyant gesture would achieve remains a little unclear. Healey had by now fallen out of favour, and the only plausible successor to Wilson from within the Labour Cabinet was Roy Jenkins, the Chancellor of the Exchequer, whose

14 Crossman diary, 7 Feb. 1968, in Richard Crossman, *The Diaries of a Cabinet Minister, Volume Two* (1976), pp. 669–70.

15 Benn picked up the rumour that Jo Grimond 'had decided he would like a coalition under Roy Jenkins with himself and Macleod' (Benn diary, 17 Feb. 1968: *Office Without Power*, pp. 36–7), and his name was often invoked by King.

16 Benn had earlier thought that Robens, a highly ambitious man, was actually 'playing for the premiership of a theoretical Coalition Government' (Benn diary, 2 Feb., also 21 Feb. 1968, ibid., pp. 28, 37–8).

17 King diary, 7 Feb. 1968, *King Diary, 1965–70*, p. 173.

18 On the Mountbatten episode, see Dennis Healey, *The Time of My Life* (1989: 1990 edn), pp. 336–7.

ministerial stewardship King was weakening by his scaremongering statements about the state of the country's reserves.[19] It is also interesting that there should have been no direct mention of 'coalition' in the 'Enough is Enough' article – though it included a reference to the 'unwillingness by successive Prime Ministers to make any serious attempt to mobilise the talent that is available in this once great country of ours'. Instead, the general public received the impression that King was trying to dictate to the Labour Party who should be its Leader – a piece of bullying that was bound to be counterproductive.

In his memoirs Wilson has some fun at the expense of 'the trinity', Lord Shawcross,[20] Robens and King, and their 'demands for a coalition of all the talents – Great Britain Limited'.[21] But like almost the entire Labour Party he was relieved as well as delighted when IPC dismissed King from its board on 30 May. Thereafter King was left to exchange reflections with his soul-mate, 'Alf' Robens, on the dire straits into which the country had fallen,[22] and to develop an interest in that other self-proclaimed 'Man of Destiny', the elderly Mosley (now in voluntary exile in France).[23]

How serious was the danger confronting Wilson in early 1968? To Benn it seemed at the time as though 'the City' was 'planning a coup against the Government', rather like the one which was supposed to have destroyed Labour in 1931.[24] Others took less seriously the 'King Conspiracy' and the 'rumblings of revolt' and the 'wild talk about "going National"' which continued to pursue the first Wilson Ministry. As Butler and Pinto-Duschinksy later wrote: 'Any moves against [the Prime Minister] were too clumsy to present a real threat, even if the stories of them fanned the prevailing atmosphere of discontent.'[25] Moreover, whatever dissatisfaction there might have

19 In fact, before publishing his article, King had submitted his resignation as a director of the Bank of England, which Jenkins promptly accepted – before going on to put him down publicly in a Commons debate a few days later.

20 A former Labour Cabinet Minister, then a distinguished cross-bench figure.

21 Harold Wilson, *The Labour Government 1964–70: A Personal Record* (1971; 1974 edn), p. 625.

22 In October Robens and Shawcross were still hoping for Coalition: five Labour, five or six Conservatives, and five non-party, Alf suggesting 'an outside PM' (21 Oct. 1968, *King Diary, 1965–70*, p. 213). Later Robens saw a dictatorship coming, perhaps from the Right, perhaps from the Left (King diary, 26 Oct. 1971, *The Cecil King Diary, 1970–1974* (1975), p. 144).

23 Cudlipp, *Walking on the Water*, pp. 393–5.

24 Benn diary, 8 Feb. 1968, *Office Without Power*, pp. 32–3.

25 David Butler and Michael Pinto-Duschinsky, *The British General Election of 1970* (1971), p. 36.

been with Wilson's leadership within his own party, very few of these critics can have relished the prospect of sharing power with the Conservatives, who, as the *Guardian* had pertinently observed in February, would have eaten alive 'anybody from any other party in the coalition – as they did in 1931'.

On the other hand, neither was it clear what the Conservative Party had to gain in early 1968 by taking part in 'Coalition politics'. Interviewed by *The Director* the previous November, Edward Heath had irritably insisted that he was a politician, not a technocrat.[26] And though he may have been an unpopular leader, in the months after devaluation the Conservatives held a lead over Labour in the opinion polls that was never less than 15 points: in May 1968 their support was recorded as being twice that of their opponents.[27] What incentive did the leadership have to engage in any kind of cross-party negotiations? Of course, had King's predictions of a post-devaluation collapse of sterling materialised, then, as in August 1931, the Conservatives might have had to revise their priorities. But, in fact, as 1968 progressed, the country's financial position perceptibly brightened, and with it the prospect of a 'national emergency' receded.

Yet the Robens–King 'Conspiracy' of 1967–68, for all its buffoonish overtones, was not without significance – quite apart from the short-term damage to sterling inflicted by King's alarmist talk. For the prospect, however fanciful, of a 'BMG' obliged politicians to take stock of their position. At all levels, it was clear, there was dissatisfaction over the standard of business competence displayed by government. But would this difficulty be 'solved' by bringing more businessmen into public office? A young Conservative MP, Bruce-Gardyne (a later Thatcherite), thought not. Beeching, Robens and King, he argued, would be no better at running a prices and incomes policy than the current Ministry; what needed to be done was to 'reduce the area of interference' of government in economic life and leave businessmen to respond to the signals which the market was giving them.[28] The Institute of Directors agreed: 'Business doesn't

26 *The Director*, Nov. 1967, 257–61. A year later Heath sarcastically asked King what names he 'proposed to submit to the Queen for my Businessman's Government. I protested that the B.M.G. had never been my idea but Robens's, and the episode passed over, but it was not entirely a joke nor entirely friendly' (King diary, 12 Feb. 1969, *King Diary, 1965–70*, p. 241).

27 Conservatives 49 per cent, Labour 24.5 per cent, Liberals 9.5 per cent, Others 4 per cent, Don't Know 13 per cent: *Gallup Opinion Polls*, II, p. 981.

28 *The Director*, June 1968, 470–2.

want to swap old political masters for new, it wants to run its own affairs.'[29]

This divergence of outlook was soon to prove crucially important. For whereas Robens and King clearly wanted to downplay the role of party in national political life, the implication of the Institute of Directors' critique was that economic reconstruction required the eradication, or at least the renegotiation, of the post-war settlement – something which would obviously necessitate a *sharpening* of party political antagonisms, not their supersession.

EDWARD HEATH AND THE 'GNU'

In the end the amateurish King–Robens intrigue came to nothing, and Wilson's prestige revived in the course of 1969, to the point where it seemed (wrongly, of course) that Labour might be re-elected. But there continued to be a prevailing mood of disillusionment, not only with Labour but with the Conservatives as well. Not surprisingly this translated into a loss of support for the two major parties. What the political scientists call 'partisan dealignment', that is to say, the erosion of party loyalties, might well have happened in any case, as economic change threw up new social groups who found difficulty in empathising with either Capital or Labour. In October 1974 barely half the electorate were identifying with (let alone voting with) their 'natural' class party.[30] And as class identity weakened, electors tended to become more volatile, more swayed by short-term considerations. After the 1964 Election approximately 50 per cent of all Conservative and Labour voters had declared a strong party allegiance: by 1979 this proportion had halved. Indeed, by 1979 only 10 per cent of the *electorate* expressed a firm commitment to either of the two main parties, and, as 'the boundaries of the traditional social bases of the two major parties' blurred, 'they became easier to transgress'.[31] This process was at first attributed to the *convergence* between the policies of the two parties and to the resultant debate as to whether parties really *mattered*. In fact, it probably owed more to the widespread

29 Ibid., Jan. 1968, 3.
30 Ivor Crewe, Bo Sarlvik and James Alt, 'Partisan Dealignment in Britain 1964–1974', *British Journal of Political Science*, 7 (1977), 183.
31 Bo Sarlvik and Ivor Crewe, *Decade of Dealignment: The Conservative victory of 1979 and electoral trends in the 1970s* (Cambridge, 1983), pp. 336–7.

perception of the failure of government economic policy, which had weakened voters' identification with 'their' party and given rise to 'a politics of quiet disillusion'.[32]

To the politically disenchanted citizen, the most readily available 'party of protest' was, of course, the Liberal Party, whose share of the poll had fallen to a pathetic 2.5 per cent in 1951 but which thereafter rose more or less steadily; it reached 5.9 per cent in 1959 and 11.2 per cent in 1966, before slipping back to 7.5 per cent in 1970.[33] Then in the General Election of February 1974 the Liberal vote shot up once more, this time to the significant level of 19.3 per cent.

The Liberals' mini-breakthrough in February 1974 was all the more significant because it coincided with a good performance by the Scottish Nationalists and by Plaid Cymru, both of whom successfully exploited the mood of political disillusionment. In addition, recent upheavals in Northern Ireland had led to the decoupling of Ulster Unionism from the main body of the Conservative Party. The result was the return of eleven independent Ulster Unionists, along with seven Scottish and two Welsh Nationalists, fourteen Liberals and three other Independents – by post-war standards, an unprecedented number of MPs detached from the two 'parties of government'. Indeed, for the first time since 1929, the country had a hung Parliament, since Labour (which had actually polled fewer votes than the Conservatives) had a lead of five over their main rivals but were seventeen seats short of a majority. Fears were expressed that the country was becoming 'ungovernable'. The United Kingdom, it seemed, was breaking up. Not only were governments unable to cope with industrial unrest and Irish terrorism: now even the two-party system had failed to produce an 'outright winner', hitherto its main justification.

In fact the 'first-past-the-post' system masked the true extent of the decline in the popularity of the two main parties. They secured only 75.4 per cent of the total vote in February 1974. In October 1974 this figures dipped still further to 75.1 per cent, and although it climbed back to 80.8 per cent in 1979, four years later it again fell back – to 70 per cent of the total vote, a post-war low. The unpopularity of the two main parties is revealed even more clearly in the figures of their share of the *total electorate*. For example, in the second 1974 Election

32 Crewe, Sarlvik and Alt, 'Partisan Dealignment', 133; James E. Alt, *The Politics of Economic Decline* (Cambridge, 1979), p. 270.

33 This process was not so apparent at the time. See Robert Rhodes James's dismissal of the Liberal Revival of 1962–65 in *Ambitions and Strategies: British Politics 1964–70* (1972), p. 226.

Labour and Conservatives only managed between them to secure the votes of about half the electorate. There was thus an accelerating refusal by voters to support the two main parties.

To both Front Benches any reliance on minor parties was a humiliation. It also had worrying implications for the running of the country. The 'politics of decline' seemed set fair to produce a succession of hung Parliaments and governments too weak to take the decisive action necessary to arrest that decline. Such a prospect took on a much grimmer appearance than had been the case during the phase of three-party politics in the 1920s, for then it was reasonable to suppose that the difficulty would shortly correct itself as Labour displaced the Liberals: but in the 1970s there were grounds for believing that instability would steadily *increase*.

In 1974 these anxieties found expression in renewed calls for national co-operation and coalition, but this time the demand was made, not as in 1967–68 by political mavericks, but by a leader of one of the two major parties, Edward Heath. As we have seen, the February election of that year resulted in a hung Parliament in which the Conservatives held the largest share of the popular vote but had fewer MPs than Labour. Heath initially tried to do a deal with the Liberals, but the attempt broke down when he refused to offer more than a Speaker's Conference on the electoral system. This left Wilson free to form his own minority Labour Government.

At Conservative Central Office a post-mortem took place. The party's private pollster, Humphrey Taylor, believed that much middle opinion, alienated by the Heath Government's abrasive stance, had switched to the Liberals in the recent election. Some of the leading figures in Conservative Central Office, among them the young Chris Patten and Ian Gilmour, drew from this the deduction that if the Conservatives were to avoid further reversals at the next general election (which could not be far off), they would need to outflank the Liberals. Here was the origin of the idea of a 'Government of National Unity' (GNU), a phrase first used by the Liberal Leader Jeremy Thorpe on 4 March.[34]

Against a background of acute industrial unrest, high inflation and general political malaise, the idea quickly won influential backers. In March, for example, Maurice Macmillan (Harold's son) resigned from the Shadow Cabinet to advocate a 'Government of all the

---

34 David Butler and Dennis Kavanagh, *The British General Election of October 1974* (1975), p. 43; John Campbell, *Edward Heath: A Biography* (1993), pp. 625–33.

Talents', as did Peter Walker.[35] Such demands met with a chorus of approval from the press, in particular from Bernard Levin of *The Times*, who was later joined by a number of popular and quality journals, including the *Financial Times*, the *Daily Mail*, the *Sunday Times*, the *Observer* and *The Economist*.[36]

Heath himself was understandably reluctant to do or say anything rash which would interfere with the normal play of party rivalries. In June he contented himself with the claim that only the Conservatives could 'now honestly claim to stand four-square in the centre of British national life'. But, according to Gilmour's later account, 'Ted came along quite well.'[37] In July he spoke of the public's 'great desire . . . for an end to the kind of politics which people describe to me as the politics of the slanging match', and eventually on 3 October the Conservative Leader pledged himself to bring in outsiders, *even if his followers secured a parliamentary majority*.[38]

Thus by the time the Conservative election manifesto was published in early October, the party had unequivocally committed itself to Coalition. The country, declared the manifesto, faced a grave 'economic crisis', a 'national emergency', which could not be dealt with by 'party bickering'. The Conservatives therefore offered the people 'a programme which would unite and not divide the nation' by genuinely attempting to bring the parties together to make common cause against the common enemy of inflation and unemployment'. Heath promised that, after consulting all the party leaders on what measures should be taken to meet the crisis, he would promptly 'bring into the administration people of talent and patriotism from all walks of life so that we can use all the skill and intellect at our command'. 'I have no doubt', he said, 'that the real hope of the British people . . . is that a national Coalition government involving all the parties could be formed, and that party differences could be put aside until the crisis is mastered'.[39]

On 10 October the country duly went to the polls in the second of the 1974 Elections. But if Heath and those who supported the new coalitionist strategy thought that it would enable the party to break

35 Butler and Kavanagh, *General Election of October 1974*, p. 44.

36 Campbell, *Heath*, p. 642.

37 Ibid., pp. 637, 633.

38 Ibid., pp. 638, 650; Butler and Kavanagh, *General Election of October 1974*, p. 44.

39 *The Times Guide to the House of Commons, October 1974* (1974), pp. 312–13.

back into office, they were mistaken, since Labour secured a small working majority.

It is not difficult to assign reasons for this 'failure'. Heath's claims to embody 'national unity' lacked plausibility, given his recent performance as Prime Minister and his own crotchety personality. Moreover, although some of his colleagues pressed him to make the 'supreme sacrifice' by standing down as Conservative Leader, Heath adamantly refused to do any such thing – thereby confirming his political opponents in their cynical assessment of his motives.[40] At the same time, the GNU idea was not being greeted with much enthusiasm by rank-and-file Conservatives. Some Front-Benchers also had their doubts: neither Mrs Thatcher nor Keith Joseph made much use of the GNU slogan in the course of their election campaigns – a portent of trouble to come. As for the wider electorate, it seems as though most voters wanted a *more conciliatory style of government*, but not an actual Coalition.[41] There was also a fatal vagueness about quite what a GNU would mean. The old idea of bringing businessmen into government made yet another appearance, Heath speaking of a 'blood transfusion' of practical people. Robens and Shawcross predictably applauded, but few observers were impressed by the mention of Sir Marcus Sieff and Toby Low as examples of the kind of non-party 'outsider' who might be invited to join the next Government.[42]

Nevertheless, the Conservatives did considerably better in October 1974 than most commentators had predicted (they certainly avoided a repetition of the 1966 disaster), and so it might even be claimed that, as an exercise in damage limitation, the GNU gambit enjoyed a modest success. It also, to some extent, rattled the leaders of the two other parties. Thus, the Liberals were in two minds. They felt some sympathy with a proposal which they themselves had done much to shape. But, in the absence of any encouragement from the Conservatives in respect of electoral reform, they could not afford to endorse it unless the Labour Party did so as well. And this Labour resolutely refused to do, Wilson sneeringly dismissing Coalition as meaning 'Con policies, Con leadership by a Con party for a Con trick'.[43] The Labour manifesto spelled out the party's objections: 'A

---

40 Campbell, *Heath*, p. 649.

41 Butler and Kavanagh, *General Election of October 1974*, pp. 122–3, 263–4.

42 Campbell, *Heath*, pp. 647–8; Butler and Kavanagh, *General Election of October 1974*, p. 123.

43 Cited in Ben Pimlott, *Harold Wilson* (1992), p. 646.

coalition government, by its very nature, tends to trim its policies and fudge its decisions', it argued, 'and it would be a cruel farce to suggest that the future of the country would be helped by shuffling, compromising administration.'[44] Yet Wilson was privately worried by opinion polls which suggested that some 26 per cent of the electorate favoured the establishment of an all-party Coalition and that 55 per cent of voters blamed Labour for ruling it out.[45] Wilson tried to neutralise the danger by presenting *Labour* as the servant of the national interest, its Conservative opponents as sectarian and divisive.

As a holding operation, this had much to recommend it. However, playing Disraeli to Heath's Robert Peel carried with it two obvious disadvantages. First, it alarmed many members of Wilson's own party, who feared betrayal: 'All this "national interest", "working together", "keep calm and keep cool", and "a Labour Government will knit the nation into one", seem absolute rubbish to me now', Benn had written in his diary after watching Wilson on TV in January.[46] Secondly, such talk lacked a wider plausibility. For, as Robert Skidelsky had noted five years earlier, Wilson's rhetoric about the 'national interest', along with his attempts to arouse the 'Dunkirk spirit', had become 'what George Orwell called a "dying metaphor", one no longer capable of evoking the desired response'.[47]

IDEOLOGICAL POLARISATION

In fact, far from there being a national coming-together, Britain underwent a polarisation of political opinion in the late 1960s and early 1970s. Hitherto anxieties about the state of the British economy had encouraged attempts to shore up the old 'consensus'. But now, faced by the phenomenon of 'stagflation' (a combination of low growth, inflation and high unemployment), more searching questions began to be asked about the viability of the old 'Keynesian' remedies. And as public expenditure drifted out of control in the mid-1970s,

44 *Times Guide to House of Commons, October 1974*, p. 300.
45 Campbell, *Heath*, p. 648; Butler and Kavanagh, *General Election of October 1974*, p. 124.
46 Benn's diary, 23 Jan. 1974, Tony Benn, *Against The Tide: Diaries 1973–76* (1989; 1990 edn), p. 97.
47 *Encounter*, Jan. 1969, 25.

the number of those looking for new economic strategies sharply increased.

In particular, activists within the Labour Party, disappointed with the performance of their own ministries, started to desert the centre ground in search of a more satisfying creed. They called for internal party democracy and advocated militant full-blooded socialism, along with a break from the foreign policy consensus which had existed since 1945. In short, from the late 1960s onwards, the Left, with Tony Benn and Michael Foot to the fore, made steady progress, thereby provoking a reaction from Labour's right wing, led by Roy Jenkins.[48]

The question of the Common Market emerged as the main battle-ground between the two factions. When in 1972 the party resolved to vote against the entry terms which Heath's Conservative Government had successfully negotiated, sixty-seven Labour MPs defied the party line, with a further twenty abstaining; and when, at committee stage, Labour pressed for a referendum on British membership, Roy Jenkins resigned his post of Deputy Leader. A few months later Dick Taverne, a pro-Common Market Labour MP, fought and won a by-election at Lincoln (1 March 1973), as a protest at his party's growing 'extremism' – causing one local paper to compare him with famous 'independents' of the past like Cripps and Winston Churchill![49]

Labour's return to power in 1974 partially stopped the leftward drift, as Harold Wilson, now posing as a reincarnated Stanley Baldwin, skilfully manoeuvred to contain the Left and to neutralise its main spokesmen: in June 1975 Benn was humiliatingly demoted and another left-wing Minister, Judith Hart, effectively sacked. But at constituency level and in the party nationally, the advance of the Left inexorably proceeded. At the 1975 Conference Benn was returned to the NEC at the top of the poll: a year later the Chancellor of the Exchequer, Dennis Healey, was voted off it. By the late 1970s the Labour Government could rely on only ten of its twenty-nine members.[50] Indeed, at the very time that Healey was introducing

48 For a good overview, see Martin Ceadel, 'Labour as a Governing Party: Balancing Right and Left', in Terry Gourvish and Alan O'Day (eds), *Britain Since 1945* (1991), pp. 274–8.

49 John Ramsden and Richard Jay, 'Lincoln: The Background to Taverne's Triumph', in Chris Cook and John Ramsden (eds), *By-Elections in British Politics* (1973), p. 308.

50 Dennis Kavanagh, *Thatcherism and British Politics: The End of Consensus?* (Oxford, 1987), p. 163.

the first 'monetarist' budgets, Labour activists were embarking on a fundamentalist socialist crusade. As these internal divisions of opinion widened, there thus emerged, in effect, 'two Labour Parties, one with the voice of the NEC and Conference and the other with that of the parliamentary leadership'.[51] Benn made no secret of the fact that his prime loyalty lay with the former, not with the Cabinet of which he was still a member – to the unease of his many critics who felt that this was carrying party spirit to dangerous extremes.[52]

Right-wing Labour MPs, alarmed at such developments and afraid, in some cases, of being deselected by their constituency activists, formed defensive organisations like the Manifesto Group in December 1974, the Social Democratic Alliance in June 1975 and the Campaign for Labour Victory in 1977. But in opposition once more after the 1979 General Election, the Left completed its capture of the party. Labour's programme now included a commitment to withdraw from the Common Market and NATO, a substantial extension of public ownership (along lines laid down by the socialist economist, Stuart Holland), and constitutional changes aimed at a reduction of the autonomy of MPs. Meanwhile there was a remarkable upsurge of interest in Marxism of a kind that had not been seen in Britain since the 1930s.

Within the Conservative Party a parallel development was taking place. There had always been elements within the party critical of Keynesian demand-management who urged the need to save capitalism by freeing the market from impediments. Since the 1950s the Institute of Economic Affairs (IEA) had acted as their think-tank. But these 'neo-Liberals' lacked influential spokesmen in the upper reaches of the party. True, Enoch Powell voiced their concerns; but he had put himself too far outside the political mainstream by his attacks on coloured immigration to be taken seriously in governing circles. And though Edward Heath's Selsdon Park conference (1970) briefly seemed to herald a decisive departure from moderate, consensual Conservatism, the party quickly returned to a more familiar managerial style after its U-turn in 1972.

However, the situation changed quite rapidly during 1974–75, when a prominent ex-Minister, Keith Joseph, made a series of speeches, inspired by the right-wing ideologue Alfred Sherman and

51 David Butler and Dennis Kavanagh, *The British General Election of 1979* (1980), p. 47.

52 Particularly since, if opinion polls were any guide, the 'party line' which Benn espoused did not command any great support among the wider electorate.

the economist Alan Walters.[53] Joseph, recently installed by Heath as head of the Centre for Policy Studies (CPS), urged Conservatives to seek 'common ground' with the *electorate*, but to avoid a 'middle ground' defined 'by splitting the difference between Labour's position and the Conservatives'.[54] He also argued that *all* post-war governments, Conservative and Labour alike, had pursued fundamentally flawed policies: 'We are now more socialist in many ways than any other developed country outside the Communist bloc', Joseph publicly declared.[55] These propositions, unsurprisingly, received almost no support from members of the Opposition Front Bench – except from Margaret Thatcher, the CPS's President.

Then in the following year the 'peasants revolt' unexpectedly swept Mrs Thatcher into the Conservative leadership. What this signified was the elevation to power of a politician who saw 'consensus' as a kind of treason.[56] Under her leadership, the Conservative Party, encouraged by new pressure groups like the Adam Smith Institute (founded in 1977) began to throw over the post-war settlement by campaigning for a sharp reduction of trade union power, the privatisation of nationalised industries, the reorganisation of many areas of public life on the basis of market principles, and the adoption of 'monetarism'. Nigel Lawson has recently described these developments as a 'reversion to an older tradition in the light of the failure of what might be termed the new enlightenment'.[57] But in many ways they constituted a fresh departure.

Moreover, Mrs Thatcher felt nothing but contempt for her opponents. As Roy Jenkins was soon to discover, she would have nothing to do with 'cross-party public appointments';[58] she despised the neutrality of the civil service, preferring to receive advice only

---

53 Behind these thinkers stood the Austrian economist and political theorist, Friedrich von Hayek, and the American economist, Milton Friedman. On the Joseph–Sherman relationship, see Hugo Young, *One of Us* (1991 edn), p. 85. Sherman wrote Joseph's famous Preston speech of September 1974 (ibid., p. 88).

54 Speech at Oxford Union, 6 Dec. 1975, in Sir Keith Joseph, *Stranded on the Middle Ground? Reflections on circumstances and policies* (1976), pp. 19–21. Joseph was right in the sense that many planks in the post-war consensus had never been popular, as opinion polls revealed: see Kavanagh, *Thatcherism*, p. 57.

55 Young, *One of Us*, p. 85.

56 In conversation with Sir Anthony Parsons in May 1978, she declared that she regarded consensus politicians as 'Quislings, as traitors' (ibid., pp. 223–4).

57 'The New Conservatism' (1980), in Nigel Lawson: *The View From No. 11: Memoirs of a Tory Radical* (1992; 1993 edn), p. 1041.

58 Jenkins, *Life at the Centre*, p. 524.

from those who were 'One of Us'; and she even abandoned well-tried mechanisms for engineering broad-based national agreement, such as the Royal Commission. Benn was envious, and wished Labour would follow her example – for example, by reducing its dependence for advice on the civil service.[59]

So, as the Labour Party swung left, the Conservatives moved to the right. There was to be no more talk about the 'end of ideology'. On the contrary, a sharp polarisation took place in the late 1970s and early 1980s of a kind that would have been inconceivable even ten years earlier. The socialist forces represented by Wedgwood Benn, on the Left, and the 'Radical Right' spearheaded by Keith Joseph and Margaret Thatcher, were alike in that they were proud to call themselves 'conviction politicians': each group, in its own way, wanted to escape from the compromises, the weary pragmatism and the outworn orthodoxies (like Keynesianism) which it held responsible for the country's decline. 'I had some sympathy with Thatcher – with her dislike of the wishy-washy centre of British politics', Benn told Edward Heath – receiving 'a frosty look' for his pains![60]

THE CENTRE REGROUPS

These development created a vacuum in the centre of politics, seemingly to the distress of many electors: a January 1980 poll found that 60 per cent thought that Labour had moved too far left, while 46 per cent thought that the Conservatives had moved too far right.[61] This alienation was more pronounced among traditional Labour voters, where distaste for militant trade union activity became very widespread in the 1970s – hence, in large part, the Conservative victory of 1979. But a dislike of the new spirit of ideological zealotry united many people across the boundaries of class and party, and the yearning for a more conciliatory style of politics soon found

59 See Benn diary, 29 Feb. 1980, in *Conflicts of Interest: Diaries 1977–80* (1990; 1991 edn), p. 584. On the other hand, it could be argued that the appointment of political advisers had been initiated by Labour in its 1964–70 and 1974–79 Administrations.

60 Benn diary, 15 May 1979, ibid., p. 505.

61 Ian Bradley, *Breaking the Mould: The Birth and Prospects of the Social Democratic Party* (Oxford, 1981), p. 43.

expression in novel forms of collaboration between the 'centrists' of all backgrounds.

A prologue to these new developments had occurred during the Common Market referendum of 1975, when Roy Jenkins and Shirley Williams of the Labour Party and Edward Heath of the Conservative Party had joined up with the Liberals in the 'Britain in Europe' pressure-group – an experience which, Jenkins later admitted, put all other political controversies in the shade. The country was then treated to the spectacle of such odd sights as a Conservative–Liberal team touring the streets of Durham with the slogan: 'Support your Labour Government – Vote Yes to Europe'![62]

Once the referendum was over, many activists welcomed the return to traditional party animosities. But other non-party figures who took part in the campaign on the pro-Europe side felt sad: 'We can all work together and we have proved it.'[63] Some prominent politicians reacted similarly. Reg Prentice, a right-wing Labour MP who later defected to the Conservatives, publicly noted that the co-operation between the pro-Marketeers had 'been welcomed by millions of people throughout Britain, who have become fed up with the traditional party dogfight. We must not lose this spirit of unity after June 5' – sentiments also voiced by the former Deputy Leader of the Labour Party, George Brown.[64] In May the *Evening Standard* carried a front-page picture of Thorpe, Heath and Jenkins under the heading of 'The Euro-Coalition'.

Left-wing Labour Party members, most of them hostile to Europe, found all of this highly disturbing. The Benn diaries contain several references to the possibility that the well-funded referendum campaign might be the prelude to the establishment of an actual coalition or the emergence of a new 'centre' party, bringing together Heath, Thorpe and Jenkins.[65] Wilson, for reasons of his own, played upon such fears by warning his Ministers: 'It could be 1931 all over again . . . What I am afraid of . . . is a pro-Market coalition, a Tory-dominated coalition with perhaps a titular Labour leader.'[66]

The European issue proved to be extremely important in the development of the politics of consensus. For a start, Europe cut clean

---

62 David Butler and Uwe Kitzinger, *The 1975 Referendum* (1976), p. 131.

63 Ibid., pp. 132–3.

64 Ibid., pp. 168–9.

65 Benn diary, 18 June, 14 Oct. 1975, *Against The Tide*, pp. 403–4, 446. See also Pimlott, *Wilson*, p. 663.

66 Pimlott, *Wilson*, p. 657.

across the party divide, with support for the EEC being strongest among moderate progressive Conservatives, on the one hand, and among most (though not all) right-wing Labour politicians, on the other.[67]

The reasons for this enthusiasm for Europe are even more significant. The pro-Europe Labour group had always admired the German Social Democratic Party's discarding of old-style socialism for social democracy and had sought to emulate it. But, in addition, British pro-Europeans, of all parties, could not help but notice that every single member of the Community, bar Britain, had rejected the first-past-the-post system for electoral set-ups which ensured that, in most cases, coalition government was the norm. This struck an anti-Marketeer like Michael Foot as both serious and sinister: staying in the EEC, he warned, would suck Britain into a Coalition method of running its economic affairs, since other members of the community had Coalition governments.[68]

Now, in the past it had been customary to disparage such political arrangements with the argument that they made for weak and ineffectual government. But, given the higher growth rates, better living standards and greater political stability enjoyed by many European countries, notably the German Federal Republic, the idea soon took root that the very opposite might be the case: that it was the first-past-the-post system that was responsible for Britain's relative decline and that recovery would elude governments until they adopted new electoral arrangements based upon power-sharing between the main parties of government and the socio-economic forces which those parties represented.[69]

As early as December 1967 Beloff had written: 'The fact that most of our friends and competitors in Western Europe regard coalition as normal should make us wonder whether we do not pay too high a price for our fidelity to the "Gladstone–Disraeli syndrome"';[70] and a year later Skidelsky similarly questioned whether the supposedly 'strong' governments which Britain had enjoyed since the war had been better at making decisions or at facing up to long-term problems

---

67 Gaitskell himself had come out increasingly strongly against the EEC at the end of his life. Some of his acolytes, notably Douglas Jay, continued this tradition of hostility.

68 Butler and Kitzinger, *1975 Referendum*, p. 168.

69 Britain herself had adopted a form of 'power-sharing' for Northern Ireland between 1973–4.

70 *The Times*, 7 Dec. 1967.

than the 'weak' governments of the Continent.[71] These were to become commonplaces of political rhetoric in the late 1970s and 1980s. Jim Prior, for example, argued that 'no one could seriously claim that West Germany . . . has been unstable over the last forty years, and they have had the benefit of much greater continuity in policy than Britain has enjoyed',[72] while Gilmour similarly rejected as 'mythological' the 'idea that coalition leads to weak government'.[73]

To many observers of British public life, it thus seemed to be of the utmost importance that the country should make a clean break with what became widely known as 'adversary politics', a phrase apparently first coined by *The Economist* in May 1974.[74] Two-party politics, it was widely claimed, had brought about considerable economic damage because it had artificially strengthened and institutionalised class conflict and brought about sudden policy lurches which prevented the implementation of consistent economic management – hence the all-too-evident weaknesses of the British economy.[75]

A considerable body of academic writing came into existence in support or refutation of this hypothesis. The very titles of some of these books indicate the new mood: *The Problem of Party Government* (Richard Rose, 1974), *Adversary Politics and Electoral Reform* (edited by S.E. Finer, 1975). Another academic critic of 'adversary politics' was Nevil Johnson, who, in a book published in 1977, sought both to demonstrate the longevity of Britain's coalition tradition and also to defend the legitimacy and efficacy of governments like those of Switzerland, based on the principle of power-sharing between groups.[76]

One consequence of these debates was the proliferation of new organisations dedicated to the adoption of PR, a creed to which many former sceptics now announced their conversion. Thus, the National Committee for Electoral Reform was launched in June 1976

71 *Encounter*, Jan. 1969, 34.

72 Jim Prior, *A Balance of Power* (1986), p. 264.

73 Ian Gilmour, *Inside Right: A Study of Conservatism* (1977), p. 226. See also *Britain Can Work* (Oxford, 1983), pp. 200–1.

74 See Jenifer Hart, *Proportional Representation: Critics of the British Electoral System 1820–1945* (Oxford, 1992), p. 283.

75 S.E. Finer (ed.), *Adversary Politics and Electoral Reform* (1975), Part II, pp. 99–140. As to whether this really happens, see Douglas E. Ashford, *Policy and Politics in Britain: The Limits of Consensus* (Oxford, 1981), p. 7.

76 Nevil Johnson, *In Search of the Constitution* (Oxford, 1977), pp. 70–1, 75. Note, too, the academic writing of Vernon Bogdanor.

by a cross-party group which included John Mackintosh, David Steel and Dick Taverne, the winner of the Lincoln by-election in March 1973.[77]

THE LIBERAL REVIVAL

Obviously the Liberal Party, of all the major political organisations, was the one best placed to exploit this new mood. Admittedly, there were some Liberals, like Grimond, who had spent years mocking the two major parties for being too *alike* and found that having to change 'the angle of [their] attack' was 'not an entirely comfortable change'.[78] On the other hand, the nature of the Liberal Party's electoral support gave it some claim to be considered a 'national party'. After all, the Labour Party relied heavily upon the working-class electors, since only one-fifth of non-manual voters supported it. The Conservatives were more successful in appealing to voters from a variety of different backgrounds.[79] But the Liberal vote had *always* been relatively evenly spread across the social spectrum: Butler and Stokes, writing in the 1960s, were duly impressed by 'the breadth and evenness, in class terms, of the Liberals' appeal', even though the lower working class was slightly under-represented.[80]

Naturally enough, the Liberals had always drawn attention to the fact that their party was 'more likely to unite the nation than either the Conservatives or the Socialists – locked as they [were] in what [was] really a class struggle'.[81] The point had been forcefully made in the 1959 Manifesto: 'A Liberal vote is a protest against the British political system being divided up between two powerful party machines, one largely financed by the employers and the other by the trade unions.'[82] If the Liberals represented an interest, wrote Grimond in 1963, it was because it had 'an interest – a strong interest – among the new educated class, the technicians, scientists, teachers (it has lately been relatively strong in the universities) and in

77 Bradley, *Breaking the Mould?*, p. 31.
78 Jo Grimond, *Memoirs* (1979), p. 253.
79 Between one-third and two-fifths of manual workers voted Conservative.
80 David Butler and Donald Stokes, *Political Change in Britain: Forces Shaping Electoral Choice* (1969; 1971 edn), p. 107.
81 *The Times House of Commons 1950* (1950), p. 297.
82 *The Times Guide to the House of Commons 1959* (1959), p. 256.

the growing middle class'.[83] True, as Butler and Pinto-Duschinsky say, the Liberals' centrist pitch was undercut in the late 1960s by 'Mr Wilson's play for the middle ground of moderation'.[84] But the Liberals' strategy was likely to become more widely attractive as despondency about the future of British politics deepened.

The Liberals had also, since the early 1920s, been advocates of electoral reform. But in the immediate post-war years Liberal propaganda had revolved around the claim that electoral reform would be 'fair', that it would empower the people, and that it would banish cynicism from political life. Under present arrangements, Grimond had written, the outcome of contests in most single-member constituencies was a foregone conclusion, something which not only frustrated minorities but damaged majority groups, too.[85] These arguments against the first–past–the–post system grew more plausible when the two 1974 Elections produced a Parliament in which, for the first time since 1929, over 50 per cent of MPs had failed to win a plurality of votes.

But during the 1970s the emphasis shifted: political and constitutional change, Liberals now argued, was the necessary prelude to *social and economic renewal*. The February 1974 General Election manifesto was headed 'The Crisis of Government': 'Britain cannot be governed effectively when parties continuously change their policies and principles to make cheap political gains', it declared. The manifesto went on to attack the parties for being partisan, and for 'polarising the nation into confrontation between classes whether they be rich or poor, manager or worker, house owner or tenant'.[86] The old two-party system was castigated for its sterility and inadequacy.

In October an even more pronounced note of urgency was sounded. 'This election will make or break Britain', claimed the Liberals. This claim was coupled with the warning that the government which took office after the election would 'face the greatest peacetime crisis we have known since the dark days of 1931'. The Liberals announced that they were 'unashamedly committed to breaking the two-party system in which the party of management alternate[d] with the party of trade unionism, each committed to the reversal of their predecessors' policies', with a consequent undermining of 'confidence and stability'. 'The first priority must be to promote a sense of common endeavour

83 Jo Grimond, *The Liberal Challenge* (1963), p. 313.
84 Butler and Pinto-Duschinsky, *General Election of 1970*, p. 113.
85 Jo Grimond, *The Liberal Future* (1959), pp. 38–9.
86 *The Times Guide to the House of Commons, February 1974* (1974), p. 312.

and national purpose in government. We must persuade all people to lay aside the differences which divide and weaken us as a nation', overcoming 'the artificial divisions which society inflicts on us.' 'Now is the time to decide whether we are to continue the steady decline in our national life, or whether we are going to pull ourselves back from the brink.'[87]

From the time of his arrival at Westminster David Steel had consistently used arguments of this kind. Indeed, he soon took this approach one step further by calling explicitly for a 'national government'. Thus, in a famous TV party political broadcast in June 1974 he declared that the country's crisis called for the creation of 'a much more broadly based government, backed by a real majority of public opinion', which meant that all parties would have to 'come together on an agreed programme in the national interest'. Steel predicted 'that the pattern of the two-party stranglehold on British politics [was] breaking up', and claimed that the growing 'public demand for a government of national unity' could only be realised by getting more Liberals into Parliament.[88] In the face of protests from many Liberal activists, the Liberal Leader, Jeremy Thorpe, toned down this appeal.[89] But it resurfaced two years later when, following Thorpe's resignation, Steel ran for the leadership: 'We must be bold enough to deploy the coalition case positively', he said.[90] As Tony Benn noted in his diary, Steel had now 'come out in favour of coalition in order to get proportional representation', rather than simply presenting coalition government as the likely outcome of electoral reform which was needed on some other ground.[91]

Steel's big chance came a year later when Wilson's Labour Government, secured on the basis of a mere 39.3 per cent of the popular vote, saw its slender majority eroded by by-election defeats. This was the origin of the Steel–Callaghan Pact of the spring of 1977, an agreement whereby Liberal MPs guaranteed to keep the Labour Government in office in return for certain policy concessions and the right to participate in a 'joint consultative committee' which considered future legislation. But although Callaghan, to humour the Liberals, felt bound to take STV seriously, Benn was voicing

---

87 *Times Guide to House of Commons, October 1974*, p. 335.

88 David Steel, *A House Divided: The Lib–Lab Pact and the Future of British Politics* (1980), pp. 17–18.

89 Ibid., pp. 18–19.

90 Ibid., pp. 24–5.

91 Benn Diary, 18 Sept. 1976, *Against The Tide*, p. 610.

the mainstream Labour view when he argued that 'if we introduce proportional representation it would mean the Party would never get into power again'.[92] The Liberals were therefore denied the one concession that really mattered to them. In 1978 the Steel–Callaghan Pact lapsed.

The Liberal Party suffered from another disadvantage: it still gave the appearance of lacking governmental tradition and administrative experience. Indeed, long years in opposition had attracted to its ranks people temperamentally attuned to the politics of protest. Paradoxically, the Liberals' role as 'a receptacle for the dissatisfied', actually meant that they were 'acting as a built-in stabiliser for the two-party system'.[93] If the Liberals were really to offer a serious alternative to the main parties, they needed to link up with others – either with disgruntled Conservatives or with disgruntled socialists.

THE RISE AND FALL OF THE 'ALLIANCE'

In some respects Steel's natural allies were to be found among Mrs Thatcher's many Conservative critics. After all, the convictions of the Tory 'wets' overlapped with those of the Liberals in many crucial respects. Both groups urged a return to Keynesian demand-management, preached the virtues of moderation and conciliation, were pro-European, and, crucially, supported constitutional changes. Gilmour, for example, wanted electoral reform to protect the country against 'extremism', by which he meant both sectional militancy and also the 'threat of an extremist Labour Party imposing Marxist chains upon an unwilling country'.[94] Prior agreed with Gilmour in recommending the adoption of a German-style Additional Member System; he also favoured other constitutional innovations designed to strengthen the 'moderate centre': the state funding of parties, more parliamentary select committees, and a rearrangement of the shape of the Commons on a circular pattern.[95]

Yet what did this imply for the future of the British party system? It so happened that the elderly Macmillan, now Lord Stockton, did

92 Benn diary, 21 April 1977, *Conflicts of Interest*, pp. 116–17.

93 Dennis Kavanagh, *Politics and Personalities* (Basingstoke and London, 1990), p. 133.

94 Gilmour, *Inside Right*, p. 225.

95 Prior, *Balance of Power*, pp. 264–6.

make a veiled appeal for a coalition government in his speech to the Lords in January 1985.[96] But none of the other leading 'wets' in the Conservative Party was prepared to fight for his principles to the point of breaking with the official party machine.

This failure has often been portrayed as cowardice or indecision. In fact, however, the main reason for the refusal of the 'consensual' Conservatives to break with the Prime Minister was their conviction that *they*, and not she, stood for traditional Conservatism. So much becomes clear from a study of the writings of Gilmour, the most articulate of the 'wets'. In two thoughtful books, *Inside Right* (1977) and *Britain Can Work* (1983), Gilmour sketched out a Tory 'national' tradition, stemming from Halifax and running through Bolingbroke, Burke and Disraeli onwards, up to modern Conservative 'corporatists' like L.S. Amery, Winston Churchill and Harold Macmillan.[97] 'With the exception of Sir Alec Douglas-Home', Gilmour noted, 'every Conservative Prime Minister since Peel has at one time in his political career formed, considered forming, joined, or attempted a coalition with other parties. Even allowing for the necessities of war, this surely shows a considerable propensity towards coalition.'[98] Gilmour drew from this the conclusion that 'if the occasion did arise, no doubt the Tory Party would form or join a coalition and would probably benefit. After all, the previous coalitions helped the Conservatives, though this was not the reason for their formation.' In Gilmour's view, there was thus 'nothing new in Conservatives being partners in a coalition. They would merely be once more putting the interest of the country and of Conservatism above the narrower interests of the Conservative Party.'[99]

But precisely because men like Gilmour, Prior and Pym rejected Thatcherism as alien and saw no contradiction between coalitionism and Conservatism, they could find neither cause nor justification in renouncing their party allegiance. When Healey flippantly remarked to Prior, 'You know, Prior, you and I should set up our own party', the latter did not feel in the least tempted: 'you do not merely up sticks and leave your party merely because you are at variance with

96 Hansard (Lords), 5th ser., vol. 459, 254: 23 Jan. 1985.

97 Gilmour, *Inside Right*, pp. 18–19; Gilmour, *Britain Can Work*, pp. 192–3. See also his articles in *The Times*, 2, 3, 4 May 1974.

98 Gilmour, *Inside Right*, p. 165.

99 Ibid., pp. 165, 226.

the approach and style of those who are temporarily leading it', he later wrote.[100]

Unfortunately, this stance, though logical and intelligible, had a fatal flaw: it erroneously assumed that Mrs Thatcher was only a temporary phenomenon. It also took insufficient account of the natural unwillingness of even 'consensual' Conservatives, at a time when their party was in office, to adopt electoral reform, the avowed objective of which to deprive *any* party of an overall Commons majority!

The Labour Party was differently situated, for the 'right-wing' rebels who feared marginalisation as a result of the 'Bennite' drift of their party had no coalition tradition of their own to fall back upon. On the contrary, Labour politicians still instinctively associated the idea of peacetime coalition with Ramsay MacDonald's 1931 'betrayal'.[101] Not even David Marquand, whose broadly sympathetic biography of MacDonald was published in 1977, was prepared to treat the establishment of that National Government as an honourable precedent.[102] Thus, when in October 1974 Benn regaled his constituency workers with the story of 1931 and, referring to the talk of a Heath–Thorpe deal, lambasted what he called 'the coalition idea',[103] the Jenkinsites were unable to challenge this view of history head-on – at least they could not do so while they remained members of the Labour Party.

Herein lies the origin of the breakaway of those Labour MPs who formed the Social Democratic Party (SDP) in 1981. For these malcontents the only available option was to 'break the mould'.[104]

---

100 Prior, *Balance of Power*, p. 263.

101 Such feelings, however, cut little ice with most Labour Party *supporters*, a social survey of 1983 showing that 54 per cent of Labour 'identifiers' preferred a multi-party government to a single-party one – a lower figure than among 'Alliance identifiers' (61 per cent), it is true, but significantly higher than among the more partisan Conservative 'identifiers' (39 per cent) (Roger Jowell and Colin Airey, *British Social Attitudes: the 1984 Report*, Aldershot, 1984, p. 16).

102 The most he could bring himself to say in 1981 was that 'Even MacDonald's National Governments, through savagely attacked by the Labour Opposition at the time, can now be seen to have tackled the economic problems of the period more effectively – and, for that matter, more radically – than had the Labour Government which preceded them' (David Marquand, *The Case for Coalition*, 1981, p. 2).

103 Benn diary, 6, 7 Oct. 1974, *Against The Tide*, pp. 233–4.

104 Some allege that Marquand had first coined the phrase for Jenkins to use in a speech in the early 1970s (Hugh Stephenson, *Claret and Chips: The Rise of the SDP*, 1982, p. 6). However, Grimond, seven years earlier, had written of trying 'to break out of the mould' (Grimond, *Liberal Challenge*, pp. 311–12).

What in practice did this entail? At one level the Labour defectors were trying to return to the 'sanities' of Keynesian economics and other aspects of the rapidly disappearing post-war settlement. Yet they knew that entirely new political strategies were now needed if this goal stood any chance of realisation: not only the adoption of electoral reform and a move towards Continental-style 'coalition politics', but also, as the first step to these reforms, the creation of a new party.

While serving as President of the European Community, Roy Jenkins had already mentally committed himself to some such strategy, and he divulged his thoughts when delivering his celebrated Dimbleby Lecture in November 1979. But for the other three members of what later became known as the 'Gang of Four' (Shirley Williams, Bill Rodgers and David Owen) the break with Labour proved to be much more difficult. Thus, following the earlier referendum campaign, Shirley Williams had unequivocally declared: 'I have never wanted coalition. I have never talked about coalition and I am not after coalition',[105] and almost until the moment of her irrevocable breach with Labour she continued to pour cold water on the idea of a new Centre Party.[106]

Nevertheless, events took their inexorable course. The 'Limehouse Declaration' was issued on 25 January 1981, leading to the establishment of a 'Council for Social Democracy'; then, shortly afterwards, the SDP emerged as a fully-fledged party. Finally, in early 1983, an 'Alliance' between the SDP and the Liberals was announced with much blowing of trumpets.

'We do not believe in the politics of an inert centre merely representing the lowest common denominator between two extremes', ran the Limehouse Declaration, but 'we believe that the need for a realignment of British politics must now be faced'.[107] The theme was taken up by Jenkins at the launch of the SDP when he announced the birth not only of 'a new party but a new politics'.[108] David Owen, soon to emerge as the most forceful member of the 'Gang of Four', spelled out more explicitly what the 'new politics' meant: the SDP aimed 'to create a multi-party system in Britain where coalition

105 Butler and Kitzinger, *1975 Referendum*, p. 168.
106 Bradley, *Breaking the Mould?*', p. 35.
107 Stephenson, *Claret and Chips*, p. 186.
108 Bradley, *Breaking the Mould?*', p. 4.

Governments became the norm and single-party Governments the exception'.[109]

Other 'Alliance' spokesmen linked the case for Coalition with the demand for a written Constitution or a Bill of Rights, such as could be found over most of the 'Western world'. Because the British state had never been 'modernised', argued Marquand, the British people still clung to the 'ancient view' that the country was governed by the Crown in Parliament, a conception of public life which, by breeding suspicion of 'power-sharing', had reinforced 'adversarial politics' – with disastrous social and economic consequences.[110]

The leaders of the two 'Alliance' parties also buttressed their demands with high-flown rhetoric. Much was heard of the old Liberal argument about freeing politics from dependence upon class-based pressure groups. 'A Fresh Start for Britain', jointly produced by the Liberals and the SDP, is a good example of 'Alliance' rhetoric. 'Our class-based party system, in which the Conservatives favour the board rooms while the Labour Party favours the trade unions, has deepened the divisions between our people', it declared; moreover, 'the intolerant dogmatism of the two old parties ha[d] produced uniquely damaging switches in economic policy'.[111]

Another claim made by 'Alliance' spokesmen was that the citizenry would be freed from the tyranny of the two big parties through the replacement of 'private coalitions over whose actual policy directions the public ha[d] little say' by an 'open coalition based on a public majority with authority to run our affairs'.[112] More basically still, the 'Alliance' made a patriotic appeal to Britons of all classes and backgrounds to unite through the practice of conciliation, compromise and partnership. 'A policy of pulling together', Steel argued, was 'surely worth trying in place of the policies of pulling apart which ha[d] manifestly failed', bringing in their train a 'growing sourness in our society, a turning inwards and meanness to others'.[113]

For much of the 1980s the 'Alliance' achieved very high ratings in the opinion polls. But such evidence probably exaggerates its real level

---

109 David Owen, *A United Kingdom* (1986), p. 42. Marquand argued that coalition government would bring out into the open the 'tripartism' which he believed was here to stay (*Case for Coalition*, pp. 16–17).

110 Marquand, *Case for Coalition*, pp. 13–14.

111 Stephenson, *Claret and Chips*, p. 187.

112 Steel, *House Divided*, p. 161.

113 Ibid., pp. 160–1.

of popular support. Most respondents seem neither to have known, nor to have been in sympathy with, the particular policies upon which the SDP was campaigning. Moreover, the support for both SDP and 'Alliance', though wide, was shallow. Thus, a 1986 survey of public attitudes showed that only 37 per cent of 'Alliance identifiers' could be categorised as 'partisans', compared to 55 per cent of Labour and 62 per cent of Conservative identifiers.[114] Thus, paradoxically, the 'Alliance' suffered even more than its competitors were doing from that loosening of party loyalties which had helped bring it into existence in the first place.

Where the SDP really did break new ground was in recruiting members, predominantly from the educated managerial and professional middle class, who had never previously been active members of any political party – testimony to the way in which the 'duopoly' had alienated a not inconsiderable section of British society. This gave the early SDP an enthusiastic energy which, despite the wary scepticism of many of its famous national leaders, enabled a mass party to be built up from scratch in a startlingly short period of time. But there was a price to be paid for this rapid expansion, since many of the SDP's local activists were both inexperienced and naive.

Moreover, the SDP was crippled from the start by a number of damaging internal divisions of opinion. Thus, the proponents of the 'new politics' soon collided with old right-wing trade union MPs who simply wanted to find refuge in a 'Labour Party Mark 2' or to construct a new populist working-class party. That battle was quite speedily resolved in favour of the 'modernisers'. But even the 'Gang of Four', 'modernisers' all, failed to see eye-to-eye on all points. Believing that 'political parties across the board and independently of their labels had got above themselves, and that their discipline, their exclusiveness, their hubris, their polemicism, were nationally damaging', Jenkins, the SDP's first leader, wanted his followers to form 'an anti-party party'.[115] But Owen, who later supplanted him, favoured a tightly disciplined and coherent organisation, which left Jenkins with the uneasy feeling that the SDP was in danger of replicating the faults of the old parties that it had originally set out to challenge.

This difference of opinion spilled over into a further disagreement

114 Of Alliance identifiers, 30 per cent were 'sympathisers' and 33 per cent were categorised as 'residual identifiers': Roger Jowell, Sharon Witherspoon and Lindsay Brook, *British Social Attitudes: the 1986 Report* (Aldershot, 1986), pp. 40–1.
115 Jenkins, *Life at Centre*, pp. 547–8.

over the SDP's proper relationship with its Liberal allies.[116] Whereas Jenkins preached the politics of partnership, Owen viewed the Liberals with much greater suspicion. Out of this divergence of viewpoint came the botched post-1987 merger, from which Liberals and Social Democrats alike have still not fully recovered. There were also some significant dissimilarities of style between the two 'Alliance' parties. To generalise crudely, the Liberal Party tended to be 'democratic' and 'radical', the SDP more 'centralist' and 'managerial': so that whereas the former's instinctive hostility towards authority made it responsive to new 'grass-roots' movements like ecology and feminism, the latter functioned more as a 'party of government', seeking to discipline its sympathisers 'from above'.[117]

The unanswerable question about the 'Alliance' is whether its programme, if adopted, could have done anything to reverse the country's economic decline and promote greater social and political cohesion. The cynical assessment is that the SDP rushed to fill the vacuum in the political centre by itself 'being as vacuous as it could possibly be'.[118] Indeed, the 'Alliance's' economic programme, such as it was, amounted to little more than an attempt to restore the old panaceas (Keynesian demand-management, a prices and incomes policy, and so on) which had already manifestly failed. Critics also allege that the promise '"to break the mould" *and* "return to the Centre"' was merely a 'card trick or sleight-of-hand'.[119] Mrs Thatcher, after all, had much stronger credentials to be considered a 'mould-breaker' than Roy Jenkins and his friends.

'Alliance' apologists have countered such objections with the argument that a refined version of Keynesianism *might* have worked, provided that there existed an appropriate framework for eliciting consent and promoting national co-operation.[120] Similarly, the apparent contradiction between 'mould-breaking' and 'moving to the Centre' was perhaps no contradiction at all, in the sense that the adoption of a Continental-style system of power-sharing and coalition government

---

116 Significantly, the Liberals had always boasted of their freedom from unnecessary regimentation: the Liberal Party, claimed Grimond in 1963, was 'a Party different in kind in many ways from the present Tory and Labour Parties, allowing loose discipline and accepting considerable co-operation with members of other Parties for some types of business' (Grimond, *Liberal Challenge*, p. 315).

117 Andrew Gamble, 'The Impact of the SDP', in Stuart Hall and Martin Jacques (eds), *The Politics of Thatcherism* (1983), pp. 302–3.

118 Stuart Hall, 'The "Little Caesars" of Social Democracy', ibid., p. 309.

119 Ibid., pp. 315–16.

120 Marquand, *Case for Coalition*, pp. 10–12.

would have represented a profound departure from *British* national traditions.

However, all this is necessarily speculative. For, in the event, the 'Alliance' never had an opportunity to put its theories to a practical test, its electoral progress having been damaged by the operation of the very first-past-the-post system it was committed to destroying. True, the 'Alliance' at its peak enjoyed a remarkable success in drawing support from across the social spectrum: in the 1983 Election, for example, it secured 28 per cent of the middle-class vote, 26 per cent of the skilled working-class vote and 24 per cent of the votes of the unskilled working-class and unemployed.[121] But the very evenness of Alliance support, on which the leaders so prided themselves, simply ensured that the two centre parties were grotesquely under-represented in the new House of Commons, their 26 per cent share of the poll in 1983 securing the election of a mere twenty-three MPs.

It was an additional irony that the Alliance should have unwittingly helped to falsify its own prophecies. In 1979, confounding the pundits, Margaret Thatcher had led the Conservatives to outright victory on the basis of only 43.9 per cent of the total vote – hardly a mandate for carrying out the 'extreme' policies to which the Prime Minister subscribed, or so said her Alliance critics. However, because 'Alliance' gains were made mainly at the expense of the crisis-ridden Labour Party, the 'Alliance' played a crucial role in splitting the anti-Conservative vote in 1983 and 1987, so allowing Mrs Thatcher to stay in office with a greatly increased majority on an *even smaller* share of the vote – little more than 42 per cent.[122] 'A landslide by default', one political scientist has called the Conservatives' 1983 victory.[123]

As a result, in the course of the 1980s the case for electoral reform was stood on its head. Whereas at the start of the decade its advocates claimed that majority governments were a thing of the past, after 1987 it was more commonly argued that only electoral reform could save the country from the disaster of *perpetual Conservative rule* – hence the new interest, among leftwingers, in a written Constitution or in a 'Bill of Rights' which would define the entitlements of the

121 Compare this with the respective shares achieved by the Conservative and Labour Parties: 55 per cent, 40 per cent, 33 per cent, in the case of the Conservatives: 16 per cent, 32 per cent, 41 per cent, in the case of Labour.

122 The figures were 42.4 per cent in 1983, 42.2 per cent in 1987.

123 Ivor Crewe, cited in Kavanagh, *Thatcherism*, p. 311. Crewe observes that public opinion seems not to have moved to the Right since 1979.

citizen and set limits to what an arrogant majoritarian government could do. Yet effective reform could only be sponsored by this self-same majoritarian government. How, in these circumstances, could the impasse be broken?

After 1987 talk of the creation of a new kind of coalition politics significantly abated. There are many reasons for this. The Labour Party, seemingly down and out in 1983, subsequently staged a comeback. True, there currently seems little likelihood of the restoration of a Labour–Conservative duopoly of the kind that flourished in the 1950s, since the Democrats (heirs of the old 'Alliance') seem to be consolidating their position as a strong third party.

At the same time, Paddy Ashdown's followers give the appearance of being a somewhat more effective version of the post-war Liberal Party, not the harbingers of the 'new politics' about which Steel, Jenkins and Owen were enthusing at the start of the 1980s. The earlier 'mould-breaking' rhetoric may indeed resurface from time to time: for example, in 1993 Ashdown denounced the monopoly of MPs and peers in government as 'one of Britain's last great unjustifiable closed shops' and advocated that up to one-third of all Cabinet and ministerial posts should be awarded to non-politicians.[124] But the Democrats' advocacy of electoral reform and their denunciation of class politics are usually cast in language which an earlier generation of Liberals would not have found unfamiliar. This may be because the 'Alliance', in its heyday, was nourished by a mood of 'crisis' which has now largely disappeared.

Yet it would be foolish to assume the death of 'coalition politics'. For the 'Alliance' agenda was never the 'rootless' thing mocked by its critics. On the contrary, many of the ideas which Jenkins, Owen and Steel were promulgating in the 1980s had a provenance going back a century or more. Well might the old socialist Eric Heffer detect in Alliance propaganda echoes of Mosley's New Party.[125] Academic commentators on the SDP, like Ben Pimlott, have also been struck by these similarities.[126] Yet Mosley was himself the heir to a way of thinking about politics which can be traced back into the nineteenth century. It would be a reckless person who assumed that a tradition which has proved to be so durable could never return to haunt the British political scene once more.

124 *Here We Stand* (1993), cited in *Guardian*, 3 Aug. 1993.
125 Bradley, *Breaking the Mould?*, p. 21.
126 See Ben Pimlott, 'When the party's over', *New Socialist*, Sept./Oct. 1981, 63–5.

CHAPTER TWELVE
Conclusion

INTRODUCTION

So customary is it to view British politics from a party perspective that historians have been tempted to explain away the long periods in which the country has been governed by coalitions or by party administrations lacking a parliamentary majority. Some, for example, argue that the transition from Liberals to Labour took rather longer than might have been expected: hence the three-party politics and consequent instability of the 1920s, before Labour fully established its ascendancy and 'normality' was restored.

Another 'distorting' factor, supposedly, was the existence of a number of 'third parties' which brought confusion to the dominant two-party system, without ever really challenging it. Thus, the Irish Nationalist Party, whose very existence clearly did so much to render majority government difficult in the late Victorian and Edwardian period, can be dismissed as a mere 'party of protest', operating from a secure but restricted geographical base in Catholic Ireland. Once Gladstone had committed his followers to Home Rule in 1886, the fortunes of the Irish Party were anyway closely bound up with the Liberals. The same observation could be made of the pre-1914 Labour Party, which may have had its occasional differences of opinion with the Liberals, but which enjoyed little freedom of manoeuvre since it was never going to throw its support behind the Conservatives.

It has also been possible to dismiss breakaway parties like the Liberal Unionists after 1886 and the Liberal Nationals and National Labour after 1931 as mere 'transit camps' – staging posts in the journey taken by disillusioned Liberals and socialists seeking a new home in the Conservative Party. On that reading of the situation, it is possible to treat the Salisbury–Balfour Ministry of 1895–1905 as a Conservative Ministry in all but name, rather than as a Coalition of Conservatives and Liberal Unionists. Similarly with the so-called 'National Governments' of the 1930s which, once the Samuelite Liberals had seceded in September 1932, fell heavily under Conservative Party influence.[1] In short, some believe that the emergence of the Liberal Unionists and later of National Labour and the Liberal Nationals signified a long-overdue *realignment* of the two-party system but did not offer an *alternative* to it.[2] However, as we have seen, the multi-party governments which have been in office for so much of the late nineteenth and twentieth centuries can only, with difficulty, be fitted into such an interpretative framework. They need to be explained, rather, against the background of a deep-rooted national tradition of antipathy towards party.

THE COALITIONIST CASE

Let us look more closely at the vast literature denigrating party and try to discern some of its salient characteristics. First, it is noticeable that although critics have often attacked the party duopoly, in recent times they have only rarely questioned the need for parties of *some* sort in a modern representative democracy. Outright denigration of party has been largely confined to those who have a quarrel with parliamentary institutions themselves or with the very notion of democratic self-government.

There was certainly an authoritarian streak in Thomas Carlyle, whose mockery of Sir Jabesh Windbag in *Past and Present* and whose even more scathing attacks on Parliament as the 'Talking Apparatus' in *Latter-Day Pamphlets* would seem to have influenced many readers both in his own day and later. This influence shows itself in the common vilification of politicians as 'mere talkers' and in the glorification of strong, silent men of action like Kitchener.

Carlyle also did much to create a cult of Cromwell, who, interestingly,

1 Bogdanor categorises these coalitions as 'a prelude to the fusion of parties' (Vernon Bogdanor (ed.), *Coalition Government in Western Europe*, 1983, pp. 10–11). But even were one to exclude these governments from one's list of coalitions, one would still end up with figures showing that party governments with Commons majorities had occupied office for only twenty-eight years between 1885 and 1945.

2 See Chapter 3, para. 1.

was often invoked by prominent advocates of a 'National Government'. Rosebery, who played an instrumental role in the erection of the Cromwell Statue in 1899,[3] clearly falls into this category. At around this time it was also common to draw parallels between Cromwell and Joseph Chamberlain.[4] As for Garvin, he could think of no higher praise for Lloyd George during the Great War than to present him as a Cromwellian hero.[5] Indeed, Lloyd George himself, at a crucial period of the war, took to reading Cromwell's speeches, finding that Cromwell had had 'just the same difficulties to contend with' as himself.[6] And it was with the histrionic invocation of Cromwell's words dismissing the Rump of the Long Parliament, 'In the name of God, go!', that Amery helped bring down Neville Chamberlain and inaugurate the Churchill Coalition in May 1940.

During wartime there have often been excited calls for the establishment of a 'Committee of Public Safety', a revealing phrase which acknowledges a debt to the French Republican tradition. There was certainly a whiff of the Jacobin about Joseph Chamberlain, combining, as he did, an authoritarian patriotism with belief in the 'general will'. Perhaps, too, there might be some deeper significance in the friendship which Lord Randolph Churchill formed with General Boulanger, whose cause he briefly espoused, at the time when the possibility of creating a 'National Party' in Britain was very much in the air.[7] One can even find a strain of populist authoritarianism in Lloyd George and in his great admirer, J.L. Garvin.

However, during the preceding century only a small minority of the critics of party have gone so far as to call for the establishment of a dictatorship, and there has been little to be gained by frontal attacks on 'Parliamentarism', the stock-in-trade of Boulanger's own demagoguery. Thus Mosley's lurch into the totalitarian creed of

3 J.F. Battick and N.C. Klimavicz, 'Much Ado About Oliver: The Parliamentary Dispute Over Cromwell's Statue', *History Today*, 24 (1974), 406–12.

4 J.P.D. Dunbabin, 'Oliver Cromwell's popular image in nineteenth-century England', in J.S. Bromley and E.H. Kossman (eds), *Britain and the Netherlands* (The Hague, 1975), p. 159.

5 See Chapter 5. Ironically, in his earlier Radical phase, Lloyd George had invoked Cromwell as the scourge of bishops and peers who, had he been alive, would have delivered the country from Joseph Chamberlain! (Roger Howell, Jr, '"Who needs another Cromwell?" The nineteenth-century image of Oliver Cromwell', in R.C. Richardson (ed.), *Images of Oliver Cromwell* (Manchester, 1993), p. 97.

6 Riddell's diary, 16 March 1918, in Lord Riddell, *War Diary 1914–1918* (1933), p. 319.

7 R.F. Foster, *Lord Randolph Churchill: A Political Life* (Oxford, 1981), p. 361.

Fascism very quickly extinguished his credibility with the general public. In Britain, as in other countries, there may have been a deep yearning for a 'national' union which would be neither Left nor Right. But, by contrast with many Continental countries, this objective has had to be pursued within the framework of a liberal, parliamentary state.

Moreover, in Britain advocacy of 'National Government' has by no means been incompatible with an internationalist outlook. Many supporters of the 'National Government' in the 1930s subscribed to the ideals enshrined in the League of Nations, just as 'Alliance' politicians in more recent years have been strong supporters of the European Community and of NATO. As for Edward Heath, he may have campaigned for a National Government in October 1974 on the slogan of 'putting Britain first', but he is much more of a 'European patriot' than an insular nationalist.

In fact, most British champions of national politics have been suspicious of Bonapartism, Fascism and ultra-nationalism, preferring to turn for inspiration to 'safe' figures like Robert Peel, about whom there was nothing remotely 'dictatorial'.[8] Indeed, the memory of Peel as the man who had sacrificed his career by putting country before party survived well into the twentieth century. Balfour, contemplating the prospect of going into coalition with Lloyd George in 1910, may have clutched his brow and exclaimed that 'he could not be another Robert Peel in his party'. But it is surely no coincidence that Rosebery should have written a short essay on Peel in 1899, just at the moment when he was exchanging his former role as senior Liberal Front-Bencher for that of the 'patriotic statesman' prepared to serve his country at a time of national crisis.[9] Other twentieth-century proponents of 'National Government', such as L.S. Amery, have also seen Peel as some kind of a role model. Even as late as 1986 David Owen, in an approving thumbnail sketch of Peel, could approvingly quote Norman Gash's verdict on the Victorian

---

8 Carlyle, who greatly admired Peel, presented him with a copy of his study of Cromwell a week before the carrying of Repeal (James Seigel, 'Carlyle and Peel: The Prophet's Search for a Heroic Politician and an Unpublished Fragment', *Victorian Studies*, 26 (1982–83), 185).

9 This piece, occasioned by the appearance of the last of Parker's volumes, was not entirely laudatory, since Rosebery felt that by taking personal responsibility for Repeal, Peel was perhaps lowering public morality. But he ended his article with a glowing panegyric to the dead statesman.

statesman: 'His allegiance was to an older concept than party loyalty; it was to the service of the state.'[10]

It was symptomatic of this more 'moderate' strand of anti-party feeling that 'Coalition' and 'National Government' should often have been presented, not as intrinsically desirable, but rather as a temporary expedient for coping with some pressing emergency. In fact, the concept of 'crisis' has been central to the critique of party. Sometimes the threat is supposed to come from within, sometimes from without, but in either case the country's very *survival* is said to require the abandonment of older loyalties of class and creed. Time and again one encounters the argument that, although parties may have served the country well in the past, they no longer suit the extraordinary circumstances currently facing the country. Lloyd George went down this particular track in his preamble to the August 1910 Secret Coalition Memorandum, and similar sentiments were frequently voiced during both World Wars. But in the interwar period, too, influential politicians were fertile in explanations of why party warfare had become a luxury which the community could no longer afford.

The phrases employed by those making out such a case are so similar that a Martian visitor, trying to reconstruct British public life, would almost be tempted to assume the existence of some 'Ur-Text' from which they had been copied.   Let this example serve for them all: party has 'great advantages', and 'in normal times it is almost indispensable to successful Parliamentary government. But since 1914 the times in which we have lived *have not been normal*, and *abnormal times call for abnormal measures*.'[11] The words, it so happens, are Austen Chamberlain's in 1932 and refer to the economic and financial difficulties of that time. But almost identical declarations were being made between 1919 and 1922, when the problem was said to be 'Bolshevism', and in the mid-1930s, when defenders of the National Government waxed eloquent about the need to protect the British way of life against the threat posed by dictatorships of both Left and Right. The Conservative Manifesto of October 1974 echoes the familiar phrases: 'In normal times the party struggle is the safeguard of freedom. But the times are far from normal.'[12]

10 David Owen, *A United Kingdom* (1986), pp. 25–6. The similarity between Peel and Heath, in Owen's view, is that both were 'men of government'. He also portrays Peel as the originator of the 'Middle Way' (ibid., p. 35).

11 Introduction to Warden Chilcott, *Political Salvation* (1932), p. 9.

12 *'The Times' Guide to the House of Commons, October 1974* (1974), p. 315.

It is this association between 'crisis' and Coalition which has led some Marxist historians to invoke Gramsci's concept of 'Caesarism'. According to Gramsci, 'Caesarism' was a compromise imposed from above when conflicting social forces balanced one another in such a way that a continuation of the conflict could only terminate in their reciprocal destruction. Historically, he argued, such a class deadlock had sometimes thrown up a 'strong' leader, like Caesar, the two Napoleons and Cromwell. However, Caesarism did not necessarily require the emergence of a 'heroic' individual: in modern times it could assume a variety of different forms. From this Gramsci proceeded to his famous dictum: 'Every coalition government is a first stage of Caesarism.'[13]

However, the examples cited in this book show many aspects of 'Coalitionism' which fail to fit into the Gramscian interpretation. Indeed, there is much to be said for David Marquand's contention that the reshaping of the political system so as to make coalitions the norm rather than the exception would mean a change from 'an essentially plebiscitary conception of democracy to a more parliamentary conception', since governments would then be directly accountable to Parliament and, through Parliament, to the electorate itself.[14]

THE JANUS FACE OF COALITION POLITICS

The case for coalition is full of ambiguities of this kind. Take, for example, the question of the way in which the past is viewed. A very common feature of the criticism of party is that its spokesmen present themselves as *forward*-looking people, anxious to throw off the 'shibboleths' of the past (a favourite phrase, that). Nor is this surprising since parties, by their very nature, link the past to the present by embodying memories and experiences in the light of which each successive generation tries to make sense of the world it inhabits. Parties are carriers of traditions which, though constantly modified,

13 Antonio Gramsci, *Selections from the Prison Notebooks* (1971: ed. and trans. Quintin Hoare and Geoffrey Nowell Smith), pp. 219–22. Gramsci interpreted MacDonald's creation of the National Government of 1931 in precisely these terms. For an attempt to apply the concept more widely to British political experience, see Bill Schwarz, 'Conservatism and "caesarism", 1903–22', in Mary Langan and Bill Schwarz (eds), *Crises in the British State 1880–1930* (1985), p. 46.
14 David Marquand, *The Case for Coalition* (1981), p. 7.

can only be jettisoned at the risk of destroying the organisation's identity and weakening its members' self-respect.

However, for this very reason, parties invite attack at times of rapid change, because they seem to be putting a brake on necessary innovation. This was obviously true at the end of the Great War and the early 1920s. Harold Spender was not alone in thinking that 'the old parties, with all their ancient loyalties', had perished.[15] In the post-war years politicians and journalists queued up to mock party as an 'obsolete' relic belonging to the 'Victorian age'.[16] More recently the SDP has struck a similar note, the 'Limehouse Declaration' of 25 January 1981, for example, calling for 'a new start in British politics'.

These were sentiments felt with particular intensity during the 1920s by many members of the war generation: young men who, through service at the Front, had undergone experiences which seemed to cut them off psychologically from their elders. It was to this constituency that Mosley directly appealed when he created his New Party, which openly declared war on the old political organisations – contemptuously dismissed as resting on 'women, buns and tea fights'. But Mosley was simply the latest in a long line of proponents of 'national' politics to sing the praises of the modern and the new, to deprecate everything that was traditional and old, and to appeal to Youth to throw off the yoke that had been imposed on public life by the 'Old Gangs' – a double gibe, indicating both that parties themselves were old and also that the leaders and apparatchiks who ran them ('Mandarins' was a favourite phrase) were not exactly in the prime of youth, either.

Sometimes attacks on the obsolescence of party have served as a prelude to more fundamental attacks on the obsolescence of the state. The structure of government, so goes the argument, has not kept abreast with the times, is too imbued with archaic aristocratic values, and so needs modernising – hence the calls for a 'businessman's government', a slogan that can be traced back as far as the Crimean War. Lord Robens in the late 1960s and the 'Alliance' parties in the 1970s and 1980s were still using a similar rhetoric. In other words, the movement to create a National Government or National Party has often, though not always, been linked to a managerial vision of politics and also to the will-o'-the-wisp of a 'business government'.

15 See Chapter 5.
16 See Chapter 6.

Not all these invocations of 'business methods' should be taken literally. When Goschen, himself an experienced banker, wrote to Lord Salisbury in 1891 about whom to appoint as Financial Secretary to the Treasury, he argued that the situation required 'a strong man, a good business man if possible'; but he went on to say: 'I don't mean reared in business, but with an aptitude for business.'[17] This distinction was not lost even on politicians like Lloyd George, who oscillated between admiration for businessmen and a realisation of how difficult it was to make the transition from business to politics and government.

'God preserve us from businessmen in politics', Tony Benn once exclaimed.[18] The objection to the idea of a 'businessman's government' was not just that it violated the principles of democratic Liberalism[19] or that the catchcry had been discredited by scurrilous charlatans like Horatio Bottomley. Churchill was only one of many politicians to protest that the idea also lacked practical credibility: Lord Woolton recalls a conversation after the Second World War in which Churchill, then Leader of the Opposition, mischievously argued that all the men who had come into government from a business background had been 'disastrous', an indictment in which he included Joseph Chamberlain as well as Baldwin, Robert Horne and Neville Chamberlain.[20] In 1968 the former Conservative Minister, Lord Eccles, similarly burst out 'into a long tirade on the futility of businessmen thinking they could be ministers', arguing that the work required 'long apprenticeship in the House of Commons'.[21] Even the Institute of Directors acknowledged that the task of a politician was different from that of a businessman since the former had skills which the latter lacked in the important task of reconciling conflicting interests.[22] The truth of this proposition was seemingly confirmed by the failure of John Davies, the former Director-General of the CBI, when put in charge of the Department of Trade and Industry between

17 James Cornford, 'The Parliamentary Foundations of the Hotel Cecil', in Robert Robson (ed.), *Ideas and Institutions of Victorian Britain* (1967), p. 301.

18 Benn diary, 16 Feb. 1968, in Tony Benn, *Office Without Power: Diaries 1968–72* (1988), p. 36.

19 See the comments of a Liberal dignitary faced by news of the King–Robens 'conspiracy', *Guardian*, 20 Feb. 1968.

20 Diplomatically, he made an exception of Oliver Lyttelton and Woolton himself, who happened to be present! (Earl of Woolton, *Memoirs* (1959), pp. 176–7).

21 King diary, 13 Feb. 1968, in *The Cecil King Diary, 1965–1970* (1972), p. 176.

22 *The Director*, June 1968, 380.

1970 and 1972. However, it is unlikely that the fascination with the idea of businessmen in government will ever disappear.

The adulation of expertise has been another strand in the attack on party. The youthful Walter Elliot struck a popular chord when, in the aftermath of the Great War, he declared: 'The problems of government in the nineteenth century were political; those of the twentieth century are economic.'[23] And economic management seemed to be too technical a task for handling by political parties – though Harold Wilson did later try to graft a technocratic vision of the future on to Labour's programme in 1963.[24]

These 'futuristic' facets of anti-party ideology are very obvious[25] – so much so that they tend to distract attention from another facet. For it is arguable that the quest for a 'national' government can also be seen as a novel strategy for the fulfilment of traditional objectives in a changing political environment: in other words, those who criticised party were looking *backwards*, as well as forwards, trying by unconventional methods to recover a lost world. For example, the National Governments of the 1930s were both praised by modernisers and idealised by nostalgic patriots like Trevelyan.

The 'Janus Face' of Coalition politics has been particularly evident in recent Alliance propaganda which has combined a promise of bold new departures ('breaking the mould') with the reassurance of a return to the consensual atmosphere of what seemed in retrospect a more harmonious age. In short, there has always been a certain tension between a modernising impulse, on the one hand, and a rather confused attempt to return to some earlier notion of 'normality', on the other.

The nostalgic strain in Coalition politics may seem strange. But it starts to make sense if we look more carefully at what is involved in two-party politics. After all, as Roy Jenkins feelingly argues on the basis of his service under Harold Wilson, most party governments

23 Captain Walter E. Elliot MP, 'For a Permanent Coalition Party', *Review of Reviews*, 61 (Jan. 1920), 31.

24 The link between the cause of industrial modernisation and political change is one of the main themes in Scott Newton and Dilwyn Porter, *Modernization Frustrated: The Politics of Industrial Decline in Britain since 1900* (1988).

25 Parties, in F.S. Oliver's view, formed an 'ancient and worshipful corporation that live[d] by setting its fellow-countrymen by the ears'. His hope was that 'the political fraternity [would] pass like the link-boys and cabmen of a bygone age into an oblivion for which they had long been ripe' (F.S. Oliver, *What Federalism Is* Not, 1914, p. 113).

have been, in practice, a kind of coalition, sometimes encompassing a spread of opinions considerably wider than might be found in a coalition government proper.[26] To be electable, parties have to be very broad-based. But, as a result, faced with a very limited choice, citizens have perforce to join, or identify themselves with, organisations whose programmes and priorities they only partly share. Thus there is always likely to be a considerable mismatch of individual opinion and party creed. This has always been a source of considerable moral and political anxiety.

The dilemma intensified in the last third of the nineteenth century, when voting cohesion in the Commons became tighter and organised mass parties emerged which sought power by asking the electorate to endorse their national programmes. However, there were now not only different ideological strands to accommodate, but also different levels of institutional interest: the parliamentary party, constituency officers, rank-and-file activists, and so on. If a party were to enjoy electoral success, it needed to formulate a coherent programme and strategy: teams do not win matches simply because they contain the best individual players. But the forging of a modicum of unity was likely to lead, either to an intra-party struggle for the control of the programme (conveying a damaging impression of factionalism and disunity), or, more commonly, to some sort of negotiated compromise with which no individual or group was entirely happy – in other words, to 'fudge and mudge'.

To these developments, two groups, in particular, reacted with anger. One was the opinion-forming intelligentsia. Few scholars and men of letters, valuing, as they do, honesty and intellectual clarity above all else, have ever shown much enthusiasm for traditional two-party politics, but the development of the 'caucus' and the consequential tightening of party discipline proved almost intolerably irksome to the likes of A. V. Dicey.

But, secondly, many Front-Bench celebrities, brought up in a tradition of aristocratic leadership, also lamented the loss of dis-cretionary authority which the rise of modern parties had produced. As Colin Matthew has shown, this contributed during the 1890s to the anxieties expressed by the Liberal Imperialists, who believed

---

26 Roy Jenkins, *A Life at the Centre* (1991), pp. 517–18. He comments: 'The test was whether the coalition was honest, which I defined as being whether those within the coalition agreed more with each other than they did with those outside.' See also Marquand, *Case for Coalition*, pp. 4–5.

that factionalism and caucus were destroying Liberalism's 'national' appeal. Even Rosebery was initially not so much anti-party as trying to restore an *older conception of party.*

ELITISM AND POPULISM

But this leads to another consideration. The sharpening of party rivalry left many of the Front-Benchers with an uneasy sense that they were becoming saddled with party commitments which would prove impossible or dangerous to implement. Indeed, Ministers often made little effort to carry out, in office, the party programme on which they had been elected, thereby incurring charges of cowardice or betrayal from their own backbenchers and constituency activists. Little wonder if some Ministers met these attacks by bewailing their followers' lack of a sense of what was practical, and from this it was easy to go on to harbour wicked thoughts about how much easier life would be if a combination of the experienced Front-Benchers could quietly get on with what they believed to be sensible and proper, free from the old party catchcries. Such considerations do not entirely explain the creation of the National Government in 1931, but neither were they entirely absent from the calculations of MacDonald and even Baldwin.

A better example of Front-Bencher impatience with the restraints imposed by party would be the attempt by the two sets of party leaders to reach a 'national settlement' in the summer and autumn of 1910, first, through the Constitutional Conference, and then by the more radical expedient of creating a Coalition Government. Many Liberals no longer believed in the merits of Irish Home Rule, while many Unionists now had second thoughts about the wisdom of staking all on a rigid defence of the Union. Hence, both sides saw the merits of 'Federalism', or 'Home Rule All Round', as a compromise between two unattractive extremes. But neither side dared suggest this openly, fearing to provoke an uproar from its own backbenchers and allies. Hence Lloyd George's exploration of the possibility of Coalition in the hope that this would provide a framework within which the two main parties could abandon or modify their traditional policies without too much loss of face.

But coalitions could also protect both sets of party leaders from more material dangers. For example, as Lloyd George argued in his August 1910 Coalition Memorandum, a comprehensive National

Insurance measure would unavoidably run into the opposition of the industrial insurance companies. Neither party dare tackle this obstacle to 'sound' social reform single-handed, he argued, but a combination of the two major parties could do so with impunity.

However, it was not just the machinations of powerful pressure groups that the proponents of coalition were eager to circumvent. Often the aim was simply the avoidance of political and electoral retribution. Thus, conscription would never have become a viable policy during the Great War but for the existence of a Coalition which spread the risks among all the parties involved. Even more interesting perhaps is the perception of nearly all the party leaders (including some Labour leaders) that the economic crisis of the late 1920s and 1930s required drastic cutbacks in public expenditure, specifically in the sphere of unemployment benefit. Neville Chamberlain, for example, was quite convinced by early 1931 that, sooner or later, this nettle would have to be grasped. But his colleagues warned him that to propose such economies on the eve of an election would play straight into Labour's hands. Thus, *all* the parties would have to take responsibility for Economy, or none could sponsor it – except at great peril. Edward Heath felt very similarly about tackling the menace of inflation in 1974.

In all the above instances there is an assumption that many electors lack the intelligence or the maturity to accept the need for short-term sacrifice to procure long-term advantage. If only by implication, coalition has thus often served as a device for protecting the masses from their own worst impulses. Indeed, some of the late Victorian and Edwardian proponents of National Government made no bones about wanting to restore an older kind of parliamentary system in which parties had felt free to act more responsibly because the restricted electorate of those days was itself more responsible.

This raises one of the many problems about anti–party rhetoric: it is often 'anti-democratic' in tone, yet many of its sponsors can be found, in almost the same breath, suggesting that 'the people' are yearning to be *released* from the constrictions and tyrannies of party. Garvin, for one, clearly saw himself as fighting the 'Old Gangs' and the established elites on behalf of the excluded masses. Recent Alliance propaganda, which contains both elitist and populist components, mirrors this ambivalence. In short, there remains a certain tension between a manipulative and a demagogic approach to coalition government – a tension which is seldom satisfactorily resolved.

What the proponents of 'national politics' are perhaps doing is drawing a distinction between the electorate's 'lower' and 'higher' natures. Voters know, in their hearts, that sacrifices for the greater national good are desirable, but shrink from giving expression to these convictions because the party machines have corrupted them by encouraging narrowly selfish kinds of behaviour from which they secretly desire to be released. A slightly different version of this argument was promulgated by Beloff, who argued that only coalition government, by recreating 'national pride and national self-confidence', would 'provide the basis of making individual and sectional sacrifices'.[27]

PRECONDITIONS FOR HEALTHY TWO-PARTY POLITICS

Looking back to the relative tranquillity of the 1860s and 1870s, politicians of the late Victorian and Edwardian eras came to understand that two-party rivalries could only flourish in a healthy way if, in Dicey's useful phrase, the differences between the two main parties were significant but not fundamental. (Hence, the general recognition that two-party politics cannot operate properly in Northern Ireland.) Balfour once observed that Britain's 'whole political machinery pre-suppose[d] a people so fundamentally at one that they can safely afford to bicker; and so sure of their own moderation that they are not dangerously disturbed by the never-ending din of political conflict'.[28] But in the years after 1885 these preconditions have only rarely existed, and, in their absence, even normally loyal partisans have sometimes turned their thoughts in the direction of national combination and coalition.

The problem, in fact, is this. On the one hand, dissatisfaction has arisen when little seems to separate the parties. Such a time was the turn of the century when Home Rule was in abeyance, sectarian animosities temporarily deadened, and fiscal controversy still in the future. The sharpest policy differences seemed to be taking place *within* the Liberal Party, rather than *between* Liberals and Unionists. In these circumstances, it was only too easy to mock party politics

---

27 *The Times*, 7 Dec. 1967.

28 Brian Harrison, *Peaceable Kingdom: Stability and Change in Modern Britain* (Oxford, 1982), p. 349, citing R.T. McKenzie and A. Silver, *Angels in Marble* (1967), p. 48.

and to portray it as a game played out between rival factions. The leaders, thought the critics, were, for personal or party advantage, magnifying the relatively small issues which divided them from one another, oblivious of the damage which such manoeuvring might inflict on the national interest.

In any case, once the perception gained ground that there were no significant differences of principle or policy between the parties, the way was open to claims that the only choice confronting the British people was one between competence and incompetence. Such a view necessarily stimulated a technocratic and managerial approach to politics: hence Lloyd George's references, in the August 1910 Memorandum, to the desirability of bringing together the 'first-rate men' of both parties, to the exclusion of the 'duffers'.

On the other hand, the pendulum could easily swing too far in the opposite direction, with the parties so angrily opposed to one another that neither would recognise the legitimacy of the other's position. Thus, in the aftermath of the Home Rule schism, many Unionists thought it inconceivable that the Gladstonians should ever again hold office – until, that is, they repented the folly and wickedness of their ways. But even a Unionist journal like *The Economist* was slightly worried about the implications: were a National Party to be formed out of the Unionist elements, it mused, where would an alternative government be found?[29]

Although by the end of the century these murderous passions had abated, they revived again after 1910. When Unionists came to believe, as many of them did, that Asquith's Government was no longer a true government at all but a revolutionary junta, the traditional two-party system had clearly broken down. However, the very intensity of political conflict in the 1910–14 period generated its own reaction: that is to say, the view developed that party strife, unless moderated, would plunge the country into civil war, an unspeakable tragedy, from which, once again, the only escape seemed to lie through some sort of National Government, a possibility particularly dear to Churchill's heart.

The outbreak of war temporarily defused the Irish dispute, but from 1917 onwards, with the challenge of *Labour*, a new threat emerged which cut away the common ground necessary for civilised two-party competition. After 1918 there were socialists who argued that 'democracy' presupposed enough agreement between the competing

29 *The Economist*, 18 June 1887, 774–5.

parties for each to be prepared, should it lose an election, to submit to its rival. But, according to Harold Laski and others, the development of capitalism had produced a polarisation so sharp between the parties representing Labour and Capital that the 'rules' of democratic politics were rapidly becoming inoperable. Since it was no longer possible for 'capitalism' to 'buy off' the working class with concessionary social reforms, the 'capitalists' had no option but to adopt a strategy of outright resistance. The 'Left' explained the rout of the Labour Party in 1931 in precisely these terms: as a counter-revolutionary *putsch* by the forces of 'bourgeois order', involving the judiciary and Buckingham Palace as well as big business, the City and the capitalist parties, all of them determined to deprive the working class of power.

This was but the mirror image of that 'anti-Bolshevik' rhetoric which, presenting the Labour Party as a threat to civilisation itself, announced that the 'enemy within' must be thwarted at all costs. More commonly the charge against Labour was that the Labour Party had disqualified itself as a respectable contender for power by its 'sectionalism'. One must remember that before 1914 most theorists of party, like Lowell, doubted whether the party system could work if 'the lines of cleavage of the parties [ever came to] coincide with those between different social classes in the community'. To those who took this position seriously, Labour did not seem to be a true party at all, but a sectional conspiracy against the common weal – relatively harmless as a small third or fourth party, but quite intolerable as a serious contender for national office.

Moreover, as the American political scientist Samuel Beer notes, the Labour Party has traditionally insisted on strict party discipline, a propensity which 'springs ultimately from factory discipline'.[30] Roy Jenkins, too, has drawn attention to 'a strong strand of 'democratic centralism' in [Labour's] theory', which predisposed it to believe 'in discipline, in the idea of the mandate, and of a government being elected to carry out a detailed programme which it had announced in advance'.[31] These are all serious shortcomings in the eyes of Labour's critics.

When charged with a narrow pursuit of 'class' interests, loyal Labour Party members, even those of them who are committed socialists, have sometimes betrayed embarrassment – so deeply rooted

30 Samuel H. Beer, *Modern British Politics: A Study of Parties and Pressure Groups* (1965), p. 85.
31 Dimbleby Lecture: *The Times*, 23 Nov. 1979.

is the concept of 'the general good' in British political culture. But here both Conservatives and Liberals have an advantage over Labour, since each of the older parties, in its different way, has traditionally identified its creed with the well-being of 'the nation'.

Yet leaders of Coalition governments are able to play this card with still *greater* effectiveness. Thus, as Leader of the post-war Coalition, Lloyd George could seek to discredit the 'class warriors' assailing his Government by defiantly proclaiming: 'The nation should be our party, the nation should be our class, and the nation should be our concern.'[32] A similar note was struck by enthusiastic supporters of the National Government in the 1930s and, more recently, by the leaders of the Alliance parties.

The moral to be drawn is that, for two-party politics to work to general satisfaction, there needs to be an equilibrium between controversy and consensus – as Winston Churchill recognised when he wrote of 'that line of half-chaffing half-candid intercourse which prevails between people who know each other though on opposite sides'.[33] Perhaps this situation came closest to realisation in the years of the Labour–Conservative duopoly after the Second World War. Yet, given the unusualness of this situation, it is hardly surprising that there has been so much dissatisfaction with the party system, nor that so much energy has gone into seeking a replacement for it.

CONTINUITIES

But though 'National Government' has often been presented as an emergency response to an 'abnormal' situation, this does not mean that we cannot identify what might be called a 'tradition' of coalition politics. Let us look once more at Winston Churchill's speech to the New Members' Coalition Group at the Criterion Restaurant in the summer of 1919. This was the speech in which, as part of his attempt to launch 'fusion', Churchill told the world about the 1910 Secret Coalition talks. But he also drew attention to earlier episodes of a similar nature in an attempt to persuade himself and

32 At the inaugural dinner of the 1920 Club, *Daily Chronicle*, 17 March 1921, cited in *Lloyd George Liberal Magazine*, April 1921, 429.
33 Churchill to Lord Salisbury, 21 Nov. 1904, in Randolph S. Churchill, *Winston S. Churchill, Vol. II Young Statesman 1901–1914*, (1967), p. 93.

others that his purpose had its own ancient pedigree. For example, he mentioned the 'Tory Democracy' of Disraeli and Lord Shaftesbury, before predictably launching out on a discussion of the attempt to form a National Party made in the late 1880s by Joseph Chamberlain and his father, Lord Randolph.[34]

There were also *family* traditions in the sphere of 'national politics'. Winston Churchill self-consciously carried on the torch which he had inherited from his father.[35] Two generations of Chamberlains sought to mitigate the narrowness of party by submerging them in wider national causes. Austen, for example, viewed 1931 as a vindication of his attempt to secure fusion a decade earlier, an episode which in turn owed something to his father's Radical Unionist past. Similarly, the 5th Earl of Rosebery would have been proud of the way his son trumpeted the merits of National Government in the 1945 Election. It is also fascinating to notice that, when the Conservative Party launched its appeal for the establishment of a 'Government of National Unity' in 1974, among its earliest proponents were Julian Amery (L.S. Amery's son), and Maurice Macmillan (the son of Harold Macmillan).[36]

'Coalition politics' could count among its champions some of the most famous statesmen of the twentieth century: Churchill, Lloyd George, Birkenhead, Austen Chamberlain. But its high-priest and prophet was undoubtedly J.L. Garvin of the *Observer*, who was involved in nearly all the episodes described in this book. He attached himself at an early stage to Joseph Chamberlain's chariot; he became a fervent admirer of Lloyd George and worked hard for 'fusion' in the years of the post-war Coalition; he was no less enthusiastic in his support for a National Government in 1930 and 1931.[37]

As well as these dynastic and personal continuities, one can trace other kinds of link between different 'coalitionist' periods, particularly between the 'fusion' phase of 1919–22 and what would seem to be the rather different phase of 1931–35. Take, for example, the twenty-

34 Churchill, speech at Criterion Restaurant, 15 July 1919, Robert Rhodes James (ed.), *Churchill Speaks* (1981), pp. 380–1.

35 However, it has been argued that Churchill projected his own political enthusiasms back on to his father, rather than vice versa (Foster, *Randolph Churchill*, pp. 385–6).

36 David Butler and Dennis Kavanagh, *The British General Election of October 1974* (1975), pp. 43–4.

37 See his 'credo', expressed in a letter to Keynes in 1929: Robert Skidelsky, *Politicians and the Slump: The Labour Government of 1929–1931* (1967), p. 278.

seven Liberal MPs returned in the 1931 General Election who had previously been elected in either 1918 and/or 1922. Of these, fifteen had earlier been 'Coalies', twelve 'Independent Liberals'. Yet while nine of the fifteen 'Coalies' went on to become 'Liberal Nationals', only one-half of the twelve 'Wee Frees' followed suit. This statistic, in itself, does not seem earth-shattering; but it does take on greater meaning when one realises that after 1931 there were also five former Coalition Liberals sitting in Parliament as *Conservative* MPs, as against a single Asquithian.[38] Thus the Liberals who had hitched their star to Lloyd George's post-war Coalition showed a much greater propensity to support the National Government in the 1930s than did the Liberals who had opposed him.

Amongst Conservatives, too, a 'coalitionist' tradition can be identi-fied. Of the hundred MPs who signed the 1934 Manifesto supporting the National Government, eight had been in the House at the time of the 1922 Carlton Club meeting. Of these, two had voted with Chamberlain (including Chamberlain himself) and another was a supporter of Chamberlain though absent from the meeting. This, however, gives a misleading impression, since two of Austen Chamber-lain's keenest followers in 1922 were actually *members* of the National Government and so debarred from signing the 1934 petition, which was a backbenchers' demonstration. Moreover, the two Ministers in question, Thomas Inskip (the Attorney-General) and Walter Elliot (the Agriculture Minister), had demonstrated their 'coalitionist' enthusiasm by attending Chamberlain's dinner after the Carlton Club vote.

It may make even more sense to look, not so much at individuals, as at the constituencies which supported 'Coalition politics'. First, it is interesting to observe the geographical linkages between Liberal Unionism and support for the post-war Coalition. Liberal Unionism's strength had been concentrated in Scotland, the West Midlands and the Western Peninsula (the proportion of all Liberal Unionist MPs coming from these three areas fluctuating between 47.4 per cent and 63.6 per cent between 1886 and 1895), and, as Kinnear has

---

38 The MPs who had been 'National Liberals' before later becoming Simonites were: James Ian Macpherson, Geoffrey Shakespeare, Robert Hutchison, John Wallace, Murdoch Macdonald, William Edge, Charles Barrie, Austin Hopkinson, E.A. Strauss. The five former Lloyd Georgites now sitting on the Conservative benches were Churchill, Freddie Guest, C.H.C. Guest, H.A. Evans, Spears, Hilton Young. Admittedly, Churchill can hardly be claimed as a supporter of the National Government!

shown, these were also areas of relative Coalition strength at the Carlton Club meeting.[39] The case of Scotland is crucial. Alarmed by evidence of the desire for Liberal reunion north of the border, Scottish Conservative MPs in 1922 came out overwhelmingly against the break-up of the Coalition, providing Austen Chamberlain with nearly one-fifth of his supporters at the Carlton Club, though they comprised under 9 per cent of all Conservative MPs. Scotland also saw many instances of co-operation between Conservatives and Coalition Liberals in the 1922 General Election in the aftermath of the Coalition's collapse. Some sort of pact was operational in nearly two-thirds of all Scottish constituencies, compared with under one-fifth of all English constituencies.[40] One beneficiary of such arrangements was Walter Elliot in Lanark.[41]

It may also be significant that fifteen of Austen Chamberlain's supporters in 1922 were returned by constituencies whose MP later signed the 1934 petition: these were predominantly urban working-class constituencies situated in towns such as Birmingham, Bristol and Glasgow. Here may be yet another indication of grass-roots (or at least of local Conservative) support for the politics of 'national co-operation'. In so far as generalisations can be made at all, it seems that Conservative–Liberal co-operation was most likely to occur in areas where the Liberal Party had been traditionally strong, though not so strong that the Liberals felt confident about going it alone.

A strong Labour challenge provided another incentive for the two older parties to combine. Indeed, it was in localities where strong 'anti-socialist' pacts were in operation in municipal politics – Liverpool, Birmingham, Bristol and Western Scotland, for example – that coalitionism was most marked at the level of national politics. Bristol is especially interesting as an example of a town where the Liberals and Conservatives were on such intimate terms that they had virtually coalesced. Throughout the 1920s the two parties maintained an almost unbroken united front against Labour in both municipal and parliamentary elections.[42] It may therefore be significant that

39 Michael Kinnear, *The British Voter: An Atlas and Survey since 1885* (2nd edn, 1981), pp. 98, 104–5.

40 I.G.S. Hutchison, *A Political History of Scotland 1832–1924* (Edinburgh, 1986), pp. 312–14.

41 The Liberals had also left Elliot a straight fight against Labour in 1918 and were to do so again in 1923.

42 Chris Cook, *The Age of Alignment: Electoral Politics in Britain 1922–1929* (1975), pp. 52, 57.

it was for Bristol seats that Inskip and Freddie Guest both sat. Moreover, over half the Conservative MPs who signed the manifesto in support of the National Government in 1934 represented solidly working-class constituencies which Labour had a good chance of capturing or regaining. Conservative MPs and candidates in safe seats, on the other hand, generally saw no need to compromise their independence.

Geographical continuities can also be traced on the Liberal side of politics, since twenty of the thirty-six Liberal National MPs elected in 1931 represented constituencies which had returned Coalition or National Liberal MPs in the 1918 or 1922 General Elections. Again, five of these constituencies were north of the border and almost a half were solidly working-class in composition.

Yet this account of the geographical basis of coalitionism refers mainly to defensive collaboration between the two older parties in the face of the threat from Labour. This, however, was only one of a number of types of possible 'National Government'.

A TYPOLOGY OF COALITIONISM

As this book has demonstrated, 'national politics' has never been a homogenous thing. 'Each of the British coalitions or party under-standings', writes David Butler, 'has been *sui generis*, arising out of particular parliamentary or national situations.'[43] Is it possible, then, to construct a typology of coalitionism? For some individuals this presents difficulties. Garvin, for example, was a critic of party so fanatical that he showed little consistency when he came to adumbrating an alternative, and he can be found, at various points in his long career, taking up a wide range of mutually incompatible positions.

Nonetheless, it would be useful to attempt to classify 'national politics' more carefully, because, in so doing, this may cast some light on why an enterprise which commanded so much sympathy and support did not have more substantial achievements to its credit. The basic problem was that those who talked about 'National Government' and 'national parties' were not all pursuing the same goal. Indeed, Philip Williamson, analysing the events of the summer

43 David Butler (ed.), *Coalitions in British Politics* (1978), p. 116.

of 1931, claims that the meaning of these phrases changed week by week, and sometimes day by day. So Garvin was not the only individual who repeatedly shifted his stance. All this may be rather confusing to posterity. But the more important point is that the looseness and ambiguity of 'coalitionist' rhetoric often confused the politicians who were using it.

All the same, the phenomenon of 'national politics' can conveniently be grouped under five headings. First, we have the 'permeators', of whom the key figure is Joseph Chamberlain. Historians have found Chamberlain very difficult to pin down, because, though he became a hero to a younger generation of advocates of 'National Government', he himself always had a very well-developed sense of the power of party machinery. On the other hand, by the late 1890s, if not earlier, Chamberlain had formed a clear conception of the desirability of a 'national' policy which drew both upon traditional Liberalism and upon traditional Conservatism. The Radical Unionism of Chamberlain's late years thus represented a serious attempt to create a dynamic synthesis out of apparently conflicting ideologies – one which gave equal emphasis to social reform at home and a strengthening of the empire abroad, the two things being presented as interdependent.

Yet, except briefly in 1887, Chamberlain never took seriously the possibility of creating his own 'National Party'. He certainly showed little interest in Coalitions or National Governments which would have required him to share power with his political opponents. That is why the Boer War talk about the construction of a government of National Efficiency linking Rosebery and Chamberlain proved to be so much hot air. Nor was this an approach which generated a particularly 'consensual' style of politics. Indeed, with some justification, Francis Pym has recently portrayed Joseph Chamberlain as a fanatical ideologue who did great damage to Conservatism – his implication being that he was a politician of the same temperamental stripe as Mrs Thatcher![44]

What Chamberlain was actually doing was trying to capture the Conservative and Unionist Parties with a view to imposing upon them a programme which would *transcend* traditional Conservatism and thereby give it a national appeal. It was, as Sykes shows, a brave but ultimately fruitless adventure, since the Conservative Party and its official leaders put up a dogged resistance to being transformed in this way.

44 Francis Pym, *The Politics of Consent* (1984), pp. 184–5.

It was out of disappointment at the frustration of this strategy that some of Chamberlain's younger followers later broke entirely with official Unionism and, under Page Croft's eccentric guidance, formed their own 'National Party' in 1917. But this resulted in a farcical failure, and Page Croft soon returned to the fold, where he resumed his earlier attempts to line the Conservative Party up behind a Chamberlainite 'national' programme.

Perhaps the most effective and persistent practitioner of 'permeationist' tactics after Joe Chamberlain's illness and death was L.S. Amery. Admittedly, circumstances having meanwhile changed, Amery was prepared, as Chamberlain had not been, to acknowledge the desirability at times of crisis of all-encompassing National Governments. Thus, Amery worked with Lloyd George after December 1916,[45] and called for a 'National Government' in 1930–33, although he was disappointed by the sort of National Government which eventually came into existence – and by his own exclusion from it! But throughout his long career Amery remained basically loyal to a vision of 'constructive Unionism', to be realised through the instrumentality of a Conservative Party somehow mystically purged of its do-nothing, complacent, negative middle-class elements.

The second category of 'nationalist' politicians comprises those who hanker after the creation of a *comprehensive all-party government*. Such a government has at least two theoretical advantages: it can spread risks when unpopular decisions have to be taken, and it is a good mechanism for engineering *consent*. In times of war patriots have instinctively advocated this sort of National Government. Citizens, they urge, must sacrifice their personal prejudices in recognition of the much greater sacrifices of the young men who have laid down their lives on the battlefield. This rhetoric of camaraderie and sacrifice was often on the lips of Lloyd George: in his inaugural speech at the 1920 Club, for example, the Premier talked fervently of 'an alliance, consecrated by common effort, consecrated by common sacrifice, consecrated by a common share in a great victory for a great cause'.[46]

But claims on behalf of such a form of government have also been made in years of peace, often in language which sceptics have found

45 First in the War Cabinet, and then in 1919 serving as Parliamentary Under-Secretary at the Colonial Office under his great hero, Milner.

46 *Daily Chronicle*, 18 March 1921, cited in *Lloyd George Liberal Magazine*, April 1921, 430.

embarrassingly boy-scoutish.[47] 'We must all pull together and play
for the team, not seeking the advantage of this or that little group or
clique, but the greater good of the whole', proclaimed one of Lloyd
George's supporters in 1921. 'There must be team work if we are to
retain our unity'.[48] It was perhaps no coincidence that this speaker
was a clergyman, since the principle of co-operation underlying
coalition government seemed to be in accordance with the teaching
of Christianity. Moreover, underlying such attempts to capture the
moral high ground one often finds a sincere but sentimental vision of
the nation as 'one great family', to quote the words used by Churchill
in his famous speech of March 1941.[49]

This sort of National Government, to be fully effective, needs to be
all-embracing, comprehensive. Churchill once memorably remarked
that his own wartime Administration took in everybody from 'Red
Ellen' Wilkinson to Lord Lloyd of Dolobran. Arguably, it was, for
that very reason, the most successful 'National Government' that has
ever been formed. Indeed, A.J.P. Taylor calls it 'the only genuine
National government in British history', since it 'was in the unique
position of commanding the almost unanimous allegiance of both
parliament and country'.[50]

This is where such comprehensive 'National Governments' must be
sharply distinguished from a third category, *the 'Defensive Bloc'*. The
latter is an alliance which aims at the exclusion from office and power
of 'alien' groups thought by the dominant elites to be threatening the
integrity of the British state. Before 1914 the main 'enemy within' was
Irish Nationalism, working through its gullible Liberal allies. Later,
from the end of the Great War into the middle of the 1920s, it was the
Labour Movement, or 'Bolshevism', as it was pejoratively labelled.
In fact, for long periods of time, particularly during Lloyd George's
post-war Coalition, the idea of 'National Government' became almost

47 A Conservative critic said that Heath's GNU idea 'was most strongly
recommended by those with no sense or knowledge of history and a boy-scoutish
idea of political life' (Butler and Kavanagh, *British General Election of October 1974*,
p. 265).

48 Revd Dr J.C. Carlile, 'The Spirit of Solidarity', *Lloyd George Liberal Magazine*,
(Jan. 1921), 229.

49 This fitted in well with one of Churchill's other conceptions, that of the
Government having 'a sacred trust to use [its] opportunities in the interests of the
people as a whole'. See his speech at the Criterion Restaurant, 15 July 1919, James
(ed.), *Churchill Speaks*, p. 383.

50 A.J.P. Taylor, '1932–1945', in Butler (ed.), *Coalitions*, p. 74.

synonymous with 'anti-socialism'. Such a desire to *exclude* Labour contrasts with my first kind of National Government which assumes that Labour should be *outflanked* and my second kind which aspires to disarm Labour by *embracing* it.

The distinction between exclusion and incorporation, clear enough in theory, is slightly more difficult to draw in practice. In a sense, as John Turner has recently argued, the wartime Coalitions of 1915–18 came into existence to defeat Germany, but ended up as a 'counter-revolutionary' device, the main objective of which was the defeat of socialism.[51] Such a transformation was finally sealed when most senior trade unionists, obeying Labour Party orders, formally withdrew from the Government at the end of 1918.

A similar process unfolded between 1930 and 1931. Most of those who called for a National Government to resolve the nation's economic difficulties had originally wanted the *inclusion* of Labour – by which they meant not just a handful of senior Labour figures, but *all* its powerful and representative personalities. For the whole point was to *implicate* Labour in a programme of economies, in order to remove the impression that what was being done was a capitalist, anti-working class plot, and to prevent a Labour Opposition from seeking party advantage by espousing the cause of the unemployed and of others who would be the short-term losers by these economies. Essentially, the story of 1931 is a story of how, by a complex chapter of accidents and mishaps, the country ended up, not with a comprehensive National Government, but with an anti-Labour bloc, reinforced by a handful of Labour renegades – an outcome which few had anticipated and even fewer originally wanted.

The fourth group are advocates of 'realignment', who, believing that the existing line of cleavage between the parties has become pointless, want to bring together people who agree upon fundamentals but find themselves separated by now obsolete party organisations and creeds.

At its feeblest, this simply means trying to create a 'Centre Party' composed of politicians whose sole characteristic is their abhorrence of extremes. The attempt between 1907 and 1909 to unite Liberal and Unionist moderates under the leadership of Rosebery fits snugly into this category.[52] The venture failed for reasons later given by

---

51 See Chapter 5.
52 See Ian Bradley, 'Attempts to Form a Centre Party in Britain, 1880–1980', *History Today*, 31 (Jan. 1981), 41–3.

Country before Party

Colin Coote: 'In a democracy there is nothing more logical and more doomed than a centre party. Everybody applauds it and nobody joins.'[53] Masterman was equally dismissive of such activities, observing that the very name of 'Centre Party' was 'grotesque, and could not warm one solitary human breast.'[54] Harcourt once made a gibe (often repeated) about Centre Parties being 'all centre and no circumference', and this view was echoed nearly a century later by Shirley Williams, who protested that 'a centre party would have no roots, no principles, no philosophy and no values'.[55] After 1918 it was, anyhow, arguable that the country already *had* a 'Centre Party', namely the Liberal Party, and so did not need another.

More hopeful have been the attempts to create a new synthesis of Left and Right, rearranging the chemical molecules so as to produce some new dynamic political creed. As Martin Pugh puts it, 'what is distinctive in this [centrist] tradition is not so much the ideas as the mixture of attitudes: on the one hand a positive view of the state and a tendency towards intervention in domestic affairs, on the other hand a bold, patriotic approach to defence, foreign and imperial questions'.[56] This was Chamberlain's old ambition, which others hoped to realise, not by a transformation of Conservatism, but through the instrumentality of a distinctive 'national' party.

But how to bring off the difficult feat of creating such a party? As *The Times* had shrewdly observed in 1889:

> A party worthy of the name cannot be made as a metallurgist makes an alloy, by combining certain quantities of certain ingredients. Parties, like poets, are not made, but born. They are evolved by a vital process which, like other vital processes, has a tendency to baffle analysis. The thing is done under our eyes, but, though we may chronicle more or less accurately certain of the stages of development, we can give but a meagre and imperfect account of the true causation.[57]

Starting up a new party from scratch certainly held out little chance of success, as Mosley discovered when his New Party flopped. It

53 Colin Coote, *A Companion of Honour: The Story of Walter Elliot* (1965), p. 48.
54 C.F.G. Masterman, 'The New Democratic Party', *Contemporary Review*, 117 (Feb. 1920), 153.
55 *Guardian*, 9 June 1980.
56 Martin Pugh, 'Left in the Centre? Lloyd George and the Centrist Tradition in British Politics', in Judith Loades (ed.), *The Life and Times of David Lloyd George* (Bangor, 1991), p. 20.
57 *The Times*, 19 Sept. 1889.

seemed more practicable to 'fuse' elements from both major parties. But, unless the new organisation was to be staffed by a spontaneous mass exodus from the two traditional parties, any kind of fusion would involve the support and co-operation of the party leaders and party Whips – who could not really be expected to back a venture the outcome of which would be the destruction of the very organisations of which they were the custodians. When Lloyd George pushed the idea of 'fusion' in late 1919 and early 1920, *he* enjoyed the freedom of not being the leader of a proper, long-established party. Even so, he failed to sell the proposal to the majority of his leading Coalition Liberal colleagues. Surprisingly, several senior Conservatives *did* seem prepared to support the venture. But, predictably, it quickly ran into opposition from Younger, the Conservative Party Chairman.

In a way, Lloyd George, having split the Liberals, had a vested interest in splitting the Conservatives so as to perpetuate his own premiership. Moreover, in all probability the Welshman did *genuinely* want a radical realignment of parties. The trouble was that he could not openly talk about *either* of these ambitions. Instead, the case for 'fusion' had to rest upon the desirability of continued coalition and upon the need to underpin it by a new organisation that could campaign vigorously for its candidates at by-elections. In the absence of such an organisation, Lloyd George's Coalition, like all coalitions before it, was, as Birkenhead observed in a rather unfortunate phrase, 'invertebrate'.

Yet in taking this line the 'fusionists' got themselves into a series of muddles. For a start, the ideology of 'coalition' proclaimed the importance of exorcising the spirit of party, but, to achieve this, the fusionists were now proposing to establish a new party of their own, on the ground that one could only fight fire with fire. In the words of Douglas Malcolm, who had wrestled with a similar dilemma a few years earlier, this entailed 'an effort to cast out devils by Beelzebub, the Prince of Devils'.[58] The SDP encountered a broadly comparable difficulty in the 1980s.

Putting this paradox to one side, it was anyhow questionable whether the post-war Coalition would really have been strengthened by the formation of a new Coalition Party. Younger had argued all along that the survival of the Coalition was a separate matter from

---

58 27 Aug. 1917, in Chris Wrigley, '"In the Excess of their Patriotism": the National Party and Threats of Subversion', in Chris Wrigley (ed.), *Warfare, Diplomacy and Politics* (1986), p. 99.

fusion, with which it should not be confused[59] – and he was right. For the truth surely is that National Governments of all kinds work best when they are broad-bottomed, a consideration that suggests the need, not for 'fusion' but for the existence of many parties (or at least more than one) that are clearly distinct from one another, yet willing to co-operate for the attainment of certain common objectives. After all, Churchill's wartime Coalition was far more stable than any previous National Government because the Labour and Conservative Parties, who provided it with its main support, were appealing to different constituencies and showed absolutely no propensity to fuse.

Of course, persistent critics of the party system who advocated National Governments were precisely the people who also came forward repeatedly to urge the creation of a National Party. Thus, during the Boer War Garvin had called stridently for 'a National Cabinet, a National Party, a National policy'.[60] But this betrays his total confusion. For not only were these objectives different: they were, in fact, mutually incompatible. Herein lay an important reason for the failure of the quest for 'fusion' after the Great War.

In the early 1920s the Liberal businessman, O.F. MacLagan, more far-sighted than most of his contemporaries, saw that coalition government in fact required the survival of a *multiplicity* of parties, each with its distinctive identity: 'Coalition government contains no menace to the separate existence of the great Parties of the past, nor to their complete independence, nor does it shut out the formation of new parties as the need or desirability may arise', he wrote.[61] MacLagan also made an explicit connection between this kind of government and the passing of *electoral reform* and, in so doing, he foreshadowed the fifth concept of 'national politics', that of the *'power-sharing coalition'*.

During the nineteenth and early twentieth centuries such a connection was seldom made.[62] John Grigg is right to comment upon the oddity of Lloyd George's slowness to embrace electoral reform, despite his

59 Kenneth O. Morgan, *Consensus and Disunity: The Lloyd George Coalition Government 1918–1922* (Oxford, 1979), p. 183.

60 See Chapter 4.

61 O.F. MacLagan, *Coalition Government: a League of Parties as an efficient Method of Government* (1922?), p. 6.

62 Jenifer Hart, *Proportional Representation: Critics of the British Electoral System 1820–1945* (Oxford, 1992), p. 95.

coalitionist ambitions.[63] Churchill, it is true, spoke out on behalf of PR during the 1930s, as did Balfour, Amery and Birkenhead (though Balfour's primary concern was the protection of Irish Protestants in the event of a Home Rule Bill). But Lloyd George was not the only advocate of 'National Government' to dislike PR: so did Joseph and Austen Chamberlain.[64] Yet *some* forms of PR (in particular the Single Transferable Vote), the favoured option of most British supporters of electoral change, would have boosted the chances of coalitions coming into existence by making it difficult for any single party to command a parliamentary majority.[65]

During the course of the 1970s and the 1980s Liberal and Social Democratic politicians started to talk about the need to change the 'first-past-the-post' electoral system and thereby to create an entirely new kind of political process, modelled on that of many Continental European countries, in the expectation that permanent coalition government would prove to be an effective mechanism for mobilising consensus in the interests of social and economic modernisation.[66]

CONCLUSION

The attraction of the idea of a National Government is that it appeals to such praiseworthy qualities as kindliness, sacrifice, service, and altruism. It can even be seen as embodying a wider conception of democracy than is entailed by two-party rivalry. 'Democracy means the rule, not of this, that, or the other section, however numerous, but of all the citizens', declared Gordon Hewart, a Coalition Liberal and the Attorney-General in Lloyd George's post-war Government:

> Democratic institutions have been obtained, not without contest and controversy. But . . . the question is being asked, more and more widely, whether it is not possible, now that the franchise is almost universal, for men of good will to unite upon no less nor lower

63 'Lloyd George and Electoral Reform', in J.M.W. Bean (ed.), *The Political Culture of Modern Britain* (1987), p. 176.

64 Hart, *Proportional Representation*, pp. 92, 264–5, 273.

65 However, as we saw in Chapter 1, there would also have to be a change of political *culture*, since hitherto British politicians, faced with a hung Parliament, have opted for minority single-party administrations in preference to a coalition.

66 Bogdanor (ed.), *Coalition Government in Western Europe*, p. 277.

programme than the welfare of the whole citizen-body. Away with faction, away with sectionalism, away with all the self-centred demands of groups, and inscribe upon your banners the welfare of the whole people![67]

Edward Heath made a similarly lofty appeal in October 1974 in an election manifesto which promised 'a government that [could] transcend party divisions, a government representing men and women of good will of all parties and of none'.[68]

Yet even the strongest advocates of 'national politics' have often expressed doubts about their feasibility. For example, Winston Churchill, while writing a life of his father, had a vision of

> an England which stretches far beyond the well-drilled masses who are assembled by party machinery to salute with appropriate acclamation the utterances of their recognised fuglemen; an England of wise men who gaze without self-deception at the failings and follies of both political parties; of brave and earnest men who find in neither faction fair scope for the effort that is in them; of 'poor men' who increasingly doubt the sincerity of party philanthropy.[69]

Yet in the very same book Churchill could also write:

> To build from the rock a great new party – free alike from vested interests and from holy formulas, able to deal with national problems on their merits, patient to respect the precious bequests of the past, strong to drive forward the wheels of progress – is without doubt a worthy ideal. Alas, that the degeneracy of man should exclude it for ever from this wicked world![70]

The outcome of this vacillation has been a widespread disillusionment with the political process itself, caught in Colin Coote's aphorism: 'The consequence of not loving coalitions is to be ruled by clichés.'[71]

Why, then, has coalition politics failed more often than it has succeeded? Some of its advocates have been insincere, but this has probably counted for less than an underlying confusion of purpose. Keith Joseph has clearly articulated one of the central difficulties. 'For the two–party system . . . to work at all', he argued in 1975, there needed to be 'a substantial measure of common

---

67 Gordon Hewart, 'Coalition and Democracy', *Sunday Times*, 7 Aug. 1921.
68 *'The Times' Guide to the House of Commons, October 1974*, p. 312.
69 Winston Spencer Churchill, *Lord Randolph Churchill* (1906), Vol. II, pp. 488–9.
70 Ibid., p. 349.
71 Coote, *Companion of Honour*, p. 48.

ground between the parties'. Hence, in periods of sharp ideological polarisation, voices have commonly been raised for the establishment of coalition government, despite the fact that conditions were totally unpropitious for such an enterprise. 'But', mused Joseph, 'if we had sufficiently wide common ground to make our party system, our constitutional and legal and economic arrangements work adequately, then hankering for a coalition government would cease anyway'.[72] In other words, in peacetime conditions coalitions are most feasible when they are least needed, and vice-versa.

As for party, it will doubtless elicit ambiguous feelings for many generations yet.[73] Those who hanker after what an idealised coalition government might theoretically deliver will never be satisfied. Yet it is equally true that party zealots are invariably disappointed by the way their party performs when it comes to power. The moral of all this may be that only those who lack strong political convictions are protected from disappointment! Meanwhile, as Kenneth Morgan has observed: 'One man's "national unity" is another's "opportunism". One man's "petty partisanship" is another's "principled independence".'[74] And thus it will ever be.

72 Keith Joseph, 6 Dec. 1975, in *Stranded on the Middle Ground?* (1976), pp. 26–7.
73 See *Guardian* editorial of 29 March 1993.
74 Kenneth O. Morgan, '1902–1924', in Butler (ed.), *Coalitions*, p. 51.

Select Bibliography

Place of publication is London, unless stated otherwise

1 INTRODUCTION

The general theme of Coalition is well presented in the historical essays contained in David Butler (ed.), *Coalitions in British Politics* (1978) and, from a political science perspective, in Vernon Bogdanor (ed.), *Coalition Government in Western Europe* (1983). A brilliant discussion of 'Centrism' is to be found in Brian Harrison, 'The Centrist Theme in Modern British Politics', in *Peaceable Kingdom: Stability and Change in Modern Britain* (Oxford, 1982).

2 THE MID-VICTORIAN PRELUDE

Mid-Victorian criticisms of party are discussed in Randall E. McGowen and Walter L. Arnstein, 'The Mid-Victorians and the Two-Party System', *Albion*, 11 (1979). Hugh Berrington's article, 'Partisanship and Dissidence in the Nineteenth-Century House of Commons', *Parliamentary Affairs*, 21 (1967–68), 338–73, is important.

3 CHAMBERLAIN AND THE LEGACY OF THE HOME RULE CRISIS, 1885–1906

The literature on Chamberlain is copious. The most useful study of his political career is that of Richard Jay, *Joseph Chamberlain: A Political*

Study (Oxford, 1981); Peter Marsh's *Joseph Chamberlain: Entrepreneur in Politics* (New Haven, CE., 1994) came out too late to be used in the writing of this book. On Tariff Reform I have leant heavily on Alan Sykes, *Tariff Reform in British Politics, 1903–1913* (Oxford, 1979). On Randolph Churchill, read R.F. Foster, *Lord Randolph Churchill: A Political Life* (Oxford, 1981).

4 NATIONAL EFFICIENCY, 1899–1914

My own book, *The Quest for National Efficiency: A Study in British Politics and British Political Thought, 1899–1914* (Oxford, 1971: new edn., London and Atlantic Highlands, NJ, 1990), is still useful. Much interesting material can be found in Robert J. Scally, *The Origins of the Lloyd George Coalition: The Politics of Social Imperialism, 1900–1918* (Princeton, 1975). In discussing the Liberal Imperialists, I have drawn heavily on H.C.G. Matthew, *The Liberal Imperialists: The ideas and politics of a post-Gladstonian elite* (Oxford, 1973). On Milner and the Milnerites, read A.M. Gollin, *Proconsul in Politics: A Study of Lord Milner in Opposition and in Power* (1964). Churchill's political ideas are usefully summarised in Paul Addison, *Churchill on the Home Front 1900–1955* (1992).

5 FIRST WORLD WAR AND COALITION

John Turner, *British Politics and the Great War: Coalition and Conflict 1915–1918* (New Haven, 1992), provides the fullest and most authoritative of the recent accounts. John Ramsden, *The Age of Balfour and Baldwin 1902–1940* (1978), is the best starting-point for an understanding of the Conservatives. Gollin on Milner and Scally on Social Imperialism (see above) are also relevant to this chapter.

6 THE POST-WAR COALITION, 1918–22

The best single account of the post-war Coalition is Kenneth O. Morgan's *Consensus and Disunity: The Lloyd George Coalition Government 1918–1922*, (Oxford, 1979). Ramsden is again useful on the

Conservatives. On Mosley and the New Members Group, read Robert Skidelsky, *Oswald Mosley* (1975).

7 TOWARDS THE NATIONAL GOVERNMENT, 1922–1931

The outstanding book is Philip Williamson's *National Crisis and National Government: British Politics, the Economy and Empire, 1926–1932* (Cambridge, 1992). Skidelsky on Mosley is also important.

8 THE NATIONAL GOVERNMENT AND ITS CRITICS, 1931–39

Apart from Williamson (see above), read David Marquand, *Ramsay MacDonald* (1977), Ramsden on the Conservative Party, and, for the opposition to the National Government in the late 1930s, Ben Pimlott, *Labour and the Left in the 1930s* (Cambridge, 1977).

9 THE SECOND WORLD WAR

Paul Addison's *The Road to 1945* (1975) remains indispensable. For an alternative view, read Kevin Jefferys, *The Churchill Coalition and Wartime Politics, 1940–1945* (Manchester, 1991). Addison's book on Churchill is also useful.

10 THE POST-WAR LABOUR-CONSERVATIVE DUOPOLY, 1945–74

The best introduction is Dennis Kavanagh, *Thatcherism and British Politics: The End of Consensus?* (Oxford, 1987). Two excellent biographies are John Campbell, *Edward Heath: A Biography* (1993) and Ben Pimlott, *Harold Wilson* (1992).

11 'ALLIANCE POLITICS', 1967–87

As in Chapter 10. The Nuffield College electoral studies are also important, particularly the volume by David Butler and Dennis Kavanagh, *The British General Election of October 1974* (1975).

12 CONCLUSION

As for Chapter 1.

Finally, mention should be made of three particularly valuable collections of printed documents: John Barnes and David Nicholson (eds), *The Empire At Bay: The Leo Amery Diaries 1929–1945* (1988); J.M. McEwen, *The Riddell Diaries 1908–1923* (1986); and John Ramsden (ed.), *Real Old Tory Politics: The Political Diaries of Robert Sanders, Lord Bayford 1910–1935* (1984).

Index

Aberdeen, Lord, 14
Acland, Richard, 194, 209, 216
Adam Smith Institute, 249
Addison, Christopher, 96, 98, 106–8,
    111–12, 117, 120, 125, 127, 131, 138,
    145
Addison, Paul, 198, 211–15
Administrative Reform Association
    (ARA),
    of 1855, 15
    of 1900, 55
'adversary politics', 253
Aitken, Max, see Lord Beaverbrook
Akers-Douglas, A., 36
Albert, Prince, 14, 34
'Alliance', 8, 9, 11, 12, 260–5, 272, 274,
    277, 281, 293
Amery, Julian, 282
Amery, L.S., as Coalitionist, 154, 258,
    269, 282, 287, 293
    and National Efficiency, 62–3
    and Milner, 65, 95, 96, 102, 287n45
    on Federalism, 83, 112
    and National Government of 1930s,
        150, 168, 172, 187, 189, 193
    and Churchill Coalition, 197–8, 200,
        268
Anderson, Sir John, 178–9, 188, 203, 218
anti-Labour politics, 124–6, 141, 160–1,
    186, 190, 221, 270, 279–80, 284–5,
    288–9
Appeasement, 190–1, 195
Ashdown, Paddy, 265
Asquith, H. H.,
    as Liberal Imperialist, 59–60, 63
    as Prime Minister before Great War,
        75, 77, 84, 279

    as wartime Premier, 85, 86–95,
        98–100, 103, 105–6, 200–1
    and Lloyd George Coalition, 102, 113,
        114–16, 128, 129, 132, 148
    also mentioned, 6, 122, 131
Astor, Lord, 96, 102, 108
Attlee, Clement, as Prime Minister, 225,
    229, 235
    member of Churchill Coalition, 198,
        201, 202, 203, 206–7, 208, 213,
        214–15, 217–18
    also mentioned, 193

Bagehot, Walter, 18, 19
Bailey, Abe, 163n49, 166
Baldwin, Stanley,
    attitude towards Lloyd George, 145,
        148, 149
    formation of National Government,
        158, 162, 165–8, 276
    role in National Government, 172,
        176, 178, 179–80, 182, 184–5
    as 'consensual' politician, 11, 19,
        187–8, 189, 191, 247
    also mentioned, 6, 7, 139, 140, 150,
        197, 273
Balfour, Arthur James,
    on party system, 278
    early career, 23, 42, 43, 55n9, 58
    his premiership, 48, 63, 267
    as Leader of Opposition, 52, 65, 73,
        75, 76, 77, 78, 269
    first wartime Coalition, 90
    colleague of Lloyd George, 102, 138
    a 'Coalitionist', 121, 129–30, 134, 146
    also mentioned, 6, 46, 51, 67, 80, 86,
        88, 133, 293

Index

Balfour, Sir Arthur, 163n49, 165
Bank of England, 169–70, 236–7
Barnes, George, 114
Barnett, Correlli, 212
Barrington-Ward, R.M., 216
Barry, Gerald, 157
Beaverbrook, Lord, and Churchill
  Coalition, 197, 201, 203
  also mentioned, 86, 93, 104, 112, 130,
    149, 154, 158, 162, 190, 219, 227
Beeching, Dr, 232, 236
Bell, Daniel, 231
Bellenger, Frederick, 215
Belloc, Hilaire, 10, 79
Beloff, Professor Max, 235–6, 252, 278
Benn, Tony, 237, 239, 246, 247, 248,
  250, 251, 256–7, 259, 273
Bevan, Aneurin, 206, 214, 229
Beveridge, William, 201, 210, 212, 214,
  215–16, 219, 230
Bevin, Ernest, 188, 199, 201, 204, 205,
  206–7, 208, 214, 218, 229
Birkenhead, Lord (F.E. Smith),
  and Secret Coalition Talks, 75, 76, 84
  other coalition intrigues, 68, 83, 86,
    96, 98
  and 'fusion', 120–1, 122, 124–5, 126,
    127, 129, 130, 134, 135, 141, 143,
    144n97, 146, 147, 151
  also mentioned, 68, 139, 187, 282, 291,
    293
Bismarck, Count, 42, 68, 81, 107, 124
Blackett, Patrick, 230
Boer War (Second), 45–7, 53
Bolingbroke, Lord, 80, 258
Bolshevism, see anti-Labour politics
Bonapartism, 268–9
Bonar Law, Andrew,
  as Opposition Leader, 78, 80, 82, 83
  and politics of Great War, 85–7, 89,
    90, 93, 94, 100, 102, 114, 115
  and 'fusion', 129–30, 132, 133, 146
  also mentioned, 6, 136, 140, 143, 150
Bonham Carter, Lady Violet, 222
Booth, F. Handel, 89
Boothby, Robert, 154, 156, 197
Bottomley, Horatio, 56, 138, 273
Boulanger, General, 268
Bowles, Tommy, 10
Boyle, Edward, 228, 237
Bracken, Brendan, 190, 203, 219, 227
Bridgeman, William, 104
Bright, John, 15, 19, 38
British Commonwealth Union, 110
Brodrick, George, 28–9, 40, 54
Brown, George, 230, 251

Brown, W.J., 10, 208–9
Bruce-Gardyne, J., 240
Bryce, James, 21
Buchan, John, 102, 163, 164
Buckmaster, Lord, 91
Burke, Edmund, 3, 80, 144, 258
Burns, John, 86, 89
business government, 9, 15–16, 55–6, 74,
  97–8, 103–5, 108, 110, 136–9, 163,
  236–41, 272–4
Butler, David, 8, 239, 254, 255, 285
Butler, R.A., 189, 212, 214, 224, 227,
  228
Butlin, Billy, 236
Butskellism, 187, 228
Buxton, Sydney, 87
by-elections, 223 and n13
  Oxford (1938), 193
  Rugby (1942), 208
  Skipton (1944), 209
  Orpington (1962), 223
  Lincoln (1973), 247

'Caesarism', 158, 173, 271
Calder, Angus, 210, 212–13
Callaghan, James, 234, 256
Campaign for Labour Victory, 248
Campbell-Bannerman, Henry, 6, 61, 64
Carlyle, Thomas, 14, 34, 50, 267, 269n8
Carnegie, Andrew, 55
Carr, E.H., 216
Carson, Edward, 93, 94, 96, 98, 100, 101
Cartland, Ronald, 189, 190
'caucus', 21–3, 29, 275–6
Cecil, Lord Robert, 122, 123n20
Centre for Policy Studies (CPS), 249
'centrism', 19
Chamberlain, Austen,
  and Secret Coalition Talks, 71, 72, 76,
    82, 87–8
  and wartime politics, 92, 112
  and 'fusion', 121, 126, 133–4, 135–6,
    142, 143, 146, 147, 150–1, 160, 166
  and National Government, 173, 182,
    187, 270, 282
  also mentioned, 83, 137, 283, 284, 293
Chamberlain, Joseph,
  as Radical, 22, 28, 29–30, 268n5
  and Home Rule Crisis, 26, 29, 31–2,
    71
  attempts to create National Party,
    33–4, 35–7, 282
  and 'national politics', 30, 37–45,
    49–50, 77, 286–7, 290
  and National Efficiency, 53, 58–9,
    61–2, 63, 286

Index